To the Harper - Super - Dupers.

French Letters

A journey to at least three places

Good friends deserve good words.

by

✥ Charlie Berridge ✥

You're very good friends! The subject of the last "chapter" B on your charge, or part of him. Take good care. All love Charlie

Bloomington, IN   authorHOUSE®   Milton Keynes, UK

AuthorHouse™
1663 Liberty Drive, Suite 200
Bloomington, IN 47403
www.authorhouse.com
Phone: 1-800-839-8640

AuthorHouse™ UK Ltd.
500 Avebury Boulevard
Central Milton Keynes, MK9 2BE
www.authorhouse.co.uk
Phone: 08001974150

First published by AuthorHouse 6/25/2007

ISBN: 978-1-4259-7556-2 (sc)

Printed in the United States of America
Bloomington, Indiana

This book is printed on acid-free paper.

The book is dedicated to K.B, my partner and the red head so often mentioned, and my children and grandchildren. I know too that my ex, Fut, played her part in creating the word cocktail, so thanks to her for the long stretch. These pages would not have happened without the help and encouragement of lots of kind and thoughtful people, my successful writing sister Kate, editor Mazzy and very part-time coach Jonathan Neale at Bath Spa University College and some time agent Broo. The Tour was greatly aided by the generosity of my family, Nima Reid, Mr and Mrs Smith from the U.S.A., Ian and Odd Barton, Mike and Jasmine Chadwick, Andrew Stroud, Jill Smith and Owen Leech, Jean-Pierre and Carrie Auge, John Phillips, Sean Ryan, John Hall, the Rev Alan Hogath, Coeurs a Sauver and the good folk of Sainte Marie-de-Campan, especially Tony and Louise Butler, Sylvie Coumel-Ronsin, Andrew Reid and all the individuals and businesses who supported the Plat du Jour Tour and the British Heart Foundation and La Federation Francaise de Cardiologie. Thanks too to farmer Hocken of Warminster in whose barn Peter now rests with a bird shitty tarpaulin over him awaiting, like the rest of us, his next big adventure or the scrap heap. Thank you to those mentioned in the book and to those that have purchased it or bothered to read it. In your way, you have all helped to keep my heart healthy and the hearts of many others too. Thanks lastly to all those who would with such regular patience enquire "How's the book coming along?" Like spurs they too pushed me on my way. Here it is then.

I have used a couple of extracts taken, with kind permission, from the Rough Guide to France 6th edition published in 1999 by Rough Guides Ltd. Their words explained so well what I tried to rather poorly.

Sainte Marie-De-Campan

Eclipse 1999 ⇥

I don't know what's happening to me. I'm having some sort of turn. My shoes are stuck to the wet pavement, glued there. I can't move. I'm fixed to Hyde Park corner just like that big bronze statue. Mustn't fall over. Need to sit down. Get my breath. I can hear her encouraging me. I can't move. I need more air. My get up and go, got up and gone. It can't be the drink. Can it? I'm having some sort of bloody turn. Please God no, not me, not here, not now.

Days before, Newbold put his morose head around my office door.

"Hope you've done your figures, " he said, meaning that he hoped I hadn't. I didn't respond as he moved off towards the boardroom with his only friend, his laptop, stuck up under his armpit like a limpet on a leech.

The boardroom had become a gladiatorial arena, a gruesome daily war zone where we would slog it out. Like hyenas tearing into the bloody rotten carcass, we growled and snarled at each other and like rats on a sinking ship, we hurried headlong towards God knows what and watched as the beast we had built began to self-destruct. The bean counters perched vulture-like around the polished table and chewed over the fat that was left. They gave their opinions about what had to be done, pecked at the pieces and flapped a lot, fanning the flames, turning up the heat. The whole process gave me indigestion; at least that's what I thought it was. Gaviscon became a daily used brand to be sampled alongside those from Mr Nestlé and Mr Seagram.

The days in a dying business were not much fun. Remission sometimes gave a glimmer of hope, but bedside enthusiasm was misplaced. I tried to be positive but when the "Banks" got heavy, and it was always the "Banks" that demanded change, their demands were always negative. They had given with a smile and interest. Now they were taking back with a grimace and compound interest. Redundancy stalked the factories and offices like a Biblical plague. Those that went down were never happy. Typing pools welled up with real tears. The girls on the picking line in Ebbw Vale tried to pick up the pieces elsewhere, the packers packed it in and the Welsh fork lift driver said, "Fork it!" That time he meant it. And while he thought about his mortgage repayments and spending more time with his whippets coursing on the hills around Crickhowell, I could only dream about escaping to Sainte Marie-de-Campan; could only fantasise about moving into the Grange, the mountain retreat I'd purchased ten years earlier.

We had enjoyed the Saturday, the red head and I, and the wedding that we had attended had been a generous do. We were late for the service. The red head asked me to do her up.

"Zip me up, darling," she said and within moments we were both undone on the hotel's king-size bed. One of our major customers from Tesco was getting hitched, and so it was duty that called us to town that weekend. We needed to exude confidence, we needed to press the flesh that kept the business going, we had to be there to show that all was well, that our steady hand was still firmly on the tiller. If our major customer sensed that all was not well then all would not be well even more quickly. Champagne, not an own label from the supermarket, had been quaffed at the reception. A Cuban cigar or two were taken with ostentatious relish to confirm our status as healthy.

The drink and the joviality lulled me along, gave me a false sense of my state as the blue smoke and the bubbles weaved their wicked way. Somewhere in a blood vessel something decided to slowly shut down. A thin fleshy tube, vital with red life, was becoming even thinner. Not a pile-up in a coronary motorway but a serious hold up in a rat run for the corpuscles. Constriction set in and the body reacted in several ways. The skin turned grey, as the colour in the cheeks was recalled from the front to return to the defence of where it was more urgently needed. A breathlessness set in so that each mouthful was not enough, nose breathing insufficient to feed the demand, the mouth hung open like a moron's and guzzled for the night air. Dizziness wound its way into the brain. Things that had symmetry, a photographic sureness, turned into Monets. Electric lights already blurred by the wet, melted and smeared like runny egg yokes over the darkening, dreamlike city canvass. Other people became other things.

The nightmare was confirmed by a lack of response from the willing mind to the unwilling body. There was a thirst, even though the drink had flowed, a thirst for water and a real wish to be somewhere else all together. But no matter how hard I tried, I couldn't get to the taxi. In slow motion it was there, black and blurred at the curbside, its back door open and inviting, the worried red head skipping between taxi and me, me and taxi, only yards for her but a marathon for me. It may as well have been on the moon rather than ticking over on the corner of Hyde Park. Its heavy metronomic diesel engine clicking sounded reassuring, a quick regular beat, something to be envious of. I was bundled into the spinning black hole of the ticking black cab. With concern and a running metre we headed westward. The driver thought that he had another drunk in the back. The red head wasn't sure what was going on but knew that strong drink alone was not to blame for what was happening to the man she was with. The man she was with wasn't sure what was happening either. He was tired, very, very tired. Perhaps he had over done things. Perhaps that was it.

What I didn't realise was that just like my business, I was being slowly shut down.

After a terrible few hours, and still unaware of the gravity of the situation, I was finally persuaded by the red head that hospital might help. I agreed but wanted to be nearer home. I don't know why it mattered to be near home when unwell. Maybe it was a hang up from childhood. Conversational madness set in, slap stick verbal hilarity an island in the ocean of seriousness.

"R.U.H" I said hoarsely.

"What?" she said.

"R.U.H."

"Are you what?"

"R.U.H." I said again.

"Am I rich?" The red head wasn't getting it.

"R.U.H Bath." I tried to be more descriptive

"Oh the Royal United Hospital!" She tuned in and beamed at me expecting a prize. It was an unfair request asking her to drive me from London back to Bath past perfectly adequate hospitals just because I didn't want to be there. She was magnificent and drove just like a Testarossa should.

There was a great way to get to the front of the casualty queue. Past the twists, sprains, cuts and breaks, a by-pass for a by-pass. Clutching my chest and complaining of pain, I shot up the examination chart quicker than a bleeding pop star. I found myself undressed in moments, on a trolley and wired up to the system. The young very early Sunday morning doctors and nurses who looked at me were all reassuring, friendly and helpful. They made me feel better. I didn't want it to be my heart. The squirt of Nitramin spray under my tongue to ease the angina didn't. So I felt like a winner breaking the tape and mock punched the air in victory salute. A premature congratulation. The machine, judge and jury of that particular trial, thought otherwise and the ECG read outs and blood tests blunted the celebrations.

"You've had a heart attack, " said an A&E attendant and, sadly, the more ugly the news, the less attractive the nurse. She turned and left us alone; had delivered her dreadful line. Her sentence hung in stunned silence for an incredulous second or two. Then the giant shock wave roared across us, knocked us sideways, exploded the awful truth, put into bold headlines the gruesome news that we hadn't dared to even whisper. I cried and the red head cried with me. Not noisy sobs but quiet real tears that bubbled up and out like the first drops from a new source. The sort that sprang from self-pity. Tears that were saying my youth was over, I could no longer afford to be reckless. I'd never walk in those French mountains again. In that instant my status on Earth changed. I would probably be classified in an "at risk" group. My insurance premiums would rocket. I'd be helped across the road by obliging boy scouts. I wouldn't be able to run, wouldn't be able to make love any more. The truth blended with the fiction in a confused thought cocktail. It had me nearly dead and buried, and certainly on the scrap heap. We held hands, clammy hands and were still not sure what was happening to us. It was the sort of thing that only ever happened to other people.

"He's at that dangerous age." I remember hearing it in conversation about some other fifty something. But I was only forty-nine. Why me? Had I really abused my self so much over the last four decades? I didn't smoke cigarettes and only ever the occasional cigar. True that the drink was an over friendly mate and exercise wasn't a priority. My diet was surely healthy and I wasn't overweight. The red head had seen to that with her sparrow-like portions.

Maybe it was a genetic legacy. My father had a weak heart and his mother had angina. But father was still going strong at over seventy and besides, children couldn't die before their own parents. They weren't supposed to. Stress might have been a factor, but stress wasn't a potion I could taste. It was an unknown brew in the chalice shared with the raucous Leo. But no matter what my head might try to tell it, my heart had a mind of its own.

And that was that. She sat there, the red head, on the tubular steel NHS chair, hunched over with her hand fixed to mine comforting just like the overhead drip. I lay on the clinical bed, a million miles away from a king size romp. We sipped insipid sweet tea and made small talk. Small talk in a big room.

"I can't believe this has happened."

"You'll get over it darling. You'll be fine again. I'll take care of you."

" But a heart attack. It can't be."

"They say it is."

"I don't believe them. Heart attacks kill people don't they? They at least make you fall over don't they? I'm not going to pop my clogs yet."

"I don't know darling. Maybe yours was a very minor one."

"It feels alright, my heart, it feels OK. Don't think it needs a by-pass or whatever. A twinge of angina maybe, that's all."

"You've got acute angina?"

"No you have." I trawled up the dreadful old joke and let my hand slip to her lap to gently pat the place I was talking about. My word play tried to make light when it was dark.

Waiting. There was always a lot of waiting in hospital. Once they had got me through the front door, plugged me into the monitors, attached a drip to my arm, filled out the forms, stabilised me, diagnosed my condition, they then sent me into the waiting system, stitched me up like a kipper. My turn came and they wheeled me off into a ward, a waiting room for the horizontal. I was wheeled in and I'd be wheeled out. How I did in between depended on whether my last trip on wheels was to the morgue. There were signs of life and the others in the ward were waking.

"Did you sleep well Willy?"

" Porridge" growled William removing the oxygen mask. William was a chipper eighty-two but deaf as a post.

"That gruel sticks better than wallpaper paste." William's sense of humour was a lot stronger than his breathing.

"'E 'ad a better night than last 'un" said Derrick.

"Aye," said Welsh Owen, "He only filled two bottles."

Not since dorm days at boarding school had I heard such bed banter and bodily function noise, and not since then had I felt like a "new bug" in the organisation. I had joined the dodgy heart brigade. My heart attack wasn't the full-blown televisual sort that requires the ER team for a jump-start. But none the less I'd had an attack, or myocardial infarction to use nursey speak. So there I was in the tender loving care of the R.U.H, stopped in mid life by crisis. Britain's biggest killer had tapped me on the shoulder, marked my card without sending me off. The forty-nine year old heart that had decided to miss a beat or two wouldn't have to attend those tiresome board meetings for a while, the ones that rinsed and gargled a lot but didn't ever swallow. I wouldn't have to suffer Newbold or the bank boys for at least six weeks. Institutionalised and bed ridden, just a name and a number with no distinguishing features, no trappings, no hint of where I had come from and lots of doubts about where I was going. I fell into the routine where the smell from the galvanised food trolley prepared me for my meals long before they arrived. Mass-produced portions of indeterminate flimsy meat and pulped veg, obscured by a film of thin brown liquid as tasteless as the china they were ladled on to, a million miles from a plat du jour. The Pyrenees, France, seemed worlds away.

The Leslie Hill E Ward (Block1) was my new home with William, Derrick, Owen, Rob and Sean. I was there for just over a week, awaiting my doctor's next decision. The banter made light of our predicament. It kept at bay the awful truth. It was comic relief and like schoolboys in a crocodile or soldiers in a trench; we were in this together most in fact worse off than me, the new boy.

"They don't stay in that bed very long," said Welsh Owen and I wasn't quite sure whether that was good or bad news. Pills, food and injections governed our days.

"Just a little prick," said the sister.

"I didn't say a bloody word." Sean smirked as the rest of the boys cackled to their hearts concern.

On Wednesdays God visited the ward. God, so they said, could take many forms but on Wednesdays he manifested himself as Dr T. He was the man I was under, so to speak. While the nurses gave the shots, he called them. As I looked around at my five fellow cardiacally challenged dorm mates I felt a fraud. I didn't lie in my bed making the sort of breathing noises made by

Billy Bunter after a cross-country run. My left ventricle was not as unstable as an empty plastic shopping bag flapping around a windy supermarket car park. My pulse, blood pressure, temperature and cholesterol were all as normal as could be, and the envy of the rest of the class. Two of the five were "long termers" having waited for over seven weeks to be transferred to Bristol or Southampton. In the jargon of the car mechanic, the R.U.H. was the diagnostic bay, white coats and leads, with the actual workshops and engineers based at other centres.

"I'm now number two on the list," said my neighbour Rob as though he'd just come up with five numbers on the lottery.

"And it's their new financial 'ear," pointed out Owen who wasn't even in the top ten after five weeks of waiting.

Welsh Owen was a lovely man nearer seventy than sixty who had presumably worked hard all his life and who sat or lay every day waiting for his turn. He didn't get many visitors or phone calls and he only had four get well cards strung across the line at the foot of his bed. His needs were greater than mine. Welsh Owen sobbed one night and was comforted by the night nurse. I heard the two of them having their very private moment in that all too public place.

The nurses regulated our timetable, as we must have determined theirs. In that way we fed off each other. They would appear, float almost to the bedside to perform their duty, administer, record and chat. Theirs was a job that required a bag full of personal skills. I could understand why nurses featured prominently in well males' sexual fantasies, the potent cocktail of uniform and bed. It was nearly always a pleasure to talk, flirt with the nurses, even though they were treating my stomach like a pincushion, but other visitors were far less welcome. Nurses had an easy bedside manner, professionalism around the sick, whereas friends and relatives from the outside world just didn't know how to behave.

"How are you?" was probably the most common greeting from the outsiders when they arrived. They said it with out thinking; used it as an icebreaker.

"Very well thanks" was the most common response. We said it playing the game. It was always good having the daily visit or two from the red head. She was used to seeing me lying on my back, used to me in sickness and in health. But not really the others, not until I was up and about able to walk to the bathroom, have a bath to wash away the smell of being unwell, the sickly stench of the drugs that seemed to mix with the underarm sweat. I never smelt like that at home. I never had to use cardboard bottles to pee into at home either. I didn't use them at all but rather bottled it up inside. The resultant use of the portable commode on day two gave one young nurse a tricky time, as bulk liquid on the move tended to keep moving. Nurses deserve every penny they get and more.

And as though Welsh Owens plight wasn't already bad enough, I then played my get out of jail free card. Dr T in NHS mode barely kissed the bed with his white coat. He was a busy man. If he was the sea and we the beach, we'd all still be quite dry. My moment came and I spoke but two words to God.

" I'll pay." Instantly I turned into wet sand. Dr T lingered and issued commands to his disciples and lo, straightway, I was headed for Southampton. It was better than an upgrade on a long haul jet. I was no longer a patient with a number; I was a patient with a name.

It didn't seem fair but then money, and that's all it was, had a tendency to make things unfair. My company valued me and as part of my package I got private health insurance. I was sure Welsh Owen put his heart into his job so it did seem unfair that while mine was covered, his was not. So I left block 1 of E ward knowing that within fifteen minutes my space would be filled by another dodgy heart waiting his turn. I said goodbye to my roommates, those of them that could talk to me, and just waved at Willy behind his oxygen mask. I didn't suppose that I would ever see any of them again but they wished me well.

"Don't let the buggers get you down." Welsh Owen's final advice rang in my ears as they wheeled me away to be repaired.

The arrival at Southampton hospital was like arriving at a shopping mall and the paramedics pushed me through the bazaar, past the flower stalls and booksellers and into registration. The check in process was just like those of any five star hotel, except that I was already undressed and in bed, all be it one on wheels. The questionnaire was a bit more than name, car registration number, nationality, and method of payment and departure date. I left the date of departure blank.

My room had just one bed and the biggest joy, a bathroom en-suite. Washing could once again become an intimate affair. The private room's only disappointment was the lack of a sea view. The compensation was the Sky view, just one of the fourteen channels on offer hovering on an adjustable arm beside the bed. I could see Kosovo but not the sea. And money it seemed bought bedside manners and the new God in Southampton; Dr D was so friendly I thought that for a brief moment he wanted to join me between the sheets. He looked like a merchant banker, distinguished, grey before his time and pin striped. There was the unmistakable reek of confidence and I deposited my heart with him in anticipation of a healthy return. Angicardiography was the technical term for a process that let the experts and the patient see blocked or damaged arteries. I was there for a look and probably angioplasty, which was to arteries what "Dyno-Rod" was to drains.

The premed preparation was just as alarming as the thought of the immanent procedure. Nurse presented me with a small tin of talc, a disposable razor and a large black bin liner and asked me to shave. God knows what she thought I was growing down there.

"Give yourself a nice bikini line," she said with a cheeky smile. Welcome mats were not really welcome there.

The other preparation was the Will. Dr D wasn't very flattered but apparently it was common practise for last Wills and Testaments to be finalised by heart patients. Two official witnesses were drummed up from the clinical management team. Apparently they didn't let the nursing staff witness Wills although they did witness births and deaths and much between the two. It focused the mind, made the whole thing real. Reading the ink on the page that I had written, leaving this and that to these and those, I suddenly understood more clearly than anyone had so far tried to explain that I might, just might be leaving. My faith and my doubts flooded like hidden water from a tightly twisted sponge. When I was alone I fell to my knees and begged God to let me live.

"Please God let me live." I implored through my clenched hands, my fingers white through temporary lack of thinned blood. He couldn't let me die. There was still so much to do, to get things sorted, get things done. I said the Lord's Prayer and remembered the prayers that my mother used to say with me every night in the early days, the days before boarding school. "Gentle Jesus meek and mild, look upon this little child." That was what I had become.

Then came the relaxing pills that blurred the edges and called up the drowsiness. The porters arrived, two for one. My light-headed state took me out of my body, away from what was happening and put me as an observer, a floating body in the room. I waved at the men and they waved back.

"Cheap day return governor?"

Down there I was flat on my back dressed up in a white short-sleeved backless gown, being pushed along the hospital corridors by the two jovial blokes. I followed the ceiling on the way to our appointment, spotted a lost opportunity, an advertising slot up there for a very specific target audience. "It's never too late to call the one you love."

Once in the theatre antechamber my name and number were checked. They confirmed that I'd "signed the papers" which gave them permission to operate immediately if "things went wrong". The chances of "things going wrong" were way less than a quarter of one percent. But I didn't feel inclined to enquire how the day's business had gone so far. The mouth was dry as they finally pushed me into the operating room and transferred me, with a giant Rolf Harris wobble board, to the ledge thin table over which the x-ray machine was poised. The team prepared, Dr D dressed up in green overalls with the sort of headgear more associated with a girl in a biscuit factory. He came alongside with a cheery, "Still here then, ha ha," type greeting. The team didn't scrub up. There weren't lashings of hot water and towels like in the old black and white films. These were technicians not sawbones.

A tube was inserted into an artery somewhere north west of my right testicle; hence the short back and sides, but I couldn't feel anything. I was pretty much awake, rather woozy, looking at the TV screen on my left. Liquid was then injected into the tube and it immediately showed up on the x-ray system. Whilst I was not sure what I was looking at, the experts assured me that it was my heart on the screen. My heart on the telly. My heart on the box. A starring role in its own show. Live TV and not a repeat. The infusion of liquid gave a warm sensation from within, a cross between a glug of sloe gin on a frosty morning and wetting oneself. Oozy warmth.

The cause of my heart attack was spotted, and with the sort of dexterity that a skilful Swiss watchmaker would cherish, a stent was placed in the offending closed down artery. In builder speak, a stent was scaffolding. Dr D described it as chicken wire. It was metal and designed to hold open the blockage in coronary arteries. Whether or not it made a bleep at airport security checks, remained to be seen.

Stented and absented, I didn't hang about. The next day I was back at home. Unreal. It was as if I had been taking part in some extraordinary TV reality show or dream. There I was with no obvious outward sign that anything had happened. I had simply passed from one chapter to another. Been out of action for a week or two. Didn't feel any difference other than tired. The after exactly the same as the before. The thing about having had a heart attack was that everyone expected you to be in a wheel chair. They wanted to see the marks, when there weren't any. All I had to show for the event were the photographs, like gruesome holiday snaps, the before and after print outs taken from the x-ray machine that was hovering when the stent was being sorted out. That was the only tangible proof. There were no stitches to be proud of like a schoolboy or plaster cast to gather signatures on. It was difficult to let my colleges know that I hadn't actually been on a holiday. All went well for two weeks.

My first proper day out was to visit an auction salesroom in Taunton to look at the stuffed heads and other sporting memorabilia the day before the sale. The red head and a couple who were very good friends planned the gentle day out. The four of us drove down the motorway. We got to Taunton and found the sale showroom with its collection of dead stuffed animals, hunting paraphernalia, fishing tackle, guns and sporting prints. The room had that disordered look about it where everything was out of place. Lots of lots just piled up willy-nilly. Unfamiliar and unloved clutter there, but once upon a time treasured possessions. A pair of copulating foxes, stuffed as they were doing it, caught our eyes. The catalogue entry read "Lot 47. A pair of stuffed and mounted foxes." We chuckled and moved on to look at the pike in their bow fronted glass cases.

I didn't know what it was but I suddenly felt very unwell, like a taxidermist's stiff specimen I slumped into a chair. I needed some water. I felt even more frightened than I had with the turn in London where ignorance was bliss. For a moment or two, I thought that I was going to meet my maker in the salesroom at Taunton appropriately surrounded by the stuffed. Hundreds of beady glass eyes from the Ark looked at me unblinking, waiting for me to join them. Suspended in time and motion, we studied each other. The copulating foxes, our cheap laugh, brushed aside their embarrassment and, frozen in time, invited me to eternity. The open mouthed pike pouted through their glass beckoning, razor teeth on edge.

"I don't want to die." I whispered to the red head. Animated, worried, she alerted the others. They drove me straight back to the hospital in Bath at speeds on the M5 only ever used by the police or those evading them.

The girls in the back talked nonsense, a filling for the uncomfortable gap.

"Funny those foxes."

"Fancy those funny foxes on your side board."

"Fancy those funny foxes anywhere."

My friend Barton didn't stop talking either, talked nervous nonsense but drove with deadly seriousness and our two partners in the back tried to ease the pace and froze because even though it wasn't a hot day, my profuse sweating forced the air conditioning full on. The pretty back seat occupants were chattering, their teeth moving behind anxious red lips, but they didn't complain. No hint of nagging or please slow down, just an understanding that we had to get to medical help and the sooner the better. The red head sat behind me with her arms outstretched over the top of the front seat and wrapped around my neck, hugging me better and keeping me safe. She held me tight, not wanting me to go. To anyone approaching, I would have looked like the passenger with four arms. Four arms and a dickey ticker. She spoke to me like I was a child or an old man. Nothing complicated, everything simple. Everything that needed an answer could be nodded but there weren't that many questions that needed a response. The big question on all our minds was not being voiced out loud. It was an awkward one that could only be answered by the experts.

Exactly why my system thought that it was once again under attack remained a mystery. Perhaps the brain played cruel tricks on its vulnerable body and the merest whiff of uneasiness resulted in an over reaction. I thought that I was going to die because I thought that I was having another heart attack and heart attacks do kill. If you think that you are going to die, it's not unreasonable to display the symptoms. But I didn't, thank God, and on August 11th of that year (1999) I made it to fifty. Not out.

August 11th was also the day of the full eclipse of the sun. Chaos was predicted for the south west of England as hoards of people headed for a butchers at the phenomenon as it tracked it's way across the Cornish sky and on to the Continent. Sun gazers were warned to use special glasses through which to study the proceedings. To look at it directly was to be struck blind. In the event the southwest coped very well and the cloud cover made sure that blindness was kept to a minimum.

The red head and I sat outside the Yeti, a restaurant in the concrete mountain complex of La Mongie set up at two thousand metres in the Hautes Pyrenees of France. In winter, and covered in snow, La Mongie looked almost pretty but in the full glare of summer, she lay exposed and undressed like a grotesque mannequin with her clothes off. We enjoyed our simple birthday lunch, mouton from the valley, and stared heavenwards at the sun as it fought its way through the cloud cover churning above us. A group of workmen sat at an adjoining table beneath a redundant Perrier umbrella. They were doing something to the mechanical lifts that hoisted the winter skiers up the slopes and one of them had a welders visor with him. I borrowed it and was able to watch through its protective dark glass, as the sun seemed to be eaten up until it became a bright nail clipping set in a darkened sky. The total black out was happening much further north but even at our latitude we were able to get an impression of the sun's temporary shut down. How strange that the sun too was suffering as I had. How encouraging that it was only an eclipse for the two of us. In days past, the end of the world would have been nigh. Prayers would have been uttered and sacrifices offered but in these enlightened times we just ordered another jug of house red. We talked.

"So you'd like to come and live out here?" The red head asked the question knowing the answer and understanding the implication. She wasn't a big fan of the Grange, my rustic French home, the one I'd had for ten years as a holiday retreat and the one I was planning to move to.

"Yes. I think I would," said I, praying that the answer I gave wouldn't make her eclipse totally, wouldn't break our bond. For me to move away and into a time warped French mountain valley while she stayed in England could stretch the tie to beyond its tolerance. I wanted to be in that part of France, needed to be in the mountains away from all that I didn't like about England, away from heart attacks and their causes. I didn't want to be away from the red head. But I was an unhealthy fifty-year-old with no job and a real craving for a change in lifestyle. She was a fit thirty one-year-old with a career and no desire to join the French peasantry. Chalk and cheese. Craie et fromage even.

"You'll keep in touch won't you?" said the red head.

I kissed her in the thin mountain air.

I'm not sure if it's right. Moving to France is a big step. A complete change. It's been great for holidays but can I really live in the Grange on my own full time? Stuck up a bloody mountain with no electricity. Water from a stream. I don't even speak the language. Will the red head kick me into touch? Will my heart be up for it? I don't know. I must be bloody mad, but I've got to do it.

Loosing My Wife 1997 ≈

I never thought it would happen to me.

I called her Fut, pronounced foot. When I first met her in Sydney in 1968 she didn't like shoes. When we first made love, she was only the second girl I had ever done it with, her toes twitched wildly. She said I was the first boy she had slept with. When we lay in the sleeping bag together after the first time, I said to her "I'm going to call you foot spelt F.u.t." I wrote home to England, back to my parents, explaining I had a girl friend called Fut. A year or so later when they met her they said "Hello Phut." We laughed. They hadn't understood that it was actually foot. Why would they?

"Hello Phut." My father greeted her not really understanding.

We'd met on a hot summer's evening in King's Cross, Sydney's den of iniquity. My travelling companion, Philip Van Welbergen, and I had been to the Wayside Chapel to watch a premiere of some poet's work at the little theatre attached to the Chapel. We'd invited two teachers we'd met to come with us. During the interval we left the auditorium and the teachers and went through the crash barrier exit door into the alley behind for a roll up. The doors of the Wayside Chapel backed on to the rear doors of a proper theatre. There where two blonde girls, schoolgirls still in their uniforms, having a free look at the show through the crack in the open fire doors. They were taking in a performance of "Hair" so we joined them. They were fun and certainly better company than the teachers, prettier too, so we asked them to come for a drink with us, abandoned the poet and the teachers. We went back to our bar in Oxford Street, the one under our room, but couldn't get in with the schoolgirls. Twenty-one was the drinking age so actually none of us was allowed in under the eyes of the law or Martin, the owner, and his sanctimonious stare. Philip and Jemma went up to the room we shared leaving the two of us to wander the streets for a while. We must have walked for miles. We just walked and talked. Talked and walked and step by step, sentence by sentence, got to like each other. We walked until the sun came up and then wandered back to the flat. Then Jemma and her friend, my new girl friend, caught an early bus back to the north shore and I kissed her goodbye for the first time.

We met frequently. She brought me peanut butter sandwiches at lunchtime in the Botanical Gardens where I had a job as a general gardener. We sat on one of the wooden benches during my lunch break and ate the sandwiches, threw the crusts to the exotic ducks and black swans, and watched the new Opera House being built. She'd skip afternoon school lessons and wait for me to finish my day's work and then we'd go back to the flat and make love. It was the summer of '68 and everyone was in love. She was seventeen and I was nineteen and we were falling in love, intoxicated by the love in the air, the love all around.

One day her parents discovered that she hadn't been at school, hadn't been staying with her friend Jemma when she said she had. Under interrogation Jemma spilled the beans and told her father where his daughter was staying that night. He arrived at the flat and found us in bed. He took her home. It was an awful night, the embarrassment, the shouting and the tears and the feeling of utter emptiness once she'd been taken away. After that we were more careful. She wasn't allowed out at night so I took the bus out to Mona Vale, where she lived, and climbed into her bed. Her room was in the basement of the house so I could come and go at will. Come noiselessly and go quietly, hopelessly in love.

After the summer of love, Philip and I had to move on. We had planned to hitch up to Darwin to shoot crocodile and there was no room for a girlfriend. We'd put it off because of my love life but really couldn't postpone it any longer. Philip and I had hitched over from Perth, hitched across the desert together and had only stopped in Sydney en route for our next big adventure. Philip was a Dutch man from Bogota. We'd met in a bar in Perth and struck up an immediate friendship. He'd been with a girl, a palm reader. I didn't believe in that sort of thing. I remember with horror that another couple in the bar wanted theirs looked at. She took their hands in hers, one at a time, but said rather too quickly that she couldn't read anything. The couple was dead within the week, killed in a car crash. I didn't know if she had seen the tragedy before it happened but the episode made the hair on the back of my neck tingle. I didn't know if she'd read Philip's palm before we set off on our journey. I wouldn't let her read mine.

I told Fut that we had to get going but promised to return in four months. We both cried. She wanted to come with me, was desperate. I asked her to wait for just four months, asked her to hang on until I'd saved up enough money so that we could run away together. I told her I'd be making a hat full up north, certainly better than the seventy dollars a fortnight I got in the gardens. It was hard to earn enough and save in Sydney. Four months should do it up north but four months seemed like an eternity. It was a long time for impetuous youth. I thought that I would always love her, couldn't imagine life without her and couldn't wait to be with her forever more. I took her to a little café with round tables and we drank real coffee and wept real tears as the stereo played " If you go to San Francisco be sure to wear some flowers in your hair." Saying goodbye to her then was one of the most miserable things I'd ever done in my life.

Philip and I didn't shoot any crocodiles but we did help to build a road between Mount Isa and Dajarra. I saved up my wages, kept them safe, hid them in a water bag and true to my word returned to Sydney four months later for the girl I loved. We met in the Botanical Gardens at the place we used to have the peanut butter sandwiches and we booked into the Australia Hotel, one of Sydney's finest. The assistant manager, an American, came to check me out.

"How will you be paying your bill sir?" he said suspicious of a young sun-tanned Hippie with no forwarding address.

"Will this be OK?" I said emptying a fat roll of dollar bills out on to the bed. I'd never earned so much money in my life before, never worked so hard either.

She was pleased to see me and I was so excited to be back with her again. We ran away the following Sunday, took an early morning bus to Melbourne and another to Adelaide. The Trans Nullarbor Express took us over to Perth, the remotest city in the world, where we found a room to live in. Ionic Street, Rossmoyne. We rented the room off a grumpy English man called Shawcross and his young son. The young son, Howard fancied Fut. I found a love note he'd written to her on the back of a photo of him playing a guitar in the yard. He was only a boy. Fut was a woman, my woman.

We hadn't a clue but we had each other. Her poor parents must have been out of their minds, but we didn't care. We were in selfish love and running away together to live happily ever after.

We married the following July at the Wayside Chapel back in Sydney. Her older sister was there and she thought it was all so much fun. Her parents were there too, but they didn't. Two months later we flew to England. In January 1970 our first son Oliver was born. A year later we had a daughter Abigail and in 1980 another son, Bartholomew. She brought up the children, while I worked at various things, tried to make money and drank far too much. We were happily married though for nearly thirty years.

Then it fell apart. She moved out that August and into a house in Bath. On the morning that the Princess of Wales's death was announced her mother rang me from Australia by mistake. She'd dialled the wrong number before I was awake and was surprised when I answered. I hadn't heard the news about Diana and we had a bizarre conversation.

Mother-in-law, "It's such a pity she's gone. Terrible news."

Me, "She might come back. Might change her mind."

Mother-in-law, "What are you talking about. She's dead." I sat up in bed abruptly.

How can she be dead? My God what have I done?

Finding The Grange 1989 ⇥

As we reach the clearing at the top of the steep mountain track, I know that the old building there, with its tin roof, will become our holiday home in the Pyrenees.

The first time I went to France was in the sixties. The Beatles latest song was Yellow Submarine and in those days, whatever the weather, summer days seemed very sunny. The Carpiers were the French family lucky enough to take me on for an exchange and their youngest son Bertrand was the actual swap. Dr and Madame Carpier lived in Quintin. I called it Kwinton much to Bertrand's annoyance. "Cantan" he would say. "C'est Cantan." But I wouldn't. Their summer villa was on the coast at Le Val Andre and for most of August, Madame Carpier and her three children, Michel, Maryvonne and Bertrand would move to the seaside. I can't remember but I think the good doctor stayed in Kwinton and popped to Le Val Andre for weekends.

Our Brittany days were filled with beach life. Volleyball matches, walks, talks, visiting other friends, listening to records that used to stack up on the record player like a black plastic kebab, waiting their turn to flop on to the turn table and spin at 45 r.p.m. Fats Domino (Blueberry Hill), the Stones (Satisfaction) and Françoise Hardy (Tous les garcons et les filles) who made my teenage toes curl. Some of the Carpier's friends were pretty interesting to the skinny, awkward English teenage boy. Chantille I remembered as glamorous and unobtainable as Françoise Hardy, and Odiele, with a haircut like a boy, who was so cool, so French. She smoked Gauloise and rode a Solex, a bicycle with an engine over the front wheel. If I were lucky, very lucky, she would let me sit on the back pannier while she drove, up there on the saddle driving the bike and me mad. Bertrand's big brother, Michel, was always big brother boisterous fun. He was the hero of the moment, the one to look up to, the real Musketeer. He taught me all the French swear words I would need and plenty I wouldn't. He gave me Gitanes cigarettes without filters and beer with my crepes. Maryvonne wasn't a French beauty and spent her days with horses. She terrified me on my last few days at the resort by saying one evening at the dinner table that it was a tradition, a custom in those parts, for the daughter to sleep with the departing male guest. It was a joke, a French joke shared by the whole family and not a very funny one for that particular guest. Such suggestions, if made back home by my sister, would have caused a parental riot of "Go to your room" proportions. There in foreign France it was just shrugs and smiles. So different, so continental.

Le Val Andre was about the most sophisticated seaside resort I had ever been to. It had a long promenade and a casino. The Carpiers took a table there one night and we all went to hear Jacques Brel sing his songs. There was a cinema and lots of little street side vendors of the delicious crepe, something I found equally as tasty as Odiele but infinitely more available.

Bertrand didn't seem interested in girls and I thought that his preferences lay elsewhere. Of course the exchange did little to improve my French language, which was the main reason for the trip. When Bertrand swapped the warm Brittany coast for the sandstorms of North Norfolk, the only words of English he added to his limited vocabulary were "Belchy makey". Belchy makey was the name my mother gave to fizzy drinks. "Encore belchy makey" Bertrand would say sheltering in a Brancaster sand dune during the ritual picnic lunch. Sandwiches were aptly named. The wind from off the North Sea would be so strong sometimes that if you didn't keep your head down in your sand dune foxhole, you'd get it blown off. Bertrand and I learned a sort of Franglaise I suppose with both families keen to chat, actually in my father's case shout, in an extraordinary language. "You like it ici. Yes. No." was the sort of high decibel phrase that the young Bertrand might have gleaned from my international father. He spoke up in the belief that all foreigners were certainly deaf and probably a little dumb as well. For my part, I came away with such useful expressions as "Tonight nous allons au cinema pour look at the flick" or the intriguing sentence that all French students of English used to be taught at school, the English translation of which meant "My tailor is rich."

If Le Val Andre represented the taste of sophistication then Le Peyras was probably the little inedible lump of fatty gristle that you'd spit out and try and hide on the side of your plate. It was at Le Peyras that I found the Grange. It was during the summer of '89 and my wife and our youngest son, Bart, were on a mission with me to seek out a holiday home in the French Pyrenees. I couldn't really explain what it was about the Pyrenees that attracted me. I had only ever flown over them before but they seemed to have just about everything my boyhood dreams had aspired to. There in the mountains was the secluded tree house from my childhood. There was skiing in the winter; proper skiing, and sun, hot sun, in the summer. There too was France with every pretty goatherd a potential Odiele. There was wholesome food and robust wine and there was a ruggedness to the place that made it foreign. There was rural romance and a way of life that was perhaps only a memory in the remotest parts of England. Those mountains were the homes of real working men and women, doing real jobs, living hard, honest lives. Those were the green mountains in spring and summer where I could walk all day without seeing another human being. There was a place I could live my dreams. Certainly escape there for a few weeks holiday every year.

"Tres rurale," I said in my very best French and sounded just like Ted Heath with a mouthful of marbles. We liked the region around the faded spa town of Bagneres-de-Bigorre and found that Patrick sort of understood us. Patrick (pronounced Patreek) was a laid back estate agent or Immoblier as they were alarmingly called. He hadn't looked convinced to start with and wanted me to buy what he had on show in the window of his tiny office in rue Marchel Foch. I couldn't help thinking that immoblier referred to his reluctance to move from behind his desk. Despite his appearance and his ambiguous address, Patrick soon caught on and we were out and about in his "cat-cat" looking at ruins perched up in the High Pyrenees. Cat-cat was actually quart-quart, the French for four by four, although it took me several days before I understood that. Patrick's cat-cat took us to new heights and areas of isolation and inaccessibility. We were shown heaps of old stone often without roofs and after some days I began to think that Patrick was just showing us all the landmarks from his youth and that if we expressed an interest he would then find out who owned it and if it was for sale.

"'Ere I ad Michelle." Patrick said at one deserted woodland ruin and a mischievous look brought a sparkle to his eyes and I suggested that we move on to the next before we too were 'ad.

"Pas du l'eau, pas d'electricity" was one sentence I learnt fairly early on although in most cases it was stating the obvious. Open fireplaces were as common as the open roofs and doors and windows often just a figment of the imagination. Earth floors carpeted most abodes and we developed an over optimistic attitude to doing things up. On one occasion I actually heard myself saying "Well it wouldn't be too difficult to convert that into a kitchen." What I should have been saying was, "If we could get rid of the sheep that have been living here and dig out their muck, oh and remove the tree growing through that wall, maybe we could find the floor." Patrick seemed pleased to be coaxed out of his office every day and he became a useful guide not only showing us remote piles of stone but also taking us to visit out of the way bars where we were expected to take aperitifs no matter what the time. Of course between twelve and two or three it was aperitifs followed by lunch. Much of the conversation remained unintelligible but we got the general idea that we were foreigners with more money than sense. That was always confirmed when it came time to depart and the "l'addition" was arrived at in the proprietors head and the ever helpful Patrick would count out the strange and colourful money from my wallet with the sort of generosity I remembered being associated with the board game Monopoly.

One sunny afternoon Patrick took us to Le Peyras, a tiny hamlet just off the broad and agricultural Campan valley. There was some consultation with a local farmer, grunts and shrugs, and we mounted a steep track and after about two hundred yards came upon a secluded stone barn with a corrugated tin roof and a chimney. The windows with their glass in place had wooden shutters and the door into the building had a handle and, most unusually, a key. The old place had not been home to sheep for some years and really did feel like a dwelling for people. The mountain ash trees that surrounded the place seemed to shake their green leaves in welcome and the fast flowing stream, splashing in the undergrowth, babbled to us that we should look no further.

We went in through the low door, into the cool, dark entrance room with its rows of boots and stacked redundant skis. The smell was boot room mixed with a damp mustiness, a leaf mould scent, and the sort of whiff a badger in his new sett might appreciate. From the dark beginning we emerged into the main room and there the light from the outside windows showed us the beamed ceiling, the underside of the rough cut floorboards from upstairs and the part-earth-part-concrete floor that we were standing on. The stone kitchen sink with its single tap, the hand made table and chairs, the black cast iron boiler and the prominent fireplace all gathered in that one living room. A rustic wooden open stairway lurched up into the roof and my young son rushed on to explore, find a world up there under the hot tin roof, a communal dormitory and one other bedroom with a set of windows, French windows, that looked out across the valley to the rock face on its other side. That then was the Grange.

It had been a mountain retreat and holiday home to an engine driver from Bordeaux and his female companion and their nine joint children. It was fairly obviously the residence of an employee of the French railways as much of the fixtures and fittings bore the legend S.N.C.F, the letters and logo of the national French rail network. In fact had we not been transported a thousand meters up a mountain, we could otherwise have been forgiven for thinking that we were on board some rolling stock stuck in a siding somewhere in rural France. The good engine driver was rather more the driver than the fixer and signs of his handiwork around the place were going to cause amusement and incredulity for years to come. The plumbing was a hosepipe from the stream. The wiring from the little generator (ex S.N.C.F.), the sort that was used to string together the fairy lights for a Christmas tree. The beds, arrayed in an open plan dormitory style, had previously been those that had slept some of the paying passengers on the couchette between Bordeaux and Paris. The main selling point for me was the enormous open fireplace that dominated the end wall of the living area. It was the ultimate campfire around which one could plan expeditions, tell tales, eat, drink and sharpen one's knife in readiness for the next big adventure. Sensibly, it was one of those fire places common in the mountains where the working face of the fire, the hearth, was set up at two feet or so above floor level, allowing for a wood store under the fire and heat at mid body height. The fireplace was designed to be used as a place for preparing food as well as plans. It was big enough to take whole tree trunks and I couldn't wait to light it as my own.

Buying a property takes time. In France there was an agreement to buy and an agreement to sell that both had to be signed. A small deposit was lodged with the notaire. A cooling off period then ensued just in case the parties changed their minds. The local mayor was offered the place because it was deemed as agricultural and he could, if he had wanted to, buy it instead of us. He declined the offer. The whole process took some months and having found the Grange in August, we agreed to complete the deal and take possession the following December, just in time for our first Christmas holiday in the mountains.

There seemed to be a two-tier system to pricing when it came to buying a property in that part of France. Three if the immoblier was to be believed. There was the ticket price or the price the immoblier displayed in his window. There was the price we offered and the seller accepted and then there was the price we actually paid. The Grange was advertised at the equivalent of £36,000. We agreed a price of £30,000 but "officially" paid £20,000. The 'missing' £10K was handed to the engine driver in the notaire's office when the notaire left the room to go for a 'smoke'. The notaire seemed to know exactly what was going on even though he was doing himself out of some commission. That was perhaps why notaires' fees were higher in France. Somehow it felt naughty handing over an envelope with lots of real money in it. But there I was sliding a very fat bundle of used French notes across the notaire's desk towards the engine driver. Patrick who had been instrumental in concocting the deal nodded his approval and reassured the sellers that there would be no need to count the money. It would all be there he whispered to the engine driver who looked as though his boiler had been well and truly stoked. Ten grand in cash was a lot of money that the French taxman wouldn't get to hear about. The last we saw or heard of the engine driver and his female companion was a smile the length of a railway line and a "merci beaucoup" as they headed off to the Cafe Londres to start the spending. Ten thousand in sterling was a lot of notes, two hundred fifties or five hundred twenties. In French francs it was even more. I'd transferred the money from England to France some weeks before the deal was going to be completed in the notaire's office. I had sent it from a bank account in the U.K. to one I had opened in the market town in France. So the day arrived for the deal to be completed, four months after Patrick had first introduced us to the Grange, and we arrived in town and went to the bank and asked for ten thousand pounds worth of French francs. They looked at me as though I was asking for gold bullion or my weight in diamonds.

"Is not possible," said the pretty teller.

"Is very possible. Imperative," said I looking at my watch, my wife and young son and expecting to be in the notaire's office for the completion of the deal in two hours. My use of the word imperative had sounded more like a request for alcoholic liquid refreshment. The director of the bank walked across from his desk. He was the director because he was wearing the tie. He had a smile too. Quite reasonably he explained in slow French, the branch didn't carry that sort of money and if we needed the hundred thousand francs we seemed to want, then could we come back next week. I explained the deal. My wife and son left the building understanding that some sort of French complication had occurred. One head was better than two or three when it came to sorting out local difficulties.

"Could you not bike it over from Tarbes?" I asked trying to be helpful, a bit like suggesting they fetch it from the moon. The director invited me over to his desk for a coffee; he had a cigarette to help things along. He then decided to get his two tellers to count what money they had. After three-quarters of an hour or so we found nearly sixty thousand francs.

"Will this do?" asked the director. Not at all sure whether it would or not, the day was saved when the local travel agent and the garage man arrived within minutes of each other to deposit some takings which gave me the bag full of money I needed to give to the engine driver. We sat there in the bank counting out the money and the director and his two tellers sent me off to the notaire's office with pats on the back for a good job done, a mixed bag of denominations and my hands grubby and smelling of used notes. For the money we became the new owners of the Grange and its surrounding acres, its entire contents including all the knives, forks, spoons and crockery (all S.N.C.F. stamped) and an old green four wheel drive Lada Niva for getting up and down to the place. Our very own cat-cat.

What we bought with excitement and enthusiasm one minute could on the next turn out to be an anticlimax. The green cat-cat didn't start and the generator with its S.N.C.F. endorsement was also on strike. When we'd last seen the Grange back in the summer it had looked lived in and loved. Now in the depths of winter the snow made the place cold and damp. So the first night of our ownership was spent in the Chalet Hotel down the mountain in Sainte Marie-de-Campan and not up in the new holiday home. We sat in the hotel's sparse dinning room, the only guests, and examined the vast expanse of Formica beautifully lit by the fluorescent tubes. We ate the confit of duck and razor thin chips served by a surly dwarf and thought about the money we had just spent, the dirty cash and the legal cheque, and doubt crept over our decision to buy the Grange. We went to our cold stark beds having tried to console ourselves with a local red wine, Madiran, which did nothing to bring on feelings of well being and much to encourage indigestion. What on earth were we doing?

The long night was full of dreams about the used note mountain and the laughing engine driver tossing bundles of currency into the furnace that kept his beast on the rails. Patrick's happy face superimposed onto the front of the train like some French equivalent of Thomas the Tank engine. Patrick the T.G.V. The Grange itself lying helpless across the rail tracks, unable to get out of the way, unable to avoid the inevitable, and snow, swirling snow as bright as the light that eventually told me the next day had arrived.

And what a day it was! Bright sunshine and deep snow as if all my best school boy dreams had been topped off with a bowl full of exotic ice cream. We climbed up to the new holiday home that we had purchased the day before. Up through the snow laden trees, their branches bowing under their wintry burden. The smell of wood smoke from the working fireplaces pushed up from the valley below. Farm dogs barked and quarrelled and a small dilapidated white Citroen van wove its way down the single track road, off to the bakery perhaps, its driver just an impression of stubble, cigarette and beret. He waved at us, the obvious strangers. We walked on and up, each marked footstep a print that told us we weren't dreaming. The air was so pure, so sharp; that we knew each lung full was like the word of God. Up the final steep track beside the rushing stream whose source came gushing out on our land. The sound of water as reassuring as life itself. And just when the climb started to make us weary, there, sitting on a piece of level ground cut out on the mountain side contour was the tiny house. The sun, unseen there as yet, had its brilliant influence on the snowy peaks opposite. To look at them would make us cry, our eyes watering at their dazzling whiteness or maybe tears of another kind. The Grange looked wonderful and all doubts faded away as we stood, knee deep in snow, outside our new front door and marvelled at the mountains wrapped all around us.

It is time to light that fire for the very first time.

Meeting The Red Head 1994

There is a look that two people give to each other when they first meet and feel that attraction, a look that says, "Hey I'd like to get to know more about you."

I had never liked red heads. I always thought that people with red hair had short tempers, too much Celtic blood in their veins. I didn't know why I'd carried the impression with me, but I had. I'd never been out with a girl with red hair nor ever kissed one. The red head joined the company as a designer. She worked in the studio with the others in the team. The first thing I noticed about her, after the shock of red hair, was her smile. She had a big mouth full of even tomb stone sized white teeth. It was the sort of mouth that dominated the face. It took complete control of the lower half and when it broke out into a smile, became the focal point for the whole thing. It was a big smile from a little girl, an innocent smile that drummed up naughty thoughts. Her brown eyes twinkled when she smiled, danced with fun and expelled her sense of humour. She wasn't a beautiful girl but she did have an attraction, a youthful liveliness and intelligence that popped and bubbled around her. It wasn't though precocious in any way. She'd flirt without perhaps meaning to. She was one of those people that would look directly into your eyes when talking to you. Would give undivided attention. She was one of those people that made you feel flattered, important. She almost had an aura, a static charge, about her, not a halo, but something that distinguished her from those around, those other pretty designers. She was short and slim and looked as though she had been a gymnast. When she wore a skirt, which wasn't that often, her legs looked fantastic and what ever she wore, her bottom looked perfect. She was twenty something and therefore nearly twenty years younger than I was. From the first time I met her, I fancied her, couldn't wait to get to know her, hoped she wanted to get to know me. Probably in my dreams.

We'd been to several business meetings together, some genuine where her contribution was warranted but others where she had just come along for the ride. I was enjoying flirting with her more and more and found myself thinking about her on occasions when my mind should have been focusing on other more important issues. I can't remember what the excuse was, but one evening she invited me to her flat at the top of a Georgian building in Bath. She cooked a sea food pasta and we sat together at a little round table in the flat enjoying the food and each other's company. When she came to clear the empty plates, smeared with the juice of her cooking, I grabbed her hand and pulled her down towards me firmly but not in any way threatening. As she came down our lips met and we kissed, my thin ones beautifully engulfed by her big mouth, swallowed up with our pasta tongues circling each other. Soon pushing my chair back from the table, I manoeuvred her to my lap where she sat with her back to me. I started to kiss her nape, the vulnerable flesh covering the spine just before it reaches the brain. She had piled her red hair up somehow so that her slender neck presented itself as a new thrill. She enjoyed the experience and before long the two of us were standing by the open window in the dark with only the outside streetlights to guide us. We behaved recklessly, without worrying about the consequences.

I guess that's how it is. That's when I started to fall in love for the second time. That's what led to the end of twenty-seven years of happily married life, led to the bloody heart attack and the move to France.

Farewell Party 1999

I can't leave England without saying goodbye or more truthfully "See you".

The belated celebration for my fiftieth birthday coupled with a leaving party, was held at the Bath Arms in Horningsham, a pub just outside the back entrance of Longleat. Ashley was the landlord of the place, since disgraced for having his hand more firmly in the till than on the tiller, he put on a splendid do. I guess the principle guests were my mother and father who arrived from their own separate parts of East Anglia and who ended up sharing a room together in the annexe to the pub. Divorced for the best part of twenty years, they realised their love for each other was still as strong as ever. True father had gone off with another, had thought he'd found what he wanted else where, had remarried, but in his heart of hearts mother was still the woman for him. Even his new wife must have guessed as much for the two of them were barely on speaking terms any more. At his home father took his meals in one room, his wife in another. It wasn't what he had imagined it might have been. So any occasion where he could meet up with mother, talk to her and better still stay under the same roof, in the same room, was a real treat. My sister made me laugh. When she had them to stay in her Manor House in Gloucestershire, she had to turn a blind eye when it came to keeping them to their separate bedrooms. She didn't really want to hear the creek of late night floorboards between their rooms. She was used to that with her own teenagers but not her divorced parents.

My sister, the one with the Manor House, turned up for the party. It was very brave of her as she was still getting over the death of her husband. His memorial service was only a few days before my own farewell party. His theme had been City suits with some uplifting music, mine was French with a very loud rock band. Considering her state of mind, my sister's effort was immense. The invitations I'd sent out said " Charlie's 50 and going Frog" and encouraged guests to dress up as something French. She dressed as a fine French chef in a uniform purloined from one. Mother dressed as a French maid while father wore a suit and the beret that he'd swapped for his wife's bra at an international rugby match in Paris. There were sixty-nine partygoers, a totally unplanned but wholly appropriate number, and the French theme took the whole place over and spilled out into a marquee put up over the back garden.

After the food, the band struck up. They looked the part. A friend had recommended them from Bristol. They had come to the venue fully loaded for a public concert to several thousand fans, not sixty-nine types pretending to be French. I suppose that the address might have given them the wrong impression. Longleat was the gig they'd come to play and right from the very first cord, we all knew that everyone for miles around would be able to hear their thumping compositions. Ashley, our host, became apoplectic. He answered the telephone because he thought it was ringing but couldn't then hear who was on the line because of the rock band's session. It was of course irate locals ringing to complain about the noise, only to find that the noise they were ringing to complain about prevented their complaint from being heard. The thing about enthusiastic young rock bands was that they did go on a bit. One "tune" led almost imperceptibly into another and the several gallons of rough cider the boys had been drinking before they were asked to perform gave them added bravado. It wasn't until Ashley pulled the power on them that things returned to near normality. The pub's telephone could be heard along with the ringing in all the guests' ears and in the distance the grumbling roar of the disgruntled lions of Longleat.

It was a good thrash. People were very kind and all wished me well for my new life in France. The red head met my mother for the first time and I caught the two of them, the mature French maid lecturing the young Breton top. Mrs Thatcher meets Minnie the Minx. When the last guests had stumbled out, the red head and I took to a bed in one of the Bath Arms bedrooms and slept soundly. Not for us a night (or more truthfully an early morning) of passion but rather the sort of sleep induced by large quantities of alcohol and the general relief that the party had gone rather well. It was our last night together for goodness knows how long but instead of stocking up with each other, we seemed to practise the idea of learning to live without each other.

Hotel breakfast the following morning saw mother returned to her normal English attire but with the same inquisitor's approach to the red head and her intentions.

"So will you be having children?" Mother asked her before the first cup of tea as we all sat at the same big table.

" Marmalade or children with your toast?" I said trying to make the red head relax. Father shared an interest in the exchange and moved his Daily Telegraph ever so slightly. I knew that behind it, he'd stopped reading so he could fully concentrate on the answer to mother's question.

"One day," said the red head. "If I'm lucky enough," she added and father returned to find the price of potato futures.

I felt twenty again rather than a hung over fifty-year-old. My mother was talking about my future, checking out the suitability of my girl friend. She seemed more concerned about the relationship than I was but then that was a mother's prerogative.

I loaded up my big Ifor Williams builder's trailer and hit the road for Plymouth and the ferry to Santander. I was on my own, off to start a new future in the high Pyrenees.

I didn't really say goodbye to anyone. I certainly didn't want to say goodbye to the red head. It was more like "See you." Then they all got on with their lives, she went back to hers without me, and I went off to get on with mine.

It is time to light that fire again and hope that it won't go out.

Maurice And Michel ⇒⊣

The fire is still hot. The Grange has become my permanent home. Momo is slicing saucisson again.

Colour was the only way to tell Maurice from Michel at a distance. Maurice had a big red beard. Michel's was big and going grey. The two men had grown up friends and taken on each other's mantels. Michel was older by ten years, but not necessarily wiser. He was the musician, and could play the accordion. Maurice, or Momo to those close to him, normally provided the percussion after a drink or two. They both wore berets, blue denim jeans and sharp knives on their belts. Trainers on their feet in summer and fur-lined snow boots in winter. Apart from beard colour, the only other major point of difference was their T-shirts. Slogans were essential. "Slim City" looked out of place across Maurice's considerable upper body. Michel's favorite was "Try me, fly me", an invitation only the foolhardy would accept.

Maurice and Michel seemed to have the strength of many men. While my neighbour Claude enrolled a donkey for hauling essentials up the mountain, Maurice and Michel thought nothing of bringing up an old wooden sideboard to the Grange. Or the enormous brass bed I purchased from Heals all those years ago and had shipped over from England in the trailer.

"What's wrong with French beds?" Maurice asked as he shuffled up the steep track, the foreign brass frame spread across his back.

All physical toil was undertaken in the morning and it was essential to make sure that all the tasks were completed by midday. "Aperos" always preceded the meal. Michel always drank neat whiskey. The glass tumbler, an empty mustard pot, was frequently replenished. Michel drank whiskey because he was thirsty, like a child with a glass of lemonade. The quality of the Scotch or Irish was never questioned. A fine old single malt dressed up in an elaborate bottle and worth £5 a shot was sunk with exactly the same enthusiasm as something from the local supermarket called Sir Scotch. Maurice drank Ricard, an alcoholic aniseed mouthwash that would eventually rot the brain. Both men smoked cigarettes bought from over the mountains in Spain, where they were as cheap as the mountain air although a lot less pure.

The midday aperitifs would have slaked the thirst of a Rugby football team. Then the business of lunch was attended to. Knives were taken out, opened and felt with the thumb; a glance across the steel to ensure that the edge was keen. A saucisson or two were unhooked from a nail stuck into the beam over the kitchen sink. Maurice carved. For such a big man, he was remarkably delicate with his knife. He could slice up a gristly dry pure pork sausage into thin rounds. Then he'd peel off its protective dusted skin and flick the pieces from the end of his knife across the table to spin and flop on the appropriate plate. Each saucisson was discussed and its merits chewed over with the baguette. One had too much garlic, another not enough salt. One needed to hang for a week or two longer. The other was made when the moon wasn't right, so it might as well be thrown out for the dogs or the carrion.

After sausage came the duck. Magret, the breast of a duck, as thick as a steak, its puckered plucked skin on one side riding a layer of yellow fat and tender flesh on the other, cooked on the heat from the embers in the open fire place. It was turned over on the metal griddle, branded by the heated bars. The liquid hot fat splattered into the fire, dripped and ran through the greasy wet bars. The ash below hissed and the flames sprang up and danced for the duck, singeing the meat and sending its smell back into the room and up the chimney and out into the woods. Another flash with the knife and Maurice sliced a gash into the cooking meat. The outside browned, blistered by the wood heat. But the inside was a dark pink wound, oozing duck juice.

Cooking in the mountains was always a way to complement the food, never ruin it. Heat was applied to encourage the flavour, coax it from within. "Well done" was a congratulation, not a culinary request. There wasn't an expression for it. "Bien cuire" meant well cooked, which to Maurice's way of thinking was just the way he did things. Maurice's meat caressed its heat, didn't hang about for a lengthy affair. The magret filled the plate where before it the slices of saucisson had lain and the sharp Laguioles set to work, each cut brought forth the red juices. The meat was consumed on its own, slice after slice with only a mouthful of red wine and maybe a cheek full of bread. Cheap wine never tasted so good. Daily bread so fresh. The green stringy beans lay steaming in their bowl on the table waiting their turn on the plate. There was an order for everything, no queue barging, no mixing or mingling of the tastes. Meat with maybe a knife swipe of mustard like oil paint never shared its place with a mere vegetable. The only possible exception was the chip. "Steak frit," said like it was joined at the hip.

Then last of all came the cheese. Goats, cows or ewes and the unmistakable flavour of meadows, high mountain pasture and course sward. That then was lunch.

When I'd broken bread in my home with my neighbours and been invited back to theirs, I knew that things were moving in the right direction. Maurice and Michel made me feel a part of the community. Even though we didn't speak the same language, we seemed to share a common love for our surroundings and the simple pleasures of good food and alcohol. Mountain men together, perhaps

Momo cleans his knife on a piece of bread, closes the sharp blade with a squeeze of his big fist and replaces it in the leather pouch on his overworked belt.

Butler ⇒

When I see Butler's bloody body lying in the road, I think he is dead.

Butler was the only other English man living in the valley. The force of the little Renault that hit him took him through the air like a scud missile and landed him like a rag doll. I didn't see it, thank God. But I heard it, the sound of tyres sliding on tarmac, a rubber zip, then a dull thud, a tin panel being beaten by a bag of bones and the sprinkling of broken glass. The screams of a woman like something from the news. I ran round from the courtyard of the house that we were visiting, and out into the road. The D935 was not a big road. I could probably spit across it. I couldn't really believe that there, lying in it, dying in it, on a Sunday afternoon, bleeding and broken, lay my friend Butler. I wanted a helicopter. Now, and said as much. "Helicoptere maintenant" I seemed to shout. But there was little chance. We thought he was a goner. Butler himself wouldn't have known much. The Renault driver didn't really know what to think either and wandered about in a daze. He'd had too much at lunch. His wife and little girls, standing there, knew that Daddy had perhaps done something wrong.

The moaning started, the dark blood oozing from Butler's ear. His bright red woollen sweater was darkening. Butler in the road was complaining. "My legs" he kept shouting. "My legs". From where I knelt beside him, his legs looked the least of his problems. But they weren't arranged on that road in a way that looked comfortable. In crisis, when I didn't know what to do, I was shocked. Reality became a film in slow motion. It was as though I wasn't actually there. Like a big bird high above the valley, soaring on the thermal but watching every slow move down below on the road. Butler just lay there a broken moaning mess. I held his hand and tried to comfort him. I mopped the blood from off the road in shock, tried to cleanse the Tarmac, soak up the gore. Mrs Butler was hysterical, distraught beyond measure, crying for her dying man. But I still kept calling for that helicopter. "Now" I said in a loud voice, as though Thunderbirds were a go in the next field. The experts, the Sapeur Pompiers, were on the scene in moments. Those used to it arrived and took control. For me it was a minefield, for them it was like shelling peas. They had Butler off the road and in the ambulance in no time. We followed behind the urgent flashing lights in the dash to Tarbes hospital, a trip that could take thirty or forty minutes, but on that occasion a lifetime.

All that had happened years before. I had been on holiday, staying at the Grange. It was Easter, April 27th, 1997 to be precise. Since the accident Butler had been rebuilt but the scars were there, some very visible and some even he couldn't see. His injuries were horrendous. Both legs with more breaks than a snooker player would dream of. The bones in his body rearranged; cracked and broken, with internal injuries that kept doctors busy for ages. A head that had been rattled down a Pyrenean mountain road causing fractures disturbed vision, perforated eardrums and flying teeth. The Butler that woke up on that spring morning of the 27th would never again go back to bed as the same man. He walked with a stick and would need more surgery, two new knees at least. Before that little Renault hit him, he seemed a reasonable man. Rational and calm. He was still a reasonable man but his fuse had shortened.

French bureaucracy hadn't helped his blood pressure. The Butler dossier was thicker than the Great Wall of China. He used to work at the ski resort as a lift operator but couldn't any longer. Trying to get the compensation he deserved and needed took over three years and a forest of paper. Had the accident happened in America, Butler would probably have received a hundred times what was awarded. In the UK it might have been ten times. In France if you were in your late fifties and got run over by a drunk driver, nearly died, spent two and a half painful years in and out of hospital, emerged with more metal nuts and bolts in your body than Frankenstein's monster, had your hearing, taste buds and eye sight changed, had to take heart pills, ulcer pills, stress pills, sleeping pills and pain killers for the rest of your life, you were given a settlement of £40,000. That probably made Butler sorer than anything else he had to suffer.

We first ran into each other in the summer of 1991. The local village was "en fete" and amongst the festivities was a bicycle race. Some friends were staying with me and their son Dom entered on his mountain bike. But a farm dog took a piece out of his leg and cut short his race. Dom needed a doctor and the Butlers happened to be at the village bar. Back then, Butlers and bars were like camels and oases. They directed us to the local doctor who stitched the wound with something that looked like catgut in one hand and a cigarette in the other. The Butlers could never be accused of understatement. Dom was going to get rabies.

Butler-speak was a spectator sport. It was quick fire, machine gun stuff. They lived full time in the valley for over a decade. Cabin fever probably set in years ago, after the rose coloured spectacles had been thrown down and stamped on. Butler's accident had obviously tested the relationship between Mr and Mrs to the limit. Some days I could sense that the slightest spark would ignite an inferno. For most of their days, they only had each other for company, and their cats. On occasions they had driven each other mad. Other English speakers invariably set them off, by introducing a key word into the conversation. Guest. "Think I saw quite a big wild boar trundling across the edge of the wood." Butler. "Call that big! You ought to have seen the one that came down here last spring. That was big." Mrs B. "Oh enormous! No much bigger. This one would have killed a man." Butler. "It did. Last year." Mrs B. "Excuse me for interrupting. Year before and it was two. Two men. It killed two men." Butler. "No Dick head! That was the year before that. The year when what's his face hanged himself in that tree." Mrs B. "Oh yes. But it wasn't a tree it was a barn and of course they didn't find him for weeks. Months actually." Butler. "Years. Just a skeleton." Mrs B. "Excuse me for interrupting." Butler. "Dick head."

The Butlers had hard times in France but they stuck to their guns. Others would have packed up and gone home to fall on the British benefit system. The Butlers had not. In the valley the size of a man's log pile proclaimed his status. The marque of his car and the cut of his cloth were pretty much irrelevant. You could be as poor as church mice and have a decent life. ("No you couldn't!" "Yes you could!" "Dick head!") They were big-hearted people, which was just as well with what they had gone through.

While he was in rehab at the hospital he made a breadboard. It's inset with little square ceramic mosaics. All the dark ones are grouped together in a line, which probably says something to a shrink. My name is written on the back of it with a brief message, scrawled in bold felt tip pen. He's left it to me when he dies. That says loads to me. "Ballwalks," I shout at him and know he understands.

The Bar

"Merci patron" I say as Marc shuffles another demi across the bar at me.

The village bar was "Du Bertrand" in Sainte Marie-de-Campan. Strange pieces of memorabilia and odd photographs hung amongst the bottles and advertising point of sale. There was a picture of the old bar dog, Soda, who used to chase every vehicle that drove past the place. It was a dangerous pursuit for dogs in those parts, and I saw a fair number of three-legged mutts. His indoor hobby was mounting customers' lower legs and jerking up and down on them with a Mutley smile on his hairy face. Soda was lucky. He died with all his limbs intact, and a drinker's enlarged liver. The bar was attached to the shop and run by the same family, Marc and Magalli Bertrand. When I first arrived in the village I could get a simple plat du jour in the bar. Sadly the economics didn't stack up. The younger brother Daniel the chef had to leave to find work elsewhere.

Before he departed I asked Daniel if he would prepare me a supper for about ten people. He seemed delighted. Every time I saw him before the event he would smile broadly and do that thing the French do of tapping his forefinger three or four times against the side of his nose. It was an action that said he knew what he was doing, he had everything under control, and what he was doing was his business and not open for discussion. So I left things to Daniel.

The evening arrived and the little bar looked exactly the same as always. Some of the plastic tables had been pushed together and covered in paper gingham table clothes. The pinball machine and motorcycle race simulator games were still plugged in. The radio was tuned to Nostalgie, a station that played the sixties and seventies. The bar had been the village railway station years before. It still had the look of a place where people came and went without loitering too long. It wasn't a welcoming place, no fireplace or comfortable chairs. It was functional, with three pumps for beer, cider and water, a coffee making machine, some optics and a collection of bottles. A cork notice board had a couple of dog-eared post cards, pictures from Morocco, and old photos of the landlord in a silver wig and some children playing in the snow. An out of date handbill advertised the village en fete. Two bare light bulbs hung from the nicotine coloured ceiling. The severe light provided a place where the flies could circle and watch their bar mates below. The smell of the communal lavatory out the back forced its way into the bar every time anybody went off to use it. Behind the door marked 'Prive' were the living quarters of the family and the little butcher who cut up his meat and served in the shop. The floor still had the station waiting room quarry tiles worn over the years. Travellers and revellers each adding to the erosion.

Daniel emerged. The only difference to his normal look was a white tea towel draped over his arm. There was no choice to that evening's menu. My guests looked as though they were in for a croque-monsieur, or steak and chips at best. What followed was a feast that was still talked about. For several happy hours that warm evening the drab little bar shone with Michelin stars. Foie gras, saumon fume, huitres, tete de veau, gesier de canard, truite, boeuf en croute, fromages et tarte aux pommes, tarte au citron et aux amandes et cafe. The alcohol was pression, cidre, Champagne, Jurancon, Madiran, some bottles of rather fine St Emillion and lashings of local eau-de-vie. We didn't sit down to start things properly until ten o'clock, so we were all still in the bar enjoying our feast at two in the morning. People would wander in and stare at the spread in disbelief. "Bon appetit" they would all say. Some, the more familiar, would shake hands or offer their cheeks by way of greeting.

Opening hours for the bar had always seemed at the discretion of the person running it. That evening the bar was sill jumping when the mini fete caught the attention of the cruising gendarmes. Three of them passed the bar in their blue Citroen van. The front end looked like it had be driven at speed into a brick wall and the back half had been manufactured from corrugated tin. The vehicle pulled up at the fountain opposite and the three policemen had sauntered across the road to see what all the excitement was about. Daniel explained.

They seemed quite happy about things, but a trifle concerned how the guests in the bar would be getting home. A row of our cars was parked outside. Law didn't allow drinking and driving. One of the policemen produced a breathalyser kit and gave it to Daniel so he could try it out on us. The only person who didn't turn the crystals an illegal shade was Electra, the eight-year-old daughter of one of the guests. She wasn't driving. With the gendarmes outside the bar we suddenly felt under siege. Then Daniel invited them to some liquid refreshment at a table inside the bar. They marched in and looked at us and marched past to their table at the back of the bar and sat down with their backs turned towards us. Daniel hurried back to our table and very politely wished us all a very good night. It was time to go and we didn't hang about.

"No more for me thanks," I plead in a way that I know will be ignored.

Les Deux Cols ⚔

"Well good hello young gentle man," says Jean-Bernard as he wipes his hand on his apron.

The only hotel in the village was called Les Deux Cols. Across the road from the village bar, the road that went off to the Col d'Aspen, the large square building had been made to look more attractive with a mural on its outside. The artist had depicted a bear baiting scene. The hotel's owner was a tall man with a potbelly and a prominent nose, its nostrils the same size as his eyes. He was called Jean-Bernard and he and his pretty wife and two daughters ran the place and its restaurant.

Jean-Bernard had leant all about running hotels in Paris where he had worked as a chef in the Hilton. If his front of house experience was self-taught, so was his English. He would make the effort though when a group of foreigners walked in. Anything he said in English started with the word "well".

"Well you can take a table here over there and be sitting in quietness for us to serve you before too longer." With English friends, I was afraid the giggles would start before we'd take our seats.

"Well what drinks?" our host would ask in his best English once we sat down. If his English language wasn't all that it should be, his cooking was fantastic. Four courses in the simple restaurant would normally satisfy the most discerning pallet. The reasonable price caused the English visitors to smile some more, and order another Cognac. The patron was only too pleased to serve them, take their money. He laughed all the way to his bank.

Jean-Bernard's commercial sense was better than most in the valley. His common sense wasn't. He had crammed as many tables as possible into his ground floor restaurant area. The non-smoking section was outside in the road. Between some of the tables he had placed post card spinners, wire towers, displaying picture post cards of the valley. Diners could browse them between courses, add their purchases to the bill. Most of the diners also stayed in the place and Jean-Bernard had a great way of preventing his patrons from leaving without paying. Every night he would lock them in. There was only one door at the bottom of the stairs to the upstairs rooms. Once all the guests had gone to their rooms, Jean-Bernard would lock the door.

"What happens if there's a fire?" I ask.
"Well I am insurance," Jean-Bernard says.

Peyras Punch Up

Claude doesn't look like a jailbird.

Claude was my nearest neighbour. His grange was even further up the mountain than mine, and the only way to his place was by foot. Claude was a gentle soul from Tarbes, a retired insurance salesman who coached rugby in his spare time. His grange was his bolthole. He arrived for a few days at a time, pottered in his mountain garden and chopped wood. Claude frequently left little gifts of homegrown vegetables or cepes on my outside table. He was a kind-hearted and gentle man.

On Saturday night I was cooking a fish stew in the Grange. The Butlers, Maurice and Michel, Roget, his partner Michelle, and her twenty-year-old daughter Natalie were my guests. It was dark outside, as dark as it could be in the mountains under thick cloud cover. Through the window I saw the flash of torchlight, a dancing beam. I went outside. Claude and three other men were making their way up the track to his place. I crossed the stream by the bridge and invited them in for a drink. Claude could hardly stand. He giggled like a naughty schoolboy. They had already had far too much. Nevertheless they agreed to come in, so I turned and left them to follow me. After five minutes they still hadn't appeared so Roget and Natalie went out to see where they were. Two minutes later Natalie came running in with a bleeding nose. Through her blood and tears, she sobbed that Roget was in the stream. The men ran outside. Our torch beams illuminated Roget's dripping bulk as he clambered up the bank from out of the fast flowing water. He shook like a wet dog and looked as fierce as a wild one. One of the drunken bunch had turned nasty, punched Natalie, and pushed Roget in the stream.

"I lost my footing." Roget tried not to look defeated. All four assailants had disappeared up the mountain to the refuge of Claude's grange.

I was happy to let things go. In the morning everything would be all right. Natalie's nose wasn't broken and Roget's pride was only dented and dampened. But Natalie's mother, Michelle, wanted to call the police. No one was going to hit her daughter. No one was going to push her man into the stream and get away with it. Michelle was a big woman. No one messed with Michelle. The police were telephoned.

It took them an hour or so to reach my Grange. The officer and his young assistant walked up to the Grange leaving their police Land Rover at the bottom on the hard road. The tall uniformed policeman was out of breath and sat down to hear the story. Everyone had his or her version of events. He saw Natalie's nose, her blackening eyes, and the bloody tissues. He asked for directions to Claude's grange.

"Straight up," said Michel truthfully.

About three quarters of an hour later the policeman was back looking very pale and shaken. "They pulled out a gun and told me to go away." He said it as though this was the first time he had ever been on the wrong end of a shotgun. It probably was. He advised us all to leave the Grange immediately.

"There's no telling what they might do, " he said.

I wasn't going to leave my home. But all the others scampered off, leaving me with a cauldron full of fish stew and a drunken gang of gunslingers six hundred yards away. I slept like a log and woke to a banging on the door at about seven the next morning. A dozen seriously armed policemen had arrived. The officer from the previous evening explained to his reinforcements that I was an Englishman, and asked me if I was all right in a way that I wasn't sure if the two things were connected.

The armed troop, all wearing body armour, set off up the mountain. Two of them had machine guns. There wasn't a shoot out, or indeed much resistance. The armed force returned down the track with the four hung over miscreants in handcuffs, their unshaved early Sunday morning heads bowed. All of them spent the day in the Campan jail down the mountain road towards Bagneres. Claude was deemed not to have done anything terribly wrong and got off with a warning. He was so embarrassed by the whole affair that he burst into tears the next time I saw him. The chap who had done the punching and the gun waving was fined and cautioned and had to pay Natalie some compensation. Sadly not enough for a nose job though.

Come to think of it, Claude hasn't been around for some time.

Mountain Women ⇒

"Oh Charl you are beautiful man." I think Christine is trying to flirt with me again.

Michelle, mother of the punched Natalie and partner to Roget, wasn't small. She rolled rather than walked, and she would literally smother her guests with her warm kisses. Michelle had a vast store of affection and Momo would often wink at me and join the back of the queue for seconds. I was all right with just one helping.

Michelle was the social climber of the mountain. An invitation from her to Roget's place wasn't a casual gesture like most others. Michelle planned her menu and her table setting with extreme precision. All her 'best' china and coloured glass was heaped on to the Spanish lace clothed table. But what lay on the table was only the icing on the cake. Roget's simple grange with electricity was made over to look like a chintzy grotto.

The proceedings started with a punch, not the sort that had collided with Natalie's nose, but a cocktail that Michelle deemed as sophistication personified. Most of her guests thought that the brew tasted like Coca-Cola with an added sweet sparkling wine. The frothy, fizzy, sweet brown liquid was ladled from the blue glass punch bowl into the matching blue drinking glasses clamped in their gold coloured metal holders. It was always the same. After one or two polite sips, Michel went on to his neat whiskey, Maurice his Ricard and the Butlers their wine. It was left to Roget, the hostess, the other guests and me to work our way through the mixture. After my first invitation I caught on and would politely decline Michelle's insistence to partake. I stuck with wine. Michelle's cocktail had the effect of making those that drunk it very quickly, very drunk. And she loved it more than anybody. There was nothing attractive about a drunken woman and a drunken woman her size was actually rather frightening. Roget didn't seem to mind though.

Of all the women I came to know in the valley, Christine was the warmest. She used to be the manageress up at the Yeti restaurant in La Mongie, when Annie owned the place, before her son was killed in his car one evening travelling down from the top. Christine took her role as manageress very seriously and she took her work home with her. Invited out to Michel's or the Butler's or mine, she would assume responsibility for the preparations and even the menu. Her table decorations made the thing look like the ornate high altar in the village church. She took pleasure and meant well although Louise Butler called her a busy body. Never to her face though.

In Christine, big Michelle found an adoring soul mate. The two would shop together at a popular emporium in town; an extraordinary retail outlet called 'Drop'. Keen pricing was their strategy. Cheap imported china ornaments were stacked on wooden shelves next to mops and buckets, silk flowers next to obscure brand batteries and plastic picture frames along side those little wooden sticks used to get runny honey out of the jar. Drop was one of the busiest shops in Bagneres.

Christine had a flat down in Bagneres although she preferred to rent a place higher up the valley. The flat was where she had discovered her husband's body, his brains all over the ceiling, the shotgun lying next to him, the final instrument in stopping his awful gambling addiction. Christine's late husband had been one of the managers in the town's casino, a very unlucky throw of the dice. No one blamed her for moving out of the flat and up the valley.

Roget was besotted with Michelle. Roget was a farmer in the summer and a piste basher at the ski resort in the winter. From a big family and related to lots of folk on the mountain, the big man met the big woman when she offered to manicure his nails. Michelle was an incongruous travelling beautician. The unlikely manicure led to the relationship and to Roget's bank account being drained of its balance. It transpired that Michelle was a serial gold digger and her social climbing days had allegedly been confined to prison. Roget didn't have a clue that he was being taken to the cleaners. Michelle used to intercept the postman and 'deal' with any awkward letters from the bank advising Roget that his borrowing was causing concern. One of his cheques eventually 'bounced', and it was illegal to bounce a cheque. Roget discovered the awful truth about Michelle. Every cloud had a silver lining. There were no more over-the-top supper parties at Roget's grange. Momo missed them and poor Roget went into a bit of a black hole after Michelle's sting.

I stoop to kiss Christine on the cheeks, the ledge and nesting place for her glasses, and thank her for her gift, a hand crocheted place mat, I think.

Pepe Joseph

The old man's gnarled grey hands smother the little glass. He raises the sugar sweet wine to his quivering mouth, as though it was the heaviest load he'd ever lifted.

At ninety-eight, Pepe Joseph was the mountain's oldest inhabitant. He was Roget's grandfather and local legend. Word had it that he had killed two men with his bare hands. One had tried to steal the money he made selling a cow at market. The other was an Italian wife beater. Outsiders weren't liked at the best of times.

Pepe Joseph climbed up to the Grange one day with Roget, Maurice and Michel. His drink was red wine with three tablespoons of sugar stirred into the tumbler. His teeth were still his own and he had a sparkle in his eye when the talk got round to women. For a nonagenarian his long-term memory was fantastic. After a glass or two he would start to talk about his past in an accent so heavy with old age and patois that I found it almost impossible to follow. How I wished I could understand more. I wanted to get to know that old man, wanted him to know me. Would have loved to be invited down to his one-roomed house to drink and hear him reminisce some more. Momo tried to translate the old man's words.

Pepe Joseph had been a porter in the 1920's when the observatory was built at the top of the Pic du Midi, the highest mountain in the area. He would carry fifty kilos of provisions and equipment up to the top two or three times a week for a few centimes. The mountains had shaped his life and he had shaped the mountains. He remembered the warring Germans, the uninvited ones that arrived in the village and rounded up several of the men folk and took them down the mountain to Tarbes and shot them. There was a wall in Tarbes where the scars from the bullets could be seen. Old Pepe Joseph didn't like foreigners, didn't trust them.

I don't think he trusts me.

Garage People ⇥

The air is sucked across the teeth in a way that I know it's going to be expensive.

When I first arrived in the region and acquired the green cat-cat, I wanted a place to keep it when I didn't need it. I also needed someone who could repair the frequent damage to the poor vehicle from getting up and down from the house to the hard road. I couldn't abandon it at the Grange when I wasn't at home. So I approached the first garage in Bagneres travelling down from the mountains.

It was a Citroen dealership with a workshop and some pumps out the front, and a scrap heap of assorted wrecks around the back. Monsieur Fourcarde was the proprietor, ably assisted by Madame and Mademoiselle Fourcarde. It gave me a great amount of schoolboy glee to arrive at their premises and greet them with a bold

"Good morning Monsieur Fuckhard. And how is Madame and Miss Fuckhard this fine day?"

They were perfectly polite to me and the greeting became a habit that persisted, no insult intended, just an accident of birth and a silly sense of humour. Madame wore the trousers and over the years had metamorphosed into the shape of one of her petrol pumps. The reception desk doubled as an office. She perched herself behind the desk and monitored all the various comings and goings. Miss Fuckhard was in charge of the pumps and fast assuming her mother's looks. The genial Monsieur always seemed to have his head under the bonnet of some vehicle or other. His hands were semipermanently covered in oil and grease. When I went to shake him by the hand he would tuck his palm inwards and offer the butt of his upturned wrist.

In common with a lot of businesses around those parts, jobs seemed to be done on the basis of bring it in, we'll have a look at it and then we'll take it from there. Cars were never ever booked in for a service but rather turned up and loitered until Monsieur Fuckhard could make his inspection. He then allocated one of his two mechanics to the task of sorting out the problem or doing the service. Having travelled from England, I would arrive in Bagneres and the garage Fourcarde to find that the green cat-cat hadn't been looked at since the last time it had been used. Flat batteries were a common occurrence. The hole in the petrol tank caused by a particularly rough descent down from the Grange hadn't been fixed, and wasn't rediscovered until Mademoiselle Fuckhard filled up the tank.

"Je suis desole," said her father, as we stood around the back end of the old vehicle watching the growing pool of fuel drip and shimmer on to the forecourt.

"Desole," repeated Monsieur Fuckhard removing the cigarette from his mouth and scuttling off into his workshop to find a suitable container to catch the spilling gallons. The hole was eventually patched up and the leak stopped. I needed someone with more mechanical expertise or enthusiasm.

Thierry, the car breaker, had plenty of enthusiasm but not much mechanical know how. He had a scrap yard round the back of Bagneres and lived with his wife Dominique up near Sainte Marie, so I saw him socially from time to time. Thierry would always offer to fix broken vehicles, mend blowing exhausts, and put on tow bars; that sort of thing. But when I turned up to his yard he was invariably on the phone and in a foul mood because some deal was going pear shaped. Thierry had the manner of a car breaker, but the aspirations of a Range Rover dealer. And that was mainly what he did. He would disappear some weekends to Belgium or Germany and arrive back with a nearly new Range Rover. He'd drive it for a week or two before flogging it to someone in the region. Short and stocky with a mop of wild hair, Thierry wore a pair of designer glasses with little square frames. I told him that in London or Paris they would have given him the look of someone in the creative business. After a drink or two he argued that he was in the creative business. Judging by the trouble he had every so often from the T.V.A. and revenue people, his accounts must have been very creative. When Thierry got merry he would start saying "I ham ze Count of Monte Christo," several times with a wicked smile ending in much laughter.

Thierry liked to laugh at his own jokes. Once at a lengthy lunch given by the Butlers, Louise said "Clean plates please." Thierry obliged even though it was a fish course. He picked up the entire skeleton of the trout by its tail and slipped it into his mouth headfirst. He swallowed very slowly bone by bone. The onlookers retched and complained. Thierry didn't bat an eyelid. He swallowed the whole bony carcass, drank another tumbler of red wine, and said with his usual big grin, "I ham ze Count of Monte Christo."

Thierry also had an obsession with blowjobs. Actually he wasn't alone. It seemed that the blowjob was the mountain man's preferred sexual practice. I too joined their ranks because of my lack of fluent French. I was building a cave at the Grange, a place to store bottles of wine. I was using round clay drainage pipes, ideal for holding an individual bottle horizontally. The pipes were supplied by the local supermarket, and I had ordered forty-eight to finish the job. I went down to town to collect my order. At the customer service desk I saw a pretty young girl with a badge on her bosom that told me she was part of the supermarket team.

"I've come for forty-eight peeps and I'd like them in the back of my car please."

The girl with the badge went red, then white, then burst into tears and ran off into the back office. I stood at the desk. A more mature woman came out of the back office door. I repeated my request.

"I am here for forty-eight peeps and it would be good if I could have them in the back of my car which is parked right outside."

The mature woman looked as though she was going to hit me. I sensed that she was rolling up her sleeves in order to prepare her self for the imminent strike.

"Peeps" I said again quite loudly. This time people at the nearby check out stopped what they were doing and stared at me.

"I've come for forty-eight peeps." The waiter I recognised from the Café Londres was in the check out queue. He smiled more broadly than usual and put his thumb up to his mouth in a gesture that I began to understand. I'd seen Thierry make the same sign when bragging about oral sex.

I left with the cat-cat full of the clay pipes I needed. I bought the pretty girl with the badge a box of sweets and tried to apologise for my mistake.

I hadn't been so embarrassed since childhood. Went as red as the organic beetroot on sale just behind me. Couldn't shop there again for months.

Thierry was a car breaker rather than maker, so for anything serious one went to see the Twins. The Twins could fix just about anything. If Thierry's yard looked like a bombsite, the Twin's garage was even more disturbing. Opposite the defunct railway station in Bagneres, their building housed their work and their homes. The Twins both had wives and children and scruffy looking Alsatian dogs. Their homes were old caravans without the wheels kept inside the building. So in the morning the Twins would get up, open their caravan doors, and instantly be at work. The workspace itself was the clear patch in the middle of the building. Around the walls were the remnants of past jobs, body shells, axles, wheels and bits of engine no longer needed. The floor itself was littered with empty cans and tools and piles of dried dog turd. The Alsatians were allowed to go anywhere and did. I had to watch my step at the Twins'.

The Twins were the best mechanics, panel beaters and car sprayers for miles. And so they were the busiest, with every breakdown truck in the region towing the disabled or damaged to them for their attention. Their work spread itself out of their premises and across the main road into the old station's car park. Butler and I, the two 'English', got on well with them. They were helpful with the various jobs the cat-cat needed to keep it on the road. We would arrive unannounced and loiter with the others until one of the Twins spotted us and greeted us like best friends. I had given them a three litre bottle of whiskey after the first repair job. Once they lent me a car for a week whilst the cat-cat's engine had some major work. The 'courtesy' car turned out to belong to one of their other customers and was itself waiting to be looked at for a passenger door that wouldn't shut after a prang. It was tied up with some string whilst I used it.

The nearest local garage was on the road up out of Sainte Marie-de-Campan, the road up to La Mongie. Gerrard's garage was really a filling station that sold snow chains in the winter and ice creams in the summer. Even though Gerrard had a workshop, it was used as storage for his JCB and his Toyota tow truck, the two vehicles in his life that kept Gerrard busy. Both came to my assistance on New Year's day.

My eldest son, Oliver, and his new wife, and some of their Australian friends, were staying with me for the Christmas holidays. We went into town and were going back to the Grange in the cat-cat when I decided to show them the scenic route. I turned off the main road at Campan and we made our way in the snow and up through the forest that lined the valley walls. The narrow forest track got more difficult. The higher we went, the deeper the snow. It was picture post card stuff, the snow-laden trees still wearing their make-up from a white Christmas. Almost at the top, the cat-cat got stuck on an incline in the track. I ordered all the blokes out so they could give me a push, leaving the girls in the back. I reversed the cat-cat back a bit so as to get a run up at the incline. When I tried to stop the reversing vehicle, I couldn't. We slid backwards in slow motion and left the track and started off in the snow backwards down the mountain. I saw the faces of my son and his friends as they stood on the track watching the cat-cat and me and their women slide off down the mountain. Open-mouthed disbelief on one, a bit of a smile on another and wide eyed amazement on the third.

Gravity grabbed hold of us. We gathered speed as we slid through the deep white snow and bumped down the mountainside. There was nothing I could do. It seemed to take forever until the girls in the back started to scream. We punched into a large rock and rolled sideways into a tree that stopped the backward slide.

"Everybody out," I said, unnecessarily. The cat-cat rocked on the two wheels that were buried in the snow, its others way up in the cool air. We bailed out and climbed our way back up to the track and the worried spectators. The cat-cat had tobogganed for a hundred feet. In only twenty more we would have plunged over the edge and dropped down into the Campan valley some thousand metres below us. It was a thought that didn't really sink in until later that New Year's Eve. Singing of Auld Lang Syne actually meant something. The girls and I were lucky to be seeing in the new, lucky to be alive and we hugged each other in real appreciation. I was very happy to be with my son. I went out into the frosty night and looked at the stars so clear from those mountains and thanked whoever it was that kept me safe. I shed tears for the old and tears for the new, tears for what I knew had happened and more for what I didn't know was going to.

The next day, New Year's day, a hung over Maurice and Michel called on a hung over Gerrard and persuaded him to get out his tow truck in order to retrieve the cat-cat for me. On its own the tow truck wasn't man enough, and so we needed the JCB as well. The cat-cat was eventually hauled back up on the track with much advice and encouraging applause from the small crowd who had gathered. Of course everyone was invited back for a celebration after the successful recovery and New Year's eve was re-run all over again up at the Grange.

His big hand rubs his stubbly chin and the air is sucked across the teeth in a way that I know it's going to be expensive. I pour another glass for Gerrard and say thank you to him for the umpteenth time. "How much do I owe you Gerrard?"

Saturday's Market

"Bonjour Monsieur. Try my cheese." The blond cheese lady gives me a piece to taste, and straight away I want everything she has to offer.

Every Saturday was market day in Bagneres-de-Bigorre. The old spa town hummed with trade and on a sunny day the streets turned into a colourful bazaar. In and around the market hall it was mostly food and drink on offer. In the elongated central square under the plane trees it was pots and pans, hats and clothes, music cassettes and leather goods. Down around the town's public swimming pool was everything for the garden. The giant tool trailer sometimes parked up opposite the trackless railway station. Working types called to top up on spanners or wheelbarrows. There were, of course, exceptions to this general rule. A shoe trader was found among the shrub sellers or a potter lurked between an olive merchant and the fruit and veg man.

Like the old town itself, nothing much had changed about Saturday mornings for hundreds of years. One Saturday I saw a sad troop of dancing bears, causing as much interest as was the man from Toulouse selling his miracle glasses cleaning cloth. New and improved formulas wouldn't wash with the Bagneres punters. They liked their Saturday mornings as they had always been. The small farmers were all there, one with a box of leeks to shift, another with some potatoes. An old misshapen peasant woman had some fresh misshapen eggs and four big bottles of milk for sale. The duck confit brigade eyed each other up and tried to persuade the passing trade that theirs was the best. Half a duck cooked and preserved in goose fat with lots of salt and garlic, squeezed into a vacuum-sealed glass jar and sold for 65 Francs might have sounded awful. It would taste just fantastic. The paella stall prepared a feast, a giant dish full that said Spain wasn't far away. The chickens turned on their spits, quail too, and as they roasted their sizzling smell made mouths water and dogs lick their chops. Their live sisters, clucking in wooden crates, looked on hopefully, not understanding why. The town's public address system played Euro pop. People met and kissed and shook each other by the hand, nodded and shrugged and talked about the week just gone, their ailments, the weather and the price of things.

In Les Halles, the market hall, the old men congregated on one side to take a drink, and perhaps something to eat. Maurice and Michel and Christine too had arranged to meet me, and we shopped for eggs and bacon, sausage and cheese and bread. Momo gave the food to the chef, the little man in the dirty apron who ran the market bar. He and his toothless wife prepared the mornings feast. They cooked it and served it up for us on one of their tables set out next to the bar in the market hall. Breakfast never tasted so good, surrounded by the gentle buzz of commerce, the "Bon appetites" from passing strangers, the handshakes from those that we knew. We drank red wine from clear glass bottles and chunky tumblers supplied by the bar and sweet black coffees and then the eau de vie. Cigarette smoke hung out with the market smells, the cut flowers and the cheese.

There were lots of cheese stalls. One just sold goats cheese on its own. Little rounds, like chess pieces, lined up on a table. The blond cheese lady though was the place to go. Her stall was just outside the main hall, on the side nearest the thermal baths. Every Saturday morning she was there looking like a Parisian, pert and as sexy as a nurse in her white get up. "Bonjour monsieur dame," she said to all her customers when they joined the queue. But when it was my turn I knew she was getting personal. I bought lots of cheese, pointed to pieces in her display that she then had to pick up, handle and give me a thin slice to taste.

"Oui," I said trying to communicate to her that I thought she was wonderful. The taste of the cheese was irrelevant. It could be hard, old, bland cheese but in her hands, cut, sliced so thinly and offered on the end of her blade, stretched across her stall, her taut white overall, those eyes meeting with mine, it tasted like an apple from Eve in the garden of Edam.

And after the market breakfast we sauntered through the streets stopping frequently so that Maurice or Michel or Christine could meet and greet their friends. I was always introduced as 'the English' who lived in Le Peyras or ' the green cat-cat '. I shook the hands and then stood on the edge of the conversation, catching the odd scrap. I was nearly always taller than they were but never superior; bigger but of less significance. We eventually found our way into the wine cave with its small smoky back room full of wooden tables, benches and chairs. The wiry mountain men were there drinking. Their weatherworn faces and working hands buffed up for market day. A cleaner pair of blue overalls but the same beret perched on their nodding heads. The owner of the cave or his brother passed among the tables with a bottle or two and poured the drink whether or not it was wanted. Wine or something stronger, and we all took some and clinked our glasses in the thick friendly air. Maurice lit up another cigarette. Front of house was the 'shop' where people came and went with their bidons. Arrived empty, left full, topped up for another week. Alongside the cheap plonk lay majestic bottles of old claret. Expensive white burgundy, dusty and aging in it's wooden case, waited for the discerning pallet and thick wallet that might materialise some day. The accents there were even more difficult to understand. But everyone knew who I was and where I was from even though I was not sure.

Come home with me pretty cheese lady. Come up my mountain track and let me taste your wares.

Lourdes Horse Market

The gruff Spaniard in his dirty trilby hat wanted two hundred francs for the tiny donkey. "One hundred and fifty," say I, which is about fifteen quid.

Lourdes was only about half an hour car journey away from the Grange. Dominique, the wife of Thierry the car breaker, said that she would take us to the horse fair. Domo liked horses and kept two or three herself for riding. Most of the horses in those parts were reared for their meat. So the horse market wasn't the best place to go to find that lovely little pony. The Butlers and I set off in Domo's old Range Rover from Sainte Marie and made our jolly way through the foothills. On our left as we travelled west we saw the high tops of the Pyrenees dusted with snow as they ran off towards the Basque region.

"Look at the view you folks," said Louise Butler from her seat next to Domo. Domo's English was better than most, but she thought that Louise had used the f-word at us. Domo was somewhat perplexed until we put her right. She was then in hysterics for the rest of the journey; the tears rolled down her cheeks so much she turned the windscreen wipers on to clear her view, which caused her even more mirth. A laugh was a laugh in any language.

The horse traders gathered on the outskirts of the town, around a large brick, open-sided but covered market. It seemed to be mostly a man thing, but difficult to understand. There were open pens full of wild horses. On the outside, around the edges of the main action, the beasts looked tranquil. But as business progressed towards the centre, they became frenzied. Their heads tossed and their nostrils flared. The noise and smell of horses disturbed, the unmistakable movement, the swift grace even in that confined space, the pounding of many hooves in the dirt covered concrete wasn't right somehow.

For cattle, sheep and pigs this was perhaps the norm. But horses looked so out of place being herded and forced, lot by lot, into the centre, like water pulled down a plug hole. Too noble, too familiar, to be treated like that.

The auctioneer, like those he was selling, tossed and danced and bayed in a restless performance. The deal was done by a nod or a wink or wave of hand from the earnest ranks of scruffy traders. A truck or trailer backed up to the central enclosure and the whirling mob of a dozen, maybe more, were beaten up into the vehicle, hit with sticks, banged up inside. I remembered their eyes as they were forced up into the transport, for most of them a lift to the abattoir. More whites to them than colour, dilating with terror. Perhaps distressing for those who had grown up with The Pony Club or played with My Little Pony, but to these folks it was a way to earn an honest crust, just horse-trading.

Louise spotted it first. Tied up to the back of a trailer the little, grey donkey stood stock-still. The frayed rope that tethered it wasn't needed. Amidst all the hustle and bustle of the market, the optimism of trade, the little grey beast was the quietest thing. Like Eeyore, only much more sad, much more real. It wasn't the rope and halter that kept it there, rooted to that place, but stubbornness.

"Go on" said Louise "Let's buy that donkey." Louise was upset and wanted to buy them all, take them home with her, keep them as pets. Not an option trying to break the food chain without the means.

A makeshift bar for the market traders sold burette, the first drop from the barrel of maturing wine, a heady brew that looked impotent but carried a disturbing kick. We had indulged. Louise's courage grew by the glass full.

"Go on," she said, "Please let's buy it." I sauntered over to the tiny creature and sensed its pathetic life, saw the cross of Jesus on its back which meant nothing. Its absurd ears were the only sign of movement when they turned, one at a time, to catch the sounds of cousins baying as they were corralled for sale. The big sad eyes implored me to do something. For a moment we stood facing each other and in a disturbing way wanting to swap places with each other. Me the donkey, the donkey me; taken back to some dusty Spanish hill side for back breaking chores and meager rations, no love, no comfort much, but a purpose.

The donkey's owner saw me. Such a big man for so small a beast. Over his broad shoulder he watched me approach and touch his animal on its velvety nose. He was talking to a group of four or five others, all Spanish, all felt hatted and all Gypsy through and through. I stood my ground. The inconvenience of my presence got to him. He had to stop what he was doing, stop talking and come over. I smelt the owner's heavy breath as he lurched towards me. I knew the man beat the donkey. He was weighing me up.

"Two hundred," he said, tossing his head in our direction.

"One hundred and fifty," said I almost too quickly. The stocky Spaniard spat and said something I didn't understand and turned to go back to the group. Turned his back on us but didn't ignore us. I knew that he wanted to trade, that's why he was there. But he knew I wasn't being serious, that I couldn't handle the responsibility, didn't want to. The donkey, too, must have guessed as much, for it didn't move, didn't change position, just resigned itself to its uncertain future.

"Too much," I lied to Louise condemning the donkey to a continued life of unease and another flogging for not being sold.

We ran into several locals. Philip Roi, the man who ran a horse trekking business, was there trying to sell one of his sturdy Appalachian ponies. He kept several of the firm-footed animals and visitors to La Mongie would see them for rent, standing like docile dummies waiting to be kick started. Up at the top of the mountain, his horses looked mangy. Down at the market, Monsieur Roi had preened his pony, plaited its mane and brushed its tail. Scrubbed up to look like a Thoroughbred, every time a prospective buyer showed the slightest interest, he and the pony would run off together, attached by a rope. Both trotting, both on show.

On a glorious weekend in October, the mountains aflame with autumn, two friends of mine popped over from England for a horse trekking expedition I had arranged with Monsieur Roi. He was a short man with a short temper and a moody Spanish girl friend who would help him - when they were talking. My two friends, the Captain and Sean, arrived and we set off from La Mongie along the very steep old track. It was the narrow route that old Joseph would have taken to the top when he was a porter.

"Av they ride 'orse before?" asked Monsieur Roi.

"Bien sur," said I, wickedly committing them both to an experience neither had ever had. Going over the top from La Mongie on the back of animals we had never ridden before was quite an adventure, an adrenaline rush. Bringing up the rear I was amused to see the Captain and Sean leaning heavily up the mountain, pulling on the left-hand rein, trying to steer their horses away from the precipice. They believed that would prevent their mounts from tumbling down into the gorge below. Of course the horses had done the trip countless times before and were sure footed on the rocky paths. The Captain and Sean were both good skiers and mountaineers. My smug satisfaction came because there was something I could do better than them. It was cruel schoolboy stuff.

After about an hour in the saddle, the Captain and Sean started to look more relaxed. Trekking through the high Pyrenees on horse back in October's sunshine was simply marvelous. Off the beaten track, each new view was spectacular, familiar peaks seen from a new perspective. We rode for several hours and then emerged into a clearing where Monsieur Roi's Spanish woman had laid out our lunch of barbecued duck hearts. We felt like pioneers, cowboys without the cows, three Englishmen and their guide on horseback, conquering the mountains and claiming them for Her Majesty. Overnight we stayed in mountain refuges, simple stone built dwellings with slate roofs and big fireplaces. No hint of running water or electricity but as warm as toast and a dry place to ease the saddle sores, eat, drink and be merry.

One night we pitched up at a remote mountain hotel and the joy of real beds with sheets and the shower down the corridor. Monsieur Roi found a guitar and we sat in the bar with a small group who had come by car. We sang the songs we knew, and got happily drunk. Our horses slept outside in the cold night air. When at last we went to bed in the early hours and closed our eyes it felt as though we were still up in the saddle. In the morning Monsieur Roi and his Spanish girl friend saddled up for us. One of the animals wasn't keen and played up so Monsieur Roi hit it on its forehead with a hammer. It seemed to us rough justice. A short man with a short temper.

Monsieur Roi had no takers for his pony that day at the horse market in Lourdes. We rolled home back in Domo's cat-cat and that evening as I climbed up the track to the Grange I heard the unmistakable and ugly bellow of a donkey. "Heeeehore" came the noise from my neighbour's field. Yvette, who farmed below me, had bought the little donkey from the Spaniard and another for company.

"Heeeehore" it's saying to me and I feel guilty and happy at the same time.

Eric ⚒

Eric's sausage is the envy of the mountain.

During the winter months I could tell it had snowed in the night even before I pushed open the wooden shutters to reveal the white. I could tell by the sound of silence muffled in a great thick white blanket. No urgent gurgling rushing stream or barking valley dogs, no bird song or chain saws whine. No far off hooting from the postman's van down in the valley. No tractor's diesel cough. Nothing but a high pitched buzz from my own inner ear and the over-eager thumping of my heart before the daily pills.

I woke in the brass bed, lay for a moment then sat bolt upright and sensed the change, knew that something was different. It had either snowed or the outside world had come to an end. Beyond the shutters everything had changed. Overnight nature had dipped her brush into the giant paint pot marked snow white and not spared a drop. Snow clung to any surface that would have it. Branches and boughs bent under the weight of their new load and they stooped to kiss the same white stuff that forced them down. Growing twigs, even thinner than a little finger, were piled high with it. The strand of wire strung out between the wooden posts that marked the field's boundary was coated. Frozen snow walked the tightrope. The log pile had vanished. The old green cat-cat was white. The corrugations in the tin roof had been leveled, the indentations filled and spread thickly with the clinging white, white crystals. Even at that angle the overnight fall clung like a new thatched roof. The stream was the only moving sign of life. Even that went more quietly than it had before, its banks and big stones wrapped, cushioned against the boisterous liquid's rough and tumble. Animal tracks from fox or dog showed where the scavengers had skipped and sniffed around the dustbin and gone off. The world had been frozen overnight and the child in me came rushing back to take me out to play. Made a snowman. Put a beret on its head. A carrot for his nose and another for his penis. Just for a laugh.

The sun didn't reach the Grange until nearly mid-day. But I could see it's brightness creeping down the mountains opposite, eating its way towards me, coming across the whiteness, turning the snow into a dazzling white furnace. Too white to look at. Sunshine on snow made me squint. Pupils contracted caught constantly by the photographer's flash bulb. It's the brightest light I'd seen since birth and, like birth, was a precious moment that would all too soon become a memory, in the drawer, a photo in the box marked nostalgia.

The snow changed everything. Local bank accounts changed colour too from red to black, as the snow brought the cash to the slopes. Skiing brought jobs for the boys and girls, working for the 'regie' as piste bashers or lift operators. Pampering the winter tourists, selling them sunglasses or renting them skis. Local peasant farmers became glamorous ski instructors working for the French Ski School. Or there was always a call for just doing the washing up in one of the many catering establishments in La Mongie.

Monday was always the best day to go skiing. I arranged to go up to La Mongie with Michel and Momo. To ski with one of them was great but to have them both was greedy. On terra firma the two big men had a slowness of pace and a rolling gait. On the snow they acquired a sleekness, speed and style. Growing up in the mountains had taught them well. To follow Michel and Momo around the slopes of La Mongie and over the Col du Tormalet down to Barages was like trailing in the wake of my own professional mountain guides and ski instructors. With my eyes firmly fixed on the very backs of the skis in front of me, I could go anywhere. I wouldn't realise that what we were attempting to do was a mountain side so steep that not even sheep could manage it when the snows disappeared. Momo and Michel made me feel like Jean Claude Killy, and the three of us covered many miles on that Monday morning before retiring to Eric's for lunch.

We arrived at the shepherd's restaurant at about midday, parked our skis outside, and stamped into the bar to meet the Monday crowd. Handshakes were obligatory for all and for some it was kisses on the cheek as Michel and Momo joined the locals. Whilst I had of course done kissing with the red head, I had never been over 'touchy feely'. Brought up to shake hands firmly and look people in the eye, the lesson hadn't included kissing. Certainly not between men. I don't think my father ever kissed me and I couldn't remember ever really kissing my own boys, sadly. I was beginning to learn that on meeting the females in the valley I should probably go for a cheek if it was offered and that if I hadn't seen Michel or Momo for some time, I might even give them a peck and a hug. I remembered the first time it happened and it was like learning to swim. Momo's bristles against my own, a clash of whiskers, me stiff, awkward and embarrassed but Momo, natural, easy and casual. There was no shame there in showing your affection for someone. I did get it wrong once when on entering the little bar in Sainte Marie I shook all the men by the hand and kissed all the girls. I didn't really know them that well; in fact a couple of them were just passing through. But I had been drinking at Butler's house, which had given me an impression that every one was my friend.

Eric, a shepherd from Campan, ran the best place to eat on the slopes. It was a cabin, another tree house without the tree, stuck up like a wooden and concrete pimple between La Mongie and Barages, just below the Col du Tormalet. The altitude may have had something to do with it being the best, although 2150 metres wasn't Everest. Thick wine was more likely than thin air to have caused the light headed feeling. Or Eric's general pleased-to-see-youness. The wooden slatted sun terrace with its green tin tables and injection molded red plastic chairs certainly had something to do with it. Especially when the sun was shinning. If it wasn't, the rooms inside filled and fugged up. The menu was scribbled on a black slate, simple fare, with delicious meats from the valley cooked by Eric's wife out the back, behind the bar. She would appear from time to time, her head of black curls bobbing around Eric like a French gun dog. Anything eaten or drunk tasted better outside up in the sunny snow, overlooked by the craggy tops of the white mountains and the bright blue sky. A bowl full of hot soup inside when the weather turned evil would chase away the chill, see off the cold. The effort to get there would give appetite a sharper edge. The place had no unnecessary trimmings, but if you knew the patron, perhaps a free glass of eau de vie.

Like all the best restaurants the company it kept made Eric's better. Holiday makers over from Blighty; the Leeches, the Ryans, big John and Kirsty Hall, the Captain and Deirdre, Michella and the Edwards girls. Catherine Edward's brave boy friend, Tom, who had never skied before, stuck with us like glue, followed us falling down the slopes like an unhinged shadow. Weekend skiers down from Bordeaux shared a tin table with us, aloof at first, not sure of these foreigners, but soon in the groove sharing the laughter, passing it around the table with us. Mondays were the best days to go when all the working locals would take the day off, shut their banks and shops and garages and head for the slopes. All helped to make the place special. Our long lunches filled with skier's chat. This wipe out, that off piste run and did you see those kids on the four-man lift, Spanish snow boarders they were, hooligans on the slope. We laughed and drank and fit Michella tried to flirt with Eric, imagined what it would be like to bed the big man. Big John, the rugger bugger, arm wrestled with him across his bar, a clash of titans and a draw. Much huffing and puffing and through the gritted teeth swear words that neither knew but both understood. The big men had mutual respect for each other. Another bottle of Eric's red please, and what about some fromage du pays, and then we really should be getting on. Eric gave us a bottle of '99 Chateau de Marsan which after a simple tasting and toasting ceremony was taken out back to the kitchen and stood next to a steaming pot of garbure to warm it up. He needn't have cared, but he did.

Nearly everyone who arrived at Eric's walked like a robot. People clunked in on the wooden floorboards like Mr & Mrs Michelin Man padded against the weather and the falls and clumped up to the bar in their bulky plastic foot wear. For a sport that needed standing up to make it work, ski boots on their own did their best to encourage falling down. Ski clothing was made to keep the body warm and dry. Great for on the piste but not so good for having one. People queuing at Eric's loo, an unsavoury hole in the ground that went straight to the centre of the earth, started the undressing process before they got to the door marked WC. Men and women, boys and girls, all used the same facility at Eric's. All-in-one ski suits had to be unzipped. What looked reasonable on the slope transformed into a half-peeled banana standing outside Eric's lavatory. On any day at lunchtime a bunch of them gathered all pretending that this wasn't really happening to them. The Armani ski suit half undone, zipped open to the waist, the empty sleeves hanging around, flapping, dangling to the floor. Some in the queue were more anxious than others. Some bladders stronger. For men it could be easier than for women but that was just nature's way of being kinder to men. Some men, impatient in the queue, ducked outside to find a patch of snow up against the wall that they could make yellow. Women were not so lucky. But Michella didn't care who saw her squatting, perhaps even enjoyed the idea.

Another troop of skiers arrived and even on their tiptoes, tilted forward by their robot boots, on Eric's wooden floorboards, they sounded like a herd of moose. The tape machine and its brass band mountain music had to give way to the thunderous footsteps and more orders for vin chaud or café or Eric's magic sausage. Eric's sausage had always been the talk of the valley. It wasn't just ordinary. Eric's sausage was blessed with mouth-watering qualities that others could only dream of. Size mattered to Eric, and Mr Big Portion was always at home. It was rather ironic that whilst Eric's pure pork or lamb monsters would satisfy his customers, his wife wore a somewhat lean and hungry look.

On that particular Monday at Eric's everyone was my friend and the lunch time session developed into an afternoon of epic proportions. Bottle after bottle of red wine arrived at our tin table. Eventually the eau de vie came out and Eric joined us. We drank until the sun went down and I was beautifully and happily drunk. Then came time to leave. There was only one way to leave from Eric's - down hill on skis.

Walking out of the bar was fine. So was putting on the skis. Trying to follow Michel and Momo was impossible. Off they went at high speed, singing their happy way down to La Mongie. I heard them go, heard their shouts of "Bon courage!" as they disappeared, assuming that I was right behind them. I travelled the first few yards trying to keep up in equally happy mode. Then my ski tips crossed and I took the first fall headfirst into the snow. I lay there laughing. Got up to have another go. Called out to Michel and Momo who were long gone. Ten yards more, then over again. More laughter. Up again and another ten or fifteen yards down the mountain in the dusk. Another fall. I lay in the darkening snow laughing my head off. I realised I had completely lost the plot. There was no way I was going to be able to ski down that mountain. They say it's far easier and safer to ski down a snow-covered mountain than it is to try and walk down one in your ski boots. I ignored the advice. I soon found myself sliding helplessly out of control into an untidy heap in the snow, a confusion of arms and legs, skis and poles. Each time I went over the laughter came loud and strong. Not yet quite hysterics.

The evening became darker. The pistes were shut. There were no other skiers in sight. I wasn't really worried. The alcohol gave me a false sense of security. I'd get down somehow and besides Michel and Momo would realise that they had lost me once they got to the bottom. Wouldn't they? I tried to ski once again and got going quite well until the fading light fooled my vision and I hit a mogul without seeing it coming. I crash-landed in a heap that took the wind out of me. Even though I wanted to laugh I couldn't. Perhaps things were serious. I lay there looking up at the darkening deep blue sky and the diamond bright first star of the night. I had visions of being stuck on the mountainside all night. I remembered the ditty my ex-wife used to say to me when we first met under Australia's sky. "Star bright, first star of the night. I wish on you I wish I might make a wish on you tonight." I made a wish. I wished that I could be in the arms of the red head, safely off the slippery slope. I lay sobering up, hurting a bit from the tumbles. Maybe I'd have to dig a snow hole. Maybe I'd get frostbite. Maybe my heart wouldn't like what I was putting it through. Maybe I'd die.

Then the lights appeared. The buzz of an engine and Eric on his Skidoo. He pulled alongside me and with a huge grin under his beret, suggested that I might like a lift to the bottom. It was one of the best suggestions I had ever heard. I was very pleased to see him and kissed him firmly on both his cheeks. Michel and Momo were pleased to see Eric and me at the bottom, so much so that we had to go for another drink in the Yeti Bar to celebrate our reunion and the safe descent. My moment of vulnerability was washed away, chased off by another glass of something proofed.

He shouts his orders through a hatch, scribbles everything down on scrappy bits of paper. Without a till the only calculator sitting under its beret, Eric knows what's what and who's who. He's the king at this altitude and I enjoy attending his winter court. I wish the red head could be here with me to enjoy it too.

Loirs And Loneliness

I miss the red head and telephone sex is no way to conduct a deep and meaningful relationship.

I knew I was getting lonely when I made a stew and it lasted two weeks. It took a particular type of human being to enjoy being on their own. I didn't mean for the odd week or two. I was talking about month after month. I loved being in the Grange but sometimes I would rather not be there all on my own.

I had the loirs for company. The little furry critters had invaded the house. They came in from the woods around. Hannibal first introduced them for his moving soldiers to snack on. I couldn't eat them. They looked like a cross between a squirrel and a big dormouse. With very long, quite bushy tails and dextrous 'hands' and 'feet', they could climb up walls and across ceilings like Spider Man. At night they came out to play and the noise up under the tin roof was ludicrous. Trying to discourage them from using the Grange as their own was very difficult. Poison would kill them and leave their rotting bodies up under the eves, decomposing and smelling. A cat might frighten them away. But I was more of a dog person and a dog wouldn't sort those things out at all. I did have a trap, like a mink trap, a fairly large wire caged construction into which I placed some bait, a piece of apple maybe. The unsuspecting animal went for the fruit, triggering a trap door that slammed shut catching the beast alive in the cage. I caught dozens of loirs like that. Each time I heard the cage trap snap I rushed off to have a look at my latest captive. Their big eyes looked back at me, a picture of innocence rather than a nocturnal hooligan. The next morning I then took the trap down the mountain with me and released the prisoner into the valley to go and find some body else to pester. The thought occurred to me that maybe the released loirs were finding their way back to the Grange. I daubed some white paint on to the back of one. Sure enough, some nights later the varmint with the white painted back was once again taken prisoner. I abandoned the trapping idea after that and learnt to live with them.

It was an uneasy truce and war broke out between us from time to time. After they found their way into the bread bin one night, I had a few too many drinks, and lost the plot. I took my .22 rifle down from its place on the wall and loaded it up. I sat in the candlelight drinking and listening to my wind up radio with the gun resting ready in my lap. A sheriff waiting for trouble. Guns and alcohol don't mix. But I sipped and waited. There was a spot right above one of the wall cupboards where they usually appeared. It was a good vantage point high in the middle of the main room. From there, the nervous loir could survey the scene, and check out if the coast was clear. The only way I could tell if there was one up there looking at me was by turning on my big torch every so often. Like one of those searchlights in prisoner of war films, its beam cut across the room and illuminated everything in its path.

The radio played classical music. I sipped the red wine. Flicked the torch. Nothing. My trigger finger itched for action. Brahms played, as the candle flames trembled ever so slightly. The torch beam lasered out across the room and up to the top of the cupboard. Two eyes shone back at me. A motionless fur ball, it sat mesmerized by the bright light. Its whiskers twitched but it didn't blink or move. Very slowly I raised the gun, so the barrel and the torch were both in my left hand. The light from one pointed the way for the other. I brought the butt up to my shoulder and took aim. It wasn't easy with the torch but I thought that the loir was right in my line of fire. I took off the safety catch. Slowly, nothing done swiftly. I squeezed the trigger. There was a loud report as the bullet headed off across the room. The torch shot out of my grip and hit the hard floor with a clatter. The high velocity bullet went through the top door of the cupboard, smashed a rather fine glass into smithereens and exited through the back of the cupboard into the old stone wall. There was no sign of the loir dead or alive. Brahms carried on as though nothing had happened. The air was full of the smell of cordite. The next night I didn't miss because I used the four ten shot gun, which was a real mistake. The mess was dreadful with bits of loir mixed up with bits of cupboard and ceiling. Served me right for using a shotgun inside.

When the days were heavy as a wet blanket and the mists and damp clung to the soggy mountains, there was not a lot to do. I lit the fire and the boiler and then I read and I wrote and I thought. I thought too much. I thought about my friends and family. My children and grandchildren in Australia and Hawaii. My ex-wife and how much I must have upset her. Broken her heart as I had broken my promise. I thought of my childhood and my grandparents. I remembered their farm; the one I'd spent so much time on during my school holidays. I didn't know why but I thought of suicide. Not for myself but I could understand why it was quite common in those mountains. How could such a beautiful landscape cause such an ugly state of mind? Death by gun or rope was a big killer in those parts. Bodies hanging in the trees not as bad as those found in the home. If a life was taken inside, it was a black mark against the family, a sign that things weren't right at home. A quiet drop out in the orchard and the family at least could hold their own heads up. I remembered when one of grandfather's men did himself in.

At the time it didn't really seem tragic when Franz the German hanged himself. It was as though Franz the German wasn't allowed to play with us any more. As children we were never told the whole truth. The whole truth might somehow taint us: turn us into monsters, affect our ordered upbringing. In the same way that Gladys in the kitchen or old peg leg Jack in the garden were never privy to 'family discussions', we too were kept in the dark. "Not in front of the servants," my grandmother would say in French or Russian in front of the servants, like a pantomime dame. They would hear whatever it was they weren't supposed to at the village shop anyway. In church on Sunday it was never just the Word of God being spread. Grandmother preferred it that way though. Old school, where children should be seen and not heard; and where the things that went on this side of the green baize door were certainly not for open comment by those that worked beyond it. As children we were somehow floaters between the two worlds.

That side of the door we seemed to have respect, privilege even. We could speak without being spoken to. We could run and laugh and slide down the corridors. We could eavesdrop in the back kitchen every Tuesday afternoon when Miss Waite the younger would come up the fairy path from the village to clean the silver. We weren't supposed to but would accept wrapped sweets off old peg leg Jack and in exchange he would rub his enormous vegetable hand through our hair, roughing it up like a seedbed. Gladys would let us scrape the mixing bowl with an eager finger and lick it clean. The wooden spoon too and our childish lips would smack with the sweetness.

The old house was the fulcrum of Castle Farm, the homestead where all the comforts and benefits accrued from the acres that rolled around its walls. There were, I think, about fifteen men on the farm. They didn't have cars - didn't need them I suppose - and walked or rode on their bicycles to work each day. Their homes were in the village. Cottages that would feature on picture post cards now, country retreats for a couple of hundred thousand pounds. But then they were tithe cottages with vegetable gardens and yapping Jack Russells, rabbits and lazy cats. Not a patio or barbecue in sight. Franz the German lived in one such with Sheila, his English wife. Theirs had a thatched roof with low doors and old beams. When grandfather went to visit, he had to bow before going in. Franz the German had been a prisoner of war. I suppose that a new life in poor post war Britain seemed a better option than one in a leaderless and ruined Germany. He had become the dairyman for grandfather's Friesian herd. Franz was good with the animals: understood them. His favourites were horses; he'd learnt all about them in the German army. It was to him we would turn if we were having trouble with our pony and we were always having trouble of some sort or another. He was a big man, like the advertisements for Charles Atlas the body builder. When he got hot he would take off his shirt and show us his muscles. We would see the tattoo: the skull and the SS marking. Hitler's own brand, he'd say, with a proud smile we couldn't begin to understand. He would flex his muscles, pump up his biceps and say in his broken English "Next time ve vill beat you. Next time Germany vill vin the vor." Although it may have sounded like a joke, something a crackpot from a cartoon comic might say in his speech bubble, he meant it. Franz the German could afford to tell us. We were the next generation. We were there to be beaten or to triumph like our father and grandfather had before. I can't remember if Franz ever worked with his shirt off in front of my grandfather but I should think not. The Germans had killed my grandfather's youngest son, the uncle I never knew, only weeks before the armistice. It did seem strange to have an enemy in the camp. But then that was just a child's way of looking at things.

Franz had met Sheila in the village. Her dad also worked on the farm, and wasn't best pleased his daughter ended up marrying "a kraut". The wedding celebration was a low-key affair with a cold buffet and a few bottles of beer in Sheila's dad's cottage. Of course P.O.W's were nearly as common as Cabbage Whites and they were, according to grandfather, very good workers. Franz was good with his hands (a rhyme that we never sang in front of him) and he liked to make things out of wood. He made us a pair of stilts and showed us how to walk with them. He had us, his own child army, goose-stepping round the cow shed, innocently strutting while he looked on. The stilts took us up to his level so that we could see eye to eye. But what those blue eyes might have seen, what those big hands had done we never knew. Shall never know. Franz the German was kind to us and unaware of his past we liked him for the present. He was in a way just like one of us. A child that is.

Franz the German was late for work one morning and the assistant cowman had called them in, mustered the black and white herd, the first few to the collecting yard, udders full. He still hadn't appeared by seven so grandfather jumped into his Land Rover and drove to the village and Franz the German's cottage. Franz the German was hanging from one of the old beams. Sheila and he had had words the previous evening and Sheila had walked out, gone across the road to her dad's cottage where she had stayed the night. I overheard that grandfather couldn't cut Franz the German down on his own. Sheila's dad had to come and help.

In the drawing room at Castle Farm there was a meeting. The colonel, my grandfather, stood with his back to the open fireplace and announced that Franz was dead.

"I am afraid that he has taken his own life and we should all pray for him," was how my grandfather put it. Words so grown up that we never questioned them. We never asked why. And to this day I don't know where Franz the German was buried. Perhaps they just had him cremated and his ashes spread by the wind.

I imagine the red head at the other end and with the telephone jammed up against my ear; I masturbate into the handkerchief and know that from on top of the cupboard a loir is looking at me.

Arrival ✈

God, I hope she's pleased to see me.

She arrived at Biarritz airport on the hot Thursday and I met her in the cat-cat. It was exciting going to meet the red head. I didn't sleep much the night before. I was up and showered long before I needed to be; lathered up with expensive cologne, squeezed into my cleanest jeans and the shirt she liked. It was a two-hour drive to the coast. At the dinky airport I could watch each departure and each arrival, see every single passenger in transit. I bought an English newspaper from the bright kiosk. The girl behind the till looked like something off one of the glossy front covers surrounding her, tousled hair and too many white teeth chewing gum. I went to the bar and grabbed a thin aluminum table that looked as though it too was in transit somewhere. I'd order a coffee, a long white one, and leaf through old news. I'd read everything, the ads, the obituaries, the financial pages, the gossip, the comment, even the sport and then I'd go back to see what I had missed. Passing the time, reading the Times, waiting for the red head to arrive. Anxious, excited, nervous, happy, jealous, lustful, worried, bored, pleased, bothered, confident, uncertain, eager.

Eager had once spun her own yarn. Years ago, when I had been a young farmer, I had been going out with a pretty girl from Peterborough. I called her Eager Eager. She was always pleased to see me. She would commute back from her week's work in London to Peterborough every Friday evening. I would be there to meet her off the train and take her off in my dirty mini pick-up to the Lantern Club or the pub or some party before returning her to her Mummy and Daddy's house out on the Fitzwilliam Estate. There was nothing wrong with Eager Eager. Her eagerness was great for my ego and her kisses were as good as it got. I don't know why it was that on one Friday evening I just didn't turn up to meet her off the train. I can't remember. I just didn't turn up and never heard from her again. She married and had twins I think. What a coward I was, how disrespectful. But maybe she wasn't on that train; maybe she was going to dump me.

The anticipation in the airport was almost something I could reach out and touch; an anxious invisible cloud that might ignite with the right spark. That great indicator, the impersonal machine that clicks and whirs on its own, displaying the times of take offs and landings, was looked at, studied by the passer by. Some lingered as if at an art gallery, taking in what's on offer, not sure perhaps of the message really intended. Some, more urgently, rushed up and scanned, found the detail in an instant and moved off accordingly. The Tannoy warned of unattended baggage and asked for Monsieur so-and-so to please report to the airport information desk. Boredom made me people watch, guessing who they were, their names and what they did. A guy in a suit had a cardboard sign awkwardly tucked up under his arm that said Monsieur Balamory. The guy was in IT. Did Monsieur Balamory have this man's name filed away somewhere or was this Monsieur Balamory himself? What happened if there wasn't a Monsieur Balamory? Maybe men with signs hang around at airports for eternity. Maybe I was one of them. One without a written sign though. The airport cleaner (Madame Nettoyer?) swept the marbled floors with an enormous v-shaped mop that harvested all the dust and fluff, the particles of dirt brought in from Paris or Nice or Stanstead or the car park right outside. Biarritz seemed to have more holiday traffic than business types. More casual clothing than suits. Surf boards wrapped up in their protective carriers, fishes out of water really, some bigger, longer than the blond guys carrying them (Hank and Rudie?). The uniformed girl behind her car hire desk, bored too, face like a smacked arse (Mademoiselle Raseuse?). "What Hertz love?" I wanted to ask but didn't. Two gendarmes (Bill et Ben?) were stepping in time together along the concourse looking for trouble but hoping not to find it. Their guns in their holsters just in case.

I could hear it when the plane landed. I could smell the distinctive perfume of spent aviation fuel. From the aluminum table in the bar area I could see the runway and the puff of smoke that the wheels made when they kissed the hot tarmac for the first fast time. The red head's plane had landed.

The great indicator spelt out, "Landed" next to the flight number. The heart beat a little bit faster, squeezing sticky blood through the stent. The plane taxied to its stop and the steps were pushed up against the doors, front and rear, so that the people could walk out and down across the shimmering concrete and into the building. The temperature was nudging towards forty and the new arrivals undressed as they walked. I couldn't see her in the crocodile crowd. Didn't catch a flash of red. The mind played a game. Perhaps she'd missed the flight. Perhaps she'd done an Eager Eager on me. Then I saw her as she came into the arrivals hall. A thin piece of plate glass between us but she and the others around her still not yet officially in the same country as me. Red head, sunglasses, denim jeans and T-shirt top, shoulder bag, the brown leather scruffy one, and a look that showed she hadn't, couldn't, see me. It didn't matter. She was there, had arrived in one piece, had come to see me, be with me, if not forever, for a few days at least. She cleared, was let out and in and we met face to face, clumsy lip to lip in the hustle and bustle of people moving. I grabbed her bag, a squashy hold all, and a large round hat box and we headed off for the cat-cat and the journey east back to the Grange where we could finish in private what started as a public display of affection.

The drive back to the Grange is unbearable. I'm like a kid with a present under the Christmas tree. I can't wait to tear off the wrapping and start playing.

Wedding

Every time I go to somebody else's wedding, I remember my own.

I got married on July 11th 1969 when I was still a teenager. At the time it was a romantic adventure. My bride should have been in the sixth form of her smart Sydney girl's school. She'd left early, run away to Perth with me and decided that I was the boy for her even though her parents, her father in particular, couldn't have agreed less. She was pregnant, which didn't help the relationship with the new in-laws. Our wedding was at the Wayside Chapel in Sydney's King's Cross. She wore a dark green dress with a fox fur borrowed from her mother. I wore a white suit I'd had made. A copy of John Lennon's from off the Abbey Road album. I arrived on the back of a motorbike. We left in a Holden Monaro GT and spent our honeymoon at the Hydro Majestic Hotel in the Blue Mountains. One night only in a twin bedded room. It was all we could afford. We looked like a couple of school kids, not newly weds. It wasn't a good honeymoon because my new bride had violent morning sickness. She stayed in bed for most of the time, for the wrong reason. The marriage lasted for nearly thirty years, lasted until the red head came along and tempted me over a bowl of pasta, used that hideous strength only women posses.

My wedding vows came rushing back. Saying, "I do" in front of God's representative and the congregation was solemn. Breaking the vow wasn't funny. Listening to others going through their words made me think about my own. Even if they were in French.

Once upon a time Michel had been married. Although it didn't last very long, he did produce a son who grew up and met a girl and they fell in love and decided to get married. Michel was a mountain man, but his future daughter-in-law came from a military family. She herself was a military nurse and it was during their period of National Service that she had met and fallen in love with Michel's one and only son. Between the families it was agreed that the main celebration should take place in the Campan valley.

Michel was beside himself with the planing. For months before the big occasion he would be seen hurrying here and there with a brief case under his arm (beret always on head) on a mission to the wine sellers or the Marie or the caterers or the people who were doing the music or the photographer. There was so much to do and once done it had to be gone over again and again just to make sure that everything would run like clockwork. My invitation arrived in due course via the postman who of course knew what it was he was delivering long before I received it. I replied and accepted the kind invitation to the civil ceremony in the Campan Marie and the Salle des Fetes afterwards. I would be taking the red head with me and she had arrived for a long weekend to coincide with the festivities. French country weddings were similar to the English variety. There were guests from the bride's side and the groom's, a ceremony and the signing of a register and a kiss perhaps. After the 'solemn' bits everyone piled into their cars and toured around the local community sounding their car horns as often as possible until they arrived at a suitable place for food, drink, toasts and general celebration. What made Michel son's wedding different from others was its length. Michel's son's do was a three-day event.

Thursday night was the first gathering for celebration. Michel had decided to cook a sheep on a spit outside in his field. The hot day became a sultry night. Momo was head chef and made sure the roasting beast was turned on its giant skewer at the right time and with the correct number of cranks over the glowing embers. Michel, in charge of the drink, took pride of place behind his little cluttered bar in the corner of his downstairs room. Used to some pretty heavy duty concoctions, on this occasion the guests were evenly split into those who imbibed and those that wouldn't. Those that wouldn't turned out to be the future brides' friends and relations. Of course all Michel's friends drank like fish. So pretty soon two distinctly different parties were developing and rather than forging links between the two sides of the new family, eye brows were raised and looks dared to question the suitability of the imminent match. Too much alcohol deadens the senses, drives decorum out of the window, either turning its recipient into a new best friend or worst enemy. When Michel produced his accordion and the songs started, there was little to cause offence. Some of the lyrics were admittedly colourful. But military people must have encountered boisterous sing-a-longs before. I thought the reference to an amorous shepherd and his love for sheep was very funny. The dancing was perhaps ill advised and the future bride's mother was probably not impressed by the impromptu can-can. Grown men dancing without their trousers can present a dilemma for a stone cold sober audience. And so it was that balmy Thursday night, the first to celebrate the coming together of two families.

Friday lunchtime saw mouton on the menu. The previous evening's leftovers had been considerable on the basis that the food wasn't ready to eat until about two in the morning by which time the sober had departed and the drunk were too drunk to eat. The two groups reconvened and after a rather stiff beginning, began to make the best of it. What prevented the whole thing from going pear shaped was the fact that the bride was the drinker, while the groom wouldn't touch a drop. Each was therefore the ideal ambassador in the other's camp. After lunch the women folk set off in an excited gaggle for the Salle des Fetes and its adjoining mini marquee where the bride and groom were to welcome their guests, receive their envelopes of money and display the wedding presents. The hall and its canvass appendix needed to be decorated for tomorrow's festivities. A combination of paper flowers and paper chains had been decided upon as the most colourful and cost effective way of cheering the place up. In Michel's book you couldn't eat or drink decorations so there was little point in spending too much time or money in that direction. The red head was invited to join the decoration party and she spent the afternoon cutting and gluing bits of coloured paper; bonding with the other female guests.

Saturday was the wedding day and it poured. Pyrenean rain was the wettest. Cruelly, a big wind had sprung up to lend support. The red head and I emerged from the Grange done up like dog's dinners. She was wearing a smart short black dress that revealed the true extent of her slender legs. On her red head was a very decorative violent pink and black straw hat with thin quivering feathers trailing to front and rear. I was in my old dark morning suit with a pink waistcoat to compliment the red head's hat, the stained Royal Agricultural college tie, and my own tall black silk topper. Thus dressed, bouncing down the wet and wind swept mountain track in the old cat-cat, we must have looked like a pair of aliens. At the Marie the wedding party had assembled. A sea of uniforms greeted our own and the brides' lot had dug out their best ceremonial rags as sailors, soldiers and policemen. It was difficult to recognise some of them in their peaked caps and the gold braid dripped over shoulders and swept down fronts just like the wet wedding day rain. As far as Michel and his friends were concerned, the dressing up box hadn't been opened. True there were cleaner than average trainers about on feet and both Michel and Maurice were wearing ties, but apart from that their wedding attire was pretty much the same as for every other day, berets included. The bride had spared no efforts in trying to dress up. Every inch, she had become the fantasy shepherdess incarnate. She looked like something out of a Gainsborough painting, something from a bygone age, an era where women wore bonnets and frills and buxom bosoms, visible heaving chests, were there to be seen, proud white pillows leading the rest of the body in procession. The hooped skirts to the floor gave her the appearance of gliding when she moved. She didn't carry a crook but gripped her groom with a fierce resolve that displayed to all her ability to catching and keeping a man.

"La belle mariee," said one overcome female relative to another. Only the red head and Louise Butler got the giggles.

"It's Little Bo Peep," whispered Louise and the two shook gently side by side. The party dripped its way into the Marie and up the staircase into the main room. The mayor, also the local doctor, performed the ceremony and we all stood around the happy couple. The bride's mother shed the obligatory tear at the letting go of her little girl and she mopped her cheek in a public display with her wedding day handkerchief.

After the mayor's words and the newly weds promises, the entire cast emerged and scuttled across the road into the old covered market. A mini grandstand had been built for the photographs. Who went where was a logistical nightmare, but the bride, like the good shepherdess she was, soon had us mustered into the right place. The red head's hat obscured one of the aunts from Toulon. Momo was asked to put out his cigarette. At last the bride took her place on the scaffolding next to her new husband and between her parents and Michel. Her hooped skirt had to be forced into the tight gap, squeezed into an unnatural shape, which took away the symmetry of the bride's composition. Up there on the scaffolding, surrounded by uniforms, brocade and berets, I didn't really belong. I was an extra on a crazy set, absurd with a top hat and a red head on my arm. As I looked around, Gilbert and Sullivan sprang to mind.

The Salle des Fetes hadn't moved but disastrously the mini marquee had. The wind had carried it off down the valley and all that was left when we all arrived were two sodden trestle tables standing alone outside the entrance to the hall. The newly marrieds formed their welcome committee in the entrance and we pushed in as quickly as we could in order to get out of the wet gale. Introductions and greetings were rather shorter than had been planned because of the crush, people out in the wet trying their best to get into the dry. I stood with the red head in the pushing queue. The uniform next to me looked agitated and mentioned something about the inclement weather.

"Les tringles d'escalier." I said with a sympathetic grin nodding heavenwards. The uniform obviously hadn't understood why I was talking about stair rods.

"Chats et chiens." I tried again but with no effect.

"Tant pis." He said.

"Oui." I replied thinking for some reason that he was referring to the missing tent. "They'll find her wrapped around some tree in the morning." The sentence should never have been tried in French but I was keen to have a go. The uniform pushed off rather quickly and for the rest of the day avoided even eye contact with me.

The generous meal eventually arrived, a great relief for the non-drinkers. Course followed ample course. All the guests were seated at trestle tables. Each had its colourful paper table decoration somewhere in the middle, a floral representation or an abstract collision of torn colored paper. Momo's cigarette put paid to one of them. Christine's quick thinking and the jug of red wine prevented a more serious conflagration. Liberally spread about on each table were typed song sheets with the words for the songs that we all had to sing between courses. At first there was a degree of timidity. But once the wine had started to take effect, especially on the bride and her Father-in-law's guests, fierce competition broke out between singing tables. The bare light bulbs hanging from the Salle des Fetes ceiling rattled in their sockets. Dust from previous gatherings slid gently from where it lay and, unnoticed, floated very delicately down amongst the new partygoers. After the meal and the cutting and serving of a huge white cake that looked like Mount Blanc, there was dancing. The country band was rather good and the floor filled with happy wedding guests. At their centre the shepherdess spun and floated on her hooped skirt like a frilly white hovercraft encouraged here and there by her shiny, grey, smiling husband. The couple looked radiant. They could be together for more than thirty years.

It was a good wedding. Symbolic of its success was the coming together of the two sets of families and their friends. One of Michel's male friends, Jacques, disappeared outside with one of the bride's girlfriends, a nurse from Lyon. I remembered my best man trying to get off with our principal bridesmaid. He failed. I could tell that Jacques had had his end away because of the smug look on his damp face when he returned. The nurse too looked happy and when she danced with somebody in a uniform, we could see the tell tale sign. On the back of her dark skirt were the distinctive marks of whitewash rubbed from off the outside wall of the Salle des Fetes.

"Taxes and a nurse," says the red head to me rather unkindly I thought. "Life's two certainties."

Jesus ⇌

I'm not a left footer but I give it a go.

I used to get something from attending the tiny country church back in Somerset, the one on the island at Orchardleigh where I assisted Fred Chant as number two Church Warden. It gave me that contemplative hour when I could talk to Jesus, get a direct line to God. I'd pump the handle, provide the air for Mary, the eighty-year-old organist, every other Sunday and found a sense of real satisfaction with those straightforward Prayer Book services. I was hoping for a similar experience in rural France. I wanted to find something that would give me the same inner feeling of well being, the impression of really belonging in a community.

Occasionally I would venture down to the village church for mass on a Sunday morning. The old building in Sainte Marie was by far the most prominent in the commune. The road curved around it on two sides, climbed up at its East end and then spilled into the centre of the village before again clambering out and South off up the mountain, over to Spain. To the North a neighbour's grass field ran away down the valley. It nourished a flock of a different kind. The well tended, walled graveyard lapped up to the thick stone wall at its West end. There the locals came to bury and talk to their dead. They placed flowers on the extravagant marble slabs and kissed the photographs of the departed. The church's stark grey exterior gave it a municipal look, business like, not really welcoming like the village bar and shop across the road. The faithful would enter the cavernous place of worship and dunk their hands into the Holy water making the sign of a cross on their foreheads as they went to their seats. Some made a sign that looked more like the 'Nike' tick and plenty didn't bother with any sign language at all. Many of the women seemed to sit apart from the men and some arriving at their place wouldn't sit, but stood as if waiting for a bus to arrive along side the rustic pews. The congregation trickled in as it suited them, most on time, but quite a few souls arrived after the service had started unaware and unconcerned over punctuality. Attendance was a casual affair, like going to a museum. Some had dressed up for the Lord but most wore what they normally got up in, trainers, tracksuit bottoms and casual gear. The old all wore black. During the summer months tourists in t-shirts and shorts swelled the numbers and children were made to join in, pray with their parents. I dressed up in collar and tie, cords and a Keeper's tweed jacket and stuck out like a leper even at the back of the church.

Theatre like, the church was concentrated around the altar. We had entered a black and white movie that then became a technicoloured extravaganza as the show started. Up at the front was the ornate gold embellished set. Vast twisted candlesticks with their lighted white wax poles giving out shimmering pinpoints of light and the smell of old religion. Painted panels, ancient oils, of Our Lord, or the artist's impression of him, being crucified surrounded by the agonised. Another of the same artist's hero being exalted with his head in the clouds sung to by chubby cherubs, dead children with wings. The priest from neighbouring Campan strolled on to centre stage dressed up in full-length vestments. The brightly coloured, almost iridescent robes had him wrapped up like the toffee from a tin of Quality Street. He held his arms outstretched, white palms open, as a welcome to us all and greeted us in French. I shouldn't have been surprised but I was. I had expected the universal language of religion, had thought that there at least I might understand everything that was being said. But I didn't. The Lord's Prayer had a rhythm that gave it away and the Creed was fairly obvious but much of the rest, and especially the sermon, were gobbledegook. Sadly they didn't sing hymns, something I loved to do. Communion should be communion in every language and lines of the faithful went up to take bread and wine from the priest and his helper, a woman who looked as though she should have been the local schoolteacher. She glowed with importance as she administered Jesus' wishes. I couldn't join in, felt that it wasn't for me.

There was a place not far from the Grange where I could walk to find Jesus without the trappings I didn't understand. Just Him and me mostly. The cross at Peyras overlooked the Grange from a mountain above it and Jesus hung there on an exposed wooden cross set into a cracked three tiered concrete plinth. Just a tiny dot as seen from the Grange, but the hour or so climb up to him brought me closer to God. It was a place where only walkers and shepherds would go, an isolated spot, bruised and battered by the weather, covered in frost and snow for most of the winter and beaten down on by the unshaded hot sun in August. Soaked by the rain, shaken by the wind. Jesus looked more than crucified. The weather had scarred him too, flaked and cracked his body, disfigured him even more than the Romans. But he hung on, his mottled head tilted to his right; he hung on as a symbol against adversity from man and nature.

I could sit at his feet, placed together, as they were one over the other, nailed to the wooden block that itself was fastened to the cross on which his body was so awfully stretched. I could perch on the cracked concrete and look up at him if I wanted to and say what I had to. Talk man to Son of Man. There, where shepherds passed, was the Lamb of God who takest away the sins of the World. He was a good listener. He had always been a good listener. Never interrupted so I could chat away. I couldn't remember every conversation I had with him although most of them would have started with the same sort of line.

"Hello Jesus. Still there then. Had I thought about it I'd have brought up some body filler and a tin of paint. Given you a good going over."

I took the red head up to meet him when she had come over for Michel's son's wedding. She was brought up a Roman Catholic so was dully reverent in front of him. There was a ruined barn not far down from the cross, just a pile of old stones really and we went to explore and ended up making love.

"No not here," she said to me at first. "I can't do it here with Him looking at us."

"But can't He see everything anyway?" I was trying to be a clever dick.

Being a good Catholic girl the red head makes sure that Jesus can't see what was going on from on his cross behind us.

85

Logging On ⚒

"Timber!" Butler shouts as loud as he can, but I don't hear him.

The wood draw changed things for me, made me question what I was doing. Every other year the community had a wood draw. All full time residents who entered were entitled to a load of community wood. All the names were pitched into the draw with an entry fee of two hundred francs. At an evening gathering in the Salle des Fete, the lot numbers were pulled out of an old tin. Some of the locals felt that I shouldn't really be included because I was "a foreigner". A discussion about my eligibility was short and sharp and the piercing looks of those that didn't want me to have a part of their community wood made me feel like an outsider. I was a foreigner.

Despite my efforts to become one of them, I would never become a mountain man. I understood a little of what it must have been like for Franz the German. I sat at the back of the hall feeling like the fraud I was. What arrogance had spurred me on to believe that I could join that exclusive club, could by rubbing shoulders with them, somehow acquire their way of life? I was as different from them as it was possible to be. I had bought my way into their community, a rich Englishman, rich by their standards. And I was playing at it. The game was turning sour. Always welcome in the bar of course, I was never going to be a peasant farmer or postman or baker or mountain guide. I was always going to pop back to England to see mother and father, my friends and the red head. So I was just play-acting, down in the Pyrenees trying to find something that actually wasn't available for me.

Michel spoke up for me and the Mayor knew that I paid my local taxes like the rest of them, so my name was allowed to go forward. Put forward in name only, I didn't really deserve their French wood. In the valley, without wood, you'd probably freeze. Wood, the getting of it, cutting, splitting, carting, stacking and burning filled many hours of many days and nights, but only when the moon was right. Wooders would tell you, you couldn't wood if the moon wasn't right. I wood with Butler, the blind leading the blind. Or in our case the man with the dodgy heart sharing with the man with the walking stick. How on earth could a man who lived with a walking stick, take to the steep hills in an attempt to chop down trees? Butler needed the exercise, the encouragement and the stimulation a day's logging could bring. He needed to be coaxed away from his fireside or TV or Louise and taken up, out of his house, into the woods where we pretended to be lumberjacks. It was positive therapy for our minds and bodies. Butler in action, both his knees braced and bandaged so tightly, moved like a wooden soldier. A stained towelling band wrapped around his head sucked up the sweat before it deluged down and stung his eyes. He looked like a wooden soldier with a head wound. We managed and sweated our way through the pathetic loads. It was good for him and for me. It was no wonder they had invented electricity. The amount of work involved in gathering about you a few sticks so that you could sit by them as they burnt was totally out of all proportion to their value. Time and motion men would laugh. Just the kit alone needed to mount a wooding expedition would cost more than a brand new generator and the diesel to run it for months. And yet wooding was still performed. The same way women went to the supermarket to find food; men went to the tree covered hills to get wood. Women shopped, men chopped.

It was absolutely knackering to the muscles. Wood muscles weren't really used for anything else. It was strenuous physical activity climbing up the steep side of a mountain with a chainsaw, its spanner and fuel, working bent over double, balancing mostly on one leg. Pulling the starting rope on the saw's engine, pulling it again so that the metal teeth spun furiously around their guide. Making the first mark and cutting through a tree in the hope that when it cracked and fell, it wouldn't crack and fall on me. What had happened to all the trees on the flat ground was obvious. The ancient inhabitants of those parts had got to the easy stuff when Asterix was a Gaul.

I shouted "Timber!" - lumberjack dramatics – and hoped the several tons would fall where I wanted them. A real lumberjack would know. But I was just a novice, an apprentice, a sapling jack. I was perched on a slope where mother gravity had been pulling at me all the time. The cut tree should have headed south. But if I'd sawn it incorrectly it could just as easily have fallen up hill, wrong footing me and sending me and my hot saw tumbling out of its way and downwards. I dripped sweat with the effort. A tinge of fear added to the perspiration matting my hair and the river of cold sweat down the back of my shirt. If there were big wild animals in those woods, with sharp teeth and hunger, they could have smelled the fear above the two-stroke mixture and chain oil. I could have been lunch.

We took lunch or caisse-croute up in the woods. A man and a chainsaw can be a lethal combination at any time. A man and a chainsaw and two or three litres of rough red wine can set up an afternoon of war zone proportions. Lopping off limbs after lunch didn't bear thinking about. But we did and thanked the patron saint of loggers that only tree limbs crashed down the mountain slopes to the waiting trailer. Butler and I tried to work well away from each other. Once the tree was felled, we had to work together. A chainsaw got jammed in the piece of wood it was trying to eat through. The sheer weight of the wood and the way it lay on the ground made the cut close behind the advancing saw, pinching it tight within the tree trunk. The chainsaw was stuck fast like Excalibur. We had to use the saw that wasn't trapped to try and cut out the one that was, so if mine had become stuck, Butler would be called over to come and help and vice versa. "Us foreigners must work together aye?" Butler said reminding me that we shouldn't really be there at all.

Once we were trying to release a stuck chainsaw from a chuck of wood the size of a small car. Suddenly, with gravity's help, the section broke off from the rest of the fallen tree, the trapped saw flew out and the sizeable chunk of wood started rolling off down the mountainside. I wasn't quick enough and it rolled right over my legs, spinning me around and throwing me down the slope. Apparently Butler had tried to warn me, or so he said after the event. But I hadn't heard him over the chainsaw's awful whine. I wasn't hurt, bruised a bit but I had lost my glasses in the fall, which try as we might we could not find. The steep floor of the forest was littered with thick leaf mould and debris that had cushioned my legs when the log ran over them. To find the tortoise shelled frames would have required a fingertip search by an army. That day's wooding ended. Without my glasses, the exercise would have turned into a massacre.

Of course we could have bought our wood, split up ready for the fire, but Butler and I preferred to cut out the middleman. We had the chainsaws, axes, splitters, sledge hammers, ropes and coins (French wedge shaped bits of metal) to do it with. We'd got the old cat-cat and a robust trailer. The main woodman in those parts was Alpha. He was the middleman. In the valley wood was often the measure of a man's wealth; the bigger his pile, the bigger his pile. Alpha acted like high street bank manager. It was about three hundred Francs a stere and nothing for a look and it was Alpha who decided whether you'd be 'stereing' or just looking. No matter if you'd got the money. No matter if you hadn't. Alpha the woodman decided. Madame Wood, Alpha's wife, worked like a Trojan. Allegedly she was sixty something with nine children but she could split and toss a log better than any. Alpha was the woodman though and he didn't say much other than it usually started with "Non". His wood went where he wanted. Some had even tried to steal their stere waiting and watching for Monsieur Wood to go out in his truck while Madame Wood was busy with chores or tending her horses. It was rumoured that the flimsy fence to the yard was taken out and logs had flown. But it was also rumoured that Monsieur Wood had got wise to these clandestine wood lice. He planted spiked pieces of wood in his pile. Placed on the open fire or in a wood burning stove, they would explode in the heat. These bangs would, so it was said, take doors of their hinges and people from their seats. Don't ask me what a spiked log looked like. Honest paying punters would just have to hope that Monsieur Wood remembered to remove the charged logs before his seventh Pastis. He did grin very occasionally and with his toothless smile confirmed that he sometimes provided a chimney sweeps services without the need for brushes. A case of bang and soot alors!

At the wood draw evening Alpha the woodman hadn't look pleased. It wasn't a bad night for his business. Some locals, having received their allocations, did a deal with him. Alpha would cut and cart their load and keep half to sell on. I needed all mine and when my name came up and the lot was drawn, I was allocated seven growing trees, all numbered so I could find them in the forest. A load was supposed to provide the recipient with enough fuel for a winter or two. My load was going to take me all winter just to gather it in. And that was with Butler's help. The main problem wasn't in felling the trees or cutting them up into manageable pieces. The main problem was carting them up the track to the Grange because the cat-cat and trailer laden with wood just wouldn't negotiate the steepness. With a load in tow, it was as difficult to climb as a fireman's pole smeared with Vaseline. The answer was Bar-Bar.

Bar-Bar was an unfortunate name for a man with a stutter. When I first asked him his name, I thought he was talking about a flock of sheep. His heavy mountain accent, his staccato speech and his stutter made it difficult to understand. Bar-Bar got his nickname because he liked to go from bar to bar. He owned a big cat-cat, an agricultural vehicle with a flashing orange light on the roof. It would go anywhere. The back tipped up using hydraulics, and it was just the sort of toy that I would ask Father Christmas to put in my stocking. So Bar-Bar and his cat-cat brought some of my logs up to my house in exchange for a bottle of wine or two.

I was so impressed with Bar-Bar's machine that I went out with Butler in search of one. I didn't want to have to rely on Bar-Bar's good will to keep me supplied with my wood. A stubborn streak in me wanted to show that I could be totally self-sufficient. If I was a foreigner then I'd better act like one. Butler and I often went off on missions to find things. We'd travel to Tarbes or Lourdes or even Pau in search of what ever it was we were looking for. An antique bed on one occasion, some carpet on another, decent wine once, building wood the next and the current quest, a large four wheel drive machine that would get up the mountain to the Grange, fully laden, no matter what the weather. The idea was to do the searching and the business in the morning and then return to the Cafe Londres in Bagneres in time for lunch. I'd treat Butler to the plat du jour and the two of us enjoyed each other's company. We had a strange relationship, more like father and son than friends. Had we met in England, we probably wouldn't have been friends at all. Thrown together in those mountains, our mother tongue the mutual bond, we hit it off together. Butler had much more French than I. He could usually explain what it was that we were after and it was better hunting as a pair, two Jonny Foreigners together.

There was only one occasion when I remembered thinking that it would have been better if Butler hadn't come along. We had called to see a Depot de Vente, a large depository where people would bring their furniture and leave it there in the hope of selling it. I was curious and so Butler and I called in to have a look. Some days Butler's body seemed to work quite well but on others it was erratic. On this particular day a new batch of pills had given him a serious and violent bout of diarrhoea. The Depot de Vente had the old style French lavatory, one of those holes in the ground that had to be hovered over. Butler with his bad legs wasn't good at hovering and when he eventually emerged from the WC with his anxious walking stick and found me looking at the old furniture he said rather furtively

"We ought to be going."

"But we've only just got here," said I keen to explore further.

"We must go now," Butler said grabbing me by the arm and leading me out of the building back to the cat-cat.

"What on earth's the matter?" I asked as we accelerated off towards Bagneres.

"It's my arse." Butler said.

"What?"

"My arse exploded."

"Oh dear," said I sympathetically visualising the new pebbledash finish to the walls of the Depot de Vente's smallest room.

"We won't be welcome back there." Butler said as though his accident had made a difference.

It was in Tarbes that we found a twenty year old UniMog made by Mercedes and so I bought it, which meant that my log pile wouldn't run out and I needn't be dependant on local good or bad will.

"You've done what?" says the red head on the phone. It strikes me that my latest investment makes it look like I am planning to stay put.

Meeting Peter ⚒

"Six hundred francs. You've got to be bloody joking."

It was probably like any other Friday and I slipped down to the village shop and bar for a loaf of bread and some company. Magali was there tending to the business while her husband Marc was out meeting with the local chasse. He liked his shooting, liked talking about it, and was fortunate his wife took care of business. But he wouldn't have seen it that way. A small group of locals perched like old crows around the bar drinking and smoking. The radio was tuned into Nostalgie as usual. A scruffy little man sat at the corner of the bar right next to the noisy coffee machine, deep in conversation with Thierry the car breaker. I joined them after the run of handshakes; Magali poured me a beer from the china pump and slid the wet glass towards me. Thierry explained to the scruffy man who I was and said that I would buy his car from him.

"What?" I said.

"You will buy his car." Thierry repeated what I thought he'd said.

"But I don't need another car. I've got the cat-cat and a Unimog. I don't want another vehicle."

"You will buy his car." Thierry seemed insistent. "Come Charl, come look at the car."

The three of us went out into the back yard of Du Bertrand's and there next to Marc's Renault Espace taxi was a three-wheeled Piaggio. It was tiny. It was rusty blue. Its wheels were about the size of dinner plates - one at the front and two at the back. It had a cab with a bench seat for two, a steering wheel, three pedals on the floor just like any normal car and a simple gear lever that slid either forward or backwards. Behind the cab was an area about the size of a decent wheelbarrow, open like the back of a pick-up truck. The current owner, the scruffy man, used it to carry his goods to market. It reminded me of a Tuk-tuk, those colourful little taxis running around Bangkok. And there was something of a dodgem car about it. The power apparently came from a 125cc two-stroke Vespa scooter engine mounted over the back wheels, so it's top speed was probably thirty miles an hour at most.

Thierry forced himself into the cab behind the steering wheel and started the engine. It hacked into life with a high pitched cackle. Once the cloud of blue smoke had cleared, the scruffy man and I watched as the pathetic vehicle spun round and round in a tight circle. Dust sprang up. Thierry, its mad controller, beamed at us through the tiny windscreen shouting "I ham ze Count of Monte Christo" at the top of his voice.

Thierry was right. I did buy the car. I bought it so that I could take off on an absurd journey around France. That inadequate three-wheeler was to be my means of escape. It was to be called Peter. Jesus had used the name to describe his "Rock".

"Five hundred and fifty then. Not a cent more." The scruffy man is smiling and I am wondering what the Patois word for sucker is.

Tree House ⚔

"I love your villa." Father means it.

Getting father down to visit the Grange was a major operation. Against doctor's orders, he was to fly to Toulouse, and then catch the train to Tarbes. He missed his flight because he had forgotten his passport.

"I didn't need one to go over there and fight the Germans," he told them at the check in desk. It didn't matter. He needed a passport. He had to travel a day later, which unfortunately meant that the French trains were on strike. I said I'd meet him at the airport but there was a misunderstanding and he took a taxi to Tarbes. Anyhow we eventually met up in Tarbes, at the café opposite the railway station. I saw him before he saw me. He was sitting at an outside table nursing a glass of beer. He wore his old Panama hat with the regimental colours proudly tied around it, just above the brim. The linen jacket looked travel worn, but the club tie was still knotted around his neck. He was reading the Daily Telegraph. He couldn't have been anything else other than English. He looked a lot older than I remembered. Hadn't over wintered well. We shook hands.

"MFU," he said firmly.

"What?"

"Monumental fuck up." I knew exactly what he meant.

"Well you're here now."

"Hmm," he made that noise of some one only partially appeased. He offered me a beer.

He loved the place. He'd been there before, once with the stepmother. She hadn't liked it at all. It was too rough round the edges for her tastes. But father, like son, loved the Grange. When describing it to his friends back home, he called it "Charlie's villa". What a picture this painted! How so unlike a villa it was!

"Of course there's no electricity and you can't drive your car to the front door." He didn't want people to get the wrong idea even though he used the wrong nametag. He inspected my improvements and seemed to approve. He then unpacked his bag, the little suitcase on wheels that followed him where ever he went. He was at home.

"What about a drink?" He was always thirsty.

The first time I remembered my father smacking me, was when I swore. Before I had grown out of short trousers and grazed knees, I understood all about tree house living and that was the way I wanted it to be forever more. My first was constructed when we lived in Moor Park, north and west of London. Riley and I built it in a hedge on something our parents called the green belt that ran between the Vaughns next door and us in Wolsey cottage. Actually it wasn't really a green belt at all because one-day pylons appeared marching down it like conquering steel giants. We all hated them and I remember saying "Bloody pylons" out loud, in the back of the car. My father stopped it and turned around and smacked me on my bare legs as I sat on the back seat trying to express what everyone knew was the truth. The simple tree house stirred up something in me, left indelible traces. In a tree house a boy had his own space. He could swear and his legs wouldn't get slapped. He climbed up and away from the mundane and entered the kingdom of tree house. Homework or prep were consigned to the bin marked "not needed" along with baths and having to eat up all your food while sitting up straight at the table. In a tree house I could eat as many penny chews as I could afford and no one would complain if I slouched like the tower of Pisa.

When I was thirteen my father decided to get to know me. I think that I must have had a reasonable school report and this was the excuse for a father and son trip to Scotland for a long weekend during term time. Father worked hard at pre-packing vegetables for the developing supermarket business and the quality time spent with his family was pretty limited, so a long weekend together, just the two of us, would be invaluable. He sought permission for the exeat from my headmaster and he planned the sortie with military precision. We set off from Cambridgeshire in the Wolsey and headed up the Great North Road. The first over night stop was Dalkieth, on the outskirts of Edinburgh and a large red brick town pub run by one of father's old army muckers. The language at the bar was unintelligible but the natives were friendly and father spent a happy evening drinking the whisky and reliving the war with his friend while I sipped shandy and ate heavily fried food. Father had planned a trip down a coalmine in Mid Lothian for the following day through another of his army chums. I remember before going to bed that night, leaving father at the bar, the advice given to me by a local who knew of our itinerary.

"Yill ken if yers too fer doon if yers meets a wee rad mon wi two herns, a lang pointy tail and a ferk in his hond."

"Thank you and goodnight," said I like a polite public school boy should. Down the mine we didn't meet the devil but we did crawl to the coalface and watch as the glistening black-faced men picked their way under the earth's crust. It was an image that will stay with me until I die. A privileged, precocious, privately educated teenager with not a real worry in the world, as out of place as a weed in a seedbed. Those hardened, tough, working men with their bright smiles made pure white by the black dust, and the pale rings around their eyes, pandering to the Coal Board for their shillings. It must have been so hard. My father, like the fighting man he had been, was probably more at ease. He would have understood, felt the bond, the struggle, and the foxhole experience. We surfaced in the cage and washed together in the communal miner's shower block, just my father and me under a shower for twenty or thirty. I hid my private parts from him and tried not to look at his. A father and his son stripped naked in the white tiled room, embarrassed beyond echoing words, the two of us total strangers. Soaped up, our sooty suds mingled and ran off down the drain. Pink again, the rough towel not nearly big enough to hide the embarrassment of a naked boy in that watering place for working men.

Next he took me to Culloden and the mists swirled so that you could have cut them with a claymore. It was there that I saw the house, a croft, a simple rectangular stone building with peat on its roof, a home to die for. That was where I wanted to live and like a spoilt child, I wanted it badly. There in the Scotch mist was my tree house without the tree. There, standing grey and solid and ageless in a whirlpool of uncertainty was a beacon, a lighthouse where dreams could be illuminated. Perhaps the lonely croft offered reassurance to the confused schoolboy, the boy who had tried to run away, the boy who didn't like being a schoolboy. I took a photograph, a colour transparency, of the building with my new Kodak Instamatic that father had made a part of the treat. In taking the picture I was staking my claim, seizing ownership of something I wanted so badly, something I had in my tree house once and something I was in danger of losing forever. We moved off and once again I couldn't say what we really thought.

It was a Boys Own holiday for both of us. The seed sown then had germinated and grown into the Grange, where we sat and looked at each other. Father had climbed up into my world.

"How you getting on with that girlfriend of yours?" He asked the question I knew he would sooner or later. He'd met her. Father had liked my wife though. They were both Pisces, shared the same birthday. He didn't like to think of us as apart. Maybe didn't want me to make the same mistake he had.

I get up, pour father a whiskey, and add some water drawn straight from the mountain stream, cold as ice.

Spitting Image

It's not just the memory that plays tricks. It's not just the dreams. The photographic evidence is inconclusive.

Sometimes I'd just sit and stare at photos of the two of them. I had several I could use. There were the black and white wedding shots of Fut standing outside the Wayside Chapel looking as vulnerable as an uncertain child. There was the one of the red head on Brighton Pier, bubbling with laugher for the person behind the camera. Then there was the shot of Fut, radiant and happy, laughing as only she could, and the one of the red head looking insecure, lost almost, caught on film by a stranger in a strange place.

Squint and each could become either, either each, their moods as interchangeable as pieces of Lego, their colouring the only distinguishing mark between them.

I had the "naughty" shots too, the ones taken with Polaroid and decades later by digital technology. One lay full length on a chaise long naked and neat like a Goya. Not a smile on her face but a reserved look that said "Go on then if you must", a reluctant pose but full frontal none the less. The other was camera shy too but coyly offered what she thought was her best, undressed feature towards the lens. If anyone else had seen the shots by mistake, they would know right away that they were private, not meant for general consumption, for my eyes only. Asked to describe their different features, I'd expect they couldn't.

The longer I stared at the images the more the two became one. In that light, the dimness of the inner Grange, I couldn't be that sure just who was who.

When I was lying in a hospital bed after the heart attack, Fut came to see me once. She left and when I opened my eyes again the red head was there, next to me asking the same questions, showing the same concern.

Maybe the red head had been arranged. Maybe she had been there so that Fut could leave, could return to Australia after nearly thirty years of serving her time. A life sentence, her parole, being hastened by the red head's willingness to take her place. Maybe they'd agreed it. Worked out a deal between them. Maybe it was only fair that her parents should have her back at last, that she would see her grandchildren, that they would grow up knowing who their grandmother was. Their grandfather on the other hand, would never be a hero for them.

Perhaps the red head was a clone, a clone for a clown for another thirty-year stint.

Perhaps I still loved them both.

Father's visit unsettles me, stirs up my guilt and uncertainty.

Father's Pudding ⚬

"You need the right sort of sugar." Father was being adamant.

The locals took to father. They called him Daveed. He nearly always got their names wrong and couldn't tell Maurice from Michel. They respected him because of his age, his generosity towards them, because he fought the Germans, and I like to think, because he was my father. He liked them too, or most of them. He suggested that Maurice and Michel might like to travel over to England to watch a game of rugby football at Twickenham. The two big men seemed keen on the idea. But that would be in the following Spring.

I asked the usual suspects up to the Grange for a Sunday lunch. We'd barbecue some steaks I'd bought from "Du Bertrand". The leaves from the big mountain ash tree by the bridge over the stream gave the dappled shade necessary. The big outside table was positioned under one of its long boughs and the hot afternoon sun couldn't get all the way through the green canopy, as it wanted to. The Butlers, Maurice and Michel, Roget and Michelle and Christine all arrived in a breathless convoy at midday. Apart from Butler and the two big women, who needed me to meet them in the cat-cat at the bottom of the steep ascent, the others climbed up to the Grange. 'Aperos' were taken by all. Father sat at the end of the table with his straw hat on and held court, rather like a great white hunter meeting a bunch of natives. He raised his glass at every drink and said "Cheers" loudly. The assembly stopped their talking and turned to him, raised their tumblers and replied "Chin chin". Maurice tried an English toast of his own. "Buttims op" he said. Michel wanted to trump that. "Op years" he said with much mirth. Father thought they were talking patois and raised his glass to theirs in genuine appreciation. The pre-lunch drinks lasted until well into the afternoon when Momo decided that it was time to light the barbecue. The steaks were delicious, somehow even better eaten outside under the shady tree.

Father had a pudding that he wanted to make for us. He wasn't a cook but wanted to have a go. The ingredients were bananas, sugar and brandy. The sugar had to be the right sort. We had spent some time the day before trawling the shops in Bagneres for the right sort of sugar. He eventually settled on a box of something that he thought might do. His simple, unusual pudding was enjoyed by all. He used the hot embers of the barbecue to heat up the sugar, the sliced bananas and the brandy, so that the three became one in a cacophony of brown, caramelised sugar, hot, mashed banana and an after kick that left most speechless.

He never ceases to surprise me. Sweet and sour, sour and sweet.

The Plat Du Jour Tour

"When are you going to get a proper job darling?"

My mother would ask me on several occasions throughout my life and hers. A proper job was a profession. A doctor, lawyer, accountant, bank manager, vicar, soldier or teacher. These were acceptable pigeonholes in which the previous generation built their respectable lives. These were jobs where a mother could be proud of her son. Stopped in the street by an acquaintance, she could smile and cluck about her boy's assured place in the community. There was somehow safety in having a child on the ladder.

My mother was always very proud of my brother-in-law who started out an accountant and became the chairman of a bank. "He's very big in the City," my mother would say, playing to the new rules created by Mrs Thatcher. Making money became more important than what you did, as long as you did it with your brains and not your hands. Mother was devastated when he died quite suddenly. We all were. Mother was, I think, never quite sure what to say about me. While my brother-in-law's life had been composed, mine had been improvised. In the end she knew I had something to do with making the greetings cards and Christmas crackers for Tesco. She used to visit the branch in Peterborough, her nearest, and go and interview the staff to find out what was selling and, more importantly, to let them know that her son was responsible. Getting 'a proper job' had never been important to me. I guess that my mother and father must have been disappointed from the day I left my expensive schooling prematurely with six O levels and became a ten-pound Pommie.

After the heart attack when I upped and went to France, my parents both thought that I had "dropped out." Was it possible to drop out at fifty? If the red head had been consulted, she might have called it "running away". I'd run away from prep school. Father had said sternly, "Maintenance of the objective. Berridges don't run away." I replied in my pre-pubescent voice that this one did, which must have hurt him quite a lot. Actually I hadn't got very far. Mr Simms found me on the wrong platform at Billingshurst station and escorted me back to the school. God how I had hated that place! When mother and father had dropped me off there after a Sunday's exeat, I remember running down the drive behind their car, watching the two rear lights getting smaller and smaller in front of my liquid eyes, crying out loud and praying, pleading, that the red brake lights would blur, the Austin Westminster would stop and that my mother would leap from the passenger seat with her arms outstretched ready to catch me up and take me away, back to my own home. The lights disappeared altogether and I stood in that long Sussex drive surrounded by wind blown trees, the saddest and loneliest little boy in the world.

I'd run away from the Vietnam draft out in Australia, probably quite a wise move. Young men were being killed in Vietnam and those that were not, looked scary when I met them on their R 'n R leave in Sydney bars. They had a spaced out look. Worse than tired. More than drained. Not drugged nor sedated. A distance to them like old men on park benches. They had seen things, done things that young men shouldn't and most of them didn't want to talk about it. One day my travelling companion, Philip, and I got drunk and went to the Army recruiting office and volunteered to join up for active service. We'd hatched the misguided plan over a few cold midis and believed that by offering our services to the Aussie armed forces, we'd dodge the draft. Reverse psychology was how Philip summed it up. How can we be called up when we've volunteered? The best form of defence is attack was how I thought of it. Anyhow we actually signed the papers that meant we'd be available. When and if the call came, I was safely back in England, having done a bunk. I didn't know where Philip had got to.

I had let my marriage of twenty-seven years just fall apart. Probably not a good idea. At the time I stumbled into marriage and parenthood and for many years was blissfully happy with it. Had three wonderful children, couldn't say that I raised them because I was too busy with other less important things. At its end I sort of stumbled out of the marriage too. My unhappy wife came to me one day and we sat down at the dinning room table. The polished table top between us reflected our hopelessness. We, I, had let things slide too far. We did little together anymore and what we had once had in common had dissolved, melted away. Mutual respect wasn't there anymore and the slightest breeze would fan the fire and burst us into destructive flames. We'd blaze away at each other in a senseless crescendo that upset our youngest son, the only one still just at home, and damaged our lives forever. I had found the red head, "the flibbertigibbet red head from Hell", and I was letting myself be pulled in that direction. Across that gate-legged table we decided that we should live apart. In that one moment we sealed our fate. I could have said that I would make an effort to get things right between us again, could have apologised for slipping into bed with another woman. But she, my wife, had already devised my epitaph. "Never say you're sorry. Never admit you're wrong." So what God had brought together, man had put asunder. It was then, across that table, that we took a decision as casually as going to the shops. One minute married, the next not.

It seemed that the course of my life bobbed about like a small cork in a vast ocean. The winds and currents tossed and turned me, not any charted navigation or steady hand on the tiller. Ingrained in the cork however was an unfailing enthusiasm and a stubbornness that kept it afloat.

I had been thinking about escape. I hadn't discussed it with the red head because I knew what she would have said. I'd told my father on his visit. He had taken the whole thing on board. He'd returned to England and would be busy drumming up support from his friends. He'd have a file with Plat du Jour written on it. Cabin fever was taking a grip over me. I had to do something. I didn't want to hate the place I loved. I had to take action to prevent a complete breakdown, to save the relationship. As always the easiest solution seemed to be to run away. School, Australia, marriage, heart attack, England, the red head and now the Grange. I was going to run again.

The three-wheeler, my new car, if I could call it that, acquired the nickname of Peter. Peter the Piaggio to give it its full family title. I think it was Louise Butler that christened it.

"What the bloody hell do you want *that* thing for?" she said.

"To go round France," I replied as though it was of no consequence what so ever. A bit like having a shower.

"Silly bugger" said Louise. Tony backed her up with a look over his glasses.

The Plat du Jour Tour came to me up at the Grange one grey and drizzly day. Housebound for the fifth or sixth consecutive day, all I wanted to do was scream. Cabin fever crept up slowly, wound its wicked way around me like ivy crawling up a tree. The first symptom was staying in bed in the morning to read. I read page after page lying down so that the words had to be taken in vertically. Words were not designed to be taken in vertically. Words were meant to be read horizontally. When I emerged back into the right way up world I would get up to light the fire. It smoked in sympathy with the mood, hissed and booed at the audience. I lit candles at midday because the gloominess in the house was like a shroud. The week old stew was as thin as a school lunch and yesterday's bread rock hard. To go outside was like leaving a dull dry room and moving into a dull wet one. Lethargy grabbed the joints and the brain. There wasn't another soul to talk to, not another pair of human eyes to look into. Not surprising in those parts and under those conditions that the bottle often became the comforter. Dreadful despair frequently danced at the rope's noose or blew a man's face away with a cheap cartridge.

My escape was going to be different. Real not imaginary. I would set off on a journey right around the circumference of France. Every day I would take a plat du jour. I'd travel in the little Piaggio called Peter and I'd take a year to complete the tour. I'd write about it. The people I'd meet, the places I'd see. I'd try and raise some money by sponsorship to cover my expenses. Any profit I'd give to the British Heart Foundation and the French equivalent. There must be one, as French men must have heart disease too. I'd set about creating a project plan. It would be great to get some good PR out of the venture, to show people that there was proof positive that life went on after a heart attack.

Bit by bit the Plat du Jour Tour took its shape. I told the locals who shrugged because I was a mad foreigner anyway. But Michel offered to help. He was going to form a committee called "Coeurs a Sauver" which would raise some money to support the venture. The committee met one evening beside Michel's smoky fire and we drank and talked and decided to open a bank account. It seemed to Michel a positive move. The committee (Michel, president, Momo, Louise, Christine, Roget and large Michelle, secretary) looked to me to start the ball rolling and so I donated a few hundred francs.

I was warmly thanked by the group for my donation and told that whilst I could not receive any payments from the fund, I could perhaps put in a claim for genuine out of pocket expenses such as postage. They meant well.

Peter the Piaggio went down to Thierry's yard in Bagneres for a make over. Butler thought that Thierry would be OK and besides Thierry had offered his services for free. "Fir ze art Charl, fir ze art, " Thierry had said with his hand firmly placed over his 'art. A new shade of blue was chosen for the paintwork. I designed a secure metal back so I could carry two tin trunks for my belongings and a tent; sleeping bag and small cooking stove. The brakes too needed looking at. They would be an important feature in the mountains and hadn't inspired a lot of confidence on their first test run. I pored over the Michelin map of France and marvelled at its three hundred and nineteen pages. The equivalent map for England wouldn't stretch to a hundred. I dug out my Rough Guide, a guide to French camp sites and one for gites and cheap hotels. I filled my head with ideas of trying to stay my way around France with friends or friends of friends. I could become a sort of pass the parcel. I tried to work out a route, fuel consumption and a budget. I spent hours writing letters to companies and individuals I thought should be interested in sponsoring the tour. I produced a brochure and took it off to a meeting with the British Heart Foundation in London.

At first they weren't terribly interested. Ideas flooded into their head office and they had to be very careful about who they became associated with in public. A slightly eccentric Englishman who'd survived a heart attack and was planning to travel around France in a motorised wheel barrow wasn't seen as main stream corporate fund raising. Yes, it was a bit of fun and yes; the story had been presented in a professional manner. Yes, it might catch the imagination of some of the media and yes; it might raise a bit of cash in sponsorship. But who were the sponsors? It was absolutely out of the question for them to have anything to do with tobacco companies. I don't think they liked my flippant remark that without cigarettes there wouldn't be nearly so much heart disease. After several meetings and phone calls, a thorough vetting of my background and a visit with their head nutritionist, I got a letter saying that the British Heart Foundation would be pleased to be associated with the Plat du Jour Tour. It could not give any financial help whatsoever. But I could use their official logo on my letterheads. I would need a full medical report to say that I was fit enough to take on the venture and full health insurance just in case I wasn't. They would, however, be pleased to accept any funds or donations made by the Plat du Jour Tour and they would put me in touch with their French counter parts, the Federation Francaise de Cardiologie in Paris. Nevertheless the Plat du Jour Tour, born out of cabin fever up in the misty mountains, had somehow become official.

For 561 francs one way, I took the couchette from Tarbes to Paris to go and meet the French Federation. The overnight experience was fine for someone who didn't need any sleep and I arrived for my meeting with the Federation Francaise de Cardiologie looking like a crumpled cardboard cut out. The Federation's boss was ex-military and looked as though he had indeed served for many years in the Foreign Legion. His handshake obliterated mine completely. His PR manager was Sylvie and even though I couldn't feel it, I sensed her handshake was altogether a far more refined affair. Sylvie had film star qualities, blond hair and a flashy white smile and a way of speaking English that made her sound like Bridgitte Bardot. It was Sylvie that had apparently persuaded her dour bosses that my ideas were worth supporting. They had read my proposals passed on to them from London but were not really sure what I was suggesting. If the British Heart Foundation was Britain's third or fourth biggest charity then the French equivalent was a tiny pinprick on France's money-giving conscience. Heart disease in France was statistically nothing like heart disease in Britain, although I did sometimes wonder who was doing the counting. The two bosses at the Federation however had been persuaded that the Englishman might raise them some money and would probably get them some publicity as he wound his way around their country.

"We only went goud piblicity," said the military boss. He pointed to a piece underlined by felt tip pen in my material that explained I would be meeting many different people on the Tour. "Priest, poets and prostitutes," the sentence had claimed amongst others. "We dun't went yew wiz prostitutes," he said in a way that implied he had sole rights. Sylvie smiled her way through the meeting and at the end of it I emerged with an agreement that the Federation would contribute towards my travelling expenses in exchanged for the publicity I would try and get for them. I had become an ambassador.

"I'll sponsor you for a thousand pounds darling," my mother says to me on the telephone and I love her. I talk to the red head. *"An ambassador for the heart?"* She is presumably wondering where that leaves hers.

The Year Started With A Lurch

"The longest journey begins with the shortest step." I am thinking of the words from the fortune cookie given to me at the Chinese restaurant in Bagneres.

There was an endemic affliction in that part of France, a condition in English called 'Litalap syndrome'. Litalap stood for Leave It Till As Late As Possible. Thierry suffered from it big time. Peter the Piaggio was delivered to his yard at the beginning of June, which should have provided plenty of time to get the little car ready for the departure in mid July. Butler and I pestered Thierry lots. Every time he'd say that things were progressing fine. The vehicle would be all done up and ready for the off.

"Dent wirry," he'd said, "I ham ze Count of Monte Christo." So we let him get on with it.

July the first arrived and with it fourteen more days to kick off. Butler and I once again went to the breakers yard to inquire about progress. Thierry was in a foul mood and grunted at us. The Piaggio was nowhere to be seen.

"Is not here," said Thierry darkly raising my blood pressure to levels that the heart surgeon wouldn't have liked. There followed what could only be described as a brief moment of interrogation, Butler and I as good cop and bad cop trying to get a confession out of our suspect. He coughed without the need for too heavy a hand and explained that Peter the Piaggio was in the tender loving care of the Twins. Butler and I scuttled round to the Twins joint and sure enough, there in a dark corner sat Peter. He looked dejected and had become a receptacle for mechanical junk. He looked as ready to hit the road as a flattened hedgehog.

The Twins beamed up at us. We explained that the world's press would be arriving in Sainte Marie in fourteen days time to watch as the Piaggio and its driver set off on a journey right around France. The Twins looked at each other in order to confirm what they had just been told. They looked back at us just to make sure and their smiles stretched to breaking point. For small men they conjured up big laughs. Like two machines they roared in unison, their laughter pumped out at us, gushed around the chaotic building like a boisterous invader. Their bodies doubled up and the two little men did a sort of dance, a gig of joy, where their feet stayed firmly planted but the rest of the body moved and shook as much as it could. It summoned their families from out of the caravans and passed on the hilarity. Tears rolled down their cheeks and even their scruffy Alsatian dogs looked amused. Butler and I stood there surrounded by the laughing and like a gas it got to us. Just a smile at first but pretty soon we too had joined in. We all shook and shrieked and slowly, very slowly the fun subsided and we stood looking at each other, the Twins stained cheeks smeared by their tears.

"C'est pas vrai." said one of them.

"Oui. C'est vrai." said Butler. And off they went again, absurd laughing puppets whose strings were being jerked out of control.

It was July 15th 2000 and the mayor turned out, which was nice. Michel and the association had planed a farewell lunch in the covered market area at Sainte Marie de Campan. Posters had proclaimed the event, a public barbecue with a band of musicians from Campan. Sixty francs for food and wine. All welcome. It had been a wet summer and that Saturday in mid-July was no exception. The weather seemed to match my mood and I didn't know why I felt so down. Numbers were down too. Jean-Bernard from the Hotel Deux Cols in the village had been roped in to cook the food and he needed an electric hairdryer to get the damp barbecue to fire up. It was that sort of a day when flames needed coaxing, when there was smoke without fire.

I had told the red head. I had given her the detail, such as it was, about the Plat du Jour Tour and she had seemed to take the idea on board without a revolt. My journey around France would take a year and so would she. She would wait for another year. Another year away from the man she said she loved. It wouldn't be complete isolation, we would have some time together but we wouldn't be a couple, the couple that she had hoped for. It had been almost a year since the eclipse and her fingers would have been firmly crossed in the hope that the separation might pull us together. In her heart she would have been praying that I had had enough of living in France and that I'd come home. Come home and live happily ever after. Her biological clock was ticking on and the word "baby" was featuring in her vocabulary more than it ever had. That was something that I wasn't sure about. Wasn't at all sure. She didn't travel over to France for the farewell do. She couldn't stand the idea of kissing me goodbye and I too was grateful for that. Sad she wasn't there with me but pleased I wasn't saying farewell to her. Not knowing exactly when I'd see her again was a painful experience; reminded me of standing in that lonely Sussex school drive or of going to San Francisco with flowers in my hair.

Jean-Bernard's barbecue of lamb and rice au sechoir a cheveux went down rather well with the forty or so that showed up. The band played their mountain music and even attempted a rendition of "God Save the Queen". The Brits stood to attention and sang loudly. The line "long to reign over us" was the most appropriate as the rain lashed on to the market hall roof and dripped and whipped its way into the open sides to try and dampen the spirits of the small crowd. Momo banged a drum and Michel sang along without understanding a word. A wooden collection box was passed around and Michel looked pleased with the 170 francs, two damp cigarettes and piece of string.

Monsieur the Mayor, Marc Chicoulaa, said a few words then shook me by the hand while the local news hound snapped away. The mayor looked sun-tanned, handsome and important and when I explained to Alyson and Deirdre, visiting English friends, that he was also the local doctor, they both thought about not feeling very well. There were hugs, kisses on the cheeks, slaps on the back, take cares and bon courages and then I climbed into Peter and turned his old key. The scooter engine fired and rattled into life and as I slid the tin gear lever forward and took my left foot off the clutch, we lurched into the wet road and took that first three-wheeled step on our new journey together.

Picasso's picture postcard sits sellotaped to Peter's dashboard. His quote stares up at me. "Si l'on sait exactement ce que l'on va faire, a quoi bon le faire?" "If you know exactly what you're going to do, what's the point of doing it?"

France

Sarlabous

First gear is so slow but it's the only way Peter will be able to get up the hill.

The Baronnies were a bunch of foothills that spread away from the east of Bagneres-de-Bigorre like a lumpy green eiderdown. Villages had names like men's sins or conditions. Lies and Prat just two of them. It felt good to have broken out from the valley that I knew so well and to be on the move at a snail's pace. My enthusiasm was running as high as the distant peaks to the south, the high Pyrenees where I had lived and played for the last year. The excitement of the Tour had kicked in. I was off. On the road with not really a care in the world. My life travelling with me. Where I went, what I saw, where I stopped were all as unpredictable as the mountain weather. Cabin fever had flown out of the window. I was doing something. Going somewhere. Slowly.

Peter and I meandered our way up and down, through wooded valleys and reached our first overnight stop at Sarlabous. On the edge of the babbling L'Arros, the purpose-built gite and camping complex had everything other than food. I had packed quite a lot into Peter but none of it edible. I went to bed hungry after my first day on the road. So much for the Plat du Jour Tour I thought. I wouldn't starve.

The news tonight is about the Concorde crash in Paris. Travelling is a risky business.

St Bertrand - De - Comminges

Handprints on a cave wall, some mutilated, like a sophisticated security system waiting for the exact palm match to allow access to whatever.

The target for the day was to reach the old settlement of St Bertrand-de-Comminges, going via the Grotte de Gargas where cave men and women had left their marks. Now, while I certainly could see the hand prints, albeit that some were short of a finger or two, the rock etchings of mammoths, bison, horses and the like were more difficult to discern. Our guide drew them out for us with his pointer. Cave art or more than that. Early expressionism or communication for other cave dwellers. The modern graffiti was easier to read but of less interest to the archaeologists. They perhaps wouldn't have wanted to know that Jean loved Florence back in 1957 or that Claude had been there on August 23rd 1968. The cave wasn't busy and our tiny tour was a family of four and me. Warm outside, once under the ground in the hillside, the temperature dropped dramatically and a cold dampness cut through to chill. Headroom too was at a premium and we three grown ups had to watch we didn't leave our own marks on the cave ceiling. The two little girls were obviously not impressed with what they were supposed to see and one of them added to the future mysteries of the underground workings by dropping the dummy out of her mouth into an unexplored chasm. That would fox the anthropologists from Toulouse in a millennium or so.

The run from the Grottes to St Bertrand-de-Commiges was quick with Peter, like me, seemingly keen for a plat du jour. The cathedral came into view before the little town around it and I knew that the Romans had been there before me. Sensibly the authorities made most cars park outside the old town and it was either a walk up to it or a seat on the Disney-like road train. My plat du jour was taken at La Vielle Auberge in the lower town where Monsieur and Madame Prey produced a crispy confit de canard with veg and salad.

At the next table, outside in the shaded sunshine, was Paul Esswood with four of his pupils. I had heard the Englishman talking to them, telling them about his life back home and after the meal when the little cups of coffee appeared I went over and introduced myself. Paul was over from Worthing in Sussex and rehearsing singing talent for the festival there. He was big into Baroque and handled his Handel with the touch of someone who knew his craft. Not an easy thing trying to coach French singers when you are English and some of them chose to sing German arias. I spent a very pleasant afternoon listening and watching them work up their different pieces in an old church just behind the Vielle Auberge. The singer's youthful enthusiasm was much to be admired. The twelve disciples under tuition had come from Japan, Switzerland, Italy, Tours, Grenoble, Paris and other parts of France to perform for one night in the music festival. Each of them had paid for the chance to be there for a week and the long hours of rehearsals were a prelude to a few minutes of hitting the right notes with the right feeling and the right "shapes". Paul was keen to see them succeed.

As a lad it was expected that I would become a choirboy. My early voice was angelic enough and every Christmas at Castle farm I would be goaded into singing the Lord's My Shepherd for my Grandmother. She loved it as only a Grandmother could. When it came to a voice test years later at school and a chance to join the Cathedral choir, I croaked at the man who played the piano. I blew my chance and disappointed my family who had thought that my vocal chords would perhaps get me the scholarship that my brainpower wouldn't. It wasn't to be. Father had to pay the school fees. Paul Esswood's voice was still pretty angelic. It could reach the sort of heights that most male singers couldn't attempt.

After lunch the vocal chords needed warming up so the group formed a semi circle around their teacher and did their scales en mass and one at a time. Before the afternoon was out, Paul had to decide which students would be performing in the cathedral. They all got to do a piece in St Jude down the road but only the best would brave the nave of the big one on top of the hill behind us. Paul's choice was empirical and he wouldn't be wrong. He had been doing that gig for three years and his c.v. was pretty impressive. They wouldn't argue with him. As a counter tenor he should have retired years ago, but he could still show his pupils how it should sound and he could still move the paying public. He was doing a recital in Krakow cathedral soon. He'd done most if not all the decent venues in London. He'd sung for the Pope and the late Princess of Wales and followed Tina Turner on stage. He'd made over 150 records, done films and TV, and conducted at the Chichester Festival. All that to his credit and he wasn't a 'luvvy', just a fifty something enjoying bringing Baroque music to that part of France.

Admiring the talent, I push off in Peter, singing as we drive. Maybe something of what I have been listening to has rubbed off on me.

Aspect

I haven't pitched a tent for years.

Peter and I headed off for Aspect, which was a fairly easy level run through the foothills. After the excesses of a night at L'Oppidum Hotel in St Bertrand-de-Comminges and the 469 franc bill, I needed to find a campsite. Monsieur and Madame Daffis raised tents at their farm in the summer months and plants for the rest of the year. With a surname like that it's a good job they didn't produce confit de canard – Daffis Ducks would have been a silly brand.

I hadn't put up a tent for many years and I hadn't practised with my new one, so quite soon a small crowd of two boys, their little sister and their furry dog gathered to watch. It was pathetic really. A fifty-year-old struggling with two bits of nylon and some strung together poles was keeping the audience enthralled. Even the dog was having a laugh. I got the thing up before dark and ate some bread and sardines inside. Quite an appropriate end to the day.

Tent pegs in France are known as sardines.

Audressein ⚒

Pigeon never tasted so good.

Its a lot easier taking a tent down than putting it up - even with the aching back I acquired as a result of a night on my "comfort mat". Who on earth gave it that name? Its inventor had obviously never slept in a proper bed and probably grew up on a park bench. "Comfort mat" - it was honestly like spending the night on a very narrow cattle grid. The benefits of the site were the facilities: hot showers and loos and the extremely noiseless neighbours. Presumably they were all so knackered after hiking up and down the mountains, that none of them could raise a whisper let alone speak.

About 10k from the campsite was Audressein. There was nothing remarkable about Audressein other than its church and its hotel. Both had their good bits and their bad. The outside of the church was much better than the inside. Underneath the arches and above the cobbles there were some murals that were obviously old and full of religion. The church itself stood on a junction of two rivers and had a prefab construction on its roof in which sat the bells and, as an afterthought, a clock.

The good bit about L'auberge d'Audressein was its cooking. For lunch and dinner the place was full and I had never enjoyed such a wonderful taste from such a common bird, the pigeon. The very best restaurants in France were the same as the very best in Britain. What gave France the edge with a better reputation for things culinary, was what happened in the run of the mill eateries. In Britain, standard 'pub grub' was pretty average. In France it wasn't. It was nearly always excellent. The bad thing about the hotel was its accommodation. I shared the bathroom with the family that ran the place;

had to move their drying washing from over the bath before using it. Brushed my teeth over a wash basin surrounded by the bits and pieces of strangers' ablutions. I had room 10 and decided to go for a decent walk rather than loiter for the afternoon between its dull walls. Madame told me exactly where to go and I did. For three hours, almost to a minute, I walked alone without meeting anybody else en route. I drove Peter to Ayet, donned the walking boots, straw hat and stick and did the round walk to Lac Bethmale.

Walking in the Pyrenees was always special. One minute I was in bright open meadows of lush grass and wild flowers, the concert of the crickets playing me along. The next I was in ferns up to my waist. Suddenly I plunged into the darker woods with the musty smell of rotting leaves and bark, and the rush and babble of the mountain stream. I criss-crossed past ancient tracks and long forgotten paths, old stone walls and granges, some with roofs of tin and slate, like mine, and some with no roof at all. I heard the noise of a working man, smelt his new turned hay. Caught the distant "tonk" of the cowbells. The constant sound that accompanied my own heartbeat was the noise of water as it pushed its way to the basement of that enormous mountain store. And when I had walked my round, I felt good, like I'd confessed and been forgiven.

Perhaps some of the food in these parts is too rich for the heart. Comforting for the soul maybe. Walking in these parts is most definitely good for both heart and soul.

Aulus-Les-Bains

I see an inscription on a war memorial that asks forgiveness for the crime committed at Aulus-Les-Bains. I think the French imprisoned their own here.

The route to Aulus-les-Bains had been up and down and up and down and Peter performed brilliantly in the sunshine. He climbed the 1395 metres to the Col de la Core, virtually freewheeled, or three wheeled it down to Seix, a bustling little town covered with trippers and surrounded by mountains. Another climb through the Vallee d'Uston and beyond and then down into the Old World charm of forgotten Aulus-les-Bains.

When the grandfather clock in the corner of the big dining room struck midnight, it made so much noise that I thought that there was a blacksmith inside belting the bell with his hammer. Apart from the twelve direct hits, none of the other guests seemed to worry that it was actually only ten past eight, even though the hands on the striking clock showed twenty to. The Hotel de France reminded me of my dear Auntie Rosemary's home. She was actually my father's cousin but I'd always called her auntie. The building was nothing like Auntie Rosemary's but rather the way the inside had been arrived at. I knew for a fact that Auntie Rosemary couldn't have had a hand in it because she wouldn't dream of visiting France. As she put it, "They eat horses and don't have proper lavatories". Never the less her influence at that particular hotel was uncanny. Minimalist it wasn't. There were things everywhere. On a big iron radiator that looked as though it had been cast in a shipyard, a surreal nativity scene was frozen. It was right next to my table. I loomed over the wooden shepherds and the wise men grouped in adoration around the crib.

I marvelled at the extras. Two plastic figures from the Magic Roundabout, a foreign legionnaire, a space man and three oversized penguins. It was probably not a bad thing to be reminded about baby Jesus all year round.

There was a collection of taxidermy perched on the walls. A wild boar's head hovered above two diners. It looked down on them fiercely; looked like a gate crasher at their table. A couple of scrawny birds of prey were stuffed on top of the heavy wooden sideboard. They too glared at the dinner guests while keeping a glass eye on the stuffed bear lurking in an alcove. Bears used to be big and alive in Aulus-Les-Bains. The pictures on the walls were a mixture of faded photographs, needlework, paint and print. The flowers man made. The cutlery, china and serving dishes wouldn't have looked out of place on the Titanic. Not a floorboard in the place fitted. The gaps between contained history's little bits of fluff and more solid evidence of the past. There were as many dogs of various breeds and agility in the dinning room, as there were paying guests. I loved the quirkiness around me.

The evening meal, a five courser of vegetable soup, a hot pastry stuffed with goats cheese, roast pork with peas and gravy, a green salad and ice cream was the fixed menu for 50 francs. It included a small carafe of red wine and gallons of mountain tap water. I walked it off afterwards and visited the church where there was a free concert given by a band from Bolivia.

I returned to the hotel with pan's pipes still whistling in my ears. The big clock made its own noise from the dinning room. As I creaked my way up the wide stairs it struck five times.

The Amiel's giant clock is wrong again but who's worrying?

Auzat ⇌

Trying to hammer a tent peg into solid rock just doesn't work.

I tried to have lunch with a doctor in Aulus-les-Bains because the place was called "La Station du Cholesterol". This title wasn't bestowed because Aulus-les-Bains was the capital of the clotted cream industry but rather because its water, when taken under treatment in the local Therms, was supposed to have a beneficial effect on reducing the cholesterol. Sadly the doctor couldn't have lunch with me, but he gave me some information on the place and the name of a professor in Toulouse who I should speak to. I would like to know more. If the water was so good for reducing cholesterol, why didn't they bottle the stuff and flog it? Why was the place only open from May to October? Perhaps cholesterol took a winter break. Cynicism drove out of the little town with me that day.

I pitched my tent at a campsite in a place that sounded like an appeal to the umpire, Auzat. It was only 30 francs for the night and I soon knew why. The lack of tents should have warned me. Caravans fine. Caravans didn't have to be fastened to the ground. Tents had to be, just in case the wind got up in the night. The ground in those parts had topsoil that was thinner than a slice of ham and rock underneath that bent tent pegs double. Because the area was so rich in ore-yielding rock, there was an industrial plant just across the river mining the natural resource and turning it into aluminium. There were two fishermen standing on the bank, casting into the river. The fish they were hoping to catch would already be tinned.

My neighbours had created a tented village between several caravans drawn up in a rough circle. It looked as though they were expecting trouble.

The noise was extraordinary. Zinc mine come factory on one side and a very large family and their friends in the tented encampment on the other. Every so often there was a public address announcement.

It makes me want to scream "Hi de hi" or something much worse at the top of my voice, but with the general din no one will hear me.

Cazalas ⇌

"Turn left at the yellow sign for donkey milk." Patrick gives me directions.

In the early 70's the community of Cazalas set in the foothills of the Pyrenees between St Girons and Foix, became an enclave for hippies. I could see why. The region was so laid back that if it didn't have the mountain range to lean against, it would fall over. At about the same time that Le Cazalas was being hippyfied, Patrick and Veronique Moore were being born and raised in Toulouse, 70 miles north. They were the owners of one of the homes in the settlement having moved from a rented flat in Foix three years earlier so that their daughter Lucy, twenty months old, could have space to grow up in.

Patrick and Veronique were both teachers, which gave them lots of quality holiday time with Lucy and Dog, their dog. Patrick was improving the three-storey house a bit at a time but it was good enough for them to move straight into before Lucy's arrival. House prices there were "sensible" and the forty thousand pounder would have been at least five times that in Britain. The region was still a backwater of France and a good place to get lost in, which was what I did. Monsieur Michelin had managed to leave out the road to La Cazalas on my copy of his map, so the mobile phone and local landmark of the bright yellow sign offering donkey milk for sale put me back on course.

Veronique's plat du jour was organically reared chicken with tomatoes, onions, garlic and rice. She bought all organic food and wouldn't give Lucy any red meat at all, organic or otherwise. I thought that in those parts all the local food would have been organic but it seemed that it had to be searched out. We had intended to eat outside in the garden, but the first big August thunderstorm put paid to those plans.

It rains cats and dogs. Not donkeys though.

Foix ⇌

I've got money in my account but the bank in this town likes to say, "Non".

I left Patrick, Veronique, Lucy and Dog shrouded in misty drizzle and set off for Foix on the back road. After about an hour and a half of climbing the sort of road that wasn't used very often, because there was a healthy crop of grass growing down the middle of it, we suddenly came across a large truck loading tree trunks in the thick fog. There was no way to get past the beast, so we turned around and went back.

It was wet in Foix but I didn't think it was the damp that caused the hole in the wall cash machine to say "NON" to my request for funds. There were phone calls to try and find out why and how "NON" could be turned into "OUI". The upshot was that if I returned to the bank in the morning, I could have my money. Tent time beckoned again and after paying for my pitch, I had 72 centimes left.

I wonder what sort of night out I can have in Foix for 72 centimes?

Hill's ⇌

Those that can, do.

After a thunderous night in my tent, which served to prove that at least the thing was water resistant, if not sound proof, I emerged to a very wet, misty day in and around Foix.

Peter and Mary Hill lived a few k's south west up in the hills at about one thousand metres. They were both Brits who used to teach in Devon. Peter had a long relationship with mountains and very nearly met his maker falling 1000 feet down one in Scotland. Their eight year old daughter, Harriet, and younger son, Shorty, were friendly outgoing children who would talk to people because they wanted to and not just because it was polite. They had their place there for over ten years but actually pulled the pin on life in Britain three years previously. The decision to move to France full time was an easy one for Peter to make. He had become frustrated and fed up with his lot as a teacher and at fifty decided to take his pension of £5000 a year and go.

Mary was less convinced and spent the first year of her new life quite homesick. While Peter missed the pub, Mary missed her old girlfriends but both seemed very happy with their new lives. Peter even believed that the change would prolong his life. It still had its stresses but building, DIYing and logging were preferable to marking, DOEing and slogging.

The Hills' main income came from holiday letting. Like all good builders, Peter's estimate for doing up the barn as a gite next to their house was totally wrong, so having advertised, they had to move out of their house and into the half-done barn, allowing the paying holiday makers the use of their home.

The children went to the local school and had made friends there. Harriet was fluent in French but at home they all talked in the mother tongue. Mary and Peter were critical of the French State education system saying that it didn't do enough. It seemed that it taught almost parrot fashion and worked to a set curriculum and performance judged by frequent exams. The Hills were deciding whether Harriet should go to a Steiner School that they had found about an hour away.

They were good hosts and the plat du jour included vegetable soup, followed by lots of salads, home grown runner beans, a rarity in those parts, some cold meats with pate and cheese.

It's a pity that the weather is so bad and the views hidden. I hear their views though.

Botas

German Mike has fallen out with the local chasse. Not a good idea when they've got all the guns.

We made it to Toulouse, the home of aerospace technology, Lautrec, quite a good rugby team and the sausage. It was the biggest city that Peter had entered and it thundered and lightened by way of fanfare for us. The petrol light came out in sympathy, flashing lots as we hit the centre of town. Its behaviour was exactly opposite to that of children on a long car journey. They inevitably wanted to stop just after the start. Peter's flashing fuel light demanded that I stopped just before I was about to finish. I was not sure which was the most infuriating.

Peter and I left the home of the Wintzers (pronounced Windsors) at 5pm and arrived in Toulouse two hours later. The undulating countryside between the foothills of the Pyrenees and Toulouse was where farming started to become more serious with crops growing in sizeable fields with sizeable tractors and, presumably, sizeable subsidies.

Mike and Anja Wintzer had 45 hectares but they were not farmers. He was a retired engineer who used to do things for the European Space Agency. He didn't look as though he should be retired but assured me he was 63. Mike was German and Anja Russian. While he was driving through Holland, where he lived, he tuned into an offer on the radio to make contact with girls in Russia. He wrote off but heard nothing for six months. Then Anja's letter arrived. After a period of courtship by post, he took the plane to Moscow where his future wife was standing with a white carnation waiting for her man. They married in Moscow having paid the officials and the Mafia for the privilege.

They lived in their home at Botas, which could either mean dancing, gumboots or hay bales. Mike bought Botas 25 years ago but it had been their permanent home for the past three. Mike had two older children and two small ones with Anja, Raymond, 5 and Luba, 3.

Life in France was not idyllic for the Wintzers. They would both rather be somewhere else. Mike in Florida and Anja back in Russia. It was difficult. The language alone was a mixture of German, Russian, French and English, so they would never be quite sure which country they were in. Never quite sure which language to argue in.

Luba means love in Russian. The chasse won't care what it means.

Zebda

He has taken the words of the President's speech and set them to music.

There was a poll taken recently to establish who in Toulouse knew who. The number three most talked about person in the city was the lead singer of a band based there called Zebda. Zebda had been the most popular band in France and their hit "Tombier la Chemise" was number one for months. The lead singer and writer of their songs was 39 year old Magyd Cherfi. He'd rather not be known for the catchy hit but more for his lyrics that pleaded the case for ethnic minorities and the French left. Magyd deemed even Monsieur Jospin as being the man who had taken ever such a slight bend in the road verging imperceptibly towards the centre. What Magyd wanted was a political earthquake. He was a millionaire pop star who, rather than spending his income on Ferraris and furs and face lifts, was spending it on La Tactik Collective. He was putting his money where his mouth was.

Magyd's parents came to France from North Africa 40 years previously. They were not allowed to vote in France, which upset Magyd and his collective. He felt deprived on behalf of those that were, and some of the words to his songs reflected his attitude to the system. Magyd had a vote, but stronger than that he had a following. His roots, like his voice, grew deep but for the moment, his message was for the French ear and conscience only. I spoke and recorded him for over an hour at the Collective office.

I don't understand everything he is saying, but it's all down on my tape and somebody else's conscience.

Toulouse ⇌

I sit on Jean Paul Belmondo and watch the street life pass by.

The mobile didn't stop. Sylvie's press release must have landed on a few desks and stirred up some interest. People seemed keen to meet the Tour and offers were stacking up just like a queue of Airbuses. The conversations had been with a girl called Florence in Paris, or Paris in Florence. She was only really interested in the famous people I'd be meeting. Another was a T.V. man in Normandy and another; a Federation member in Bordeaux wanted a rendezvous. When would I get to Bordeaux? It was a question I couldn't possibly answer. There was someone from Champagne too. My French couldn't really cope with quick fire telephone conversations but I hoped that between us I'd got their numbers right so that I could get back to them.

A girl from La Depeche was interviewing me in the Cafe Florida, opposite the pink Capitole building. She spoke slowly to me; I spoke slowly back so that we started to understand each other. My mobile rang with another garbled French request. I handed my interviewer the phone and let one journalist talk to another for a while. She didn't speak slowly on the phone but rushed ahead in a language that sounded beautiful. How I wished that I too could produce such sounds and understand their meaning. I had given myself a serious handicap. I'd justified my lack of fluency by saying that language only got in the way. By not being able to understand, I'd have to form my own opinions. A fair degree of selfish conceit.

Then came the photo call for the newspaper and Peter was let out of the Capitole car park. His slot there had cost as much as my bed at the Grand Balcon. I put my leather flying helmet on for the cameraman and stood next to Peter. It seemed appropriate. I had been staying in the same hotel as St-Exupery once had. He was a flying pioneer in the 1920's and delivered letters out of Toulouse, off down to Africa. Flying French letters. The father of air mail. I too felt like a pioneer, carrying news of a different kind.

The evening sunshine made the Capitole building look like a giant pink wedding cake. I wandered the streets looking at familiar shops like Tie Rack and M & S. I spent time sitting between Catherine Deneuve and Paul Newman with Dustin Hoffman and Juliette Binoche just opposite me. Le Cardinal in Place Wilson was where I supped a large cool beer for 30 francs whilst sitting on Jean Paul Belmondo. All the chairs there were named after film celebrities, so it was as close as I was ever going to come to Stanley Kubrick. Le Cardinal and the cafes in La Place Capitole were tourist traps.

Down by the Baronne, Le Cafe des Artists and the little restaurants near by (in English, the Spoilt Children and the Silly Cat) were a pleasure to be caught in. The great thing about Toulouse, or the central bits of it, was that I could walk them all with ease. It was best to walk. I made the mistake of taking Peter to the Cafe des Artists one evening for a photo opportunity. The photo opportunity developed into a drinking opportunity and so I left Peter parked on the street outside for the night. One of the major pastimes was graffiti and the three-wheeler became an overnight victim or canvas. I didn't understand some of the words. All of the drawings were self-explanatory. All explicit and not in keeping with my sponsor's aspirations. Water and a good scrub worked like magic and, whilst some smudge marks remained, the message, whatever it was, disappeared.

One day I had lunch with an ex magician. The tricks he performed were far more believable than they used to be. Laurie Mort had swapped the magic circle for God and it couldn't get more mystical than that. The Rev Laurie Mort was the gentle Anglican who looked after the needs of his flock from Pau in the west to Cahors in the North, to Montpellier in the east and down south to the Spanish border. His "parish" boundary was the size of several small countries and his faith continental in proportion. He bought me a healthy salad, plat du jour at the Green Magpie, a subsidised canteen in the community of Cornebarrieu. We talked mainly about his boss (not the Bishop in London) and the way he moved in mysterious ways his wonders to perform. The Rev Mort loved his competition, the RC's, and couldn't work without them. I supposed it was like banking with Barclays and using the

Nat West hole in the wall to get your money out. After lunch he said a little prayer of blessing for the Tour. I was more touched by that simple act than if he'd pulled a rabbit from out of his cassock.

Purpan was a hospital like Russia was a country. It was big, had an underground secret, was state run and probably had more workers (9000) than patients. Casim had worked there for 26 years. There was nothing medical about Casim. He was there in support. He was a hospital porter and the two of us met up for a lunch together in a hotel opposite. He found me some surgical spirit that took the remaining blemishes off Peter.

The liquid removes the final traces of Toulouse altogether.

The Lot

*France isn't all old cobbled streets, jolly bereted peasants and dappled sunshine.
It does neon Motels and takeaway pizza too.*

On the16th I set the controls for the North. By six that evening we had
reached Montauban and had left the Haute Garonne for the Tarn et Garonne.
There was nothing memorable about Montauban and after several circuits of
the town I settled on a Formule 1 Hotel. For one hundred and fifteen francs it
gave me a room with a double bed and a single one suspended over it. I wasn't
sure if this arrangement had been designed for couples who didn't get on, or
for the family of three who did. My room smelt of dull cigarette smoke that
by morning, had become a part of me. The big mirror that stretched around
the corner over the wash basin confused me. It made me look as though I was
going when I was coming and coming when I was going. My body told me
I was moving one way but the mirror threw me. Beware, I thought; beware
of rooms with wash basins only. Previous occupants would all most certainly
have relieved themselves into the sink rather than face a walk down the
passage in the middle of the night. I had, so I bet they had as well.

The plat du jour that day was a take away pizza over the corner table of
room 226 in the Formule1. It masked the smell of stale smoke. I didn't like
pizza. I didn't like taking it away.

The 17th was Saint Hyacinth's day, which seemed rather apt as we
ventured into a landscape riddled with fruit and flowers. The corn really
was as high as an elephant's eye and the odd vine was thrown in for good
measure. At Moissac, I marvelled at a millennium of man's Masonic mastery
and at his myopic malevolence. In 1100, the Romanesque cloister was created

along side the Abbey. It and its refectory managed to survive a siege in 1212, English ownership during the Hundred Years War, a major revolution and several attempts at serious suppression only to fall foul of the1856 train from Bordeaux to Sete. Those forward-looking planners took out the refectory but were, thank goodness, prevented from turning the church portal into the entrance to platform four.

I enjoyed my plat du jour at Le Florentin right in the face of one of the masterpieces of 12th century art. Salade de filets de canard, persillade, lardoons, poeles, tomatoes, asparagus and lettuce, all for 59 francs. Every time I looked up there was the sculptured scene of St John's Apocalypse. Just the thing to help the food go down. The afternoon saw Lauzerte and Montcuq, two delightful little towns in the Lot region.

The whole area is popular with the British. Perhaps too popular. I'm on my way through the rolling wooded hills to meet some of them.

Prayssac

The Plat du Jour Tour is in danger of turning into the Brit du Jour Tour.

Jen and Nigel Heggie had had a holiday home in the Lot for fourteen years. Nigel, ex-army long and straight as a tank gun barrel, spent four months every year there and Jen, voice just like Joanna Lumley, fitted in two or three. He didn't really want to buy the place but egged on by her, they did in preference to a hide away in Wales, Cumbria or Scotland.

"The area here reminded us a bit of the Kenya we had lived in," said Nigel on the terrace by the pool as he turned the tuna over the white-hot charcoal. There were no wildebeest or elephant roaming through the scrub like trees that stretched to the horizon on the hill opposite, but we did see goldcrests and heard a nightjar at dusk like a helicopter preparing for a sortie.

Nigel, who'd had a go at property developing, had developed that one over the years. Nearly top of the list was the aforementioned pool that appeared, from the house, to be missing out on one side. The water apparently cascaded over the edge and off down into the thirsty valley. It didn't really. It was a clever touch, but then Nigel was a clever bloke. Jen was bright; brighter even than one of her pool side lanterns. She was a consultant who helped businessmen communicate with each other. Her advice presumably didn't fall on stony ground unlike the firing Acanthus that catapulted its seedpods with a rifle crack into the pool and onto the terrace. The Acanthus, its leaves made famous by the Romans and perpetuated by William Morris, was exploding at the Heggies.

Nigel used to look after tanks in his army days and his latest construction, his garage and workshop, looked as though it would house four or five of them.

I enjoyed Heggie hospitality for two nights and it was great fun catching up with the Leeches, en route from Bath down to their place in Bagneres-de-Bigorre.

The Heggies's neighbour was a bank manager. He had the sign of the Black Horse engraved on his heart. Bob Davis came to France with Lloyds in 1957, so although he spoke English, he was actually more French. Bob did banking by the sea in Nice and Biarritz, which must have been a tough assignment. When the Black Horse threw him out of the saddle, Bob set up I.C.B, a business advising ex-pats what to do with their money. At 59 years old, he ran the business from an office with an ambience and view that an impressionist painter would have given his right ear for.

Bob and his wife Josianne, who was big into real horses of any colour, had a beautiful home in the Lot hills. It had mini chateau pretensions with its own tower. Bob was obviously a victim of his own medicine and the gravel drive outside his house was so thick that Peter's little wheels got bogged down. I couldn't remember the last time a bank manager had helped me out, pushing my car.

Not far away, the Friday market in Prayssac was bristling with Brits and although the Lot's population of about 150,000 souls had only 4,000 Anglo Saxons, the language at one trader's pitch was unmistakable.

"Timothy. Take your hands off that tart!" It's pomme of course.

Dreaming Cahors ⚓

Sleep is difficult camping on the banks of the Vezere in Montignac. I feel that I am floating off, being carried away by the swollen waters.

It was impossible to do anything other than just lie there. The tent was being subjected to the full force of another mighty French rainstorm. The noise was like a belligerent gang of kids outside throwing handfuls of gravel at my little igloo. The wet was trying to seep through to me. The ground sheet, attached to the sides, was actually floating like one of those plastic covers on a swimming pool. I hoped that I wouldn't be carried away in the night to eventually join the mighty Garonne.

I did drift off and was once again taking tea with Elizabeth Espitalie in Cahors. She had been there for fifty years. Married to a retired French garage owner. She reminded me of a jolly good aunt as she guided the silver teapot.

"Can I see your M.B.E?" I asked as though I wanted another slice of cake. She left the cluttered, faded room and returned with the medal that the Queen had given to her in 1984. She had queued up back in London. Stood along side Dick Francis.

Compton McKenzie was standing on the old bridge, looking up at the square tower. He helped put the place on the map. Its dark purple wine mixed with the swirling waters of the Lot below. It flowed in a rage under the 14th century Pont Valentine.

On the Cathedral steps, a bride in white waited for her man. She was nervous with her friends. Tourists came and went, climbed up the steps and went into the old sombre house of God that smelt of spent candles wax. The white bride, full of hope, didn't look as though she should be there. She was totally out of place. The bride became the red head or had been her all along.

I am awake. Half dream half not. This rain is ridiculous. I ring the red head. Tell her I'm missing her. She's missing me too.

Peters Out

Nearly every other car I spot on the roads has British plates. The Dordogne is awash with them.

Unfortunately Peter's numberplate (9212 QA 65) would not be spotted on any roads for a day or two. On route N21 between Sarliac s-l'lsie and Sorges (North East of Perigueux), Peter ground to a halt at eleven a.m. There wasn't a nasty clunk or expensive bang. It was just a decreasing lack of power, as though we'd run out of fuel. We hadn't. I wished that I'd been more attentive to farm machinery lectures at Cirencester all those years ago. I was mechanically challenged, couldn't identify the problem. I accepted that things worked when they did, but didn't understand why they went wrong when they did and it wasn't obvious. Peter gave up the ghost not many yards from a roadside SOS phone point. It wasn't a phone in the traditional sense but rather a metal obelisk with a grille into which I spoke and out of which I was spoken to. With my restricted roadside French, it was a credit to all concerned that Peter was winched up onto a recovery lorry and the two of us run down to Perigueux before anyone could say "Nervous breakdown".

We had been going along very nicely through the region of France that was not dissimilar to parts of Sussex other than the buildings and, at last, the sunshine. I could understand why the English had taken to the place. It was abroad but not too abroad. Peter had done over one thousand trouble free kilometres since leaving Sainte Marie- de-Campan. He was allowed a hick-up provided of course it was just that and no more. One of the set backs with a breakdown on a Sunday meant no action, in the fixing sense of the word, until Tuesday. The French liked Mondays. Many of them didn't go to work on Mondays. The rescue truck dropped me at the Ibis Hotel in Perigueux after tucking the lame Peter up for a night or two in a secure yard.

I walked to the Eglise Saint-Etienne where Henry Aristizabal was at his organ that evening. I walked to the place early expecting a bit of a crush because it was advertised and free, but there were enough seats to accommodate a freebee from Johnny Haliday himself. The concert didn't raise the hairs of the back of the neck like Dr Arthur Wills and his beast at Ely cathedral used to do when I was a schoolboy. I looked up at the roof and noticed some pretty major cracks in the otherwise uninspiring ceiling. Maybe that was why the maestro didn't dwell on the loud bits for too long. We all clapped but not too loudly on account of the performance or the cracks, but he looked pleased from his lofty perch up by the pipes.

At least his organ is working whereas Peter, sadly, has run out of puff.

Perplexed In Perigueux ⟤

There isn't a street, crook or nanny that I don't know in this ville.

The pineapple-capped Cathedral was right next door to the Ibis. When I opened my double-glazing, I could just catch the organ practice over the noise of the dustmen accompanied by the high-pitched throttle cries extracted by gangly youths astride their two-wheeled screamers. Perigueux might be the capital of beautiful Dordogne but after two and a half days of enforced habitation, the place was wearing a bit thin. Familiarity, they said, bred contempt and even with my generous broad brush, I could see just why some had been less than respectful about certain aspects of the town. One guidebook suggested that the Cathedral roof had sprouted nipples. I thought they looked more like birdcages that light up at night.

It was difficult not to take some solace from comfort food but I was a good boy and stuck to salads, which were both good for the heart and the pocket most of the time. Some of them could be covered in foie gras, goose gizzards, bits of bacon, ham, duck and if money was no object, truffles.

Without Peter I felt a fraud. I still ventured into the offices of Sud Ouest, the regional newspaper, but they too didn't want to see me on my own. I didn't want to be on my own. Peter's full recovery became further removed on Tuesday morning. Monsieur recovery man rang to tell me that help was at hand. Not in Perigueux though. I had to go to Sarlat. I had been through there the Saturday before. I felt as though I was playing Snakes and Ladders.

It seems that mechanics in Perigueux are even more difficult to find than truffles.

Piston Broke

The most pressing thing that prehistoric man worries about is where his next meal is coming from.

There were two early morning calls. The one I had programmed on the hotel phone went off at 5.45 a.m. The one the man who was going to meet me that morning had arranged with the hotel because he knew I was foreign and therefore not working to his timetable went off just after. Jack was on time at 6.30 as Monsieur recovery man had promised and Jack dealt with Piaggio scooters in Sarlat. That was where we were heading. We loaded Peter onto a trailer behind Jack's van and got to Sarlat at eight after a pleasant drive through the morning misty countryside. We passed a prehistoric site where our Stone Age forebears use to live up in the caves that honey combed the rocky cliffs. Mechanical malfunction wouldn't have worried them one bit.

Jack was the owner of two businesses and he commuted daily between Perigueux, where he lived, and Sarlat. He dealt in chainsaws, strimmers, mowers and scooters, selling them as new and looking after them when they didn't work. He had three men who worked for him in Sarlat and could have, certainly on the servicing and repair side, done with three more. One of them got to grips with Peter as soon as we arrived while he was still on the trailer.

There was an international language for motor mechanics used to convey to the waiting client that things were not as good as they might be. Peter's mechanic was fluent in it. It started with a tut. Then there was a sigh, an "Ou la la " something, a nod of the head with another tut and a pained expression with gritted teeth and wide eyes. A black greasy pointing finger emphasised the words, " Kaput, casse, is broke". Finally there was a swear word. That was thrown in to express my feelings rather than his.

Basically, Peter's spark plug had become too hot, had had enough and had decided to pull the pin. In doing so it was going to take the piston and cylinder with it. Selfish those bits of engine. So it was going to be two nights in Sarlat waiting for the new bits to arrive and a repair bill of over four hundred pounds.

There is an international language for people who have just been confronted by big bills.

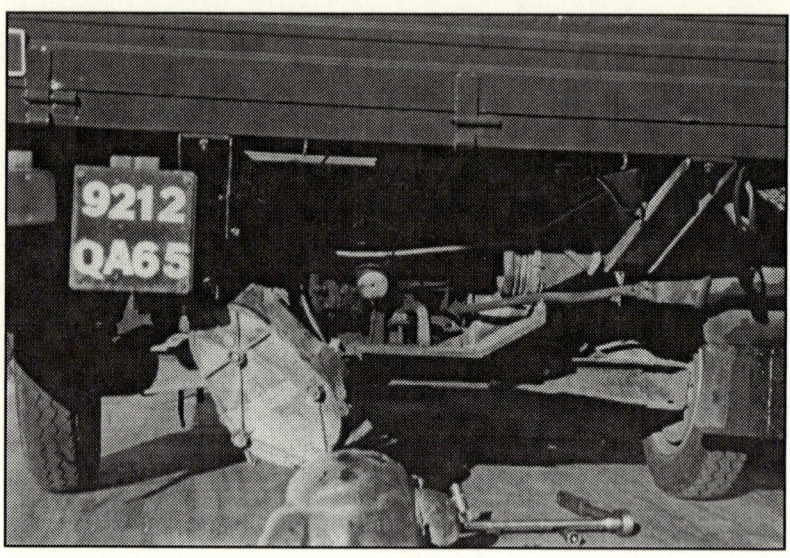

Sarlat

It's Thursday so it must be Sarlat.

Sarlat-la-Caneda was its proper name and it had a town within a town. The town within the town, the old bit, was what the tourists flocked to gawp at. At times, because of the throngs and those trying to flog to them, it was like visiting a medieval themed shopping precinct. I cut away from the very busy little streets that ran to the East of the main rue de la Republique. They scarred the old town like a clumsy surgeon's stitches. I saw the place much as it was intended in the fifteenth and sixteenth centuries. It was amazing how some of the steep roofs kept their heavy tiles and the stone work of many of the buildings, its soft honey colour.

The Cathedral was slightly less remarkable than the buildings and squares around it but nonetheless I marked my request for a prayer, for Peter and I as we journey around France, in the book used for such things. The biro provided started to run out of ink before I had finished which wasn't an encouraging sign.

For ten francs I visited an exhibition to celebrate the life and work of Jean Cocteau who could, with a very few strokes of his pencil, create anything from jewellery to film sets. His talents made the humble street artist outside, scribbling portraits of tourists' kids, look like a kindergarten impressionist.

I took a plat du jour at Le Gargantua for 75 francs in a corner of the Cour des Fontaines. They had a front but I chose their backside because there were more empty tables. At some venues the management should provide a bag full of colouring books, a large box of conjuring tricks or a loaded shot gun dependant on the volume of noise from the children on the next table.

One's own children making a din - fine. Other peoples - unacceptable. Peter's condition was turning me into a grumpy old man. His piston bust, mine liable to snap at the slightest aggravation. The Armagnac mellowed me.

The narrow streets of old Sarlat provided an excellent catwalk on which may be displayed the latest fashions of the tourist. I noted what was generally to be seen on a hot afternoon as I sipped a coffee and Armagnac or two. I became the compere in that none too sophisticated fashion show.

'Good afternoon Ladies and Gentlemen, mes Dames, Monsieur. Welcome to Salat 2000 street fashion. Tourist fashion at its most colourful. We'd like to start at the bottom. Feet, Ladies and Gentlemen. Feet. Those vital appendages at the bottom of the legs. Those plates of meat on which we march or skip or plod. How does the well-turned heel look today? (Pause for a drink).

Here comes Mr Older with his Roman style sandals and ankle length white socks. Perhaps not the most practical colour for the dusty thoroughfares, but nine the less quite charming. And for Younger Male esquire what could be bitter than the sporty trainer? Its designer label clearly visible and not a starting block in sight. You'll notice Ladies and Gentlemen, mes Dames, Monsewers, that these expensive statements can be worn with or without accompanying sox. Next we can see the sensible footwear of Mrs Older. There's a hint of design but flat common-sense has won the day here. Miss Younger has picked designer sandals with sick platform soles to give her a few more inches of height. Vital for spotting those street side bargains. Her friends are in trainers and flip-flops; those bright flips of rubber that are held on to the foot by a fred forced between the big soe and its neighbour. (Pause for a drink).

Moving ups wiv like to draw your tension toss the middle grind. What's covering the fashionable tourist's bottom? Here's Mr Older again. Hez in shhort shhorts or lang longs. Myster Younger on zee ither hund is in long shorts or short longs. Please dint get confused Ladies and Gentlemen. Mes Dames Monsieurs. You'll natice that some of the young menz wear jeanz or those highly colourful tracksuit bittoms with patterns of an Afro-Caribbean inflatuence. Masses Older saunters past us in her baggy shorts. Her sister is in the biggy dress. Miz Younger over there is in sshhort sshhorts. Her friends are in sshhort dressess, sshhort sskirts and jeanz, often torn to sheads. (Pause for another drink)

New Lodies und Gintlemen, mes Dames, Monsters, we come to the stop. Mr Older has a shirt sleeved short on and his fiend with him, a T-shirt with or without a logo. Mr Younger always has his T-shirt with a logon. Misses Older loves her blouse or T-shirt without a logon or the tip half of that boggy dress you zaw. Miss Younger has the tit half of her tight dress or T-shirt with or without logon or shit T-shirt that reveals hertummy. You'll note that if they're sleeveless, it's very important to show off the steps that provided the underwear zupport, if indeed there is any. With or without logons. (Pause for another drink)

Fennelly, Laddies and Gontlemen, messy Dames, Monsters. Heatgear. Itz invariably sim sort of straw hot or baseball cup or a fleppy canvas affair or nithing at all. This tourist fushion show has provided canfirmation that marketing wirrs. It has been made pissible by several spunsors and we'd really like to spank all those that have ticken fart. It's well done to Nike, Lacoste, Adidas, Polo and Mr Kelvin Clean. A pat on ve beck too for Yachting Style, Street Crazy, Numbers 1 to 15, I'm a fit one and Police. Liddies and Guntleman. mes Domes et Monsewers. I thunked the list one was genuine rather than a fushion stotemont becuss he was corrying a gun. That's folks all.'

Armagnac and warm afternoon sunshine were a potent mix. The fashion show became a happy blur, like a procession of scrambled eggs really. The cat walkers would have seen a fifty-year old English man slumped in his chair with an absurd grin on his flushed face.

I wonder what Saint Bernard would think of it all. In 1147 he visited here to perform some miracles. Perhaps it's time he called again if only to pick up a T-shirt, with or without a logo and join me for a glass or two.

Back To The Grange ⇌

"What do you mean next Tuesday?"

It was Friday morning and I booked out of the Hotel Saint-Albert having spoken on the phone to one of Jack's men who told me the good news that Peter's new parts had arrived. The plan was that I would amuse myself until they rang me on the mobile later that afternoon to arrange for the joyous reunion between Peter and I and the resumption of the Plat du Jour Tour.

I telephoned the Rooks in whose direction I was headed on breakdown Sunday. I arranged a rendezvous for the evening and they confirmed that they would be pleased to see me. For a couple with whom I'd only ever had a telephone relationship, I felt that over the last week we'd got to know each other rather well. Sadly and with much "Je suis desole," I wouldn't get to taste the Rook pie.

At 7pm on the Friday evening I got a call. At 7pm, not 3, 4 or even 5, when there was still some time to plan the rest of the day, but at 7 the phone went. I was informed that Peter wouldn't be ready until the following Tuesday at the earliest. 'Litalap syndrome' had reached Sarlat. I bellowed like a bull but that only seemed to encourage the gladiatorial crowd. There was nothing they could do about it. So what did I do? I booked back into the hotel and arranged to take a train from Sarlat to Bordeaux, Bordeaux to Tarbes the next morning. A bus would take me to Bagneres-de-Bigorre and then a taxi the last leg to find my cat-cat to enable me to climb the mountain to my home. I needed a familiar place to lick my wounds for a few days.

In the hotel bedroom I watch the remake of Dial M for Murder on the TV. It's badly dubbed. Gwyneth Paltrow kills an intruder with a sharp instrument normally used to tell if the joint is cooked. Afterwards they show three bullfights and three bulls are killed with sharp instruments. That isn't dubbed at all.

Reflections In My Bed ⚞

I'm just skimming the surface. Not really getting to the heart of things.

Mr Heal's bed that Momo had carried up to the Grange was the best bed in the world. The Staples mattress with it was the most comfortable. I slept on it for hours, caught up from the nights on the thin comfort mat and the strange contours of some hotel mattresses and other people's beds. I lay there reviewing the trip so far, a month and a half of travel. That was all.

Travelling in the stupid blue machine, I was floating from town to town like a lost butterfly. Sure I was meeting some people, the sort of people I already knew. People who could speak some English. But I wasn't discovering anything. Not really. I was a tourist moving amongst tourists. Not an adventurer. Not the pioneer I had tried to emulate with that daft posed picture in the Place du Capitole. Dressed up in a flying helmet. I wasn't flying anywhere. Who was I trying to kid?

I read my notebooks. The first entry faithfully recorded every day were the number of kilometres travelled. I was clocking up the distance. I reported what I had eaten, kept the receipts to prove it. I was gathering quite a collection of photographs. Friendly faces standing next to Peter. Friendly faces in a foreign land. But I wasn't discovering anything real about France, the French or myself. What had I expected? Perhaps there was nothing left to find. Maybe I was learning that. I was probably in too much of a hurry. The idea made me laugh. I should learn to slow down. Did it matter? Wasn't travelling enough?

I went down to the Butlers. Took Louise a big bundle of dirty washing. She would have it sorted and out on her clothesline, a string of flapping shirts and underpants dancing for the valley folk. They had a bundle of post for me. Bills. Birthday cards from last month. Some T-shirts from Rowena at Men's Health magazine and a letter from America.

Back in July, before the Tour had started, I happened to be in the village shop when an American guy came in. He asked Magali where he could find a garage. Magali didn't speak American. She saw me browsing her meat counter and so passed the gentleman my way. He had a flat tyre on his rented Mercedes. It had been flat for miles. He and his wife had been touring the mountains.

"Gee but they're wonderful," he said as though I didn't already know. I called Gerrard up at his garage and he came down in his big tow truck. Had the wheel off and changed in no time at all. The American and his wife and I sat in the bar next to the shop. We had small beers and the wife took a soda. I told them about my plans for driving around France. The couple liked the idea. They said they'd like to help, would like to support the heart cause. I could tell they meant it. They gave me their address back home in the States and told me to drop them a line. I did. In the envelope waiting for me at the Butler's was a money order for $2000. A stranger's faith in me was greater than my own. I couldn't let them down.

Autumn was coming to the mountains. The evenings had a chill and I sat on the hearth bench seat in the chimney of Butler's smoky fire. We drank cheap wine, the sort that turned my teeth blue and ate Louise's supper. She'd cooked a fish pie, some for us and some for the cats. Only the seasons changed in the valley.

Father's words come to me. "Maintenance of the objective." Like a wood louse crawling across a thick carpet, I'll stick with it, get going again.

Rouffillac

A pinch and a punch for the first of the month and no returns.

We used to do that at school along with spitting on the best biscuit before we were allowed to have it. Spit would usually ensure that no one else would want it. The house prefect, Yentob, would get into a right bait if he saw you spitting. He'd punish spitters. I'd blanco his cadet force webbing white instead of regulation army green. That pissed him off even more. Bandsmen wore white webbing. Yentob wasn't in the band though.

It was wonderful to open the diary and see a number one. A new beginning. The first of September. A pinch and a punch for the first of the month and no returns. I said it again out loud but emphasised the no returns. No returns to mechanic's workshops in Sarlat. No returns to roadside rescue phones, tow trucks and bigger bills than I'd find on a pelican.

I had to pay out 8054.69 French francs. Because I paid it with a French franc cheque, it felt like monopoly money, somehow not real. It was certainly very real. Peter's repairs cost over eight hundred pounds. It would have been even more had not Jack caught me crying while interpreting his two-page account. Twenty-four hours for labour alone, which Jack cut to twelve with the press of a button on his calculator to make me feel a little better. Peter had got new everything in the engine department.

The day was a long one. Up at six. Nearly missed the 8.33 train from Tarbes because of dustmen and roadwork's. Had lunch in Bordeaux at a café opposite the station. Arrived at Sarlat at 4.32 to be met by Fredrick, Jack's salesman. Had a road test with Peter and Eric, Jack's mechanic, because he couldn't believe how slow Peter actually went even with new bits. Finally after seventeen kilometres, found a campsite in Rouffillac right next to the Dordogne. The pitch for the tent cost four pounds fifty, which made Peter's repair bill the equivalent of 180 nights under canvass.

The Ibis hotel in Pereguex was missing one pillow and I had nicked it. It was a spare I found in a drawer but that didn't diminish the guilt one jot. I couldn't say that I was full of remorse, in fact I was looking forward to resting my head on its plumped up form in my tent rather than on a crumpled shirt or plastic ground sheet. If the Ibis hotel wanted it back then they could have it after the Tour or maybe they'd like to sponsor me a pillow. Happy campers right around France would see their logo. It was amazing just what could be seen through tent walls. I went off to the loo after dark leaving the tent light on and realised that my flimsy shelter was as see through as Tony Blair's politics.

I turn the torchlight off in my tent before undressing and trying to take the rough edges off my toenails with my penknife.

South To Najac

Empty barrels make the most noise. So they say.

We crossed the Dordogne and headed for Rocamadour, a place that seemed to have been created by covering a large cliff with super glue and throwing old houses, churches, castles and gift shops at it. Most appeared to have stuck and most seemed to have turned into sticky flytraps for tourists. The old "cite" even had its own tourist train with rubber tyres and flashing lights. I pushed on pretty quickly deciding not to go on my knees up the steps to the black Madonna.

Lunch, a salad with a hint of goose gizzard, was taken at Labastide-Murat in an hotel that could have been on the Hog's Back just outside Guildford. The term had been used before, but the Braying Brits were there. The place had twenty or so lunchers but that particular quartet were the epicentre of the dining room. Their language wasn't really English at all. It was called *huppercrusty* and was spoken at several decibels higher than any other tongue and from the front of the mouth somewhere just behind the teeth or dentures rather than purely from the vocal chords. *Huppercrusty* like French, Spanish, Italian or English had its own grammar, nouns, verbs and declensions. Some had tried to document it. Examples included cresh (the act of vehicles colliding). Cash (T-shirt and shorts). Hice (a building in which people lived or belonging to her). Hause (a four legged animal for riding or betting on or the first word uttered to an umpire at a cricket match when appealing for LBW). And so the list went. *Huppercrusty* was a language for show rather than useful personal communication. Hence the need for its volume. Participants therefore tended to use it when they were 'height and a bite'. When they were on their own, with no audience, they normally reverted back to the common grunt, pretty much like the rest of us. I caught one sentence of *huppercrusty* during my meal. It ran "Cause ustard haddock pipe" and it was only after some time that I realised what the gentleman was shouting. "Cahors used to have a Pope."

Not everyone shouted, thank goodness, and some when they spoke softly could actually deafen with their words. Peter's livery was such that he attracted attention. That was what it was for. A couple came up and said hello. Susan and Michael Powell were on holiday from Tamworth and very generously gave me twenty pounds towards fundraising. They told me about a place I ought to try and visit called Taize and a man called Brother Roger. It was there that they went or were sent as a result of seeing their eldest son die in a glider crash right in front of them.

I cannot begin to imagine their experience and the brief encounter with them leaves the hairs on the back of my neck tingling most of the way to Najac.

Nine Hour Drive ⟞

I sing to myself. Sing out loud which looks a bit silly for those overtaking.

Alphonse of Poitiers, who really put Najac on the map, sounded like a 1970's French hairdresser rather than the 13th century brother to the King of France and quite a big cheese. The place was much visited because of the Alphonse influenced castle that lay perfectly in the Aveyron valley.

I lay fairly perfectly in room 22 of L'Oustal del Barry hotel, the view from which surveyed the whole medieval scene. The hotel and its restaurant were rather up market. The chat at breakfast wasn't about chef's skills the previous evening, but why hadn't England brought on Owen sooner so, that instead of a one all draw, we could have taken the smugness off the French at the Parc de France. Defrocked them in their current ludicrous run as global champions.

The day was a real test for Peter and from Najac to the little community of Villelongue in the Aude; we drove for nine hours. There were several games I played en route to help while away the time. When we were children we used to play a game we called Tibbit to amuse us on those eternal car journeys. The first occupant of the car to spot either a telephone or post box would shout Tibbit. Only red ones counted. The game was only good fun when fellow travellers didn't know why the rest of us were shouting Tibbit at the top of our voices. The uninitiated were never told the rules and had to guess why our family had gone completely barking. Playing with just the family never lasted that long and the winner was the person who had said Tibbit first the most times before those immortal words "I'm not playing anymore." Another favourite was I Spy. Since I was on my own, neither game would be much fun.

I invented another. I called the new road game Frog Stacking. The rules were pretty straightforward. I had to see how many French vehicles I could get consecutively in a slow queue behind me. It was only French numberplates that counted. If a German or a Swede got into the long tail back, I couldn't count them, although I'd get a deal of pleasure in knowing that my slowness was annoying them every bit as much as the French. I scored when the queue started to overtake me. Each consecutive French numberplate was worth one point. My highest score was twenty-six just the other side of Albi.

When I eventually arrived at the Elliott's, I emerged from Peter in the sitting position having become stuck like that after the too long trek. It was stupid. I'd bitten off too big a bite. I didn't deserve to succeed mistreating Peter in that way. The warmth of their welcome soon had me straightened out though.

I knew the Elliotts before I had my heart attack.

Domaine De Camus Nau ⇒

"Sharlie it's so vunderful to seize you." Gunilla's generous smile and warm embrace makes me feel welcome before I'm even over the threshold.

The region of L'Aude I was visiting was attractive, being neither too hilly nor too flat. The landscape was interesting and resembled one of those chunky patchwork duvets in greens and browns, blues and yellows, which had been tossed over a sleeping body or two. The undulations were covered either in trees, vines, sunflowers or dry prickly grass on a sandy coloured soil. The trees, like the people, came in all shapes and sizes. Olive and quince, pine and acorn, fig and fruit, short and tall. It was a French jungle out there. Where the trees and scrubby grasses didn't grow, the faded sun flowers with their bowed heads or grape vines did. The vines stood in neat rows; their juicy bunches held almost in secret.

That week saw the start of the vendage and the Chardonnay was being picked around us. The Elliotts harvested theirs by hand in order to produce quality wine. The yield was slightly down on the previous year but the quality was up. The neighbour was using a harvester, a fairly brutal machine that sat astride the wired up vines and travelled along them shaking them senseless until they yielded up their fruit. The machine was noisy but then so was the gang of Portuguese pickers working at Camus Nau. There were eight of them. They were keen to work and would each earn about five pounds an hour for four weeks or so. Each should return home with over one thousand pounds, which really was a small fortune where they lived. Meryvn and Gunilla were not the usual patrons and gave their pickers the sort of living conditions that many holidaymakers would willingly pay for. Not all grape pickers were treated with such respect. Each picker was given three litres of wine a day as a part of the wage. The pickers would prepare their own evening meal and we'd hear the result of the wine ration as it took effect and helped their singing.

The Elliott's grapes were shipped off to the local cave co-op in Limoux, where they were turned into wine. The co-op would pay up but getting the money was a gradual process and one calculated to make cash flow predictions easier to assess with a crystal ball than an abacus. The final amount of money Mervyn was owed for his September 1999 harvest wouldn't boost his bank balance until March 2001. It made that old slogan – "It's all at the co-op" – somehow rather real.

Mervyn (because he was conceived in Wales) and Gunilla (in Sweden) became the new owners of the thirty-three hectare domain two years previously. They and their Labrador, Victoria (the only dog of its kind that I'd seen eating grapes off the vines) led the sort of life that many from Britain dreamt of but few achieved. They sold up in Bath and moved into the new life having the kind of adventures that Peter Mayle filled one or two books with. Mervyn was passionate about his wine and will grow and bottle his own one-day. The temptation to call it "Mer Vin" will, I'm sure, quickly pass. Meryvn was far too serious a vigneron for that. He enjoyed sharing the results of his labour, both red, white and sparkling, with his guests, which went down well with me, in moderation of course.

The move to France wasn't without its anxieties, its doubts, homesickness and what-on-earth-have-we-done questions. But to look at them, and I'd known them for over a dozen years, I thought they were ten years younger than when I last saw them just before they moved out. France certainly seemed good for their health and sanity.

Gunilla's skills as the original Swedish chef were legendary and paying guests to the gite could, if they were lucky, dip into her culinary hospitality after dipping into the pool.

Mervyn and Gunilla had only one regret. That was they hadn't moved ten years earlier.

"Valkies," says Gunilla. It's time to walk the grape-eating Labrador again.

An Archer ⇒⊢

Dum de dum de dum de dum. Dum de dum de da da.

One of the main reasons for high tailing it down to the Carcassonne area was to keep an appointment with Jennifer Archer. She was the one that was married to Brian Aldridge. Jennifer otherwise known as Angela Piper had a holiday home not far from Castelnaudary. It was quite uncanny talking to Angela and if I closed my eyes, I could have been having an Aga-side chat with Mrs Aldridge at Home Farm. We talked about Jennifer because Angela had been Jennifer for over thirty-seven years. After studying at the Royal Academy of music, she won a BBC prize and went into radio and worked in rep with two of the then Archer characters. The then Jennifer Archer or rather the person who played her, went off to do Emergency Ward 10 on TV and Angela (a Midland's girl) auditioned and got the part in 1963. Back in the sixties the programme was more about giving farmers and small holders agricultural information than it was about producing good radio drama. The acting profession looked down their noses and frowned at a part that was designed to tell the listener when to call in the AI man or the date to start drilling the forty-acre. Now with the soapsuds of Ambridge well and truly lathered up, actors would give their eyeteeth for a chance to get their own tankard at the Bull.

Angela had become Jennifer although she had done voice overs, did Points of View with Barry Took until the BBC post bag suggested that she had only taken the job because Brian Aldridge wasn't giving her enough housekeeping. She also worked with Derrick Nimo in a comedy series. Angela had produced two cookery books and Jennifer Aldridge's Archers cookbook sold over 40,000 copies, which for someone who wasn't the Naked Chef or Delia Smith, was pretty good going.

I asked her would she, given the time again, still have chosen the Jennifer Archer role for her life. Yes she would she said. And what was the most memorable episode? Probably thirty-four years ago when Jennifer had to tell the vicar about her pregnancy. Angela herself was pregnant with her first child.

Where Angela seemed to take over completely from Jennifer was when she talked about France and her love for the place. She and her husband Peter, also a BBC long termer, felt so much fitter and more refreshed in France. The air and sunshine, the lack of people and traffic noise, the food of course and perhaps the fact that Jennifer was safely back in Borsetshire.

It was great meeting the two of them, Angela and Jennifer, and Angela's friend Felica Heaton-Armstrong who very kindly came to my rescue. As Peter and I approached the village where we were to meet Angela, the engine worked fine but the power that it generated didn't want to get to the wheels. We seemed to be all talk and no torque. I set off walking because I knew my rendezvous wasn't far away and over the brow of the first hill I found Monsieur Rey behind his petrol pump. He also seemed to be a fixer and breaker of vehicles by the look of his yard and fairly soon we had Peter towed into the sanctuary of Monsieur Rey's shed for a going over.

Felicia came to fetch me and we left Peter until after the Jennifer Aldridge light lunch. Monsieur Rey was well versed in the French school of "Je suis desole" and the shaking of the hand in such a manner as to make it appear completely detached from the wrist.

Once again Peter's future is in the hands of a Gallic mechanic.

Barricades And Bemmy

It is beautiful walking along the dusty tracks that dissect the fields. There are vines in every direction and the warm autumn sun makes everything mellow.

It was ironic. If Peter was repaired, he wouldn't get very far because there was no petrol. The French, who hadn't forgotten how to revolt, had taken to the streets in order to stop the flow of fuel to persuade Monsieur Jospin to reduce the tax he made on the stuff.

The Lambs from Marshfield in Wiltshire were also guests at the Elliotts. We were digging in and being forced to enjoy our prolonged stay behind the barricades. It was very difficult putting up with the rigorous daily routine. It started with breakfast outside in the sunshine at about ten (tea or coffee, toast, fruit, cheese, jams) followed by a leisurely stroll and maybe a midmorning dip in the pool. The lengthy luncheon outside under a big sunshade normally took a hellish two or three hours and the afternoon's strenuous activities might include another gentle stroll or siesta, with perhaps another swim in the warm pool. Aperitifs were simply awful and always followed by supper (maybe barbecued tuna fish with lashings of salads, that sort of thing) normally taken outside and then, quite exhausted, one made ones way to ones comfortable bed. On top of all that arduous stress, one might be forced to play the odd game of boule in the gravelled courtyard or leaf through a novel or two. Frankly I hoped the unrest out there didn't last too long, as I wasn't sure how much more I could take.

One day I walked across the valley to meet the neighbour. I entered the World Peace Kingdom. Bemmy was its president or king. He looked like a nutter. He was a nice nutter, not scary in a Norman Bates sort of way but certainly several grapes short of a bunch. His name was Benny but he didn't ever use the letter N. He didn't believe in N's for some reason I couldn't fathom. Bemmy had lived in his World Peace Kimgdom for many years. His home looked more like a sixties theatre set and was a colourful house resplendent with rainbow painted outside walls, mystic eyes, the smell of dope and a full size Indian tepee. He celebrated sunrise most days from within the tent, squatting on its floor and chanting as the sun's first rays shone in through a special hole made in the hide. His ancestors came from Villelongue and so he was 'called' back to the area. Symbols and Catharism surrounded his life. He didn't trust the governments of Britain, Germany or France and felt that they were conspiring against him. He'd fallen foul of local law when he went down to the town hall and dismantled the statue standing outside. He was put in prison for a short spell but his family, who were apparently 'well connected', arrived in a sleek black limo and got him set free.

The land around his house was littered with stones of significance, altars, symbols and a pyramid through which he found inspiration. The view from his front door was inspiring enough for me. I didn't need any more proof of the guy's eccentricity but just in case I did, he put on a gold cat mask for the photograph I took of him. He said he didn't want to be recognised by the governments of Western Europe. They wouldn't recognise him at all.

The hum of the vemdage doesn't disturb the Peace for Bemmy.

Villelongue ⇒

What becomes of yesterday's revolutionaries?

Depending on where in the world they were revolting, some were shot, some became gurus, some leaders, some bank managers and the rest, ordinary people. The one I took afternoon tea with had become one of Sweden's top theatre costume designers. Gunilla Norlund looked like a cross between Zandra Rhodes and Ulrika Johnson. Back in the 1950's and not yet sixteen, Gunilla went to London as a Swedish au pair. Working in the austerity of that post war period, she thought that the U.K. was still in the dark ages. Her young Swedish style was not appreciated in old-fashioned Britain and she hated it, so she skipped over to Paris.

Having finished her education in Sweden, she revisited Paris in the 60's and "hung out" with the likes of Ginsberg, Keroac and Corso. She remembered the impact of the first airing of Bob Dylan's "The times they are a changing" and the way the anthem was received. She enjoyed her street life and was, in her own words, a beatnik who drifted from experience to experience. Whilst she perhaps didn't dive into the deep end and immerse herself totally in the free love, free drug culture of Paris in those days, she was certainly splashing about in the shallow end as one of its disciples. She admitted her part in the '68 Paris riots and her aim with a cobblestone against the French riot police was probably more accurate than the aim of the U.S.A.F. on their targets in Vietnam. She, like all the "soixante-huits" who had ended up scattered in the remoter parts of France, was fiercely opposed to the Vietnam War.

She earned her living as a freelance theatre costume designer, having slipped out of the fashion business. She spent about three months every year at her village house in Villelongue and the rest mainly in Stockholm. That part of France first came to her attention via a celebrated Swedish chef and she bought on a whim nine years previously.

Villelongue was perched up on a bump to its surrounding countryside with a solid square church tower as its centrepiece. Like hundreds of settlements up and down France there was nothing breathtakingly stunning about the place, but it did have a wealth of higgledy-piggledy charm. Narrow streets with old buildings all on different levels were suddenly and occasionally pockmarked by modern monstrosities and misconstructions. Mayors had presumably turned blind eyes when the planning applications had come up. 'Euro boxes' were sprouting here and there. Some, when choosing their exterior colour schemes, obviously went shopping in the paint shop called "Inappropriate."

The place and the countryside around were full of foreigners with Dutch and Belgians fairly thick on the ground. It was a Belgian band that entertained the few of us with the inclination or petrol enough to get there one evening. The indigenous French were thinner in numbers than new comers. The band nearly outnumbered the audience and performed on a specially built platform illuminated with a string of fairy lights. The eleven players put up a good show. Tom-toms and bongos, flute, guitars, accordion, fiddle and a mouth organ played around a girl with a saxophone that she didn't manage to blow all night. Her turn would come one day. For a band of its size it actually made very little noise, but it was the focal point for the evening's unsophisticated fun. That was what struck me about the evening in Villelongue under the shadow of the old church tower. The people enjoyed themselves, young and old, from the blacksmith mayor and his serious wife to the local winegrower. From the leather-clad bikers to the middle aged Dutch hippies. Everyone was happy. Some danced, most drank, a few even slept but it was the sort of Saturday night that the rural French took for granted. It wouldn't happen in Britain quite like that.

I am still unable to go very far without petrol

Carcassonne ⇌

I wonder. Is this where Robin made Marion?

Monsieur Rey had patched up Peter and petrol and two-stroke mixture was plentiful again. Monsieur Rey, who must have spent most of his life flat on his back under broken vehicles, had sorted out the problem with the gears. He made a new bit to replace the old thingamajig that dove tailed into the fluted collared sprocket drive half shaft gearing housing mechanism or what ever. Good old Mon Rey. What ever he had done, Peter went forwards and backwards at the switch of the lever and all for forty-five pounds. The engine over-revved violently between gear changes, but we had motion, which was necessary for a tour to be a tour.

We also had rain, the first for some weeks and although the vine's roots were too far down to appreciate it, the leaves would be sending wet messages below. The downpour was accompanied by a storm of thunder and lightening, a spectacular fanfare for the open road. Leaving the Elliott's, I felt as though I was being sent back to boarding school after a long summer holiday.

I drove through Limoux and stopped at the cave where the Elliotts' grapes (and loads of others) were being transported and turned into wine. Out the back were queues of tractors and trailers each with their plastic bins of picked grapes. There were twelve bins to a fully laden trailer waiting to be tipped into the processing plant. Out the front were queues of tourists in trainers each with their plastic bags of bottled wine. There were six bottles to a full bag waiting to be tipped back into the touring coach. I purchased two bottles of "good" Merlot Grenache for the journey, at less than thirty francs a bottle. The label mentioned the words "Toques et Clochers" (chef's hats and clock towers). It was a local wine trade organisation. Every year the toques and clochers gathered to raise money to preserve or restore the bell tower of a local church. There was always an auction of wine and a feast prepared by really good chefs in the chosen town or village. It cost about a thousand francs for a ticket to the 'do' but they were worth it and kept the church towers in the region looking good.

Carcassonne lost its importance as a fortified citadel in the middle of the seventeenth century when the Pyrenees became the official border between France and Spain. The thick walls had been breached and what their ancestors died trying to keep out, their predecessors were dying to keep in. Nowadays the walled city was besieged with tourists. Instead of boiling oil, giant boulders and arrows raining down on the invaders, it was hot cassoulet, soft scoop ice cream and post cards. The old city of Carcassonne was number three or four most visited tourist attraction in France. I didn't know where Euro Disney came or if it even counted, but when I first saw the turrets and walls from a distance, I could have been excused from thinking that Walt's creative boys had had a hand in building it.

I met Hugo, a French civil engineer, who knew all about the place and we walked the old walls together. Hugo, actually Hugues Droulers, had studied architecture for years. He was based at the local hospital, overseeing their building work. He was able to point out and explain the scars of centuries of construction and deconstruction. He explained the fairy tale conical roofs on some of the towers. They were the work of Viollet le Duc, the man who also recreated the Notre Dame in Paris. The slated cones were literally plonked onto the old battlements to make the citadel look less fierce. The heavy metal rings set into the pillars on the inside of the ugly basilica were put there during the French revolution when the church was used as a stable. Cows chewed the cud in the blue glow of light from the thirteenth century stained glass windows.

Hugo recounted the legend of Dame Carcas. When the city was under siege and the population was down to its last pig, she decided to throw the poor animal over the walls. The besieging army outside, who were hoping to starve those inside into surrender, took the gesture to mean that there was plenty of food left in the city and decided to pack up their bags, tents, sling shots and battering rams and go back to their own homes. The people of Carcassonne were saved thanks to the Dame, who presumably didn't much like pork anyway. In celebration they rang the bells and hence the city was christened Carcassonne, after Dame Carcas and the sonne of the ringing bells.

The place looked as though it was riddled with history and it was a legend that was perpetuated. The film Robin Hood, Prince of Thieves was shot on location, which seemed to impress some American visitors much more than the two thousand years of real history.

"Gee, just imagine honey. Robin Hood stood on this bridge," I heard one say.

Hugo lived in the new Carcassonne with 48,999 others. There was nothing of note other than the river Aude, the very straight streets and the Canal du Midi. The town hall was pure art deco and looked like a 1900 and something cinema, complete with giant square wristwatch clock face set in its tower. Hugo rented but his girl friend Valerie and her three young sons had a house where she gave us a supper. Hot goats cheese salad, fillet of beef with a hint of blue cheese and ratatouille. Hugo had known Valerie, who was a nurse in the same hospital, since last October and they were in love.

Hugo put me up for the night on his sofa. If I visited Carcassonne again maybe I'd be able to stay on his barge on the canal. He had a plan to convert one into a houseboat and have paying guests.

Americans included.

Central Hospital ⇌

Peter is in another garage where a rather nervous Monsieur Guitard is trying to sort out his over- revving.

Sick or not, I extracted Peter from Monsieur Guitard's scooter workshop and drove him, via a car wash, to the Central Hospital. A misnomer, the Central Hospital was outside Carcassonne. It was built about twenty five years ago and I could understand why it needed Hugo and his talents to keep it from falling down. It was definitely a utility building rather than a prestigious public monument. There were no fountains or statues, sweeping marble stairs, large clocks or breezy public rooms. Just French functional non-fripperies with one small flowerbed in the entrance lobby.

Doctor Jean Chounet had been at the hospital since its cement was drying and was one of the five heart men there. He was not a surgeon, for that sort of thing one had to go to Toulouse, but he attended to the cardiovascular needs of the 57 beds occupied by those needing cardiovascular attention. Ten years previously, hearts took up 72 beds, which indicated that things might be improving. The other statistic that hinted at improvement was the length of stay. It used to be twelve days, now it was six. I assumed that the good doctor was referring to the number of days a patient stayed before being allowed back into this world rather than the next.

The hospital had 936 beds and 110 doctors and I got the impression that the system was not as over worked or as over stretched as its British counterpart. Doctor Chounet shook his head when I asked about a waiting list and told me that he had been looking after an increasing number of British patients who really didn't like queuing, especially when the sick ticker didn't understand the principle of time.

He did not look like a heart doctor. In his jeans and rugby football shirt, he was nearer sixty than fifty and could be taken for a teacher, taxi driver, plumber or train driver. It was probably a toss up which way the young Jean Chounet would have gone. It could have been hearts or trains. The telltale signs that he was a doctor were his white coat and stethoscope but then he lit up a cigarette, which shunted me temporarily into a railway siding somewhere. The shelves of his office were stacked in equal proportion with tomes about veins and trains.

"Aorta know better" sat easy along side "Getting up steam".

In a peaked cap and with a whistle, Doctor Chounet's bedside manner would take on platform proportions. He had actually built one or two steam engines and when asked about his most memorable encounter with the railway, he told me about the Paris to Venice stretch of the Orient Express with the sort of expression a young train spotter might have had. I guessed there was a link, a branch line, between engines and hearts and one that Doctor Chounet steamed up and down admirably.

The hospital boasted its own garage and Hugo arranged for Peter to be admitted. Richard, whose name was pronounced like the alcoholic aniseed drink and whose breath smelt of it too, was the chief doctor in the mechanical clinic more used to ambulances than over- revving three wheelers. He had the problem diagnosed in twenty minutes but, just like the patients who get referred to Toulouse for the actual surgery, Peter would have to return to Monsieur Guitard for his operation. The over-revving might need some more bits from Piaggio, so once again it looked as though Peter would be helping Italy's balance of payments.

I spend another night on Hugo's sofa.

Carcassonne Chef

A pig's trotter tart with Fitou. Roll on winter.

Imagine an above average, professional French chef and some of the following key words might appear in the description. Arrogant, self opinionated, bombastic, rude, above criticism, proud, emotional, short tempered, always right, unapproachable, fussy but none-the-less a jolly fine cook. Pierre Mesa was a jolly fine cook and, as far as I could tell, didn't have an ounce of any of the aforementioned ingredients. He ran his fine restaurant in the old walled city of Carcassonne and it was a place where for about twenty pounds a head, people could wine and dine on some of the best that the region had to offer.

Pierre Mesa served his apprenticeship in Knightsbridge, Holland Park, the Place de la Bastille in Paris and Carcassonne. There were no airs and graces with Pierre and his aim was to provide excellence to local dishes at sensible prices. He bought the restaurant in the Rue St Louis because it was where he started to cook as a boy. His Mother and Father used to be there and it was somehow fitting that Pierre's nursery was now his kitchen some thirteen years after his parents had left. He loved what he did and his enthusiasm and infectious high-pitched laugh made him a good guy for his eighteen staff to work for.

He invited me into the kitchen where I watched him create a new dish for his winter menu. The main ingredient was minced pig's trotter and Pierre produced a light pastry tartlet into which he layered his cooked mixture together with sliced cepes and a sauce which used laurel leaves as a part of creating the flavour. Together with an atypical red Fitou, the result was wonderful and I envied the restaurant's winter clientele already.

Because he was experienced both sides of the Channel, I asked him who was more difficult to please. Whilst the British were keen to learn more about food, the French thought that they knew it all. There were differences in taste. The British preferred their smoked meats, iceberg lettuce and mushrooms of the Paris variety. Frenchman wouldn't know what to do with a smoked chicken. An iceberg was what sunk the Titanic and mushrooms came out of woods, not out of tins. The food culture gap was getting much narrower and Franglais cuisine was equally at home in Brighton as Bordeaux.

The restaurant, Comte Roger, didn't have a plat du jour (it did have a mouth-watering dessert du jour) because Pierre thought that that would make his establishment too ordinary, more like a bistro than the fine diner with a reputation he was intent on growing. Cassoulet was his most popular dish and his was really special and should be enjoyed when two or three are gathered together. It's not a meal for a man on his own but needs "conviviality" as Chef Mesa put it.

Pierre Mesa gives me a sauce recipe, which he believes is classic, simple and good for the heart. He writes it down for me on a scrap of paper. Cream of garlic country sauce. Peel the garlic and cut each clove long ways in half. Remove the little "pip" (le germe as he calls it) from each clove's middle. These will be found more easily in really fresh garlic. Blanch the cloves. Place into cold water and bring to the boil and repeat the exercise three more times. Take the blanched cloves and mash them with a pestle and mortar. Add crème fraiche. Cook for 10 minutes on a very low heat. Stir the mixture and add salt and white pepper. This sauce will go with lamb, veal, fish (especially tuna and sea bass), vegetables of the summer (as he calls them) and potatoes. Use a complete head of garlic and 125 grams of crème fraiche to provide the sauce for four people.

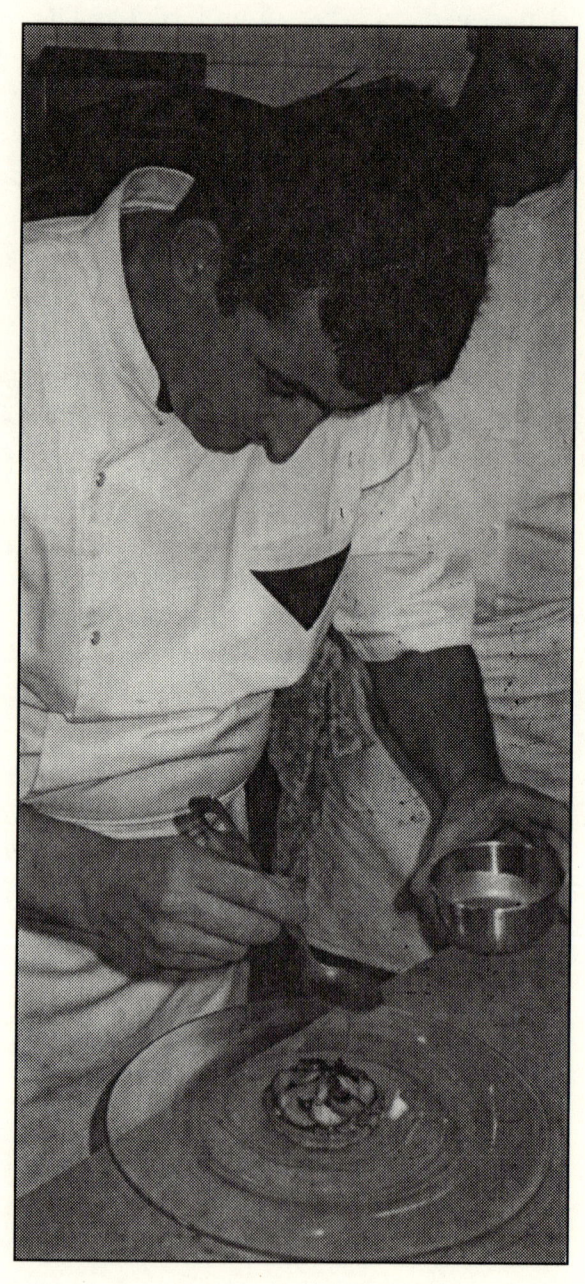

Beziers ⇥

In Beziers's Hotel of the Poet,
there's a loo in which you can't do it.
To make it with ease,
needs a hole for your knees
in the door to poke them both through it.

It was the evening. I was strolling through the narrow streets of Beziers with the smell of the Golfe du Lion wafting in from the East, stirring in the thermals above the old city to mix with the vent of the vendage from the plains and hills out to the West. I'd booked into the Hotel des Poetes, room 40, up three floors and very adequate. What wasn't quite so adequate was the loo. It was a communal one for the top floor. It was smaller than a fridge. To use the thing sitting down, I had to leave the door open. Either that or my knees would have been up around my ears. Not very comfortable and nor was it desperately comfortable with the door open. There were some things that should only be done in private. The name of the Hotel prompted a Limerick, which should have be sent to the charming landlady:

Beziers's current Cathedral looked a bit like a Gothic castle and in the warm late September evening sunshine there was no hint of De Montfort's massacre of five thousand people eight hundred years ago. When he was on the warpath against the Cathars, the locals refused to hand over twenty fugitives and so he killed all of them. Just another incident in the rich history of civilisation and the part played by holy wars.

I took a meal on the pavement at the Vieux Siege with a colourful bird who kept me amused all evening. She whistled the opening bars of the French national anthem and every so often would ask in her funny French accent "C'a va, c'a va?"

The red head need not be jealous. The bird's a parrot.

Nimes

It's where denim came from. So presumably jeans can be worn anywhere.

Leaving Beziers with yet another Piaggio "Non" and that funny but familiar sucking noise of air over mechanic's teeth, we headed for the coast at Agde. There the fish smelt stronger than the wine and torsos of tuna lay waiting to be sliced up on fish mongers slabs. Some of the old buildings looked as though they could have done with a decent clean. Their blackened facades were not the result of polluted air, but because the local volcanic building rock was naturally that colour.

Between Agde and Sete, along that flat bit of land, which gently greeted the sea, I did the same and stopped, like an excited child, for a paddle and a photograph. The Mediterranean looked like a lake. I could imagine that the landscape hadn't changed much since the ancient Greeks, or whoever, first caught sight of it. Landing on the beach and before going off to civilise the natives, new invaders would be forced to pull over for a plastic plate of frites. The signs for them were littered along the coast road.

Montpellier sort of came and went as we headed north east for a garage in Castlenau-Le-Lez. The Monsieur who ran the set up was willing to help but he couldn't fit us in for three weeks. It was my turn to suck air over teeth. I couldn't hang about. We pressed on slowly and on the relative flat for Nimes.

Perrier water shouldn't be flat and the water bottling plant (they call it a source) was a giant factory at Vergeze. It was owned by Nestles, one of the worlds largest food companies. Its water products accounted for 15% of the world production of bottled water and during my brief visit of half an hour, the plant churned out another ninety thousand green bottles of the stuff.

The bubbly water supposedly came straight out of the ground. The well-kept gardens around 'Chateau Fizz' contained some hilarious bottle shaped topiary. It's branding gone mad. Watch the ad, enjoy the drink, buy the sweatshirt, sit under the umbrella and cut the hedge.

Dependent upon how Nimes was approached and from which direction, the city looked a lot like Milton Keynes. There were some wacky-looking structures with lots of metal girders; glass and so on and modern influence could be found even in the old bits of the town. Roman met Norman as the Mason Caree (first century AD) sat just across the road from the Caree d'Art designed by Norman Foster. The two looked well together.

To my mind the very best thing about Nimes was the amphitheatre. It was very nearly breathtaking. From the outside it was what everybody imagined a Roman arena would look like. The familiar architecture sprang to life from the pages of illustrated school history books and words like Sparticus and Ben Hur hit the tip of my mind's tongue. Circumnavigating its outside, I had to pinch myself because I didn't think that it was real. I'd never seen one before. For 28 francs I was given ticket number 184144 and I wandered around the inside of the place in a sort of stupor. There were times when I expected a centurion or toga-wrapped citizen to stroll down one of the many honeycomb passages towards me with a "Hail" or "Pax" or something mumbled in Latin. Two thousand years ago, a capacity crowd would have been 23,000. That was probably more than the population of Londinium at that time. The sport then, as now, was gladiatorial – then it was lions and men – now it was bulls and men. I wandered the old building with my mouth open in wonder, for an hour or more.

The second best thing about Nimes was the Hotel Lisita, which was right next door to the amphitheatre. Its proximity made it the place where bullfighters pitched up for the night. The reception was littered with pictures of the colourful characters. Some had colourful matador type names and some sounded like Scottish footballers. Denis Lore was one. Saved by the acute accent over the last letter, his surname was pronounced lorry.

The Hotel Lisita was old and jaded but my room (12) was fine and nothing like a modern bedroom at all. It was colourful, romantic and cheap. I didn't run into any matadors in the lift (max capacity two) or on the stairs but I heard one in the room next door. He sounded like he was practising his fighting technique with a lot of noisy encouragement from a female fan. She grunted lots. Would have been what the red head called, a screamer. The headboard to their moving bed was only inches away from my still one. I shouted "Ole!" at the banging thin wall separating us, not because I wanted to spoil their fun but because it was about three in the morning. It did the trick. They shut up and he presumably put away his cape or whatever.

Nimes street cleaners were noisy too. They were given two jobs to do by the City Fathers. One to clean the streets and the other to provide the early morning wake up call. The noise they made for about an hour between five and six a.m. was a testament to their thoroughness for scrapping up every last speck of dirt and waking up Nimes sleepers.

I enjoyed a meal in the restaurant Lisita. It wasn't related to the hotel although it was right next door. I only mentioned it because of the starter. I ordered squid, octopus and artichoke all together in a light wine sauce and altogether very good. The wine was local, red tieres de Nimes from Chateau de Rozier, just outside Manduel some 10 k's east of Nimes. Its proprietor was on my list of people to visit.

Louis de Belair was an artist and ex bank employee and the owner of Chateau de Rozier. He was a short, sun tanned wine maker with an obvious enthusiasm and pride in what he did. The chateau's 22 hectares of vines produced about 65,000 bottles of the little known red. Louis had pioneered his export business and over 70% of his production went abroad. Belgium and the Low Countries, Germany, Switzerland and Ireland were his biggest customers. As a result of his efforts at a Shanghai trade fair and with the help of President Chirac, he sold 13,000 bottles a year to the Chinese. His best vintage so far was 1985 but the latest crop, available in his labelled bottles in 2001, should be every bit as good, if not better or so he said with a warm smile.

Louis was a leading light in a new approach to wine growing and he talked a lot about FARRE, an organisation that promoted responsible commercial agriculture and respect for the environment. I was not sure what made a chateau a chateau and a domaine a domaine. Louis wanted his photo taken in the shadow of the tower on his property, which perhaps helped to make his chateau a chateau.

"The man I sell my wine to in England. He is slow to pay my bills." Louis tells me hoping I can do something about it. I'm embarrassed because I know the man in England. I should be embarrassed even if I didn't.

Avignon ⚞

I sing a new song in anticipation as we chug along. "Sur le pont d'Avignon, en y danser, en y danser."

Mention the word Avignon and most would start whistling the tune to that ditty "Sur le pont d'Avignon". It was probably the third most sung French song outside France. "Alouetta" No1. "Frere Jaques" No 2, "Sur le pont d'Avignon" No 3, "La Marseillaise" No 4, "Sank evans fer lille gulls" by Maurice Chevalier at No 5 and anything by Johnny Halliday at Nos 6,7,8, 9 and 10.

Forget that the city used to house the Popes and that it had a great summer festival following its tradition as a major centre for the arts. Forget that the city walls still went all the way round it. All I wanted to see was the bridge and it wasn't there. It was a pier. What a let down! It didn't cross the Rhone. Didn't even reach half way across. I sulked with all the other tourists in one of the cafés in the Place de l'Horloge. I read up on the history of Avignon but developed my own theory. The Pope of Avignon was getting mightily fed up that the populace was more impressed with the bridge than their Pope. Of course the Pope of Avignon wasn't the real Pope. The real one was back in Rome, so Avignon had to satisfy itself with Pope Two. So it was Pope Two, fed up with being ignored in the street by people rushing to work over the bridge, who said knock it down. He thought that he would get more attention. But his plan backfired and the good people of Avignon kicked him out in favour of Pope One in Rome. They also named Pope One as Pontiff just to keep him on his toes and in case he ever tried to turn any more ponts into piers. Having rewritten the history, I've had to provide new words for that ditty. Same tune but new lyrics for the end bit.

'Sur le pont no you can't, en y danser, en y danser. Sur le pont no you won't, en y danser it's a con.'

I looked at where the Popes had lived and it was impressive. I found my way to a municipal campsite across the river using a proper bridge and spent the evening with a book.

The trip to Chateauneuf–du–Pape turned the landscape into Provence. The late September sunshine made me want to become a painter, an artist. The sunflowers had gone and where they had been harvested, the fields looked like they were sprouting a crop of short sticks. The village that gave its name to the famous wine smelt like a brewery and where I expected to see hairdressers' shops, those being the most common retail outlets in any average French settlement, in Chateauneuf–du–Pape there were more wine sellers than any other artisans. The local bar and brasserie only seemed to serve English or American speaking individuals and instead of the "hat check girl" or "cloak room attendant", they had a guy who'd take your wine purchases away and look after them while you lunched.

In Carpentras, Carrine had booked me into the Hotel du Fiacre. It was a good choice and my room (17) sat off the courtyard on the ground floor. Carrine was one of the people who had been telephoning lots and she had arranged "a gathering" in Carpentras for the next day. It was going to be in aid of the Federation Francaise de Cardiologie.

That evening I walked the town and rather liked it. On Mondays not a lot was open and I meandered without ending up as a trophy on the bonnet of a Citroen. The Passage Boyer was a 19th century shopping arcade with most of its shops still offering 19th century merchandise. Its high glass and metal roof must have been the talk of the town back then. The cathedral's outside was better looking than its inside and that was, sensibly, where the restoration money was being spent. There was scaffolding and work going on at the West face with stonemasons and builders having a laugh whilst they did their best. On the South side, over the main entrance or Porte Juif (The Jews Door), stonemasons from the 14th century had had a laugh too or had been very symbolic with their stone carving. There was a round stone, representing the world, with rats running over it.

I hope Carrine is as pretty as she sounds on the phone.

Carpentras ⇌

She is.

The 'picnic' at L'Espace Fenouil in Carpentras, which had been organised by Carrine, was a great success. The Tour collected fifteen hundred Francs for the Federation Francaise de Cardiologie with one thousand from the good members in Avignon. Two reporters asked me questions and took pictures for their papers. One of them was also a healer, the laying on of hands type. It seemed an odd job combination somehow, a newspaper journalist and a healer. Bit like being a spendthrift and a bank manager.

The representative from Avignon, Jean Claude Pestour, had been through it with his heart. He gave the gathered thirty-two a talk about leading more healthy lives. My garbled effort, which tried in very bad French to explain the Tour, gathered pace. I stopped to consider the word I needed to complete the sentence. Couldn't find it. The audience clapped. I took it as a sign to shut up and sat down.

Guy Largier and his wife Chantal ran l'Espace Fenouil as a business. It was where people went if they wanted to do evening classes. Theatre, art, dance, photography and a list of lessons that read like the menu of a Chinese takeaway. Nin-jutsu, ju-jutsu, aikido, tai chi chuan, chi kong, yoga and qi gong. The centre catered for all ages and had an official capacity in the community. It took in groups of the long-term unemployed. It tried to give them back their self-esteem and confidence. Adrienne Reed-Coissard put her students through a twice-weekly, three-month course, called P.N.L. (Programmation Neuro Linguistique). Adrienne came to France from England when she was one year old. Her Father moved to make briar pipes for tobacco smoking. She enjoyed her job at the centre. The satisfaction she got when her pupils went out and held their heads up with renewed confidence to try and find work, gave her a real buzz. P.N.L. was all about positive communication and the time spent at the centre was, apart from my brief speech, just that.

Carrine worked in the centre's office. It was a pleasure to meet her soft-spoken Irish husband and eleven-month-old daughter Emma and her Mum and Dad and all the people she got together for the Plat du Jour Tour picnic. Guy and Chantal invited me back to their house for supper in the evening and I met their three children and the puppies. They appeared to be good people and Carpentras must be a better place for them and L'Espace Fenouil.

I think of the rats running over the world, the carving over the Jews door at the Cathedrale St-Siffrein. It's an inappropriate image for the people of Carpentras I met.

Vaison-La-Romaine

But is it art?

One of the journalists at Carrine's picnic suggested that I head North to look at the Dentelles and Mont Ventoux. If Peter had overheard he'd have blown another gasket. More hill climbing was just what he didn't want. We headed North and reached Vaison-La-Romaine and the modern campsite appropriately named Camping du Theatre Romain.

The run out from Carpentras towards Vaison-La-Romaine wasn't that arduous on the tarmac roads. Innocently, and because I wanted to see Seguret, I turned off at Crestet. As I wound my way up and out of the medieval village into the woods that covered the hills, I suddenly came upon the signs that said Crestet Centre d'Art. I thought "But I'm in back water Provence, up in the Dentelles, surrounded by woods. What's with the art centre business?"

Le Crestet Centre d'Art was funded by the government, employed seven people, had ten thousand visitors a year and was probably as good a way as any for using the woods and French tax payers money to promote the arts. Currently on show in the white thirty-year old concrete studio was the work of Ricardo Brey. The centre gave a personal guided tour. Mine explained the work I was looking at. I imagined that she must have been to the school of "Believing-what-you-are-saying-and-not-bursting-into-laughter-when-what-you-are-describing-and-what-the-viewer-is-seeing-bears-no-relation."

Most of Ricardo's works were untitled, which wasn't a surprise. I understood "Nest", a collection of branches and leaves in the middle of which were several broken ostrich eggs, cracked plates and an old saxophone. I didn't understand the lion skin in a glass case, its mane on an old pillow with an electric fan, its body covered with a quilt and scattered around the sleeping beast, buttons and dice. One thousand and one gloves (untitled), as a statue deserved a big hand. The fire hose spread out across the studio floor, with a small rug under one end, was just what I'd call lazy art. Ricardo Brey was part Cuban, part Belgian and part rather wacky artist. He was clever though because his stuff was on show up in the hills overhanging Vaison-La-Romaine.

When I left the white studio building, I wandered around the woods where I was supposed to find eleven different commissioned sculptures in between the trees. Amongst those that I found and could identify were "Les Parques" by Vincent Barre, "Le Portique des Gemeaux" by Francois Stahly, who started the art thing off there, and "Le Pont" which I foolishly skipped across thinking it was a bridge rather than a 1972 sculpture by Dominque Arel. There was also a rusty red Alpha Romeo (untitled) parked at the back of the studio and a picnic table and chairs (untitled) with an empty plastic water bottle (Evian). I hastened back to the public car park just in case Peter had become an exhibit, but there he was, thank goodness, all on his own (untitled).

The road from Crestet towards Seguret got thinner and thinner and eventually tarmac gave way to stone, gravel and sand. We were, for a mile or two, on a footpath, which was great for two feet but jolly awkward for three wheels. Peter's central front wheel was either riding all the big stones in the middle of the track or off to one side. His two tiny back tyres were therefore straddled over the track. One might be in the centre bumping over the stones, while the other was on the track, which tilted us at an alarming angle. We bounced our way very slowly through the woods of Seguret and along the edges of fields of vines. There too the stones were abundant, heaped up under the vines to store and radiate the heat of the sun and so help natures ripening process. Just as the shaking was becoming an enjoyable routine, the footpath became a road once again and Seguret appeared.

If the little hillside village were female, she would be a super model. Nothing was out of place, not a smudge here or a blemish there. The locals must have got up every morning before dawn and cleaned the place with their toothbrushes. The streets were paved with the cousins of the stones that Peter and I had just trundled along except the stones were much smoother and very set in their ways.

Eight years previously, almost to the day, the river in Vaison-La-Romaine burst its banks causing mayhem and destruction in the town. I couldn't believe it possible looking at the gentle flow way down under the old bridge on a bright September evening.

Looks can be deceptive.

Mont Ventoux ⇒

I can see it from miles away, long before I reach its base and the two thousand-metre ascent.

The climb up le Mont Ventoux took Peter forever and when we were only 7 kilometres from the summit, a burley gendarme with dark glasses, motor bike and gun stopped us. He told us we couldn't go any further as there was a film blocking the road. It sounded like an excuse.

Our journey was halted where the road reached the Hotel Restaurant Chalet Liotard. There was a marquee erected in the road outside and inside much activity, shouting, running about and general preparation for the feeding of the film crew and the extras. Three hundred of them descended from the summit and straight away I was back in 1970 surrounded by the dress and the vehicles of thirty years ago. The dress might have changed but the habits hadn't. After a morning's filming the queue to use the two loos in the restaurant was longer than the queue of traffic waiting to go up the mountain. But then the law decided that the road would remain shut for the rest of the day. It was best not to argue with gendarmes. Peter looked positively relieved as I booked into the hotel bit of the Liotard and mingled.

I had an extra lunch or lunch as an extra and thought about slipping into a pair of my plus fours and donning the old flat tweed hat so I too could play a part. The film being shot was called "Le velo de Ghislain Lambert". It was about a Belgian cyclist who was brilliant on a bike in Belgium but absolutely dismal in the Tour de France back in the late 60's and early 70's. As French films went it was fairly big budget stuff being made by Lazennec Productions of Paris and due out for general release in September the following year. The talk in the bar was that the spend for the picture was eight hundred thousand Francs a day and the Patron, Coco, looked as though he'd been paid a fair slug of that day's budget for the catering he'd put on. He'd mustered help from friends and relatives and, as I was the only paying guest staying in the Liotard for the night, they invited me to join them for supper. Not surprisingly we had what I had already had for lunch.

I climbed the stairs to Mount Blanc (room 3) and as I went to bed, the wind got up.

I wasn't sure what sound it was that woke me first the following morning before light. It was either the banging of the swinging shutter or the extraordinary noise of the wind. It was like a wolf sitting on the bedside table howling. By breakfast there was no let up and the force of the gale was such that Peter would have been blown off the road on the way to the summit.

The patron, Coco, said that it got up to 200 kilometres an hour which, if we had been silly enough to venture out, would have put Peter and I somewhere else all together. The name itself should have been warning enough. Mont Ventoux, vent being wind and presumably oux meaning more than just the light passing of. So the day blew by and the only entertainment was whether or not the marquee which was flapping wildly outside like a twenties Charleston dancer and had cost Lazennec Productions of Paris twenty five thousand Francs to house the feeding of the three hundred, would last the day. Chef seemed to be running a book on it and if it blew away before noon the odds were set at 5 to1. Before one, 4 to1, before two, 3 to1 and so on. Punters would get their money back if the thing took to the air at 5pm. After that all bets were off as the weather forecast spoilt the form and predicted a more peaceful night. In fact all bets were called off at 3.20. The owners of the tent arrived to remove the canvas bits which was probably just as well, as a 4 o'clock gust would have undoubtedly carried the thing back to Marseille for them, although probably not in as neat a bundle as they would have liked.

There was something binding about being forced by inclement conditions to stay somewhere unplanned. It was bonding, like I imagined the sort of spirit cocktail shaken up and served when the people of London took shelter in the Underground during the Blitz. Not that the wind on Mont Ventoux was anything remotely like the Blitz. But the same spirit was probably prevalent. The singing, the chat and banter, the "Wow that was a big one", the general passing of time with people who had never met before and who would never meet again. The bonding, united by the common enemy, the big wind.

Waking the next morning to find the sun was shining and there wasn't the faintest breath of a breeze, I felt, as I paid the bill and my share of the previous night's tabs, a bit of an anti climax. The roof of the hotel wasn't in the next valley and Coco, the patron, and his family were perhaps no longer the very best friends I'd ever had in my whole life.

A few windy hours and a few glasses of alcohol and the world put to rights.

Aix-en-Provence ⇒

The perfume of Provence is lavender.

From the very top of Mont Ventoux I thought that I could smell it wafting from the plains below, coming up from Sault. The spicy air peppered from Sault. Although reaping should have finished by mid-September, the perfume lingered. It reminded me of chests of drawers and old wardrobes and my Grandmother's handkerchiefs.

The climb to the top of Mont Ventoux was steep. It was quite amazing how cyclists took it in their stride. They were fit. I'd never seen a fat racing cyclist. There weren't any. It looked like hell and was a notorious part of the Tour de France. Going down the other side, the side the touring cyclists usually peddled their way up, I paused at the stark, rocky, roadside memorial to Tom Simpson. He died there on 13th July 1967 while on the Tour de France. His heart had had enough. Thirty years after the racers death his two daughters, Jane and Joanne, had added their own thoughts "There is no mountain too high". I guess that pretty much summed up the spirit with which the dedicated peddlers performed their arduous ups and downs.

There were still ripening olives on their olive trees and we meandered our way through the sort of country side that probably hadn't changed much since Paul Cézanne depicted it in his paintings. It was to the town where he worked and died that I went and pitched my tent.

Aix-en-Provence was very aptly named. It was aptly named because Aix-en-Provence was an omelette. Someone had gathered all the different eggs of Provence, cracked them open and tossed them into one beautiful bowl about 30 kilometres away from the Mediterranean, whisked them up, cooked and served the result. Eggs-in-Provence made one of the best French omelettes ever. It had art, music, architecture, markets for everything, shops for even more, street cafes, American students (mostly female), beggars, graffiti, plane trees, narrow streets and wide boulevards, performers, posers and truck loads of tourists, fountains and more squares than a chess board, noise and Provence excitement, more than a hint of style and sunshine in October. Cézanne could have painted even the campsite I chose. My little tent between two impressionist trees stuck out like a colourful dab of oil paint.

I had discovered snobbery involved with camping. The ancient nomadic act of wandering and pitching at will, should be without some of the more nasty aspects of the twenty-first century. Not so. There was a pecking order. Those with caravans look down on those with camper vans, who look down on those with tents. Everyone in the campsite looked down on me, on my own, in my little tent. I didn't have a satellite dish, an annex, a solar shower, potted plants or cut flowers outside my opening, extra motor scooters or jet skis, dog kennels, nameplate, trouser press or a man servant to bring me my tea in the morning. I had seen most of them on the campsites of Southern France. Far from the sentiment of the open road, the great out doors or hunter-gatherer instinct that the modern day camper tried to emulate, he could not. He actually took everything he had at home, what he had worked for and what he was used to. He had packed it up and transported it to put it somewhere else for a week or two. I didn't actually see any one with their secretary or P.A. but then I couldn't tell.

I expect they're here with somebody else's.

Marseille ⇌

I look out of the window from my room in the Hotel Pavillion and see a collection of used condoms amongst the general filth gathered on the murky ledge beneath.

I'd been doing a lot of pavement pounding. Once again Peter had become indisposed. Actually he worked, he could go forwards and backwards, but sadly it was only in first gear. Like some of the T-shirts I wore for a tad longer than I should, Peter had chosen his favourite gear and stuck in it. The upshot was that we left our campsite just outside Aix-en-Provence and motored into the centre to find the Piaggio dealer.

The journey, three kilometres, took an embarrassing hour or so, with pedestrians crawling along the pavement with more haste than we could muster. The over-revving made things worse. We spoilt the peace of several Sunday morning residents but thanked God the roads weren't that busy. I left Peter outside another showroom with Piaggio emblazoned over the shutters, where he would sit for two days waiting the return to work on Tuesday. And Tuesday arrived as Tuesdays did every seven days, and the young guy at the garage got to grips with the problem. I called it an opportunity. Like his driver, Peter had a screw loose. Within minutes he was back in the right gear and Marseille was only a couple of changes away.

I was sure there was a back road to Marseille but we took the motorway. The three lanes of major road encouraged users to move along fairly swiftly. 110 kilometres an hour was what the signs suggested. Most drivers seemed to achieve the requirement. Peter did try his best and on one down hill stretch got up to a very scary 60 k's. But our progress was obviously not quick enough for some that hooted and gesticulated at us as they flew past. The best response was to smile and wave back, which got them even hotter-collared. Once I'd got used to my rear view mirror filled with the flashing headlights and gnashing teeth of vehicles and their occupants coming from behind at speed, then having to brake hard or swerve to avoid me, I could relax. If there were not a law preventing the likes of Peter on motorways, then there should have been. He just wasn't good for the blood pressure and covered as he was with signs promoting the British and French heart foundations, he was certainly testing the roadworthiness of several hearts during that journey. Mine not least of all.

Marseille arrived after the motorway madness and we took an exit that dumped us into somewhere reminiscent of Brent Cross. It wasn't pretty, very fifties and sixties, tower blocks and roads, concrete and commerce. I was bent on finding the place that allegedly would sort out Peter's over-revving problem. After several wrong turns and several false leads and driving through the sort of scenery I remembered in the film "The French Connection", I eventually found Frederick. I left Peter hoping very much that he wouldn't be broken up or melted down and sold on the street bit by bit.

A taxi took me and my overnight kit to the Vieux Port. I felt like a salty sea dog. I trawled the area for a bed. There were several I could have had for an hour or so, or even a half day. I knew what sort of neighbourhood I was visiting. The Hotel Pavillion was the first with a room available at a daily rate. There was a woman behind the fitted desk in the entrance hall. She looked a lot smarter than her surroundings. She smiled like a proper receptionist. Payment was strictly up front she said. I paid for two days and regretted it once I'd seen the room in more detail than was initially allowed.

The double bed looked very well used. It sagged in its middle like a soup bowl. Hadn't got the more comfortable flatness of a side plate. A transparent, plastic sheet suspended like a cheap theatre curtain, screened off a corner of the room. Behind it was a wash basin and a shower. There was no lavatory. That was down the hall behind a combination lock. There weren't any pictures on the walls. Clients didn't come there to study the art. They would create their own ambience, draw their own conclusions from the space around them. The window looked out onto the back of another building and there was only a hint of dreary daylight from above. I opened it and turned up that noise, the sound of people living in close proximity. Raised voices, radios or television sets, a dog, a food mixer, some one chopping something, a banging, a shout, the explosion of a pigeon taking off. I looked down and saw the filth on a ledge below. Cigarette packs and used condoms, pigeon shit and broken glass. A room with a view.

Marseille, France's second city, was a different kettle of fish. That was what it smelt like from my hotel in the old port. Bad breath bouillabaisse. The place was big with 800,000 people and the space that they needed to live and work in. There were lots of suits and ties which I hadn't seen much of on the Tour. A suit normally meant serious and Marseille was the most serious city I'd visited so far. Although there was plenty of evidence around to show that it did have its tongue in its cheek sometimes.

Its sea-sideyness was not kiss-me-quick hats and candyfloss but merchant shipping and traders. For rock and deckchairs read stock and Bourse shares. Before I'd had a chance to sip my first cup of tea, I was offered a beaten copper tray, a decorative and useful penholder, several lighters and a rose. I'd barely got a few yards off the motorway and there were guys offering the kerb side windscreen washing service although even those traffic light traders were not quite sure what to make of Peter's front window. There were beggars too and dog dirt, which most seem to step around although both stuck with equal persistence once contact had been made.

Marseille had been a trading post for two and a half thousand years, one of the natural valves between Africa and Europe, through which a two-way traffic ebbed and flowed. It was no wonder that I could find hemp, hash, haddock, haricots and harlots in the same arrondissement. There were sixteen to choose from compared to the twenty in Paris. Arrondissements that was, not harlots. It had style and I wandered the Cours Julien and felt "Villagey". I'd slip a few streets back towards the port and I was in a North African market with fruit and footballs, Pokemon and pineapples side by side in cardboard boxes. What I saw was what I got, guaranteed to the end of the short street. Within a couple of blocks, I was cheek to cheek with chic and the labels shouted at me from the halogen enhanced windows. Marseille was a bizarre bazaar.

Some traders tried and played it rough and I came across my first would-be muggers. Two guys, both in their teens, rumbled up to me and asked for a cigarette. I said I didn't smoke but they wouldn't take no or go away as the answer. Their tactics were classic. One grabbed my attention while the other grabbed my goods. My mobile was firmly fixed to my belt and I wasn't carrying a bag or anything and both hands were free. So when I felt some fingers trying to get into the pocket of my jeans, I knew they weren't mine. I didn't want to lose my wallet, so I pushed the owner of the prying hand away. Pushed him hard, sent him reeling across the pavement, so he knew I meant it, and shouted very loudly at him. They got the message, didn't get their knives out for the lanky English man.

Crime was only a minor problem for Ian Davies, Her Majesty's Consul General in Marseille. In fact he didn't seem to have any problems or none that his diplomatic training couldn't cope with. His P.A. Janice made us a pot of tea (from M&S not many blocks away) and I talked to "our man" in Marseille and everywhere between the Italian and Spanish border down in the South East of France. He looked after two million British tourists to the region every year, thirteen thousand officially registered ex-pats, a staff of ten, an annual budget of four hundred and fifty thousand pounds and most importantly, the business interests of U.K.Ltd. He was really our regional Chairman and he came across as a steady hand to have on the tiller.

Marseille's importance as a cosmopolitan community and its mix of Muslim, Jew, Christian and others, was reflected by the presence of twenty career and forty honourary consulates from all over. China and Russia were represented there as well as the U.S.A. Britain was the second biggest investor in the region, after America, and Ian's job was to push Britain and things British. B.P and Shell (40% British) represented our biggest chunks of investment but there were other familiar names like Camel Laird the ship repairers, Virgin the music sellers and Marks and Spencer the tea providers.

Ian Davies got into the job because he wanted to travel and at 44, he'd already notched up some air miles. Bolivia, Paris and Moscow had all been his diplomatic bag and in July of the following year his four year term in Marseille would be up, so he would be off opening the doors, networking and bringing his quite "John Major" like style of public diplomacy to another outpost.

When it came to the game of football, I was an intellectual hooligan. I did know that France was currently enjoying what might be termed a good run. Olympique de Marseille was one of France's, probably the World's, most famous clubs established in 1899, notorious in 1993 when the then owner Bernard Tapie introduced some of his business management practices and cost the club its place in the premier league. Under the ownership of Robert Louis-

Dreyfus and new President, Eves Marchand, the team was currently lying in 9th position half way up, or down, the first division. The club claimed to have five million supporters worldwide and its web site enjoyed 5000 "hits" a day. Under their new presidency the club was clawing back some of its glitter. Its financial deficit had been reduced but the path to glory simply needed goals and goal makers and those cost money. Marseille didn't have any megastars with the likes of Zidane and Petit going to where the buck wouldn't stop. But OM had all the potential to get back on top. Their impressive stadium, owned by Marseille city, held a crowd of 60,000 and their marketing and communications programme included their own cable T.V. channel. They seemed to have got what it took and all they'd have to do was take what it gets.

Nathalie Paoli ran something called OM Attitude and had been doing the job for a year. She headed up the social programme for the club, its mission to respond to demands from associations and organisations that believed they could benefit from a link to the club. The club in return got some good press and more supporters. Her main target audience, not surprisingly, was youngsters and Nathalie worked with social centres to encourage fair play and the right team spirit among its young people. She was the funnel through which the club may help the community and through which the community could gain access to the club.

With Nathalie's magic key Peter and I gained access to the impressive stadium. Peter was back off the bench having been declared fit to play again. The crowd roared their approval at the news (actually I sang Jerusalem) as we processed majestically without a hint of over revving from one side of Marseille to the other to keep our rendezvous with Nathalie.

After Marseille and a final farewell from the fake Michael Angello David and the thumbs up from another less famous but more original statue, probably more typical of the city's real attitude, we headed off along the coast to Cassis and La Ciotat with the mistral playing vigorously.

The plastic palms in the Cours D'Estienne D'Orves spin around as moving sculpture. Sometimes in their crazy cycle, they are upside down, dangling from their pots. They never need watering, just looking at from time to time.

Cassis And La Ciotat ⚔

*There's a restaurant in La Ciotat that used to be a pharmacy. It has lots of
little wooden drawers where they must have kept the pills and potions. They
are spread across one wall of the dining room. My table is next to them. I
have too much to drink. Take out my notebook and write a message to the
red head. Tear the page out. Open one of the little drawers and post it there.
I don't suppose she'll ever see it.*

The mistral blew and even though it was not cold, it was windy and
whipped up the sea into a relative frenzy, simmering not boiling its head off.
Someone told me that in winter when it blew off the Alps, the cold blast could
cut like a knife. Apparently it only happened in ones (one day), threes, sixes
or nines, never in two's, four's or eight's.

Mistrals and rain apart, the Tour had entered a more exotic zone as we
pushed on to Cannes. Red Ferraris, pink flamingos, haute couture beach
wear, no beachwear, Bono at the next table and whining jet skis in unison
with the whining motor scooters. The vegetation had become more tropical
with palm trees, cacti and oversized pineapple-shaped bushes. The rows and
rows of vines had given way to ranks and ranks of masts with an armada of
boats all tied up with no one to play on them. It was extraordinary just how
many floating vessels there were along the coast. Who owned them and who
used them was one of the great mysteries at that time of year. They'd sit there
rather like Mrs. Marcos's shoe collection waiting for their turn to be tried
on for an hour or so. The money tied up in tied up yachts and floating gin
palaces was amazing.

The glitzy legend was greater than the reality. There were undoubtedly some very beautiful bits to the coast and I could see why, over the years, creative types like the Lumiere brothers of La Ciotat (the Eden cinema in the town screened the world's first movie) and galleries full of painters, had seen the light there. It was a unique light and when the sun or moon shone, the sea reflected its special colour back and the beach glistened like someone had sprinkled caster sugar over the sand and pebbles. The Mediterranean climate was as mild as an English complaint and its coves and crevices had coddled those with enough cash to cling there. But its legend was also its downfall and the easy cheap jet to Nice meant that anyone could be David Niven or Grace Kelly for a day or two. The Cote d'Azur was a Cote d'Allure with Corniche routes and camper vans, caviar and karaoke, Coke and coke, chips and chips, rich and Porsche, Gucci shades and roller blades all revelling on the Riviera. There were bits of it that were truly smart, up together, tip top, beautifully painted and decorated, but there were also some rather nasty damp patches where the wallpaper was peeling.

The red head is coming over to see me.

Cannes ⇌

"God that's so good."

She had arrived at Nice airport and I was so pleased to see her. The red head too was pleased to see me but not so delighted to be introduced to Peter, our three-wheeled transport and mobile home for the next week or so. It was their first meeting. She'd seen photographs of the three-wheeler but this was their first face to face. She walked around the little blue machine with the look of a jealous lover. So this was the 'thing' that had taken her man away from her. She tossed her red hair in contempt, muttered something about size and then pulled open the passenger door and jumped in. She slammed the thin door shut with a biscuit tin clank and Peter rocked fiercely. It was the first time that I had had someone sharing the cab with me, invading my travelling space. The two of us squeezed on to the tight bench seat like two peas in a pod and left the airport car park to head off to the Carlton in Cannes for the romantic reunion. The elation of having her there next to me was almost too much to bear. I was so excited and talked like an animated machine gun, drowning out the two-stroke engine noise and anything the red head might have wanted to say.

I had booked into the Carlton Hotel in Cannes, one of the Rivera's most legendary icons. It was the hotel where Grace Kelly walked through the lobby in her beachwear and large sun hat "to catch a thief", namely Carry Grant. In more recent movie history, Meg Ryan and Kevin Klein used the place for "French Kiss". Narjiss Slaoui-Falcoz, who sounded like she should have been in the movies, was the Public Relations Manager for the Carlton. She had been handling the likes and dislikes of Michael Jackson, Rod Stewart,

Sharon Stone, Kim Basinger and a cast of would be stars when they decided to twinkle awhile at the hotel. Narjiss had been doing the job for ten years and therefore knew exactly how many lumps Arnie liked in his tea or what Claudia meant when she asked for a nightcap. I had been to meet her to talk about the famous old place and ended up booking a room.

The red head, Peter and I made our way, like an incongruous menage a trois, along the coast road from Nice via Antibes and into Cannes. The surprised doorman in his Carlton livery was more used to sleek limousines than the pathetic three-wheeler, but he took the keys anyway and after brief instruction squeezed into the cab to drive Peter off to safe hotel car parking somewhere.

"No need for the valet," I said to the fellow who looked so embarrassed behind the small steering wheel.

There was something undeniably naughty about going to bed explicitly for sex in the middle of the day, a working day for every one else. The two of us, pumped up with desire, stripped off and jumped into the big crisp cotton sheeted bed. "Kerplosh!" head first under the covers. Foreplay an unnecessary element. Pretty soon getting lost in each other's delicious company. Rediscovering the tastes and smells, the trembling excitement of the warm touching, the moist kissing and coupling. The inevitable, eventual climax. We had our moment, a perfect reunion. Coming together. Being together. Laying entwined afterwards was of equal importance, the lazy chat, casual words that meant so much, said how much she loved me, how much I missed her. We drank fine wine.

"God that was good."

The Carlton was born in 1909 when Russian and British aristocracy gathered on the sea front to discuss what to do with Europe and Faberge's latest egg. For the last fifty or so years the film festival had given Cannes and the Carlton the sort of branding a product manager would wet his or her knickers for and branding like that didn't come cheap. The Imperial Suite was 400 square meters and came with its own lift. It cost 45,000 Francs a night. For slightly less you could have Dirk Bogard or Roman Polanski or indeed another similar two-roomed suite named after some of the presidents of the film festivals jury. The room I had booked was called 249; so in film speak it was just an extra.

The place didn't really have a high season or a slack time with Cannes being the venue for so many business gatherings and conventions all hoping presumably to scrape off a little of the glitter left by the film stars twinkling there in May. Its current guests seemed evenly divided between those on business and private individuals and the place did have an international feel to it with American, English, French, Italian, Spanish, Japanese and other Babel tongues all being tried out. The only way we knew that we were not in Manhattan or Mayfair was that just across the road, the Promenade de la Croisette, the Mediterranean was lapping at the tables of the Carlton beach restaurant. Even in October, the dress reflected the location with men in shorts ordering shorts and women dressed for swimming feigning breaststroke in the elevator. Going up of course.

The hotel had as many stories to tell as it had expensive knick-knacks on offer in its concessions. I didn't remember Grace Kelly gliding through the lobby on her way to the beach and pausing to browse at the Persian rug on offer in the Oriental carpet shop window. The Carlton had also become an up market shopping emporium, a millionaire's mall or billionaire's bazaar. It was an impressive place with a young General Manager more staff than beds in its 338 rooms and some pretty wacky items left behind by guests. For some reason lost property came up in conversation. An exotic list of forgotten belongings hinted at their former exotic owners. Misplaced trinkets of the rich. As we checked into room 249 our luggage had been delivered before we arrived and along with our meagre two or three items, there was a smart black camera case with a video camera inside, the property of someone else or a welcome gift from the management. Encouragement to make a film perhaps. Tempting though it was, I returned it to the porter in the hope that if it were mine in the wrong place then someone would do the same. Presumably it was added to the stash of Rolex watches and other cameras in lost property. There must have been rows of humble false teeth stacked along side more glitzy Hollywood bits and pieces. Perhaps that was where Sharon Stone mislaid her underwear or where Harrison Ford lost the lost ark. There was a load of aluminium cladding brought by an Arab Prince for security. He left his truckload of tin behind presumably together with his insecurity.

Apparently the most dazzling event in Cannes after the film festival was the Duty Free Show. It had been running in the town and we had seen the signs. It was a trade show therefore no to Johnny Public but, "Hello and what can I get you?" for Mr. Duty Free Shop Buyer. Firms that supplied the tax-free sector were nearly always associated with luxury or indulgence or down right bad for you products. Watches, perfume, booze and tobacco all fitted neatly into the pigeonhole and it was those corporate coffers (or coughers in the case of the tobacco boys) that paid for the extravagance that was the weeklong jamboree of buying and selling.

The more up-market exhibitors at trade shows would charter a yacht for the week. It would be moored along side the convention centre in Cannes, a floating board room, come show room, come hospitality tent, come hotel for the reps. One such was the motor yacht Perle. Its owners Andy and Anne Baillie invited us on board after their show charter guests had departed.

Yachts, big ones, conjured up a picture of affluence and gently rolling luxury with the pop of Champagne corks in the bright sunshine, shaded, of course, on the aft deck and waited upon hand and foot by staff that think the recipients were heaven sent. The people that had chartered the Perle were actually in the scent business, but probably not from heaven. Their brands were apparently big in the East and not the sort of thing found at Kennedy or Heathrow and having smelt the lingering brew I could understand why. It must have been a very specialist market or maybe they had created a unique and combined product that made its user smell reasonable at the same time as keeping the flies off their camel.

To hire Andy's yacht for a week would cost twenty thousand pounds with all food and drink on top. For that sort of weekly rental the client could come aboard with five or six people and stay alongside the Cannes Film festival or the Monaco Grand Prix. Less prestigious events cost less. If the thing was used for what it was originally built in Italy for, namely cruising, then twenty one thousand dollars would get a week in the Med. Further costs of 700 francs an hour would be added for the fuel needed to drive the two 650 horsepower engines. It had got its own tender behind from which water skiing was possible or if preferred, the on deck crane could lower the jet ski into the water for a different bit of wet fun. If there was a warm Riviera breeze then maybe a spot of windsurfing could be arranged on the Perle's windsurfing boards.

As working owners Andy and Anne made sure that their clients were really well looked after. They were in their first season and they were keen to make the business work well. It was very hard work and Anne did all the cooking in the galley, which was very nearly the smallest room on the boat.

The previous week she had to magic up a decent four-course luncheon for eight people every day and a substantial spread in the evening as well. The five people living on board for the week were working, selling their perfume, and they brought customers or potential customers back to the yacht to be entertained, which was yet another job for Anne and her antipodean helper who worked on the Perle for six months of the year.

Andy was Royal Navy trained and had been "on" yachts for twenty years, the biggest being 150 feet with a crew of 13. He bought the Perle from someone he knew, who had been in the charter business. Both he and Anne had said that they wouldn't get into it, but they had. Anne was a Brummie and told it as she found it. She missed Sainsburys and didn't like chartering to the French. All her old mates back home and her family, thought that she must be having a wonderful life. Well they would, wouldn't they with a yacht in the South of France? It was near the top of every lottery winners shopping list, that and the trip to Disney Land. Anne would tell a different story. Looking after her clients was a twenty-four hour a day job and as about as glamorous as being a waitress in a Little Chef and they got to go home after their shifts.

Andy wouldn't change his life. He'd worked for other owners and there was always a degree of uncertainty with the job. A yacht was one of the first toys a rich man threw out of his pram when things got tough. Crews tended to go down with their discarded vessels. The Mediterranean waters were not difficult to navigate and Andy said the main hazards to navigation were idiots with money. Apparently anyone could turn up to the boat dealer with a wedge of cash and drive off in something that could do 60 knots at the press of a lever. There was no need to pass any sort of test and of course as often as not the first provision taken aboard the new toy was booze. There were no drink driving laws and the French police were powerless anyway if a foreign flag was flying from the blunt end. Every year several people died.

The red head and I sipped our bloody Marys under Hitchcock's haughty stare in the Celebrity Bar at our hotel and then stepped out in search of seafood. There was a glass-fronted restaurant on the front overlooking the sea that seemed to have what we thought we wanted. A table for two the man asked, stating the obvious, and we sat down to enjoy a feast of another kind. A cool bottle of Sancerre was uncorked and the talk got real all too quickly.

"But I've had mine. I don't want any more."

As soon as I had said it I heard that pause, that moment of silence when neither of us knew quite what to say. Then we both spoke at once.

"If you don't want children then it's over."

"You know I'm not sure about kids at my age." The two statements collided. Their words bounced off each other and made no sense to their intended.

"It's not fair," said the red head. "You're spinning me along."

"I'm just not sure that's all." Pathetic defence. Neither of us liked the way it was going.

"But I've had mine. I don't want any more." I made the statement again without much real conviction and, despite the words meaning, delivered it in a way that left room for interpretation.

"Well you'd better let me know." She said it as though she meant it. "And soon." She sounded sad, looked on the verge of tears.

The conversation fell apart and I was left with that feeling like the onset of flu. That feeling where the head thumped and the throat got dry. I knew that once again in my life I had reached a crossroads. Many times in the past I hadn't seen the signs until I'd gone way beyond them, but there would be no excuse over the baby issue. The red head's ultimatum on the edge of the Baie de Cannes was crystal clear.

The words from my PA in pre heart attack business days come to me. Marian is her name and she has a way with words that can sum up a situation fairly succinctly. Shit or get off the pot is what she would say.

St - Tropez ⇒

The doorman at the Carlton hands me the keys to Peter with a look of relief on his face. I give him a broad smile and a tip. He gives me one back. "Get yourself four wheels sir," he says with a salute.

St -Tropez was backtracking, heading west when the Tour was generally going east. The red head and I bought some provisions, two pieces of steak and some fresh vegetables that we were going to cook beside the tent. We sat in a café across the road from the redundant yachts and sleek motor cruisers. They complained in the wind, those with masts rattled their stays at us; tink, tink, tink, the sound of wire tapping aluminium.

We found a campsite, pitched the tent and then headed off to the beach, Plage de Pampelonne. There was a break in the weather. It had stopped raining. We walked for miles along the edge of the sea. Held hands. Played silly games, tried to trip each other up on the empty sand. Threw stones and bits of wood into the waves. Thought that we could smell Morocco across the sea. Neither of us wanted to think about the awkward conversation of the day before. No mention was made of it.

There was a man standing on the beach fishing. He had long grey hair tied in a pony tail and his skin looked as though he fished there a lot. Not just in October. He was naked except for the sandals. His skin wrinkled like a walnut. He held his rod in his hand while his tackle dangled towards the damp sand. He didn't seem to notice us, kept looking out to sea. We walked around him, took a wider birth than we would have done with a clothed fisherman. Didn't ask him if he'd caught anything.

It started to rain again before we were off the beach. We returned to the tent and looked at each other. We were damp and it was pouring. We didn't want to cook outside. Peter took us inland to Gassin where we found a little bistro and had someone else cook us supper in the warm and dry. Heavy condensation on the windows though.

Peter's passenger door has been forced open and the basket the red head left sitting on the bench seat has gone. The thief has got himself a new basket with a plastic bag containing two pieces of raw meat and some local vegetables.

Antibes. ⇌

The Mas Djoliba Hotel gives us more comfortable lodgings than the tent. As the song goes, "Out side it's raining, inside it's wet."

Not far from where Pablo Picasso used to paint some of his pictures was an English bookshop. Had he stepped out side of the Chateau Grimaldi to flick his brushes dry, he may well have unwittingly created a masterpiece right on their front door. Behind it, Heidi Lee had created her own masterpiece with English language books. The place felt like a library and several browsers were sitting down reading. They were engrossed, well on their way into chapter four of something they were still not sure about buying.

Heidi used to be a professional actress in Australia and the thespian in her still performed when there was an audience. In the '80's Heidi and her husband Brian visited Antibes from Manchester. Heidi refused to get back on the plane and threw a tantrum on the tarmac until her husband, then a pilot for BA, agreed that they would move to France. The Antibes bug had bitten. They moved and Brian became a business consultant and Heidi, who also used to write children's books, set up a book selling business. It was a business based in a cupboard with two shelves and a ridiculously optimistic sign outside inviting people to come in and browse. After three months it was fairly obvious that the market for English language books in Antibes was there and its size demanded more than a cupboard full. The business moved into 90 square meters and after another six months into its current home of 450 square meters which, allegedly, made it the biggest bookshop outside Paris.

Ninety eight percent of their customers were English speakers and the other two were lost or French speakers who liked to read English. They didn't have a number one best seller, as their customers were a very varied bunch. Harry Potter sold by the boat load and esoteric books, arty stuff, Margaret Atwood, Salmon Rushdie and David Hampshire's guide to living and working in France all got a mention in dispatches of best performers. Guide books and self help tomes and books for students studying at the International School in near by Sophia Antipolis, all found their way on and off Heidi's shelves.

Graham Greene used to live there and he would probably have approved. Celebrities breezed in and out of the place. Cindy Crawford can read, or at least she bought a book or two. For those on more meagre incomes than Cindy, Heidi had a big second-hand book department.

Gilli is the font of all knowledge at Hedi's bookshop. She's like a friendly buxom bar maid. Takes your money with a smile and chats.

Nice ⇥

La Perouse is in a great position right under the Chateau between the sea and the old part of town. It's a shame about the noisy road works.

Nice was France's fifth largest city and it put on a very English front. Promenade des Anglais ran between the town and the sea and it was where the old English used to stroll to take the sea air in a more genteel age. People still sauntered along the broad concourse and took in the sea air but it was a lot less leisurely. More hazardous and resembling an assault course, it was likely that a French kid on one of those small silver scooters would take us out, or we'd get roller bladed or worse still, take sudden painful delivery of a skate boarder's helmet in the groin. And that was out of season.

The voices we heard were mostly British but I didn't expect to run into one I knew by sheer chance. I hadn't seen Alex Garret for over two years. He'd left the old firm as a thrusting young sales exec to take up the fresh challenge as a snow-boarder in the French Alps. Various stories about him and his exploits had filtered back and I was looking forward to seeing him and his friends when the Plat du Jour Tour got to Chamonix. So it was with a double take that we eyeballed each other in a Thai restaurant just in front of the flower market. Of all the bars in all the world, it was one of those moments. We had an unplanned evening out in old Nice. Drank some beer and reminisced and looked forward too.

Garret had been to the Grange. I think that it had had a big influence on him. Shaped the way he thought he'd like to live one day. He'd always been interested in killing things for food. Read a lot of SAS survival books. Would disappear off into the woods around the Grange to build a shelter, make a mantrap. I'd have to check the area out after he'd gone just in case. Shepherds and woodsmen still wandered those parts.

Alexia Maulkin owned another British voice that we encountered. She was speaking in French but I could tell. She was working as a "welcomer" at a bistro in the old town. It was her job to pounce on punters as they sauntered by and maybe paused to glance at the menu for a second. If they did, like a swooping bird of prey, she'd force them to sit down as her partner in entrapment, the waiter, thrust his order pad under their nose. Before they could say "just looking thanks"; they had committed themselves to a hundred and fifty-franc meal. She was very good and "welcomed" the red head and me without any resistance from us.

She was just 19 and arrived from Poulton-le-Fylde with her friend Beth and five hundred pounds in her pocket a month before. For the first two nights they stayed in hotels and then found an apartment advertised at four hundred pounds a month, which they got for three hundred on a short rental through a friendly estate agent. The small flat was fully kited out including the obligatory thin nylon duvet, which wouldn't keep them warm but would provide enough static light at night to help them save on electricity.

Next Lex and Beth needed to find work so they trawled the many pubs and bars of Nice looking for jobs. A close encounter with a pimp nearly got them into the oldest profession in the world. They rumbled the bar room interview when their potential employer asked if they minded working naked. She got the job as a welcomer, got to keep her kit on and took home seven hundred pounds a month plus weekly tips and two meals a day. Her hours were 9 to 2.30 and 6 until 11.30 for six days a week and she loved it. She travelled everywhere on her roller blades and played the hours she didn't work. English guys, she said, were afraid of looking stupid but French boys said it and meant it.

The drug scene in Nice was not nice but she knew it was there and how to avoid it. I suspected that Lex was rather short on sleep and big into young Nice fun. The following August she was going back to the real world of Bristol or the LSE to do a degree in economics where she could snooze all she liked through those lectures. Catch up on the sleep.

The red head and I went to the Negresco to rendezvous with a character who looked a bit like Mr Magoo. He was the news hunter and gatherer for the Riviera Reporter, an English language magazine that emerged every two months.

Patrick Middleton was 64 and had been resident in France for 27 years. He and a friend started their ex-pat newsmagazine in 1985 and had allegedly built up a readership of 35,000 with sixty percent being ex-pats. The Riviera Reporter had a fairly sharp tone to it. It was serious because it wasn't fun being bland, said Patrick. It certainly didn't kow-tow to the French. It had a go at corrupt or incompetent mayors, local dishonest taxi drivers, the police, Prince Rainier, local radio, Jose Bove (the French dairy farmer who was leading the protest against globalisation) and even Niece's sea gulls. All came in for critical broadsides in the October/November issue I was given.

When I talked to Patrick, who was the main mouthpiece of the Riviera Reporter, I could understand why he wrote the way he did. He just didn't like the French.

"They're mean," he said very quickly talking like Patrick Moore, the Sky at Night man. "If they do you a favour, a bill will come in eventually." Patrick judged the French meanness in the texture of everyday social life against the generosity of the Americans or Australians. But to use the Australians as a benchmark was way off beam. Your average Aussie was as generous as a fruit machine stuck on maximum payout. He also found the French lacking in humour. Patrick was Irish. He quoted the case back in 1985 when Nice was covered in the sort of snow that allowed skiing on the beaches. Patrick was not a driver, hence his greater reliance on taxis and his loathing for them, and he had walked to the university technical college where he lectured. No one was there because of the snowfall. The note he left on the door didn't make the French laugh. "Now I understand why France has never won its wars," it read.

Patrick Middleton was also Amanda Segrave, Jill Penton-Browne, Dr. Walt Ambruster (a retired American doctor with an Oregon license that was not valid in France), Alice Gladwell and Phil K. Heinlein. They were his pen names. He had interviewed Peter Mayle, "A modest man who liked to lunch and who's bored". France's first British mayor, "A Yorkshire man and they don't undersell themselves" and the aristocratic French woman, who lived full time in Nice airport, "You see people flying these days who'd never have flown when I was a girl".

The Middleton career brought him to Nice from Ireland via Oxford University where he read English and social anthropology, to the police force and to Wormwood Scrubs as a trainee assistant governor to Poland, Brazil and Holland. He wouldn't end up like one of the ex-pats he despised. Like the couple from Worthing he described, who came down without speaking a word of French, loved the weather in the Summer until it turned a tad cold and who lived in a world of digital TV and each other's increasingly boring company. Patrick thought that he'd end up in Australia but he better be careful. The one thing the Aussies actually weren't generous about was the whinging Pom or Paddy.

The Hotel Negresco looked like a giant doll's house with a dome on top. The flunkey on the door wore a uniform with a hat and plume that foretold of the grandeur inside. Ornate ceilings and oils with a vast chandelier, its twin apparently hung in the Kremlin.

The red head and I take more tea and then walk the sea front back to our less elaborate hotel, and the pneumatic drill ripping into the Quai Rauba Capeu. Our time together on the Riviera is ticking away. The minutes being eaten up like the asphalt.

St Jean - Cap - Ferrat

My eldest sister knows Basil. I think they met in Hong Kong.

Just around the corner from Nice was St Jean-Cap-Ferrat. Like an epiglottis, on the map it dangled off the coast between Nice and Monte-Carlo. Stuck out ever so slightly into the Mediterranean. Stuck out but not in the sore thumb sense. Everything about St Jean-Cap-Ferrat was discreet, everything behind closed security doors. But once through them, once admitted, the seats with unrestricted views allowed the fortunate the Riviera experience, an exclusive show for the very privileged.

Basil Sellers had lived in David Niven's home for seven years. Or so I'd been told. Franco greeted us, let us in electronically through the metal gates once we had been identified, Peter, the red head and me. Franco and his wife Bianca had come with the property and lived in a cottage in the grounds. They'd been there for thirty years. Franco looked after the place, was the old retainer and acted as butler. Bianca was the cook. They had been there for David Niven, could tell a real tale or two. Their own discretion was what kept them there however. Franco regarded Peter with interest. Smiled. They shared the same nationality. Franco used to ride a scooter of the same make when he was a boy.

Basil appeared and took us to the pool where Franco poured the vintage champagne. Basil spoke Australian and looked like he'd been in the sun too much when he was a boy. He wore dark colours. He had that aura that came with years of success, the ring of confidence that highlighted life's winners. We sat and introduced ourselves in the warm October sunshine. Small talk, big view. Italy off in the distance, Monaco just a water-ski away. The private beach below us, a banana in the blue. Claire, Basil's wife, joined us. She looked like a former Miss Australia should, elegant by the pool in trousers and a knitted top. Not a sign of any Speedo swimwear that had made her husband some of his money. We became happily giddy with the surroundings and the fizz.

Basil Sellers had always been a high flyer but never more so than when he visited Thunder City in Cape Town to be launched in a lightening fighter to eleven miles above the earth at over twice the speed of sound. It was only in South Africa or Moscow that big toys such as those could be played with legally by big boys such as Basil. After lunch he showed us the video of his latest adrenaline rush over Africa. His head bobbed about in its helmet as the curve of the Earth went from ear to ear like an upside down smile.

Basil didn't need to impress us but he did anyway. The red head told him that she was a cricket fan. He showed us the cricket memorabilia that he had collected. His brother had played for Australia but Basil had the bat hanging on his study wall, the sacred piece of willow signed by Don Bradman and Harold Larwood. He knew I liked wine so an inspection of his cellar was next. There were ranks of red and white nectar and I held a bottle of 1917 Chateau La Tour without dropping it. On our way down to look at the drink, we brushed past two Picassos. The red head recognised them. Basil was a serious collector.

The Sellers spent as much time as they could at their beautiful home. They had others in the world, but this was their favourite. Their neighbours were Monsieur Givenchy, Lords Saatchi and Lloyd-Webber. It was no wonder that the well heeled wanted to drop their anchors and rest awhile on Cap Ferrat. Years before it had been the Moors who used to drop theirs and invade the place. The most important resident then, a monk called Hospice, used to look after the dying. He was saved from having his head lopped off by a miracle. Hospice became a saint and his name became firmly etched into our language.

We leave, not envious, but rather understanding that the trappings of success have to be earned. No man is an island but those with money can live on a beautiful peninsular.

Monaco

Being in Monaco is a bit like being in a virtual reality game of Monopoly without the Old Kent Road, Whitechapel or anywhere else that doesn't raise a four figure rent with a hotel on it. It's about the same size as the game board. It boasts silver racing cars, top hats and dogs just like the game pieces for Monopoly. It even has a jail but I'm not sure about the Community Chest.

Actually the tax-free kingdom had virtually no reality at all except one, and that was money. Queen Victoria used to go through with the blinds drawn down because she thought it was satanic. If motor racing, gambling, looking after and laundering cash were satanic activities, then the old Queen was right. The climate was as demanding as the taxman, that's why many of the cars went topless and there were more motor scooters buzzing around than Prince Rainier's daughters had had lovers. The police nearly all wore white gloves presumably so they didn't leave any embarrassing fingerprints. There were legions of them but they all looked like cool commissionaires rather than law enforcers.

The casinos were full of people trying to look cool while losing their shirts because for every winner there must be hundreds who played just to feed the coffers. We watched two Italians, him with the chips and her with the pen and notebook and dark glasses. They were presumably trying to work out a system to beat the roulette wheel and every so often the woman with the pad would indicate to her man that the time was right to place that bet. They lost all their chips and went off to discuss tactics and presumably revise them. I guessed the casino liked nothing better than a gambler with "a system".

My system was simply not to do it, but the casino still won because the red head and I had to pay to get in. The days of dinner jackets only and James Bond types with sultry bejewelled beauties pouting at the pile of chips had gone. I did see one or two smarty-pants but the really smart money was earned or inherited, rarely won. The buildings and rooms in which all that money moved from one heap to another were more in keeping with highbrow cultural activities or religion. I supposed to those that prayed at the altar of lady luck, going to the casino was like visiting church. Instead of God looking down from on high, the security cameras had a peek from the vaulted Rococo ceiling. When the painted nude had just winked, it was best to smile back because filming was in progress.

If Monaco was a Monopoly board then the flashiest bits in Monte Carlo were the casino, opera house and Hotel de Paris (Mayfair) with L'Hermitage tucked just behind them (Park Lane).

In Monaco's new bit, Fontvieille, built on reclaimed land, there was an English pub called The Ship and Castle. Its owner was John Haly and he and his wife Annie, from Brittany, had been running the local there for twelve years. When the red head and I went into the bar to meet him, John was on the phone organising fresh supplies of Cheddar cheese, gammon and Branston pickle. Before The Ship and Castle, John ran pubs in Bristol for twenty-six years so he knew his trade. The main difference between a pub in Monaco and one in Bristol was that in Monaco there were few regulars. In Bristol, the pub was a social club that coincidentally catered for thirst. The Ship and Castle was somewhere to go because of thirst and food was important too. Coffee was drunk every bit as much as a small beer. There were no pints or shove halfpenny boards, dartboards or details of the next quiz night. There was always the resident drunk though. The Ship and Castle currently enjoyed a Scotsman in the role and he was charming.

The French were keen to experiment and prepared to try new drinks as they appeared. They'd sup on a tin of Guinness or Crossbow cider and then headed straight back to the Pernod or biere blonde. The British, on the other hand, wouldn't dream of wetting their lips with a hint of anything their mothers hadn't weaned them on. There was a dismissiveness of strange brews in the immortal British opening pub prayer, "A pint of the usual please". John's customers were half-French and half something else. His clients reflected the Monaco mix. Inside the pub, at the bar, I could have been in any Ship and Castle, King's Head, Talbot or any other town pub in Britain. It was not distressed enough to be a country inn. All the fixtures and fittings, including the old red telephone kiosk, came over from England. John had four staff but more in the summer when the seating and eating outside really took off. It overlooked the new harbour and "the rock" opposite, on top of which sat the old bit of Monaco, Prince Rainier and the old town.

On Friday it was fish, chips and mushy peas on the menu. Even though the chips were French fries, the fish in its batter was lovely, the best I'd had outside England and generously on the house, which always added a certain hint of extra flavour. The red head agreed. Thick and tasty. She liked her batter like she liked her men, so she joked.

From batter to battery and Peter's was as flat as a skate when I tried to start him up after our lunch. The red head had to leave me. Peter's battery trouble meant that I couldn't run her back to the airport. The red head had to get back to Nice and her plane home to England. I felt as flat as Peter's battery as I kissed her farewell. She boarded a coach. I hated saying goodbye. Didn't want her to leave but didn't make a fuss about it. I couldn't stand those lingering departures. Just a short "See you soon" would more than do for me. It wouldn't express what I really thought. I couldn't do that. She made me promise I'd go home for Christmas. Waving goodbye to someone I loved was one of the hardest things. Especially when I didn't know when we would meet again. I'd done it with my children. Waved them goodbye to America and Australia not knowing if I'd ever see them again. That was not much fun. It was important to say farewell with a happy face though. It was always good to go up to bed with a smile, just in case you didn't ever wake up again. I tried to do that most nights. Couldn't that night though. I missed her awfully but hadn't resolved what to do about it.

The man in Monaco with a Piaggio not unlike Peter was Joe-Bill Bartling. The next day he rode into sight like the 7th cavalry. Joe-Bill looked and talked like a much younger version of Colonel Saunders, him of Kentucky Fried Chicken fame. Of the 4,000 natives (Monegasque) and 27,000 others in Monaco, Joe-Bill seemed to know about 29,000 of them. Joe-Bill was exactly like a horse trooper with his blue jeans, T-shirt and braces. He even chewed tobacco. He'd left his horse back in Fort Laramie and used a Vespa to get around Monaco's canyons. He'd been there for thirty years so he knew everything there was to know.

Like John, the landlord, he didn't own his home there but rented. A modest two-bedroom apartment in Monaco would cost as much as a decent flat in nearly fashionable London. Six to eight hundred thousand pounds was what was needed and unless you were a successful racing driver or other tax exile, renting was on and buying was off. Property prices had been pretty static in Monaco for the last decade, so the likes of Joe-Bill were quite happy to rent from the likes of Coulthard or Costa (him of the coffee) who had bought. Joe-Bill trained as a pilot in the U.S. air force and just finished at about the time the pin was being pulled on the Vietnam War. Like all good Americans, Joe-Bill spoke in a language that told me he used to fly fixed wing. I understood that. The 150's, 172's, 310's were all a mystery. So were Moonies who I thought were a sect and Aztecs, big in Peru once. Joe-Bill's Dad was a pilot for T.W.A. so the take off and landing thing were in his blood. He came to France and worked near Paris and in Cannes, on the boats, before starting a clothing boutique up on "the rock" in Monaco in 1972.

His interest in woodcarving and silkscreen printing got him into printed T-shirts and JB's were Monaco's biggest and busiest T-shirt wholesalers. His premises were spread out like a rabbit warren around Monaco and he sold all over France and in Italy. The point of difference was that he could personalise the design for his customers and they didn't have to order a shed load to get what they wanted. In Monaco he could normally design, print and deliver within 48 hours and putting his money where his mouth was, JB's came up with some shirts for the Plat du Jour Tour, no charge, which was very kind. He had done the Grand Prix T-shirt for 29 years but next time Mr. Ecclestone apparently wanted a slice of the action by way of a royalty. JB products were designed for the Hotel Negresco, Grand Hotel Cap Ferrat and the Royal Monaco Yacht Club. There was also a range of cute pussycats for the bucket and spade fraternity.

Joe-Bill and his Danish wife Henry (short for Henrietta) and their two daughters were really friendly. I ate with them at their home, rode on their motor scooters, and went on a Sunday morning bike ride with them as they showed me around. I saw the new convention centre, the tranquil and very orderly Japanese gardens, the sporting club and at the Cap d'Ail end, where Beaverbrook had his pad and the walk Winston Churchill used to take when he stayed there.

Joe-Bill introduced me to his friends and the three-wheel Piaggio that he used to cart T-shirts around Monaco, his Vespa scooter, his electric motor scooter, his 1000cc Russian motorbike and sidecar and his Piaggio dealer. Sadly his Piaggio dealer was just like all the others I'd seen on the tour so far.

Joe-Bill Bartling was like the free parking square on the Monopoly board when all around people were shouting, "Rent!" He was a rare breed in Monaco and a good guy to run into.

I thought I could grow to like Monaco and anywhere that had sunshine in Winter, the seaside, was income tax free with virtually no crime, no beggars and had a really good heart hospital couldn't be all bad. But if I had to live there all the time, I would go mad. I'd need a place to escape in order to top up on sanity.

I sat at a harbour side café for a cup of tea for one. It was a cup of hot water with a tea bag on the side. I was feeling sorry for myself. Lonely as the tea bag. An old guy with a heavy gold chain around his open neck, its links mingling with his climbing grey chest hairs, sat at the next table. He looked like Charlie Drake, the dead comedian. A mature woman who obviously enjoyed more money than taste soon joined him. The conversation between the two was unreal, Monaco speak.

C. Drake look-a-like. "It always has a dust jacket over it in the garage but I keep a feather duster in the boot."

Mature woman. "The automatic doings that work the awning on my balcony have packed up, so I'm in the dark until the man comes."

C. Drake look-a-like. "Midnight blue with a cream upholstery is so Rolls-Royce but leather gets very warm with the roof down."

Mature woman. "The Brazilians have arrived because the motor racing season has finished and I'm out every night. I'm at my wits end. "

C. Drake look-a-like. "I got her a mini convertible but she won't go out in it and she's got five or six mobiles because she leaves them all over town. " And so on and so on. The dear couple that was sharing the tea and conversation would have seen absolutely nothing wrong with what they were talking about and in the context of Monaco there was nothing wrong. Before they parted company they spent about five minutes arguing over whose turn it was to pay for the tea, all of two pounds, because neither of them wanted to, which was infuriating or sweet depending on the point of view. I'm sure if I had lent over and offered to pay the bill for them, they would have accepted.

Someone else I met in Monaco who I was delighted to share a cup of tea with, was Liana Burgess. She was married to Anthony Burgess for 30 years and missed him lots. She told me that in 1968 they had left Chiswick in London, where they lived and had set off for Malta in a Bedford Dormobile. He used to like writing in the travelling home and she was the driver. At Avignon they had all their papers, passports and money stolen, which was a real bind in those days. I think she told me that because she knew I was travelling around France. She was quite envious as well. She was quite difficult to understand, spoke quickly with an Italian accent and a mind that either wandered, or was so quick, it jumped on ahead.

The Burgesses moved to Monaco in 1975 because Anthony had been in Malaya for eight years previously as an education officer and after the tropics it was sensible to find a base with a climate that wouldn't jar. Liana Burgess didn't like the Riviera and thought that the French were "Schoolmarmish". They were too quick to scold. Brought up on the Adriatic, she'd always loved travelling and had fallen in love with cities the world over. The last was Krakow. She would never fall in love again. She said it very sadly. Age and arthritis were both being cruel to her. I wanted to hug her.

She met her husband in London when she was a freelance translator and she had already admired his work. Anthony Burgess was a musician before he was a writer but he became a celebrity because of his writing. Her personal favourite work was Enderby, ("Maybe I was his dark lady") and she said her husband was his most creative when he was given one year to live in 1959. He produced five or six books then including Clockwork Orange. Liana read it in 1960 and thought it a good book. She didn't read the one that was commissioned but never published, History of London. I asked her why it was never put into print and she talked about "they" in terms of "they" didn't like what Anthony was going to say about "them".

The Anthony Burgess Society and the friends of AB had been set up to promote all aspects of his creative legacy. His writing and art, his music and work in the cinema. The society worked with the University of Angers, where his library was, but would organise other cultural events. The society published a newsletter twice a year and under its president Jean-Jacques Annaud, had attracted several honorary members including A.S. Byatt, Seamus Heaney, Malcom McDowell, Martin Scorsese and Gore Vidal.

"Would you like to join?" asked Liana. I joined up for a hundred francs because I liked her, because he liked France and because I'd like to know more about the man who wrote Clockwork Orange.

It would be difficult to forget the Principalities best hamburger joint too. Both the Princes had been to Kate Power's establishment in Monaco, but then anybody who was anybody would do. Like Joe-Bill, Kate talked with an American accent but she didn't chew tobacco or, as far as I could see, wear braces or suspenders, as they liked to call them. When I met her at her business, Stars'n' Bars, it was a bit like meeting one of the more glamorous actresses from that TV show, Dallas. She was pretty, blonde and smiled a lot. She was also pretty clued up.

Kate grew up in Monaco, as her stepfather was a symphony conductor from St Louis who worked in Europe. Aged sixteen they moved to London, which was just like life in the fast lane after Monaco's small town pace. The Lycee in Paris gave Kate more education and then she moved to Switzerland and then on to her family in Houston. In Texas they ran the Texas Land and Cattle Company that, despite the name, was in the restaurant business. Twelve years previously her mother moved back to Monaco and opened a Tex Mex restaurant and Stars'n' Bars followed soon after with Kate at its helm. Kate thought that the Americans were "real picky" about their American food, (easy over, sunny side up, backside down, that sort of thing) where as the French didn't understand American food. They tended to think of it as just hamburgers. Kate was trying to persuade the locals that spare ribs and barbecue sauce were every bit as edible and tasty as frogs legs and garlic. Kate confirmed the view that each tended to stick to their own, so even though they would all have a try, they couldn't wait to get back to the fodder they knew.

Stars'n' Bars customers came from a wide cross section, the guy who swept the street to the UBS president, from Prince (the artist formerly known as) to the Prince of Monaco (still known as). Kate was proud that her place was a family style restaurant. They had a supervised children's room with lots of play things and a games arcade which kept the kids from nagging, "Is it time to go yet?" A clever way to keep the parents eating, drinking and spending. It was mainly steaks, burgers and ribs that sold and on a busy summer's day the restaurant could do twelve hundred covers. The meat was French although Kate was working on getting some in from Argentina. Sadly none from Britain. Sixty-five francs would buy a hamburger and they opened from 11am until midnight for food. The nightclub stayed open till 5 in the morning. In the summer the bars opened until 2ish and the music stopped at 6, just in time for breakfast. During the Grand Prix week Stars'n' Bars took what it normally took in a month. Rather than the corporate boys moving in, it was the drivers who liked to book the space as a night out for their teams. The paddocks were right outside the front door taking 250 valuable spaces away but giving even more valuable customers for the week.

Inside the décor was a mixture of rock and roll, sport and American roadhouse with just a hint of Internet café creeping in. Like Texas, it was big with tables and booths on two floors and a full size racing car hung from the roof. Kate was proud of her celebrity visitors as the photos on the wall showed. She had met them all. Prince did two private gigs in the place at his request and Stevie Wonder and Chuck Berry had their moments there as well. Kate and her boyfriend employed up to115 staff, which was nearly as scary as the Halloween bash that weekend that Stars'n'Bars had become famous for.

I pay my rent at the Hotel Helvetia, roll the dice, don't go past go, don't collect two hundred pounds and make my way back along the coast to Nice. I am not the silver racing car or the dog or the slipper. Not even the top hat. I'm the little blue three wheeler once again.

Corse ⇌

I am getting on to the ferry in Nice and my mobile rings. It's my mother telling me that my ex-wife is leaving England for Australia.
"Isn't there anything you can do to stop her?" says mother as though we were still married and she was running off. There isn't. She'll be happier with her new life I hope.

Peter and I took the ferry from Nice on impulse really. One minute I was contemplating a salad du jour in a port side cafe listening to a rendition of "Midnight train to Georgia" and the next I was on the ten o'clock bateau to Bastia. Corsica was an overnight sail away from Nice.

I drove aboard in the absurd vehicle; concerned at one stage that Peter's three-wheel configuration wouldn't get up the ramps into the bowels of the ferry. Worried that one thin wheel might slip through the gap over the dark salt water below. It didn't. Everything around him was enormous. He looked like a toy dwarfed by the trucks sharing the crossing. I took out an overnight bag and went up to find the small cabin. It was claustrophobic with bunk beds and no window. I went to bed, climbed into the top berth. I felt really sad. Maybe it was the news from my mother. Somehow the real end of an era. I felt alone. The boat got underway and I was rocked to half sleep by the deep drone of the engine, the turning of the screw and the sea's swell. The cabin door opened and stark electric light wedged in from the metal passageway. Someone came in, a man, and he smelt of strong drink. He shuffled about in the dark. Got into the bunk beneath me, gruff and full of moaning complaint. We didn't say a word to each other. I pretended that I wasn't there. He had been just a shape, a featureless shadow crawling into my night. I tried to sleep with his vile body under mine, only inches away. Was it, I wondered, just like that for my ex-wife in the end?

It was French, although when I got there I could have been mistaken for thinking that I was in Italy or indeed Corsica. The graffiti and bullet holes tried to persuade me towards the Corsican vote, the language was French and the driving Italian. It seemed that the locals, their numberplates 2B or not 2B (actually 2A), liked to drive white vans. Car sized things, not transit jobs, they all seemed to be white. Whether this was because the hot sun made other colours too unbearable or whether Messieurs Citroen, Peugeot and Fiat had decided that all their white production should go to Corsica, I didn't know.

One of the problems with overnight ferries was that they tended to arrive while it was still night and Bastia at 6am wasn't quite awake. Peter and I trundled off the good ship "Sardinia Queen" and drove in triumph through a stirring Bastia and out into the hills. My preconception of Corsica included at least a handful of bandits and hot sunshine. I was disappointed on both counts, not one highway robber, other than the petrol stations on the way out of town, and it looked like rain was immanent. We made our slow way to St Florent and then on to Calvi. The countryside could have been Scottish or Welsh other than what was growing and the occasional glimpse of the Mediterranean.

There was that dreadful old joke about the chap who was on board HMS Victory being shown around and he tripped over a metal plate screwed to the deck with the words "Nelson fell here". "No wonder," he said to his guide. "Tripped over the damn thing myself." I couldn't find any reference in Calvi to Nelson or his eye, which he lost there in the 1750's whilst trying to dislodge the French. There was plenty of fuss about Christopher Columbus though, who was apparently born there in 1469. His house was a pile of rubble overlooked by a modern block in the old citadel. The centre of the citadel still had a real working fort full of Beau Jest look a likes. It was a home to the Foreign Legion and I moved on rather quickly.

Where Corsica got stunning was between Calvi and Porto. The landscape became even more dramatic than the Highlands of Scotland with steep slopes covered in lush green maquis, the local name for the thick bush or scrub. Where the rock had burst through, nothing grew. If I glanced over my right shoulder, the sea was below, foaming at the cliffs and rocks or rolling up the secluded sandy bays. The road clung to its coastal route like a mummy's boy on the first ever day of school. It was not worth thinking about the frailty of the edges or what might happen if we inadvertently veered off Corse. But we didn't and Peter and I followed the roller coastal route through the wind and rain and just marvelled that any road could be part of such spectacular scenery. The rocks in some places looked as though they had been worked on by a stone mason or sculptor, rather than nature's hammer and chisel. The November rain belied the dryness of the countryside. There was plenty of evidence of summer's cruel barbecue and black stumps and charred branches lay twisted and charcoal grey on the slopes like sooty black finger prints after the arsonist's crime. But the green, the lush green of the maquis would always win and like some sci-fi fungus or Triffid, it would spread its counterpane to smother the after effects of the fire that tried to destroy it.

In Porto, I spent the night at one of the few hotels open. I had the hotel and nearly the whole, single street, seaside village to myself. Out of season and in the driving rain Porto could have been any number of small British resorts enjoying a British summer. Its charm and its very pretty seaside with old Genoese tower must have helped to make Mr Kodak a wealthy man. In the summer I could imagine the Pizza Parlour and knick-knack kiosk doing a roaring trade. I liked Porto in November.

From Porto to Piana the coastal run continued to be breathtaking and the rock formations took up their poses as men wearing monocles, dog's heads or just as dramatic arches through which the little road cut its twisted way.

Ajaccio, the island's capital, arrived in the rain after more miles of Scottish or Welsh proportions with goats grazing in the bandit-free countryside and quite often, on the road itself.

Edward Lear visited Ajaccio in the rain and proclaimed the place to be dull. I think Lear was writing nonsense. I spent a pleasant, wet afternoon exploring. I confirmed that Napoleon Bonaparte was vertically challenged because I saw the bed he slept in. It was like a matchbox. He was born in Ajaccio in 1769 and after his French military training in Paris, returned to the family home there until 1793 when their rivals saw off the Bonapartes. He returned briefly in 1799 but there was no love lost between the Emperor and Corsica and vice versa. For the town that fathered the father of modern day France, there wasn't a great show of "Gosh look who we spawned." Spawned and spurned.

Another bit that I was surprised didn't catch Mr Lear as interesting was the little library next to the Musee Fesch, itself no dullard. I came off the hustle and wet bustle of a busy commercial street and almost immediately slipped back into a frock-coated era. Wall to wall, floor to ceiling, old books surrounded one long central island table where the books' contents were studied. The attendant was asked to fetch the required volume. I couldn't do it for myself there. A couple of oversized stone lions guarded the entrance hall to the place. They must have come from somewhere far grander, but they made an impressive pair of bookends.

At Ajaccio port "La Meridionale" found Peter and I a slot each to take us to Marseille, which in the event was just as well because the rigors of the route were beginning to make Peter grunt again. He was tired if that was possible.

We didn't quite make the safety of Frederick's workshop but the friendly breakdown truck man soon got us there. That was where Peter would be spending his Christmas.

I am returning by train to the mountains and the Grange.

Twickenham, Middlesex

"You like rugger. Yes, no?" My father was speaking his very best Franglais.

England was due to play France at Twickenham. My father, a debenture holder, had suggested that Maurice and Michel might like to fly over for the weekend and attend the game. I invited them and they accepted on the basis that I would look after them once they got to England. They had never been before.

Most men in the south west of France followed rugby football. In Maurice and Michel's case on the television slung from the ceiling next to Michel's vast open fireplace. I could just about see the picture through the billowing clouds of wood smoke. A fog of a different kind normally descended brought on by the strong drink served by Michel from the epicentre of his home, his bar. Michel's home made bar put many professional ones to shame, although the legality of much of the drink on offer was questionable. Eau-de-vie was the house tipple and just one sip made the back of the throat try to leave the body. After several, the game on the television could be anything and the outcome, well, who cared?

The appropriate weekend in the tournament arrived. I had been back in England for a few weeks. Maurice and Michel got themselves to Toulouse and on the right plane. I met them at Gatwick. The two men strolled into the arrivals lounge like a couple of big French Wombles with their berets on and black leather drinking gourds slung over their shoulders. After the hugging ceremony and the three kisses offered and taken by each of us, Michel took a twenty-pound note carefully out of his purse. He unfolded it like an old map of buried treasure. Michel waved it at me. He had been practising his arrival speech and very slowly and earnestly he said "Ear we 'av the Monet."

I drove them to Bath where I was staying with the red head. We arrived just in time for lunch at the Beaujolais restaurant just off Queen Square. The patron, J.P, himself a native of the Pyrenees, was pleased to meet and greet the two obvious French men. Lunch and some conversation they could understand lasted for most of the afternoon. Both Maurice and Michel seemed in their element. They loved the other diners in the busy restaurant and wandered off through the tables to try and chat. It was perfectly normal back home in a mountain eatery, but not in an English city on a Friday afternoon. The two bearded men were particularly delighted to run into a table of four lunching ladies, two of whom spoke good French from their days as air hostesses. For Maurice and Michel this chance encounter was like Christmas and birthday rolled into one. In the mountains a good-looking woman seemed as rare as an overcooked steak. Dragging the French men away from their new friends was not easy. I eventually got them out of town and into a little country pub in nearby Combe Hay. My friend Mike Taylor was the genial landlord. Maurice and Michel were going to spend the night at the Wheat Sheaf because the red head's flat was just not big enough for the two big visitors. That evening in the pub we enjoyed another party and Taylor's hospitality. Maurice and Michel sang songs and danced until the early hours of the morning. Taylor was keen to show the boys his cellar. They emerged clutching an old bottle of Armagnac. They pulled the cork and shared it with all of us. "No worries" said Taylor in his broad West Country way. "I'll put it on your slate, mind."

The next morning I arrived at the pub to drive Maurice and Michel to London for the big game. The only overnight guests, they were sitting at a table laden with a full English breakfast. Taylor was standing next to them looking puzzled.

"They won't eat a thing, mind," said he scratching his head. I asked the two French men what the trouble was.

"It's wine Michael," I said to the landlord. "They won't eat their breakfast without a bottle of red wine."

The Cardinal Vaughn car park at Twickenham was full buzzing with rugger buffers. The ranks of Range Rovers and shiny German cars were lined up with their boots open and the pre-match feast was well under way. We parked next to an old gentleman and his Jensen Interceptor. Already perched on his shooting stick, he was into his third gin and It. He eyed up Maurice and Michel as they clambered out of the back of my Jeep with their berets and gourds still in place and much excited French chatter. It looked like we could be from the enemy camp. Our new neighbour looked over the top of his half moon glasses, stood bolt upright like a ramrod dressed in Harris Tweed and Cavalry Twill.

"Agincourt!" he said very loudly at the two French men. "Agincourt!"

The French lost the game by a hefty margin, which put Maurice and Michel under some pressure in the car park after the final whistle. Undaunted, they were soon dancing and singing and drinking as though their nation had been victorious. Their gourds held a litre and a half of dubious alcohol each. They were offered to any one game enough to have a go. The flamboyant style and flourish needed to drink from a tanned sheep's stomach often left the inexperienced drinker soaked. The two French men continued to make new friends until their supplies ran dry and the car park started to empty.

Father had arranged a dinner that evening at a bar and restaurant in town run by a friend of his. There was a smart table of twenty or so French men from Paris who were drowning their sorrows. Maurice and Michel were not going to be out done by those fellows in their blazers, club ties and straw boaters. The two mountain men entertained all of us and even the taxi driver with their drunken strange mountain songs as we drove back to Whitehall and the Farmer's Club for the night.

Father had a bad night. He'd overdone things during the day and his heart didn't like it. In the room the two of us shared, he slept badly, groaned much and swore. In the very early hours he fell out of his single bed and crashed to the floor with a "Bloody hell!" I got him back up and made him a cup of tea.

"Life saver," he said with his thin hands shaking around the green china teacup. He managed to sip some of it.

Father's club, and mine, had a strict dress code. Even at weekends guests were expected to dress "appropriately". The sight of the two French men arriving in the member's dinning room on Sunday morning for breakfast still dressed in their berets and jeans and French rugger shirts gave the Irish steward a headache. Father put a brave face on for breakfast. He looked very unwell and the two French men looked as concerned as the steward did. Father got up from the table and disappeared to find the secretary. He re-emerged with two club ties, which he presented to Maurice and Michel. They immediately put the ties around their open necks, and enjoyed their breakfast and a bottle of Farmer's Club good ordinary claret. Father's concern for his guests welfare rather than his own discomfort was typical.

After Sunday's breakfast I returned them to Gatwick and their flight back to France. With berets, gourds and Farmer's Club ties, the two men said their farewells. Michel once again produced his neatly folded twenty-pound note. "'Ear we 'av the Monet" he said once more, but I wanted him to keep it. The weekend had cost a small fortune for Father and I but what pleasure we had had. The next time I saw Michel's bar, there was the tie my father had given to him, hanging in pride of place amongst all the other memorabilia and lethal cocktails that the wood smoke and mountain dust had made their own.

"They were in good order," father says as we go over the experience once more. Better order than he is in. I return to France with some reluctance.

Back To Marseille ⟹

The bastards have stolen stuff from Peter. Forced the back open, jemmied one of the tin trunks and nicked some clothes.

Even though I telephoned Frederick in Marseille on many occasions to check on Peter's progress, it wasn't until the end of February that he sounded as though the work had been done. A lot could happen in four months. A sow could conceive and farrow. I had replenished the woodpile at the Grange, performed some more logging antics with Butler. Did some skiing and some time at Eric's. Went over to England to the red head. Had Christmas and the New Year celebrations with her. We skirted around the big issue. In fact no mention was made of the red head's hankering for children. We got along famously and she understood that I had to get on with the Tour. Father was unwell and in hospital, then a nursing home. He wouldn't be going to any more rugby matches that season.

I was nearly on the road again. It started with a drive to Tarbes; six hours in a train and a taxi ride to get me to where I left Peter in Marseille four months previously. After four months I had forgotten how small Peter was. How ridiculous my quest to circumnavigate France in him. He stood in Frederick's yard next to a pile of scrapped motor scooters and bald rubber tyres. He looked neglected and unloved. Frederick looked embarrassed. He told me that Peter had been broken into. A local gang of young hoods had scaled the wall of the compound undeterred by the security, several signs depicting an Alsatian dog with rabies and some strands of barbed wire. There was little point in talking to the Gendarmes about it, but if I'd had the time, I could have caught the culprits. It wouldn't have bee difficult. I'd look out for someone wearing an old Saville Row tailored dinner jacket with a brown leather flying helmet and a heavy tweed shooting jacket, black lace up Church brogues and a slightly soiled G&H dress shirt. They had also nicked my chauffeur's hat, head torch and presumably other bits and pieces that I wouldn't know about until I wondered where they'd gone. I had half expected the violation of Peter in that part of Marseille, but it was still a shock when it happened. I never expected to win the lottery but I still bought a ticket occasionally.

Frederick had done his job on the engine and had fitted another new piston, a new cylinder head and had done some work on the gearbox. The bill was three thousand francs which added to the list, could turn out to prove that Peter was the most expensive set of three wheels ever to be kept going on French roads. Having paid and tipped Frederick, Peter and I spluttered out through the old wooden non-vandal proof gates and into the back street. We both felt uncertain. I was rusty but we managed to go rather well for about twenty yards and then stopped. The gears didn't really want to obey the gear stick and even though the lever pointed to first, second and even third, the result was never gold, silver or bronze. Frederick, who moments before had been wishing me "Bon courageux" and "Bonne route", had to push Peter back through the gates with " Desole" the new key word. He had un morceau d'oeuf sur son visage but assured me that it was " Pas grave" and that all would be well in the morning.

I booked into an Ibis Hotel in town, not of course the nearest one to Fred's yard. That was full and it would have been far too easy. It wasn't the best of restarts for the Tour. It could have been worse. The over-the-wall gang could have torched Peter or the gears could have "gone" several miles further away from Frederick's attention. It wasn't the cheapest of days either. The train fare was three hundred and sixty francs, Peter's repairs three thousand four hundred, taxis two hundred and fifty, hotel four hundred and a meal a hundred plus Frederick's premature tip. A total of four hundred and fifty quid. Cracking value.

That's so far. Well it is only nine p.m. and who knows what other bills will roll in before the clock strikes twelve.

Arles And The Camargue ⇌

The flat lands of the Rhone estuary are wonderful for Peter's performance. Reassuring for me.

The station clock at Arles said 1540 when Peter and I drove past. It was 1888 when Van Gogh first stepped off the train there. He arrived in February of that year and proceeded to paint the town red and other hues creating his legendary impression. He was like many a genius before and since. He put candles on his hat in order to see where he was going and cut his ear off.

Had Vincent pitched his tent at La Bienheureuse for the night, I could have understood why in the morning he might have emerged from under his canvas minus an ear. The site was the epicentre for all sorts of noisy transport with railway lines, major roads and flight paths all cunningly concealed just behind the caravan next door. Still 39 francs for the night wasn't an arm and a leg and the shower was as good as any I'd stood under.

Arles was fine as a town to take out an easel. I couldn't get overexcited about the Roman arena, having seen my first in Nimes. Your first Roman arena was like your first proper kiss and you didn't forget it, even though it might have been a bit clumsy in parts.

It wasn't until I got down into the Camargue that I stopped wondering why Arles was twinned with Wisbech back in 1964. The market town in Cambridgeshire wasn't renowned for its Roman ruins or mad artists. It did have a river running through, the Nene not the Rhone. What they both had in common was their surroundings. Wisbech the Fens, Arles the Camargue. It was the sky I could see most when the land was flat and the sky above the Camargue on that March day was as blue and clear as any I'd ever seen. Grey horses, some looked white, and flamingos gave the place the look of an exotic safari park. The scrubby marshland seemed uncertain as to whether it should be land or sea. There was more vegetation and more trees than in the Fens but the agriculture was less crop intensive and more about horses, bulls and birds with reeds, rice and a pinch of salt probably all taking second place to the great annual cash crop, tourism.

The seaside resort of Les Saintes-Maries-de-la-Mer traded on its position and had the look of a Spanish settlement. I took a plat du jour of spaghetti and moules just to add further geographical confusion. In a couple of months the gypsy pilgrims would arrive to see their Saints processed from their church to the sea, from where they had originally come. The annual ritual was apparently the little town's equivalent of the Cannes film festival. Preparations were underway with some serious roadworks and refurbishment around the Saintes Maries themselves in their old church.

There's a man wearing a Fedora astride a prancing horse rounding up a bull on a small traffic roundabout on the front at Les Saintes-Maries-de-la-Mer.

Montpellier And L'Herault ⇒

Don't sit it out, dance.

Montpellier was a bright city. It was sparky and would take my vote for the best attempt I'd seen so far in France at mixing old with new. It had got trams that looked like matchbox TGV's and a traffic-free centre that put people on the move. There was plenty of youth about with most of them busy not doing begging or graffiti and quite a lot of them studying to be doctors. The old Opera House sat without any embarrassment opposite the new Le Triangle with the new Le Polygone waiting just behind. There was some criticism that the centre was becoming too depopulated, too open, but then not so long ago the old part was slated for being too claustrophobic.

It was a city where Monsieur Cartier set out his stall selling twenty-four carets for tens of thousands of francs not far from Monsieur Bartier who was selling twenty-four carrots for ten francs. The locals, "oeufers", paraded in the place de la Comedie or "L'oeuf " with a self-confidence that confirmed the results of a recent poll. Asked where in France they would choose to live, other than in the place they lived now, over 70% of respondents said Montpellier. For a city that had been run for over twenty years by the same left wing mayor, it hadn't done badly.

Much of the talk at the moment was about elections, as France had gone to the polls to elect its Mayors and others for office. Turnouts were usually pretty poor but in the village where I was staying, the Mayor Claude Carceller, received 80% of the votes from over 85% of the electorate. His next six years in office had been assured by his competitors less than straight dealing. One sensed that in local French politics at least, a breath of fresh air was blowing away much that hinted at nepotism and dodgy dealing. Some obviously didn't help themselves. The mayoress of Octon, a community on the edge of Lac du Salagou not far away, shot herself in the foot with a pre-election meeting at which she openly criticised many of those around her. Marc Chicoulaa, the mayor from my community back in Campan, didn't get the necessary 51% majority to avoid a second ballot and so it would have to happen all over again for him. I think it was complacency in his case.

Montpeyroux was a village of 1200 people not far from the Herault and about forty kilometres west of Mountpellier. It was surrounded by lines of vines, which at that time of year looked lifeless, an invading wooden army standing too, waiting for the command to advance. Most had finished pruning and the warm Spring weather prompted the shoots that in only a few weeks would catapult the vines back into visible life. Already the wild iris was flowering and the browns on the palette would soon need swapping for greens.

Mountpeyroux was one of the many communities proud of its growing reputation as a good wine producer in the Languedoc. Quality had become a key word, though quantity was still enormous. My hostess for a few days told me that the region produced more wine than Australia and New Zealand together. It did seem that every patch of available land was wired up for wine.

Peter and Patricia Kirwan had lived in the village for seven years. Their tardis-like home looked from the outside as though there was no room to swing a cat, let alone the two Cairn terriers Horace and Oscar. Looks could be deceptive and No 4 Route Neuve was as big as a house and as welcoming as a home. Peter was ex-army (Inniskillings) and ex-city and Patricia was ex-Westminster Council. She'd had her fifteen minutes of fame on BBC's Panorama. She'd blown the whistle on Shirley Porter, the notorious Tory local politician who misunderstood the meaning of the syllable 'seller' in the word councillor. Patricia was a bulldog of a woman. She would have been what was described as a formidable opponent. She had a man's voice, which wasn't helped by the cigarettes. Peter was rather gentler.

Peter and Patricia loved the region and thrived on it. They shared an interest in wine and had a small business discovering and exporting local varieties back to England. Good health hadn't always smiled on them but they felt reassured that they could count on a more efficient health service in France than they came to expect in Britain.

When two or three expats gathered together, the conversation nearly always lead to comparisons. The debate normally split the debaters into two parties. "The love its" or "The hate its." The Kirwans fell into "The love its" category and chuckled with glee at a letter in the Times on March 15th that ran as follows: -

"Hague's Foreign Land.

Sir,

Something is bothering me about William Hague's campaign strategy. I am a Conservative and have never voted Labour. Mr Hague tells us, however, that under continued Labour administration we will all wake up one day and find ourselves living in a foreign country. Would this be one in which cigarettes are £1.90 a packet and a decent bottle of whiskey about £10; one where a journey on the Tube costs 58 pence irrespective of distance, and where for longer journeys there are 200mph trains with low fares and an enviable safety record; one where I can buy a first-rate meal for two with aperitifs, wine and coffee for less than £50; one in which public monuments are exquisitely maintained and the streets kept clean; one with first-rate health and education systems; one where rural issues are taken seriously, and where diesel is about 45 pence a litre? France, perhaps?"

The Kirwans made friends easily, got involved, and I could understand why the locals loved them or hated them. After the recent election they threw a party for the winning mayor. The night before, they provided the shoulders to cry on for the unsuccessful candidate from the next village. Theirs was a friendship genuinely given to hippie and vigneron, postman, peasant and priest. They encapsulated all that was good about the French rural community spirit and their past life in a Gloucestershire village served to highlight the changes that had tarnished the country side way of life in Britain. To quote Peter, one of the new villagers in Gloucestershire became incensed and said that, "It was a disgrace sheep were allowed to do their toilet in the road" whilst being moved from one Cotswold pasture to another. The friends they had in village England could be counted on one hand but there in village France they hadn't stopped counting. I did wonder if they hadn't become bigger fish in a smaller pond. I admired their commitment. They danced, wouldn't sit it out.

I unload some of the kit that Peter is carrying. Try to lighten his load. Store it at the Kirwans. There are more mountains to climb. Some of them big.

Uzes

When he flies back to London, he takes a bag full of truffles with him. It gets him the best table in the restaurant and a free meal.

The two gay Germans were sitting at the next table. Hans Nees, that's what I called one of them, was more Austrian than Aryan. They were pleased to be in each other's company. The couple behind them on table three were married but not to each other. They couldn't be because they were middle aged and laughing a lot. Table two, over on the left, was also animated. She (blonde, suit, glasses, thirty-two), was enjoying him, (dark, ex-rugger player, older). My neighbours (he irrelevant tie and chequebook, she Spanish-looking and eating like a bull) were happy with each other too. There was only one Billy no mates in the joint and that was me.

The restaurant with nine customers was alive. Its clientele didn't whisper. They did not shout either, but they enjoyed their evening meals and didn't act as though they were taking an illegal snack in a library. The menu (four courses) costs 110 francs and was cooked and served by a couple who really gave the impression that they wanted to cook and serve. For them cooking and serving was not a chore, not a job even, indeed it was nothing short of an absolute pleasure. A smile added more to the ambience of the place. Actually it took the mind off the extraordinary decor. The people that decorated in there last probably died in the same ward as Van Gogh and at the same time. The effect created by the random lighting gave an emphasis to each diner's face that would make an interrogator drool in anticipation. The intermittent radio music flicked from swinging sixties to swinging seventies and back again with something even older and French thrown in every now and again presumably for political correctness.

Silk flowers and a poster of Uzes reflected in the " Bitter Campari" mirror. They shouted as loud as the wooden chairs scrapping on the lino tiled floor. The lead-based paint was flaking and the dried flower arrangements on each table since V.E. Day itself were doubly dangerous fire and health hazards. The unframed art on the walls came from the brush marked broad and was crafted by the hand called unskilfully clumsy.

In that dreadful, untrendy, dowdy, badly lit, tasteless and cheap restaurant, people were enjoying themselves and having a great supper for less than a tenner a head or in Hans Nees case, thirty marks. I gave the place full marks.

The Romans were not really remembered for their catchy advertising slogans. They used their water without the need to be sold it so "Sparkling or straight our aqua tastes great" or "Soft or hard from the Pont du Gard" hadn't survived in the Latin copywriter's handbook. What they were remembered for was the way in which they got their water. The aqueduct at Pont du Gard, between Nimes and Avignon, looked mighty impressive two thousand years after it was finished. It was the best looking plumbing I'd ever seen. So too was the Tour Fenestrelle, a helter-skelter appendage to St Theodorit's cathedral in Uzes.

Peter and I trundled North through natural truffle country. The rolling land in those parts had oaks on whose roots pigs or dogs with highly prized noses smelled out the highly priced delicacies. The season ran from November through to early March and at up to three hundred quid a kilo, it was an expensive habit but one that didn't need any selling. A Mindel jingle would be inappropriate.

Not far from Pont St Esprit on the banks of the fast flowing Rhone, there was an old Mas, renamed the Mas of heather because Heather lived there. She wasn't at home when I called but her partner David Mindel and a flock of cats made me very welcome. They'd created a separate annexe for guests with everything that could be needed, including the kitchen sink.

David was a musician, well composer really. He'd made his money writing catchy jingles for ads (memorably biscuits and beer) and he'd knocked out the odd tune for the likes of John Travolta. His musical work for TV with, amongst others, Rory Bremner had won awards and prompted law suites.

Apparently EMI didn't like Rory's rendition of "All you need is love" which David had adapted. It was sorted with an out of court settlement by the TV channel but only cost the composer his modest fee. His longest running TV tune was the theme for "Jim'll fix it", so Jim fixed it for him.

For the last six years David had been writing a musical "Soul Searchers" which needed a Sir Cameron Macintosh treatment to get it to the paying public. As the name implied, soul music was the show's bag. David admitted that he'd perhaps been born too white but he'd got the rhythm and had had it since he was four years old. A Buddy Holly performance sparked the Mindel fire into life and happiness came with frets and six strings. The piano arrived later when he was thirty, which was just as well, because everything he fed into his musical making computer was via the black and white keyboard. He showed me how he composed using Blueberry Hill as the plank (I choose the tune). He turned it into a piece of orchestral proportions good enough to help sell scoops full of Blueberry Hill ice cream.

It was impressive watching the man make music. He was an artist in the same way a fine wine maker or a good chef was an artist. He had experience and nodded and talked like an old session musician, rubbing his stubbled chin every now and then. He'd rubbed shoulders with others from his profession and names like Clapton, Morrison and D'Abo were mentioned. David Mindel had the trappings of his jingle success, the house, pool and Ferrari but much more importantly, he'd got real soul. When his show hits the big time, he'll still be the sort of guy one could call up and ask for a bed for the night. He would probably say "Fine" in a cool, laid back sort of way and as long as I could put up with Tim Hardin on the CD, a well cooked healthy supper, some local wine, contented purring cats and a very comfortable guest house, I'd be all right.

Walk me out in the morning dew.

Die ⟺

We're going to Die.

When I wanted Mayle, I went to the Post Office. So I did and probably much to his relief, the lady behind the counter couldn't tell me where Monsieur Mayle lived. For three francs she'd get my post card to him. So she said. I would have liked a plat du jour with the man who, more than anybody, had given French lunches a good name. I posted the card asking if we could meet for one.

Lourmarin was a bit like Disney Provence and the prices of most of the little restaurants were designed for Peter Mayle type bank accounts. I took a quick buzz through the Friday morning market (bongos and blankets, cheese and chairs). It was spread out in an L shape between the chateau and the town. We then headed off to Apt and Sault; a journey spent most of the time climbing in second gear or less.

The lavender fields were beginning to look like lines of purple furry bolsters and the apricot trees were filling with blossom. It was tee shirt weather in Peter's cab but when the sun disappeared there was still a chill. Mount Ventoux had been looking at us for most of the day as we came at it from the south, past it on the east and then headed north. We climbed and dipped, climbed and dipped from the Luberon through the Vaucluse into the Baronnies.

At Tarendol we had had enough for the day and pulled up at the gite in the little village. The landlord farmer lit the wood burner and the four overnight guests sat at the table in its glow. Everything we ate was homemade, the pate, wild boar stew with cabbage, goat's cheese (from his herd of one hundred) and meringue with apricot preserve. The local wine came from jugs. They looked as though the farmer's wife had thrown them up on her potter's wheel earlier that week. My fellow overnighters were a mother and her daughter from St Etienne and a Pharmacist from the Ardeche, a little man with a beard and a funny way of speaking. He asked for his thermos flask to be filled with hot water at breakfast.

Gites were a good way of meeting people. For the tariff of 190 Francs for a bed and a shower, an evening meal with a jug or two of wine and breakfast, it was worth putting up with strange-sounding Pharmacists.

The following morning's onward journey from tiny Tarendol was again up and down but mostly up. I didn't think I was going to Die and then I did. Dee the French called it but the sign said Die. After Die it was up all the way and a climb which was a dress rehearsal for the real thing. We stopped for a plat du jour at Chamaloc. We struggled to the top of the Col de Rousset at 1367 metres where two gendarmes stopped us. I thought that perhaps they had wanted to give us an award for our plucky climb, a scroll signed by an official from the Parc Regional du Vercors. They wanted to see my papers. Just routine they said. The climb was anything but routine for us.

The run down the other side was refreshing and we slid along the wide bottomed valley feeling a touch Alpine. Green pastures conjured up an image of Julie Andrews and the Von Trapp family gambolling through the sward. There too, in that very pleasant place, other brave men and women fought the Nazis and seven hundred of them were killed doing so. I didn't see any German registered cars in the car park at the Grotte de la Luire, the memorial to the Marquis.

The Gorges de la Bourne that ran up into Villard-de-Lans was like a tunnel with barely room for the road and the rushing water and overhanging rocks. But like a little blue cork, Peter popped out into the breezy daylight and we came to rest in the resort town, flecks of snow visible on the surrounding mountaintops.

We have both been to Die and have lived to tell the tale. There's no word from Peter Mayle yet.

Grenoble ⇌

There is no signal on my mobile so Peter Mayle won't be able to get through. I guess the mountains make it difficult. The first phone box I come to I'll stop and ring my mother. I should have arranged some flowers but didn't. What a terrible son I am.

On Mothering Sunday, Peter wouldn't start. I probably hadn't been mothering him enough so in protest his battery was as flat as the roads he would have liked to run on. The joy of being in mountainous country was that it didn't need much effort to get jump-started. Off with the handbrake and good old Mr Gravity soon started things moving. We had to go the wrong way down a one way street but it was Sunday morning and the clocks had gone forward so most were still just getting up.

We started and did the short hop to St Nazier-du-Mouchcherotte in the drizzle. It was 6 degrees, a neon sign told me, and the mountaintops were covered in moody mists. I telephoned my mother in England but was only able to wish her answering machine a happy day. She'd probably be in church. One year I drove for three hours from the West Country to the village church in Barnwell, Northamptonshire, and slid into the pew beside her for Matins on Mothering Sunday. She was really surprised, very pleased to see me and held my hand a lot through the service. It was one of the best journeys I had made in my life.

Francois and Michel Laur had given me their number the previous year and had said, "Give us a ring when you get to Grenoble." So I did and after a moment or two of confusion, they remembered who I was. I asked if I could spend the night with them or pitch my tent in their garden, little realising that they didn't have a spare room or a garden. Anyhow they said that they would drive up to St N-du-M to meet me that afternoon. I parked Peter on a slope and climbed the mountain that gave St Nazier its name.

From up the top, Grenoble looked like a toy city surrounded by papier-mâché snow dusted mountains. It sat like a thin omelette in a deep frying pan. It was a gentle place with a gentle pace and only a few pretensions at being trendy. It had students and technology, museums and art galleries but when I tried to visit them on a Tuesday in March, all I saw was the outside. On the exterior of one of the old buildings some life-sized elephant heads, presumably in tribute to Hannibal, looked down their trunks. The bubble cable car was shut when I tried it. The Sapeur Pomps were doing an exercise evacuating stranded passengers and abseiling them into a rubber boat in the river Isere below. It looked very James Bond.

Grenoble had trams but they were not as "designer" as those in Montpellier and their bendy buses weren't working on Monday because all public transport workers in France were on strike trying to get their retirement age down to 55. Cynically, with the number of days some sectors of France's work force spent "en greve", their "actual" retirement age would probably be about 37.

The Laurs lived in Echirolles, a southern suburb of Grenoble. It would best be described in the same way as any "new town" development circa seventies. There weren't any houses that I could see, but only blocks of flats, utilitarian and not sparing on the concrete. It was all a bit shabby and grey but with very little scrawling on the walls which must have shown the degree of community pride. There were thin trees in the squares that took some of the echoes away from the children playing with the kidnapped supermarket trolleys and gave bird song in the morning. There were shops, more like market traders, with pull down metal shutters, signs for doctors and hairdressers and bikes and washing and barking dogs on balconies.

For about seventy quid a week Michel and Francois, their working daughter Alexandra and two-year old Tommy, the Yorkshire terrier, lived on the top (7th) floor in their block. There were two bedrooms, a bathroom, a loo, a kitchen, a hall and a good sized dinning room come sitting room. Michel had a lockable garage in the dark underground car park, over which the flats were built. He kept his five-year-old Toyota there. His daughter had to keep her little Peugeot out in the open car park.

Michel retired last year at 58 after twenty years working in the factory for one of Grenoble's biggest employers. Francois worked five days a week, from six in the morning until two in the afternoon. She made meals for the schools of Echirolles and with her fellow fifteen workers, put together the lunches for 1700 people every day. The meals were prepared the day before they were eaten and normally included starter, main course, cheese and pudding. Francois's job was preparing the veg that - other than for carrots, onions and endives - all came out of packets. Flavour, sadly, was sacrificed for convenience.

Taste was always a matter of opinion but there wasn't one thing in the flat that I would like to have owned. The wallpaper pre-dated the walls and a man with heavy wooden hands had designed the heavy dark wooden furniture. It would have been more at home in a large old-fashioned mountain hotel. Designer labels had no place there. Phillips provided constant TV and Sony was there in a corner. So too was a cushioned lavatory seat that expelled air when I sat, a silent whoopee cushion that presumably was designed to make the sitter feel comfortable but which alarmed me to total distraction. I couldn't go.

There were giant cuddly toys in the sitting room and dried flower arrangements, bowling cups and china ornaments like those from seaside shops that were reminders of the visit, mementoes of a good time even if it hadn't been. A smiling dolphin from Ajaccio, testimony to the souvenir potter's skill. Proud photos or photocopies of proud photos. Working men looking uncomfortable in light-coloured wedding suits, their partners done up like dolls, were stuck on the wall and incongruous, Constable's Flatford Mill. Net curtains and Jesus on his cross, as tasteless as that was.

We had lunch out on Monday and found the supermarket cafeteria comfortable. It was a help yourself affair. We pointed at what we wanted, saw the price and paid before we took a bite. We shopped at Ed, a discount food store, where the staff were more concerned with cramming the aisles with cartons of tinned goods than they were with taking the money for them through the crowded checkout. The word "Organic" was as out of place in Ed's as the word "IKEA" would have been in the flat.

If it sounded like I was being outrageous, a dreadful snob, a spoilt public school boy and an ungrateful brat, then I wasn't. Taste would always be a matter of opinion and opinions, like taste, will differ. What was far more important than a man's possessions, was what he did with them and in the case of the Laur's, they could not have done more. They gave me their bed to sleep in without question. They slept on the sofa. Heavy and wooden it may have been, but they gave me their bed, which was so unselfish an act, I could hardly believe it. I protested. They wouldn't hear of it. They'd have the sofa and that was that. Michel ran me around in his car, helped me find a place to charge up the flat battery, gave me his set of jump leads in case it happened again and let Peter have his lock up garage for the two night stay. Put his Toyota outside on the harsh street. Francois did a day's work and then cooked supper for us. Michel and Francois had something far more important than what I interpreted as taste. They'd got their own style and lashings of generosity, which was much better than any taste could ever be.

Equipped with three new tyres (pneus in French which I always thought sounded like a minor catarrh problem) and a recharged battery, Peter and I did our meeting the press bit and then headed up and out of Grenoble, escorted by the generous Michel in his green Toyota. He put us on the right road for Chartreuse.

The church at St Hugues looked more like an art gallery dedicated to one man's ego and creativity rather than a place to go and think about the Creator. It was, to my mind, done in bad taste for a place to worship God, but then Arcabas would have thought differently.

"Who's the trout?" the young waiter said with a straight face looking at no one in particular. Those present would have been able to guess with out much difficulty. She wasn't to my taste either, but then obviously made somebody happy. I looked at the view through the big picture window in the dining room. Darkening rocks with pine trees, some perched like birds on a razor's ledge. The chalet style dolls houses opposite, some with lights but most without, blending into the dark green which was Chatreuse.

I sample the Monk's green brew. It tastes like medicine. I am beginning to accept that Mr Mayle doesn't want to eat with me.

Courchevel ⇌

The young policeman looks about fifteen. He waves at me, wants me to turn off into a large lay-by and we crawl off the steep road and draw up to a halt beside him.

If you wandered down the King's Road, Chelsea any time after six o'clock on a Friday summer evening and ventured into one of its pubs, stopped and listened, you would hear Britain's bright young things at their watering trough. The sound was unmistakable. It was exactly the same sound in Courchevel, which, as some would have it, was one of Europe's most exclusive skiing resorts.

In late March the place had the distinct look of out of season to it and although there weren't loose tumbleweeds rolling with the dry dust down Main Street, there weren't too many people about. Little snow equalled little crowds. There was the odd bunch apres skiing in Le Jump Bar which, but for the ski clobber, could be a gathering at Soho House or the White Horse on Parsons Green. I didn't have to wait for more than several beats of Craig David to get my glass of Kronnie and there was no problem with the language because behind the bar it was English too. Only the money was funny but wasn't it pretty? Gustave Eiffel on a two hundred, Cezanne on one hundred and that pioneer flying chappie, Antoine de Saint-Exupery on the fifty franc note. Poor old Claude Debussy looked very undervalued on the twenty-franc note but even he beat someone who looked like Thora Hird on the folding back home.

Out of season holidays always catered for out of season holiday takers. Easter wasn't quite there just yet and the snow hadn't been fantastic, prompting the impulse cry of "Come on Darling. Let's pop over to the three valleys for a few blac   k runs."

At supper it was the boys from Limerick on the week without the wives and a good craic to be sure. The Ingams Holiday set were stuffing their faces. The rich older man with his second (or third) wife and her young child, not his, browsed the wine list. There were two such trios not many feet away from my table in the restaurant. The children in question were both boys. Both were under eight. Both had heads that were shaped like London policemen's helmets. Both were with their mummy and not their daddy. Both mummies were trying to impress the "new" daddies. Both children were precocious. Both needed a sharp whack across the knuckles with a serving spoon from the would be "Daddy". Both knew exactly how to play the game.

"Why don't you run on up and get ready for bed Josh?" asked mummy.

"Why don't you jump out of the window and break your neck while you're at it," thought the man opposite knowing that Josh wouldn't sprout wings even though his mummy thought he'd got a halo.

Courchevel was Chelski or Batterski. The young rich were there and behaving exactly as they would back home.

"We'll keep checking on you guys OK?" said one cherry-faced mum to a bedroom full of gangly teenage girls, awkward in their baggy jeans, bare tummies, and fag behind the back towards the open window.

"Have fun darlings!" and off she went back to Basil and Fee and Roger of course, whose idea it was to take the girls out of school early for the break. Their CD player turned up in direct proportion to their mother's departing footsteps. It was black rappers for those white middle class girls and like the vodka and nicotine their parents tried to discourage, it was called growing up.

"Give it to me baby are har, are har. So the marks on your shoulder are har are har. Makin' love on the bathroom floor." They knew the words and sang them with more gusto than the rappers themselves. But they couldn't mean them. It was just a chant. No one stopped to think about the real meaning.

"It wouldn't be right if I didn't tell your knee to do it." Or so came the girlie shout through the bedroom wall. And there was more.

"Hey hey we're the Monkeys." What came round went round. Even I could sing along with that one, but I resisted the temptation to let rip back through the wall just in case I got the words wrong.

Peter and I had fairly struggled to get to Courchevel 1850 and had resisted the temptation of 1550 and even 1650 in order to savour the real heights. The last few kilometres were in first gear and had the incline been any more serious, I would have been forced to get out, having found some way of keeping the accelerator to the floor, and push.

Agonisingly close to the top, we were pulled over by a municipal policeman who had obviously noticed that we were not keeping up with the rest of the traffic. Old cyclists seemed to be doing a better job. I was delighted for the break and the opportunity of putting the young guy straight. He said that we were not allowed to be on the road.

"I'm doing a tour of France." The young official didn't get it. I just asked how much further it was. He looked very confused.

"To the top," I added. "Not round France."

It wasn't far and while Peter is resting in the private underground car park with Jags, Mercs and Range Rovers, I am still trying to get my head around some of the rap lyrics that the Chelski girl's choir is performing next door.

Humet ⇥

Despite the warning, I eat in my dull room. I don't try to cook anything though.

The sign on the back of the bedroom door said, amongst other things, "Il est strictement interdit de manger et de cuisiner dans les chambres." I'd just come through a near white-out and even though my feet were freezing, I hadn't planned on getting out my camping stove and starting it up. The management was safe on that score. What I had done was to procure a bottle of the local wine, vin de savoie and a sausage, which I consumed for my evening meal in an effort to redeem myself from the excesses that had been Courchevel.

The previous night's bedroom had cost 905 Francs. It comprised two singles and I only used one, with en suite foot bath, basin and loo, a TV set and of course the apres ski hair drier. Breakfast and supper were included and apparently I was very lucky to get such a good price. The tourist office had told me that the charge would be 590 Francs. That was the price per person based on two people sharing the room. I didn't like to mention the Chelski girl's choir whom I felt I had spent most of the night with, even though they were ignorant of the arrangement. I paid up and shut up then went up to meet Jean-Jacques.

If La Potiniere was a two star establishment, then Hotel Courcheneige had two stars with oak leaves. It was up near Courchevel's private airstrip. Guests could ski right out on to the piste from the front door. Jean-Jacques ran the ski hire business he started in the hotel fourteen years previously. He was 43 years old and spoke a very good Franglaise that he learnt in India.

264

After a childhood in Lyon, he travelled for a decade and mixed it with big British motorbikes and the hippie happy Asian trail. He came to Courchevel as a dishwasher but then persuaded the privately owned hotel that it would benefit by having an in house ski hire shop. The hotel was always full and its 245 bedrooms catered for an international bunch at about two hundred pounds an international head per night. Jean-Jacque's season lasted from December until May, which gave him seven months to spend with his wife and two children and his bees.

"Fiftee sowsand wirkers in zee ive wiz out strikes". He laughed at the truism in a country where even the lightning struck in the same place twice. His bees and his family lived fifteen kilometres away from the resort mainly because he didn't want his children to mix with the wealthy holidaymakers. His young teenage daughter couldn't understand why her holidaying contemporaries seemed to posses every creature comfort they needed and lots they didn't. Drugs were used as often as chair lifts and had become a part of the youth culture that was on the piste all day, on the piss all night.

It was not only the young that had got too much money. It was the Arabs. There was one big Hansel and Grettel looking chalet with its own indoor/outdoor pool and sliding dance floor cover. The Arab that owned it brought his thirty-four staff with him on his skiing holiday and that year hired thirty-four ski instructors to give his staff individual lessons.

Money aside, the biggest change that Jean-Jacques had seen in Courchevel over the years was the weather. That season had been the worst for five years and Jean-Jacques was convinced that there was real proof of the global warming theory. He recounted to me the dreadful story from eight years earlier when at minus 32, children were not allowed on the ski lifts. One backpacked baby had developed frostbite and had to have a leg amputated. It didn't get that cold anymore. South winds, pollution and rain were all enemies for snow and the thousand pound a week skier would soon be thinking again before popping his cheque in the post and planning a trip to the three valleys, even though it might be called the worlds biggest skiing area.

There was quite suddenly a general excitement in the hotel dinning room where Jean-Jacques and I were taking our plat du jour. All the tables were buzzing like a kid's birthday party. Grown men couldn't sit still and wanted to leave the table. Jean-Jacques too was keen to reopen his shop downstairs.

He knew there was going be a run on goggles that afternoon because it was snowing quite hard and visibility was no more than a few yards.

Peter and I emerged from the hotel's underground car park and cut our way through the white covering. It was downhill all the way thank goodness, like a bobsleigh, hurrying to the bottom rather than risking being snowbound without the bank balance to cope. We made it to Flumet and the cheap hotel with the instructions on its bedroom doors.

I won't be able to get snow chains for wheels the size of side plates.

Chamonix ⇌

"You don't need to buy a ski pass." One of the lads has a business in forged documents.

Unlike Courchevel, Chamonix was a town that had been there long before apres-ski. The top of Mont Blanc was visible from the front of La Terrace and as I sipped my demi or vin chaud, I could pretend that I'd tracked across its white heights at nearly five thousand metres. The mountains around Chamonix were very serious and nature had thrown up a playground that was used and abused in winter and summer. If the three valleys offered wide pistes and family skiing, then Chamonix gave the off-pister a chance. Families were people back home who occasionally receive hotmail from the cybercafes.

Ibiza on ice, the town was run by an army of twenty something's. English was the common lingo but it could have Irish, Scottish, Swedish, American, Australian, New Zealand, French or even Manchunian intonations. A magnet whose three main pulls were booze, birds and boards (not necessarily in that order) or shots, Sheilas and skis had forced the gathering. Snow and sun threw them together in the party town although most didn't see very much of the latter before it was well overhead. Rarely out of bed before midday and rarely in it before four, the boys and girls (although boys seem to outnumber girls by two if not three to one) worked and played hard for their countries.

The wages kept them lean and hungry with maybe £700 for a good month in a good bar and therefore "tourist" prices in "tourist" places were pretty much off limits. They shared apartments, ate staff meals and paid reduced drinks prices, but that didn't mean they'd eat or drink any less. Far from it.

In one bar I visited the average monthly slate for its staff was £400 and that was at half price.

I spent four days there with the boys and girl who lived in the totally misnamed Impass des Rhododendrons. It was difficult sometimes to confirm what the wristwatch reported. Three in the afternoon could just as well be three in the morning. Lodging in their flat was a bit like staying on the set of a wild TV sitcom. My "room" was a section of the main living area, cordoned off behind a sheet and just big enough to house a sleeping bag an it's occupant. My neighbour, Nick the Manc, was another suspended sheet partition away. We got to know each other's nocturnal noises quite well.

My two hosts, Dom (looks like Jude Law) and Garrett (the guy I ran into in a Thai restaurant in Nice) also had annexes off the main room. Dom had to go up a ladder to reach his bed whilst Garrett's garret was through a cupboard door. Jo, the girl, and her extreme skier boyfriend, Ozzie Nick, had the bedroom or the only room the original architect had intended for sleeping in. The sofa provided more accommodation should the need arise and it did when Moz (I think it was him) had to stay over one night (well five a.m. until lunchtime actually)

The flat had been lovingly decorated with girlie calendars, photographs of friends behaving badly and stolen advertising memorabilia. Ski and snow boarding "kit" took up quite a lot of space as did washing up (empty glasses) full ash trays, videos and CD's, "leisure" magazines and mountain bikes. There was a balcony with things growing on it which didn't look quite so horticultural as the things propagating in the bathroom, even though those on the balcony had been planted and those in the bathroom hadn't.

The place was homely and lived in and had its very own smells and sounds. It was like being a student all over again with cries of "Who's had all the milk?" and "You're not bringing Her back here tonight" as though she had leprosy. Swearing was an important part of the language. Actually the language, swearing aside, was riddled with jargon. Snowtalk was a language on its own which would have taken more than a few days to study. In my short time I gleaned and almost understood the following gems: -
Wife = Girlfriend.
It = Girl.
Scratch = Bed.
Bro = A male friend or a cup of tea (dependent on the accent).

To pipe = To have sexual relations with.

Bean flicker = Girl who prefers girls.

A wife beater = A plain white T-shirt or singlet or a pint of larger.

Gnarly = Something to do with snowboarding but I couldn't work out what.

The names of the dramatis personae were no less strange than the terms they used. Nick the Manc, Ozzie Nick, Loza, Moz, Squaddie, Hominator, Posh Jon, English Hanna, Pat Chef, Brethren Blotch, Hankey Pankey Swedish Chef, Baron Barg, Asa Viking Princess, Rexadus, Balsa Wood Bumble Bee and I mustn't forget The Farter, the apt name given to the Suzuki four wheel drive. I found myself christening one girl behind the bar as Goophy. Another as Andhairer because her name was Andrea and there was something about her hair.

Like a conscripted army, they were a mixed bunch. Some would just do their time and move on to pastures new. There was quite a migration south for the summer and work on the boats. Some however stayed and signed up for regular service and hoped to "get their own place out there one day". I didn't believe it was just a bunch of young people having a good time. I didn't believe it was all E's, weed, snow, coke, sex and booze; "Deluded" every second Tuesday where the music was as incomprehensible as the people who moved to it (little boxes, big boxes, little boxes, big boxes). I believed that they were living life to the full, that some of them sometimes over stepped the mark and some of them died. A twenty-nine year old French dentist fell to his death the day before I left. He was up in the snow doing what he probably loved most. That group of happy players had come together because they'd got youth, ambition, enthusiasm and a willingness to get up and go, albeit at midday.

As I drove out of Chamonix and crossed the long viaduct that carried the N205 to and from the place, my emotions were mixed. I was leaving behind friends whose company I enjoyed very much but whose company needed to carry a public health warning, well certainly for a fifty one year old with an over worked heart.

In a previous life, these were the boys and girls who would have fought for King and Country. In a previous life, I had been one of them.

Lyon ✈

It is bad for the heart. It is good for the heart.

The town of Annecy seemed overrun with water the evening Peter and I pulled into the place after the escape from Chamonix. Someone described it as the Venice of the Alps, which was probably a fair call. The old part certainly had a canal or two surging through although the speed of flow would knock on the head any romantic idea of a gentle punt in a gondola. Lac d' Annecy provided the water and a pretty playground on which to take a pleasure cruiser and have a plat du jour afloat, as I guessed many did in the summer. In the rather prolonged April shower with added thunder, I found a little bistro under the arches beneath the old castle and had jambon du pays and the local tart. Bread never came with butter but jambon seldom came without it, a little pat and a few gherkins on the side. The local tart turned out in her own piping hot cast iron bowl and was a mixture of melted cheese, potato and a few onions.

After Annecy it was away from the yodelling and back to a flatter tune. Bigger fields were full of growing crops and yellow-flowering oil seed rape lay like a chequered flag across the land. And then after more water, Lac De Bourget, and more fairly level going came Lyon.

I could always tell when a town of size and importance was immanent by the clusters of roadside signs. Like colourful estate agents for sale boards, they proclaimed coming retail opportunities. Hotels, restaurants, shops and car dealers all featured and for petrol the sign said to turn right at the 'feu'. McDonald's were nearly always 'tout droit' which was disturbing if the directions were taken literally. For major conurbation's the boards would turn into hoardings, sometimes with movement. Matter of fact and not particularly mouth watering shots of a joint of veal or a French mother pondering over a shade of lipstick. There didn't seem to be any rules about the density of the advertisements. They sprouted like media plantations, fed by the volume of traffic past them.

We slipped in through Lyon's outer skirts full of commerce and giant signs proclaiming DIY or Hyper this or Giant that, grubby car breakers' yards away from Japanese car makers and roundabouts and traffic lights controlling the increased flow. There was a serious looking accident in one of the suburbs, attended as always by a healthy looking crowd of officials and unofficials.

Because much of Lyon wasn't Lyon, it could not lay claim to being France's second city. That title had gone to Marseille. Visually It sprawled for miles but with nine arrondissements (Paris had 20 and Marseille 14) it could only claim bronze. It did have two rivers running through, the HQ of Interpol, more chemists and their test tubes than silk looms. Lyon's wealth and reputation had been built on silk. It had one serious skyscraper aptly owned by Credit Lyonnais and a not uninteresting old town. It had a university and museums dedicated to textiles, puppets and Barbie, who should not to be mistaken for the doll. He was the murdering Gestapo boss of Lyon. It was also the home to Andre-Marie Ampere and the Electricity museum. Hence Amps.

Where it did knock spots off its rivals was in the kitchen. Lyon was probably the food capital of France and chefs seemed to congregate like thirsty animals around a watering hole in their Bouchons and finer restaurants. Bouchons were typical Lyonnais eating places, the bouchon being the cork and the number of corks pulled during a meal being the old guide as to the price charged.

With lips smacking in anticipation, my first night's supper between the Rhone and Saone was taken in the Brasserie George 1836. It was a bit like eating in an ornate railway station. The inside was big, the actual grazing area the size of a football pitch or ice skating rink which was spooky because the name "Beire Rinck" was emblazoned in neon on the end wall several arrondissements away. The place put the can into canteen and the brass in the word brasserie and it claimed to be one of Europe's oldest. Its clients had included Jules Verne, Emile Zola, a Dalai Lama and a Prince of Japan. Madame Jacques Chirac could nearly be described as a regular. The establishment had two entries in the Guinness book of records, one in 1986 for serving up one and a half tonnes of sauerkraut and the other ten years later for the biggest omelette. Presumably Lyon's thriving pharmaceutical industry was still working on the world's largest indigestion pill. Under the four enormous art deco chandeliers, I chose the not very healthy starter of "La Celebre Gratinee au Madere menu of

1949" because it was the year I was born. The blurb and the waiter told me that the traditional recipe would be prepared at my table. Onion soup "au gratin" egg yolk and Maderia for 54 francs.

The main course was even more unhealthy and described in French as "Veritable Andouillette Bobosse au frison de porc, tiree a la ficelle, sauce moutard, pommes frites." In English it was far less glamorous. "Bobosse baked chitteling served with mustard sauce and French fries" In any language it was a mouth full of what should only be taken infrequently. It was pure comfort food and at 79 francs perhaps an awful lot for offal. The half bottle of Cotes du Rhone at 44 francs and the Espresso at 9.50 brought the lot to under 200 francs and if the wallet felt lighter, the rest of me was rather pleased that my bedroom was in the hotel only next door.

The next morning, and despite the over indulgence, the rendezvous with the Maison du Coeur went to plan. It was with Jacques Fleurence, a retired manager from the camping gas business who looked after the welfare of Lyon's healthy hearts. His best friend was one of France's eminent heart surgeons who looked after Lyon's not so healthy hearts. Jacques and the surgeon went cycling together and the Maison du Coeur gave Jacques something worthwhile to do when he was not out on his bike or cooking. It was a shop front in central Lyon (Place Edgar Quinet) where people could go to pick up information about the heart. It was also a place where people went to learn practically how to help someone who might have had a heart attack. The French were encouraging the public to go and learn about mouth to mouth resuscitation and the other techniques required to keep a potential fatality from the clutches of the grim reaper. It was a good idea and there were several hundred Lyonnais out there who knew how to spring into action. Just as well with meals like the one I'd eaten.

After the official photo of Jacques, Yerlikaya and Metivier - two wonderful Christian names - Peter and I limped across the Soane. We took a wrong turn and found ourselves sucked into a tunnel heading purposefully for Paris. We extracted ourselves from the Paris flow and found our way to the top of old Lyon and the wedding cake like Basilique Notre-Dame le Fourviere. The best thing about the religious pile was the view from its backyard. Apparently on a clear day Mont Blanc could be seen. The highest point in view that day was the Credit Lyonnais tower.

Lyon had prostitutes although, along with the rest of France's population, they too just pointed and smiled when Peter chugged past. They may, of course, have been laughing at me. I was never quite sure what happened, how they got their work or where they did it. It was normally rush hour and on the side of the busy roads that flanked the Soane and the Rhone, they would be gathered in pairs. They seemed to hunt in twos, had their own territory. They dressed exactly like they were off to a vicars and tarts fancy dress party. Obviously not as vicars, but black and leather were the two predominant fashion statements along with minimalist coverage. Presumably cars stopped and a deal was struck. When the traffic backed up as a result of red lights did they, I wondered, offer their services like the windscreen-washing brigade?

"E'm surry ser, ther bick window is extra." I was tempted to pull over in Peter and ask for directions. I expected to be told exactly where to go.

Peter must have known that Lyon was the perfect place to have his next relapse and he did almost right outside the Piaggio dealer. I got him there with clutch and or gear trouble. The clutch didn't want to stop the engine from driving the wheels, which at Lyon's many traffic lights meant having to turn the engine off and restart it again given the green. The very helpful youthful Piaggio dealer had a look and tried to start Peter who refused. So I left him there outside in the street in Vieux Lyon.

Jacques had invited me to his home in Saintes Foy-les-Lyon for supper and he picked me up at the Villages hotel and gave me a guided tour in his Twingo. Jacques should either drive or point out the sites but not attempt both at the same time. Lyonnais hooters were on overtime as the blue Twingo changed lane and sometimes direction on a whim and certainly without any regard for those who maybe following. We got to Jacque's apartment, the home he had with Marie Therese for thirty years and spent a pleasant evening. Jacques was not only a skilful stunt driver, he also cooked. That evening was Lyon sausage and boiled potatoes with butter, another treat for the heart. In his way Jacques would be keeping Lyon's Maison du Coeur busy for the foreseeable future.

The lift back to the Villages hotel on the Cours Gambetta was performed in Jacque's other car, a Mercedes. Presumably that was used to fox any earlier swerving Twingo victims and provide greater protection in the event of actual contact, it being after super and darker than before. He got me back perfectly and showed me the coach station and which one I would need in the morning to get me out to the airport.

It's April 6ᵗʰ. I am going back to England. Father isn't well.

Back To Lyon ⇥

On June 19ʰ the prostitutes are still there. They wave and I wave back. I can't tell whether it's the same ones. Similar uniforms, same jobs.

Back in April I had visited the Maison du Coeur and had a plat du jour with Monsieur and Madame Fleurence at their home in Sainte-Foy-Les-Lyon. In June, like the film 'Ground Hog Day', I did exactly the same. The first time it was "saucission accompagne de pomme vapeur et de beurre frais", the second, veal and ratatouille. In April it was night-time, in June it was lunch.

Jacques had overseen Peter's latest repairs and I collected him from a lawn mower centre in Gennas, not far from Lyon. He was well again and we headed out along the banks of the Soane and North. I stopped briefly to pay homage at the culinary cathedral that was Paul Bocuse in Collonges but moved on again to the municipal campsite in Villefranche-sur-Soane.

As father lay in his hospital bed unwell back in England, a nurse would have asked him what he'd like for lunch. Had he filled in the form, ticked the boxes?

"I've a mind above food," he would have replied weakly.

It is good to get the disinfected smell of an English hospital blown away by a warm June breeze in France. Father wants me to get on with my life, or so he said. "Bugger off back to France" was how he put it.

Beaujolais ⇥

It is very kind of Monsieur Joseph to give me some of his wine.

The day went like a wine list. It was all red and all Beaujolais. To the left of the Soane between Villefrance and Macon there was an undulating piece of France which produced the Gamay grape in decomposed granite soil that looked like it wouldn't grow a weed. In only a few miles, we did Brouilly, Morgon, Fleurie, Chenas and Julienas.

Mount Brouilly took Peter down to first gear again but we'd climbed higher peaks and the chapelle Notre-Dame de Brouilly was not very inspiring for a first gear effort. The view was hazy but the information platform was clear enough. Brouilly, it said, had 360 growers who produced 10 million bottles of wine a year from 1300 hectares in six villages. Brouilly accounted for 20% of the Beaujolais production.

In Fleurie I bought a bottle in the little Casino shop for 40 Francs along with some provisions for lunch. At Chenas I had a picnic on the public-spirited heavy wooden table and benches that were as common in France as berets. Whether or not it was wise to be seen drinking Fleurie in Chenas or vice versa I didn't mind. It tasted just great with the fresh baguette, jambon, mustard, tomato, bulbous spring onions and green crisp Granny Smith apple.

Only a spit outside of Chenas at the Vieux Domaine, Monsieur Joseph had ten hectares of Gamay grape from which he produced and bottled both Chenas and Moulin du Vent. He very kindly gave me two for the journey and promised to send six more of each to Paris, care of the Federation Francaise de Cardiologie. He insisted that his wine was better for the heart than any other. He wanted to prove it.

Another address I had to visit was east across the Soane and away from the rows of vines and into woodland and grassy meadows full of Limousin cattle, big dirty white beasts. The village was Vonnas although it perhaps should have changed its name to George Blancville. One of France's greatest chefs, Monsieur Blanc's three star emporium even had a new enclosed bridge across the road linking one side of his establishment to the other, presumably so the soufflés didn't flop during the crossing. In case customers were in a real hurry or wanted a take away, there was a helicopter-landing pad in the back yard. I could tell the place was supposed to be very good by the endorsements on signed photographs of the rich and famous who had eaten there. The Clintons, Mr Gobochov, at least two presidents of France, Jackie Stewart, Stirling Moss, film and pop stars, all were smiling from their frames on the wall, all well fed up by George. The young flunky on the front door posed next to Peter for a photo because Monsieur Blanc was not available. He gave me a copy of the menu. It read like a poem.

De Mer et d'eau Douce.

Daurade legerement fumee beignet d'oignon mauve et caviar.

Soupe sauvage "velours vert" aux grenouilles et mariage d'herbes.

Des filets de rouget, des champignons et une royale d'oseille dans une nage au vin jaune.

Meli melo de homard eclate et legumes tendres a l'huile parfumee.

Aile de pigeon roti servie dans un bouillon corsetartine de halicot de cuisse, gnocchi d'aubergines et pata negra.

Fromages frais et affines.

Les pre-desserts.

Votre choix

Parmi la composition des desserts du moment.

Not only did food taste better, it sounded better in French. The translation made it more matter-of-fact, less like art and more like food which wasn't sure about itself.

Sea and Fresh Water

Slightly smoked sea bream mauve onion and caviar fritter

Wild "Green velvet" soup with frogs and mixed herbs Fillets of mullet, mushrooms and a sorrel royale swimming in young wine

Mixture of fragmented lobster and tender vegetables in perfumed oil

Roast pigeon wing in a full-bodied broth. And so on, and so on.

I was a bit unsure with the translation of some of Monsieur Blanc's terms. The dictionary gave eclate as confused or fragmented. There was no room for interpretation with the price. That was 990 francs. Drinks were extra. There was a menu for 550 francs or one for 1300 francs just in case.

I scuttle off like a confused lobster.

Taize ⇌

The bells control the day. The discipline is somehow comforting.

I couldn't remember whether it was swifts or swallows that whistled as they swooped. In both Macon and Cluny their happy shrills and darting shadows played over my street side table. In Macon it was coffee and a stroll to see the old wooden house in the Place des Herbes with the not so old bar underneath. In Cluny it was a 58 franc plateau repas, a sort of superior aeroplane tray that arrived containing a green salad, a hot quiche, fromage blanc (yoghurt) and a delicious patisserie. The small green china jug of red wine was extra and I knew it was time to go because the little one way street started to get busy at about 2.30 and the whistling birds played in the background to the clicking diesels and high-pitched two strokes.

The view over my "plateau repas" was an underwear shop. Second only to hairdressers, those retail outlets populated the towns of France leading me to suppose that female French drawers must be bulging with female French drawers.

The history books and buildings of Cluny told that once upon a time it was a very important place as far as religion was concerned. The Abbey and its monastery became revered in the Christian world. Only the Pope surpassed the incumbent's influence. While Cluny still enjoyed status as a tourist stop, the influential religious crown, such as it was nowadays, had passed to Taize, a village only ten k's away to the north in the Burgundy hills.

Brother Roger came to the village from Switzerland in 1940, aged twenty-five. His aim was to create a community where simplicity and kind-heartedness would be lived out day after day. His first opportunity to put into practice the aim came with the Second World War. Taize was close to the demarcation line that divided France in two, so was well placed to welcome those on the run. Roger and his sister helped many, Christian and non-Christian alike, and it was probably the shelter that they offered to fleeing Jews which brought them the unwelcome attention of the invading authorities. Warned by a family friend, Roger and his supporters left in 1942. But two years later he was back with more help and the community was rekindled.

At over eighty-five years old Brother Roger looked a saintly figure. Dressed in white robes, he and his sixty brothers ambled into the Church and sat themselves between low hedges that kept us from them. The Church was the focal point of the community. The long low building with its onion shaped domes took us out of the bright Burgundian sunshine and into a subdued theatrical pavilion with low ceilings. It was capable of holding the six thousand visitors that could stay there together. The Taize experience was mostly for the young. There were 1600 there and about 200 adults. To be adult was to be over thirty. There were three daily services at 8.15am, 12.20 and 8.30pm and all involved singing or chanting while sitting or squatting on the floor. The Taize order of service was a songbook printed in a dozen languages. Several electronic number boards flashed up the number of the next hymn. It wasn't Ancient and Modern or even pop chart catchy. It was repetitive phrases, sometimes in Latin, with lots of Alleluias sung to quite forgettable melodies with pre-recorded acoustic guitar or live organ always led by the brothers. The congregation seemed to know exactly what to do and that was the whole thing about Taize. People wouldn't go there unless they were already members of the ecumenical club.

People normally booked in for a week, so when I arrived after lunch on Thursday, I was "welcomed" by a Canadian girl and paid my "contribution" for two night's stay. She suggested I might like to pay any amount between 106 and 160 francs. I gave 150. Having pitched my tent next to a small German gathering, I then joined my afternoon discussion group. A priest from India, who was our leader, Tim a Methodist minister from Birmingham, an Australian lady who looked like an antipodean Miss Marple, one Swedish girl and one Dutch. Our topics were old age and immigration.

It probably wasn't intentional but someone pointed out that because euthanasia was legal in Holland, old age shouldn't be a problem there. The

Dutch girl wasn't best pleased and it was only Miss Aussie Marple that defused the tricky discussion by igniting another.

"Yous Indians." she said to our leader. "Yous Indians do sew much bitter in England than you dew back in yer own country."

Tim hid behind his notes and the Swede looked as though she'd swallowed an IKEA sofa. The Dutch girl glared at Miss Aussie Marple with a look that clearly thought euthanasia should be performed there and then. Our leader looked to heaven. I wondered if it was time for tea. Tea was at 5.15. It wasn't tea but a watery fruit drink in a red plastic bowl.

Supper at 7 was a red plastic bowl with water, one dollop of mash and a thin sausage the size of a pencil, one apple, two bits of bread and three dry biscuits.

"Good for the art." said Miss Aussie Marple. Whether she had meant a still life or one's medical condition, she was wrong on both counts. Brother Roger scored full marks on the simplicity scale for the food. Not a hot drink or glass of wine anywhere in sight. I kept my bottle hidden in the back of Peter lest the Germans next door got a whiff of it.

Those around me in Taize certainly seemed to believe in God and while I could not vouch for the youngsters who were there on a church outing with the school and therefore just having a bit of fun away from home, without exception the adults were club members. Comfortable as conservatives under Mrs Thatcher, happy and clappy, smug almost.

"It's my fifth time," said a retired Anglican priest from Beverly whose duty, apart from the itinerary, included cleaning the lavatories. God moved in mysterious ways. Going to Taize did nobody any harm and notched up a few more brownie points for those already well on their way to the Kingdom of Heaven.

The one thing that impressed me the most was the man who started it all, Brother Roger. The round-shouldered white haired old man sat after evening prayer in the middle of the church, which he had built with the children around him at his feet. He looked like part of the scene depicted on one of my old Sunday school attendance stamps, the one where Jesus was sitting with children around him and the words "Suffer little children to come unto me".

Brother Roger is the closest living thing to Jesus that I have ever seen. Him and Basil Hume, who did my son's school Speech Day once. I say my prayers and ask God to watch over those I love. I thank him for bringing me safely to this place and ask him to get me safely to the next. Where ever that is.

Dijon ⇥

Burgundy looks and feels like a confident, wealthy uncle. The mayor of Dijon confirms this.

The Germans were awake early and using the sort of expressions I used to read in my Battle Picture Library comics as a schoolboy after lights out with a torch under the bedclothes. "Actung". "Donner und Blitzhund". That sort of thing. I did catch the odd "Alleluia" which reminded me that I was still encamped with the God squad. After a shower and a kind goodbye handshake from the retired Anglican from Beverly and his wife, Peter and I left to the sound of the Taize community bells beckoning for Morning Prayer. Some of the faithful would already be there perched on their little wooden prayer stools facing thoughtfully towards the eight big red sails and three honeycomb banks with a candle in each hollow. Honeycomb altars. There was one simple iron crucifix offset to the right. The sunlight played through the modern stained glass slits.

It was back to the real world. The route north through the Burgundy countryside once again triggered the memory of the top shelf names at the local Majestic or Tesco. Pommard, Alexoe Corton, Gevrey Chambertin, Nuits St Georges all previously only names on labels and tastes but now bricks and mortar. Some serious piles had criss-cross patterns in different coloured tiles picked out on their steep wedge shaped roofs. I was journeying through serious vine land and it went on and on. Burgundy looked and felt as rich as the colour the name suggested, the land of milk and honey, wine and money. The aptly named Cote d'Or. Rarely seen the simple cat-cat. I was in Range Rover country.

Beaune was not in contention as I headed up the same way as the Saone for Dijon. The municipal campsite was on the Paris side of town. Fed up with tussling with Peter's gear box, which still seemed to want to go when the clutch was tighter to the floor than a carpet fitter's wife, I walked into town.

It was great to arrive at a place, park up, and then walk the streets, explore the area. I took with me my small, khaki, canvass, army shoulder bag; the one with Cpl M. Tweedie's name in pen written on its side. I found it in an army surplus store. Presumably Cpl Tweedie didn't need it anymore. In the bag were my two cameras, tape recorder, pen and notebook, the Rough Guide, half a loo roll, a compass, a lighter and the lucky horse's tooth given me by Gunilla. There was also a whistle hidden in an outside pocket, attached to the bag by a piece of string. I had an idea that if I was ever mugged; I'd pull out my whistle and blow it loudly.

I didn't dawdle. I strode out with purpose, as though I knew where I was going. I must, to those that noticed, have seemed like a man on a mission. A reporter perhaps. I didn't normally like to ask for directions because nine times out of ten, I'd find what I was looking for without help. I'd have to ask sometimes and almost as soon as I had, I'd regret it. My French wasn't good enough and I'd be left gapping like a fish out of water. The red head said that I was just like my father in that respect. He too would never ask for directions, never turn the car round when he'd missed the turn. There was always another way to get there without going back. I'd park and walk. Some days I'd walk as many miles as I'd driven.

It was the only real way to get to know a place. Take in the contours and the smells; discover the new and the old. Stumble into the backside, catch the wrong view out, as well as marvel at the well-turned out site, the place the Tourist Bureau would want me to see.

What were the chances of strolling into Dijon and meeting the mayor of the great city totally unplanned on a Saturday evening? Well I did. He couldn't have been anybody else other than the mayor. His silver hair was swept back and his smart, casual dress made him quite dashing. The women with him clucked and cooed their obvious approval. They looked over their shoulders at him. Flashed their smiles in the hope of a warm return. The men nodded at him, shook him by the hand, slapped him on the back, treated him with respect and circled around him as if to protect their champion. He had the air of a victorious fighting cock. He bought me a glass of Champagne.

The over attentive waiter was pleased to serve me, brought the bubbling flute alongside with a flourish for his mayor. Monsieur Francois Rebsamen and his entourage sat at the next tables to me in a cafe on the Place de la Liberation, so I joined them. I tried to tell him what I was doing but I don't think he believed me. He was keener to tell me what he was doing. The two of us stood there in front of his vast town hall, both of our egos as inflated as the building. Both talking, neither listening as the hot early evening sun ripened our complexions.

Not long before the mayor had arrived, I had been watching a mini demonstration outside the town hall but it was too hot to get too bothered. If the weather was as hot as the mustard, the jazz that played for the patrons of the Legend Café was cool and the evening felt like a fete. On the way back to my tent, the Cathedral St Benigne looked cavernous but with bright sunlight fanning through the leaded windows above the organ, it felt as though the Lord wasn't far away. I could have walked up any one of the solid sunbeams, followed the shafts to God knows where.

Back at the campsite I shared a bottle of wine with a neighbour and fellow traveller, Frauline Fraute, who was just finishing a week's bike tour of the region. Her English was very good and learnt at school, which put my own efforts at her mother tongue to shame. I didn't try my schoolboy war comic German out on her. I didn't want to spoil the day.

I start the day with German and finish it with one as well.

Troyes ⇌

I am pressing on for Paris, Seine-spotting as I go.

From Dijon I had originally planned to strike out right, or northeast, for Strasbourg and what I imagined would be the woody bits next to Germany. Having accepted an invitation for luncheon with Her Majesty's Ambassador at his Paris residence, I didn't think it would be polite to head off in the opposite direction. The lunch was for Thursday 28th, so I wanted to be there the day before. My blazer needed dry cleaning after the hoods of Marseille had kicked it around Frederick's yard. I couldn't turn up for a half tidy lunch looking half-untidy. So we struck out on the N71 from Dijon to Troyes and made 180 kilometres progress north and westwards following the Seine on its way to Paris.

The source of the capital's great river was a bit of a trickle among some beech trees a few k's left off the N71 mid-way between Dijon and Chatillon-s-Seine. The city of Paris owned the spot and they'd put up some wooden tables and benches for visitor to picnic. There was a grotto over the damp patch with the sculpture of a naked and reclining fat woman. Sequana was the goddess of the Seine. It was surprising though how quickly the trickle gathered pace and by Aisey-s-Seine, only a few kilometres away, it was big enough to turn a mill wheel and catch fish in.

At Chatillon-s-Seine the town seemed to be "en fete" which meant that the town square was shut to traffic and there were displays of new cars, agricultural machinery, tractor tyres and the like. It seemed too hot for much exertion so most people where sitting in the shade of cafes' umbrellas listening to the running commentary played with occasional music over the town's P.A. system. The museum was cool and empty apart from the relics and I went upstairs to see their prize exhibits from the Celtic period.

At nearby Vix, which was the highest navigable point of the Seine, they discovered the tomb of a Celtic princess who ruled over the tin trade. She had been given some wonderful gifts that were buried with her, including an enormous bronze Greek urn. It was big enough for me to climb into. I didn't. Her jewellery and gold torque looked precious. She was buried in a four-wheeled wooden chariot that had been reconstructed for us behind glass. That princess would have been a VIP in her day.

I wanted to see where Henry V married Catherine of France in 1420 but the local clerk of works had the church of St Jean in Troyes shrouded in scaffolding and closed to the public. I tried to imagine the scene as I feasted on my salad, cider and crepe in the busy bar right along side the shut church. Troyes was a mixture of ancient and modern and in some streets I could see the very old traditional timbered buildings on their own, survivors of time, fire, graffiti and town planning. In others they were bang next door to breezeblocks and concrete.

The tourist map had the town's inner ring road in the shape of a Champagne cork because we were in Champagne country. It didn't help me much. I got lost and it took me sometime to find the municipal campsite. Troyes was also something of a factory shop outlet town. It was big in the production of cloth and had become a Mecca for those keen to get their hands on designer labels at knock down prices. I wasn't tempted.

All I need is a dry cleaner and no breakdowns. Please God, no breakdowns.

Paris ⇒

Les camping d'Ile de France, Camping du Bois de Boulogne, Alle de Bord de l'eau, 75016, Paris. This is my Parisian address.

Peter and I made Paris together coming in from the south east via the N19. I had tears in my eyes. It was an emotional entry. There was only really one nasty moment when we found ourselves in the right-hand lane of a road that's left-hand lane took us to central Paris. The left lane we needed was about forty-six lanes to port with a lot of fast moving metal between. There were two ways of handling mass traffic on the move that was faster than we were. One was to look and smile and point and wave and proceed in a stop/start sort of way, picking each lane off, one at a time. The other was just to do it. I was from that school. I prayed, checked over the left shoulder for immediate danger, stuck the arm firmly out of the window, then swung the steering wheel left and accelerated. We did it. Got over into the desired lane with the pungent smell of burning rubber and the alarming squeal of French tyres mixed with the fanfare from several dozen French horns. We caused mayhem, but we did it.

Before Paris, between the capital and Troyes there were just enormous fields full of wheat, barley, oats, beans, the odd fruit and brassica. There were no hedges and not much of interest at all. It was a landscape with a big sky. I turned off the N19 at Fountaine-les-Gres and headed west through several villages that were completely devoid of the visible living. Perhaps the populace was inside servicing their combines in readiness for the harvest. At one stage I obviously turned too far south. The sun was no longer in the right place. With the lack of people to ask, I referred to the compass and the map. Country roads might be more interesting but when the only view was the other end of another vast field, the route nationale wasn't so bad.

At Nogent-s-Seine I went into the Champion supermarket to buy some provisions; three francs for a loaf of bread that would have fed a family. I stopped on the route, the other side of Provins (full of school children looking for Roman remains) and Nangis. A huge tanker truck burst past us, overtook on a long straight, rocked us violently with his slipstream, and buffeted us off course for a moment. We pulled into a lay-by with a marble look-a-like table and bench. Just opposite was a weather beaten memorial to "Capitaine Aviateur Camine" killed on September 2nd 1911. The inscription beneath his name and above his carved portrait in relief read "En tombant il s'eleve!" The French pilot was doing his best over those fields ninety years before. I had my picnic and put my left overs in a black plastic bag somewhere near where the Capitaine had put his. He died for his country. I ate for myself.

The N19 ran effortlessly to Paris via Creteil which may as well have been Paris because once there, we were there. Paris sort of arrived and at the Eiffel tower I shed a tear for the Tour. I didn't kiss the pavement even though I saw Paris as the halfway mark. I wanted to climb to the top of the famous landmark and fly a flag, tell the world that we had made it. It might not have been like landing on the moon but it was a significant milestone for Peter and me. We were the only two sharing the experience, which was rather sad. Those around us couldn't have cared less. They were busy doing their thing and we, ours. We were all travellers crossing each other's paths by sheer coincidence. I wanted to go up to someone and kiss them or shake them by the hand. I wanted some recognition, a pat on the back. A "Well done". I needed to explain that we hadn't got there on the Metro, we'd come on a troubled journey from the south west of France on three pathetic wheels in eleven long months. I didn't tell anybody. Instead we became a part of the traffic noise and the sounds and smells of Paris on a hot afternoon in June. I pulled myself together with a cup of tea. Paris prices 22 Ff. compared to 16 Ff. in Dijon and 10 Ff. back in Ste Marie-de-Campan. The tea bag on its thin piece of string was the same; what differed were the water and the surroundings. I knew which tasted the best.

I needed the Bois de Boulogne and its camp site, the nearest to central Paris and in order to find it precisely, I had to buy a map. The focal point for any Paris map seemed to be the Eiffel tower and so that was where I took my bearings. It only took me an hour and a bit to weave through the Paris traffic to the campsite next to the Seine. A Paris pigeon would have done the journey in a few minutes. I deserved champagne but I had a pichet of rouge for my trouble.

I know which tastes the best.

Bois De Boulonge

If you go down to the woods today.

When I said the Bois de Boulonge, everyone fell about laughing. It was apparently the stalking ground for prostitutes and transvestites and an area on the fringes of Paris not just with its geography. I'd only seen one odd looking bloke in chains on a bicycle who rode past me with a funny expression. He looked like a man peddling without the comfort or protection of a saddle. I think he might have been lost too. There were two enormously fat ladies, out of their car, having an argument on the wooded side of the road. Nothing odd about that except one of them was only wearing a skirt and bra and her bra was nearly the size of her car. Big was not beautiful.

I bent seven tent pegs trying to secure the tent. The campsite was probably the noisiest that I had ever stayed at, with a busy road and river only yards from my sleeping bag. During the night, a thunderstorm boiled over after the day's thirty-degree temperature.

Mademoiselle Carine Fabre wasn't having a lucky day even though it was her birthday. While our two vehicles were manoeuvring for a space fit for only one of them, the Mademoiselle lost the competition and the wing mirror off her Ford fiesta. She nearly lost her head too. Most perplexed, she leapt from her winged motor and clung on to Peter as though we were some sort of hit and run culprits. It was my fault but the inefficient clutch kept us creeping forward and the only way to stop was to turn off the engine once we'd got safely to the kerbside of the wide Avenue Charles de Gaul. After her initial upset and limpet like ride on the side of Peter, she turned out to be rather pleasant and I took a picture of her. She didn't smile for the camera. I had to record my first road traffic accident of the Tour I told her, but she still wasn't smiling. She produced and filled out the instant roadside incident insurance form that both parties agreed and signed after a prang. She did look a tad bothered because I didn't quite fit the right boxes on the form with my British driving licence. I hoped she'd get a new wing mirror fairly soon and certainly before her next birthday.

On arrival at the Federation's H.Q. not far from Gare St-Lazare in Rue du Rocher, I rang Sylvie, my main contact there, and asked her to step outside. Peter and I were parked across the road much to her amusement and pretty soon most of the occupants in the building were coming out onto the street for a look at what they had only ever read about. I had an audience with Serge, the surly boss and in fact every one seemed pleased to see me. I used Sylvie's office to catch up with e-mails on my laptop. The feeling I got when the inbox was receiving 1 of 15 messages was just like the feeling I had when hand written envelopes dropped through the letterbox. It was quite exciting. I charged up my mobile and made contact with those I needed to. I called the red head; told her I was half way there. Wherever there was.

The twelve bottles of Beaujolais had arrived from Monsieur Josepth, half of which would be served to cardiologists at a meeting the following week and the other six I'd be giving to HM's representative the next day.

Getting around Paris in Peter was not as bad as I had imagined, even with a dickey clutch, and I became quite the man about town. Parisians had a fairly cavalier attitude to other road users. They seemed to park where they liked, quite often two or three banks deep. Should I find myself hemmed in and wanting to move, I'd blow my klaxon and several heads would normally appear at nearby building's windows. The appropriate owner would come on down to move the blockage. The hooter was a vital tool for Paris driving and it was used at almost every intersection in the city along with the gesticulating hand movement. Driving was not for the timid and even if I didn't know where I was going, I had to go there with purpose.

Among the people I contacted was Ludvig Bosse, the multilingual marketing man of Piaggio H.Q. at La Defense in Paris. He seemed to have taken an interest in Peter's exploits and was able to direct me to a suitable garage where someone would actually look at the clutch. I took Peter on a long slow cross-town trek to the recommended Piaggio dealer. Within an hour and for two hundred Francs, they had the job done. No sucking of air over teeth or "Oh la las" just a mechanic who knew what he was doing to what. I drooled with envy at the bright new three wheelers in the show room and realised too that with the amount I'd spent on Peter I could probably be the proud owner of any one of them. Peter did have a certain style all of his own and when we drove off with a working clutch, I would not have swapped him. Those in central Paris that afternoon would have heard me singing my head off in a state of absolute happiness.

If you go down to the woods today, you're sure of a big surprise.

39 Rue Du Faubourg Saint-Honore ⇸

There's a frivolous TV advertisement in Britain for chocolate balls wrapped in gold paper, stacked like a pyramid on a platter, being served at the Ambassador's ball. It's the one where a glamorous, female, foreign guest says, "Whiz sees chocolates you really spoils us Mr Ambassador." The Ambassador spoils us, but not with his balls.

The British purchased 39 Rue Du Faubourg St Honore in 1814 for 35,000 pounds in gold for the Duke of Wellington to use as his residence in Paris. The seller was Napoleon's ex-wife which, would have been a bit of a double whammy for Bonaparte. First your archenemy buys a house with all its contents from your ex-Mrs and then, not many months later, he gives you a thorough thrashing at Waterloo. The residence was palatial and the decor lavish. It was the British Embassy in Paris and the place where I was going to have lunch.

I woke in less grand surroundings. My little tent on the Camping du Bois de Boulogne out on the west side of Paris, in the 16th arrondissssement, overlooked the Seine as it made its murky way north out of the capital. I showered and dressed in the communal block. Not jeans for that day, but rather a white shirt and tie, the cleaned blazer and a half tidy pair of light coloured trousers I'd been keeping on one side. The shoes were the same as always. The brown Timberland deck variety. Scuffed with the miles. Mother always said you could judge a man by his shoes. Mine looked rather beaten up but comfortable. I guessed that summed me up pretty well. Looking as smart as I could, I packed up Peter and headed off east, into central Paris. On the side of one leafy avenue in the Bois de Boulogne, a pantomime dame took her breakfast from the roof of her car. She guzzled bread and wine through her very ruby red lips. Her white-powdered face beamed out under a set of curls straight from the Good Ship Lollypop. She gave us a big wave as we sailed past, saluted a fellow trooper, my machine as theatrical as she was. It must have been a strange world in those woods, a land of sexual fantasy and reality. I waved back at the transvestite with an appetite, taking a snack between meals, before resuming her daytime trade.

Paris was busy. It was hot. I was excited. I had to rendezvous with the man from the British Heart Foundation. He'd flown over from London for the day to be at the Ambassador's lunch. Denis Christian was deputy chief of fundraising. He was a retired and well-travelled ex-policeman who had taken on the demanding role of demanding money for the BHF. What he brought to the party must work because the previous year they raised £60 million. His aim was to get giving up to a level of 10p per head of the population. At the moment it was 9 point something. The British Heart Foundation was Britain's sixth biggest charity and looked at with frog-green envy by the French who raised one tenth of the British amount. Denis was sitting outside in the sunshine and sipping a small beer at the café we'd agreed to meet in, the one in the Place Etoile, just off the Arc de Triumph. We needn't have worried about recognising each other. Peter's kerbside arrival was enough.

"I'll get a taxi." He said when the time came for us to leave the cafe.

"No. You'll travel with me in Peter." I insisted. Denis didn't look at all keen. Nevertheless he squeezed into Peter and we set off for luncheon with the Ambassador. There was no room for any mutiny on this Bounty and Mr Christian and I sweated our way through the Paris traffic on down the Rue du Faubourg St Honore. Just before the Elycee Palace we were stopped by one of the many policemen on duty. There were more than a handful of armed soldiers as well, not quite trooping their colours, but none the less fingering their triggers. The visiting Syrian President was coming and going at about the same time as we were, with the resultant traffic diversions. I played my "You have to let me down here " card by holding up to the windscreen my invitation embossed with rampant Lion and Unicorn. It did the trick and without diplomatic incident or a single soldier presenting his arms in the mistaken belief that the Syrians were arriving on three wheels, we were waved through. We slipped regally past the palace and arrived outside the heavy doors that guard No 39. Pressing the bell and being asked who is was, I was tempted to say something silly into the intercom, like "Another delivery of Ferrero Roche", but I didn't with Mr Christian looking on. In his grey suit, he looked the most business like passenger Peter had encountered so far.

We were the first to arrive and were warmly greeted by Ben Newick, the butler, and his wife Mandy, the PA. I presented her with a bunch of flowers. She'd been very helpful. Despite the traffic and the Syrians, we were fifteen minutes early. We were shown into the glorious garden where the lawn was just being perfectly mown in light and dark green straight lines. Mandy and Ben chatted to us and chilled white wine and Champagne arrived at the same time as Sylvie, the first from the French Federation.

Matthew Lodge was there. He was Sir Michael Jay's right hand man and had been instrumental in setting up the lunch, with Mandy's help. Serge Lafaye, general manager of the Federation, arrived looking very hot and bothered. Sir Michael Jay, who I could tell at twenty paces was obviously the Ambassador, joined us. Tall, lean in a smart light grey suit with white shirt , sober tie and spectacles that go lighter and darker according to sunshine, he took centre stage beside the garden table. He took his jacket off. We knew that we were in important company, in important surroundings but Sir Michael had an ease of manner that was reciprocated as a result. It wasn't going to be an audience with an old buffer of a statesman, but a lunch for eight with the main conversation relevant to things of the heart, health issues. We had drawn together the British with Denis Christian and the French led by Professor Daniel Thomas, President of the Federation. Clare was the eighth guest and she had recently joined the Embassy staff as a local liaison officer specialising in health and educational issues.

James the French chef, who didn't speak a word of English, had been there for over thirty years and because Lady Sylvia Jay had become Chairperson of the British Food and Drinks Council, much of what was prepared in the kitchens, was of British origin. They were worried that James might have taken French umbrage but he had risen to the challenge, and if our menu was anything to go by, produced some wonderful plats du jour. The four-course menu had been well thought out. The grilled Pandora was sea bream and the very special touch was the elderflower water ice, frozen and sculptured into the shape of a heart. Sir Michael was a noble host and he said some very charming words about my efforts at bringing the British and French together that day.

The British had their menu cards printed in English and the French in French. British farmhouse cheese was a very good general description as one of the three presented was Stinking Bishop from Devon. I was not sure how that would translate in French. Our Ambassador however thought Le Stinking Bishop would probably do the job. Most French thought that the British were incapable of producing cheese, other than cheddar. Sadly at that time, soft cheeses could not be a part of the menu because of foot and mouth issues, but when they were reintroduced, French guests at that table would discover what we had known about for years. The white wine was English and I didn't see a single French wince. I did smile however at the description on the menu card of the '95 Pommard. In English it was fine with the word MERODE in brackets. But on the French cards the letter O had mysteriously vanished. Every inch the diplomat, Sir Michael Jay, hadn't meant to describe the burgundy as shit.

After lunch the Ambassador showed us Lady Sylvia's herb garden. Denis Christian left to Buzz it back to Stanstead, a less cramped and smoother ride than the one he had in Peter. Sir Michael drove the little three-wheeler around his front yard with the press photographer snapping away and me praying that the repaired clutch pedal would continue to work. It did.

Sir Michael would leave soon to join the foreign office in London. He was too young and too able to retire. He had already done Washington, so he'd perhaps find London and his home in Chelsea a bit "normal" after that special corner of Paris. His houseguests will probably no longer include Her Majesty the Queen, the Redgrave family, David Hockney, Tom Stoppard, John Major and Tony Blair and I didn't expect I'd be invited for lunch again.

Peter and I left the Embassy and headed for Charles de Gaulle airport. It was a Red day on the roads and the first day of the school summer holidays with early leavers already clogging the tarmac arteries. Getting near the airport and finding a bed took a long time, but the B&B place at 265 Ff. a night had a slot, presumably because potential punters thought there was some catch. Having found my room and with no time to wash and brush up, it was in a cab and back to central Paris to Rue Theodule Ribot and the home of Sylvie and her husband Stephane and their two young sons. Sylvie had always promised me a plat du jour at her apartment when I arrived in Paris and we spent a most pleasant evening with, for the second time that day, not a chocolate ball anywhere to be seen.

Sylvie had been getting strange phone calls. For some reason she thought that the Federation wanted to get rid of her, that they were using underhand tactics to drive her from her job. The phone rang when I was there and her husband took the call. There was apparently no response from the other end. Sylvie shook her head, looked disturbed and unsettled. She was near to tears. Her man shouted at the non-communicative caller. Meant every word that I didn't understand. It was all rather strange. Disturbing if true.

Sylvie's left her job. I haven't been able to speak to her since. I hope she's all right.

Bath. ⇌

Be sure to wear some flour in your hair.

Going back to England, or the Grange, was like having an exeat from boarding school. It was a change to the routine of travelling, which was perhaps a strange concept. How could a journey such as mine ever be called routine? It wasn't often that I knew where my next stop was going to be, so I supposed the reassurance provided by familiar surroundings was welcome. Anyway that was what I did for the last weekend of June 2001. It was wonderful to swap the blue Peter for the red head. I flew back to her flat in Bath and her own special brand of hospitality. It was unsettling for both of us but like drug addicts, we couldn't kick the habit.

The trip coincided with the Bath Charity Boules festivities. The annual ritual saw Queen Square, opposite the Francis Hotel in Bath, taken over by mid summer revellers who ate, drank, danced, watched and played the game of boules. The standard of play wasn't anything like that I'd seen in the towns and villages around France, but the drinking was to the same high standard.

The whole thing kicked off on the Friday night with the Boules Ball and that year's theme was flowers. There were some wonderfully colourful costumes, some more elaborate than others. The occupants of one table all had giant flowerpots on their heads. Some had gone to great lengths to dress up as giant sunflowers. One or two of the women who apparently hadn't made any effort assured me that they were wearing flowery underwear. I wasn't prepared to verify the claims. Not with the red head on my arm. One girl came as herself and was accused of not bothering but her name was Fleur.

The red head looked like a large peony. Most had a floral shirt and shorts or a flowery dress and then there was me, dressed up as a sack of flour.

British Airways had lost my one bag of luggage from Paris and I had packed an Hawaiian shirt for the occasion. The flour sack idea came to me as a simple alternative and the red head was able to fit me up in some hessian with the word "flour" emblazoned across my sacking chest. The accompanying bag of Waitrose organic strong white flour was, as the evening developed, a real nuisance to those its contents came into contact with. It was amazing just how far a small bag of flour would go. Launched from a desert spoon and catapulted over my shoulder towards the tables behind, the result looked as though an instant snowstorm had swirled its way into the marquee. I was the loader and launcher of the air borne attacks and Phil de Glanville, one of the ten on our table, was the aimer. He couldn't actually fire the spoon himself because he only had one good arm and being the ex-captain of England's rugby team, he was probably better at giving orders than taking them. It was a good-natured evening; lots of fun, with only one bottle of mineral water emptied over my flour-covered hair. I turned into something of a cross between the Pillsbury doughboy and a very white Rastafarian with unusual "bread" locks.

It was always very good to catch up with family and friends, all of whose generosity never ceased to amaze me. On the Sunday I lunched with my sisters and Mother. They wanted the latest news and Mother loved the idea of her son having lunch with the British Ambassador. It was something she could tell her friends about at her next bridge evening.

The red head was, as always, very long suffering and the Bartons deserved a mention for taking delivery of my lost luggage when it did eventually turn up. A courier drove it from Heathrow to their house (I wasn't sure if I'd be staying there or not) and woke them all up before 7am the morning after the Boules Ball. Apparently the driver thought that my good friend Barton was a baker with all the flour still clinging to him from the night before.

I fly back to Paris with a stinking cold. Running around as a flour sack probably wasn't a good idea.

Epernay ⇥

The air is as heavy as the cold in my nose. What we both need is a good clear out. The air, a good thunder storm with some more rain and my nose something of pretty similar proportions.

It was no good staying cooped up in the slot machine world of the B&B hotel, so by mid morning Peter and I set off around the Charles de Gaulle airport. North, then east, then south, to seek out that first choice destination of every one who had ever won any money on TV quiz shows or in the National Lottery.

"And what will you be doing with the money?"

"I'll be taking the family to Disneyland." It always seemed to be the first priority. We were going there too. I expected to see towering turrets of Chateau Sleeping Beauty with exploding fireworks and swooping blue birds, tons of fairy glitter with singing dwarfs tending to the needs of bright wide eyed furry animals. Why on earth, I can't imagine. Maybe Walt's publicity machine had got to me or maybe it was the Feverex powders.

In reality the whole of the northeastern edge of Paris was a hybrid of new building sites. There were construction cranes everywhere. The new trees on the roadside and roundabouts looked as though they had been crucified. Their new branches had been nailed to wooden frames so they'd conform. I decided against parting with any cash for taking Peter through the Disneyland tollgates. Once in there, I wasn't sure what might happen to us. We took the last minute escape exit to the left and headed back down the Disney dual carriageway, away from his fantasy and fun and back to our own. Just in case we wanted to change our mind, Mr Disney had thoughtfully put in a re-entry slip road that would have taken us right back to the car parking tollgates. I could imagine how many families had run that gauntlet, been stuck on that merry-go-round.

"You're not going."

"Oh please Dad. We promise to be good."

"OK then."

"How much for a family ticket please?"

"How much! I'm not bloody paying that."

"Oh please Dad."

Round and round they'd go on the last free ride this side of Mickey's hungry mouth. I resisted and set course for Epernay.

The god between Goofy and Champagne was grain. It must be because the silos were more prominent than the churches. In some big fields harvesting had already started but most still smelt of the sprayer's last visit. Some of the wheat was lodged, not with corn circle symmetry but by rain drop damage.

If the fields between Paris and Epernay contributed to the breadbasket of France, then Epernay itself provided the bubbles. It was supposed to be the capital of Champagne country and because I'd cut the phlegm with a glass or two in my time, it did seem appropriate to visit the home of Moet et Chandon. Right then it was not the cutting of the phlegm I needed but rather the annihilation of it. Sadly that evening was not for tasting even if the buds had let me. When I arrived, the Champagne houses were shut. The Moet premises were enormous and spread over several blocks up and off the Avenue de Champagne. An empire had been built on the bubbles and they owned Mercier, Dom Perignon and other labels. If their fizz didn't get up the nose, maybe their Dior perfume would.

If I'd thought that Champagne's capital was going to feel like the so-called smarter enclosures at royal Ascot, then I was wrong. I heard more popping French scooters haring around the Place de la Republique than popping French corks in the bars around it. I didn't hear one, but then do the goldfish see the water that they swim in? I was beginning to sound like Eric Cantona and the powders were getting to me again.

I take one more Feverex and zip up the flaps on my tent.

303

Chalons-En-Champagne

The thunder storm rages right over my little shelter in Epernay. It then follows me.

Chalons-en-Champagne had only recently been renamed as such and until I got quite close it was still called Chalon-sur-Marne. There was much about the Champagne business that was image. Who drinks whose was important. I suspected that it was as competitive as the fashion industry and the different maisons (there were 120 serious ones) vied with each other for a market that was already over supplied. The scare that we wouldn't be able to get enough in order to celebrate the Millennium was a great marketing ploy.

The biggest and best, and the only one I could see in Chalons-en-Champagne was Joseph Perrier. For about 150 years that particular Perrier (not to be confused with the fizzy water) had been at home at the foot of the hill where the cellars were created in the Roman chalk pit workings. The underground caves of Joseph Perrier ran for two miles and provided the ideal nursery for the maturing wine. Humidity was on tap from the constant rising damp and the temperature gauge was stuck on ten degrees C. It was cool when I walked into the labyrinth and so too was the current boss and descendant, Jean-Claude Fourmon. He was a very dapper French man who dressed like the sort of person he hoped would enjoy drinking his brew. About 150,000 bottles of the 650,000 produced every year found their way to British sippers. Monsieur Fourman liked to play up to the photograph of him and the Prince of Wales (they both looked about twelve) and the presentation of a bottle of Joseph Perrier at a polo match. The company ties with important Britain went back to the Duke of Wellington and Queen Victoria, but in the bubbly world of spin, we were not told if the sovereign was amused or not.

Jean-Claude invited me for a plat du jour at la Medina (specialites tunisiennes) right opposite the town hall and we drank a bottle of his Champagne with the couscous. Climate was the most important factor in determining the quality of the finished sparkling drink. Bad weather in June, the flowering period, could be disastrous. Hail storms were as popular as plagues of locusts in old Egypt, but more rare. Their damage, which could be very local, might effect vines for three or four years. Some insured against freak weather damage but it was very expensive and not for Joseph Perrier.

Monsieur Fourman talked about some great vintage years, nodding knowingly like some expert who'd discovered something precious at a car boot sale. '53,'59, '62 and '66 were all worth a nod with anything any good before 1947 just sighed over as looters had seized the lot. The Pinot Noir, Chardonnay and Pinot Meunier grapes that were used to produce the finished product came from 21 hectares of family owned vineyards and that was sufficient for a third of the annual production. The remaining two thirds came from thirty different growers. Almost so as to justify the end price, much mention was made of the hands-on skill required to bring the fizz to perfection. "Remuage" was the hand turning of the bottles as they sat nose down in their special racks encouraging the impurities to the top. Between "degorgement" (removing of the sediment) and "habillage" (labelling), the bottles rested for a least three months. Non vintage Champagne was less than three years old and formed the bulk of the production.

Genned up and encouraged by the enthusiastic Monsieur Fourman to drink nothing but his fizz ever again, I clambered into Peter and drunk drove my way out of town and onto the sober roads east.

The storms seemed to follow me as I made my dull way towards Nancy. The roads were straight with the odd up bit and then the odd down bit. It was serial cereal country and the little towns and villages between Chalon-en-Champagne and Ligny-en-Barrois were often drab. The road ran through and didn't see a reason to stop. On either side shuttered up windows and grubby dwellings hugged the route indistinctly. In one, the "boutique de pain" seemed aptly named and was well worth hastening past. In nearly all of them I saw that old man, sitting on his door step, cigarette perched on his bottom lip, dangling towards the knee, an off-white vest, drab blue trousers, dirty baseball cap and trainers and skin the colour of dark tan shoe polish. As I went past his head turned in direct proportion to my progress. Speedy sports cars gave him a pain in the neck, tractors and trucks he'd take with a minor crick, while cyclists and old three-wheeled Piaggios he could enjoy, study at his leisure. He'd always have the same expression no matter what went past him. Whether Lady Godiva or a weapon of mass destruction on its motorised launcher. He was the same guy in every settlement and that was his job; the village lookout.

With the wind howling around the campsite, adding further venom to the already stinging rain as I wrote up my days damp notes, I thought that any other time, any other place, any other where would have been a pretty good option. It wasn't a Martini moment.

I won't need a shower in the morning. The rain's so hard it's coming through two layers of tent and falling as a fine spray all over me.

Toul ⇥

I remember where I was when President Kennedy was shot and when Armstrong first walked on the moon. I'll never forget where I was on July 6ᵗʰ when my mobile rang.
"You've got it wrong," I say to the red head who is in tears.

All night the wind howled. I was amazed that my little tent, the only one at the site, withstood the blasting at the municipal campsite in Ligny-en-Barrois. Reminiscent of the scene in Macbeth, the night of Duncan's murder, the trees tossed and the clouds whipped across the night sky in some fantastic race. People died in the night. Eleven crushed by falling branches at an outside concert near Strasbourg. Forty kilometres from where I was camping. For early July it wasn't right. It wasn't right for my mother.

The Sunday before I had seen her. I had visited my sister in Gloucestershire. Both my sisters there, and my mother. It was one of those English summer days where everything was bright and fresh and we had lunch in the sunny garden. Mother looked well. Maybe a little too thin but elegant. She talked about father. She always talked about father. Still loved him even though they had been apart for years. She was concerned about him, worried about his health, what he was going to do. Where he was going to die. She was worried about us too, her grown up children. Worried about what we were doing with our lives. She worried about her grandchildren as well. She spent too much of her life worrying. Most of all she worried about what would happen

308

to her in old age. If only she could have seen the future. If only she could have understood that we didn't want her to worry. When mother laughed, she had the most beautiful smile. She would light up any room. She was a good-looking woman, intelligent and witty. Her glass though was always half empty. Too many of her father's genes or maybe the Meningitis had flipped some depressing switch when she was a girl.

My youngest sister's arrival hadn't helped. We'd joke about it cruelly, my sisters and I. She was the only mother we knew who had suffered post-natal depression for over forty years. She was a complex character and I didn't really understand her. Didn't try hard enough. Perhaps that was the reason I never seemed to mention her much in conversation. I'd talk about "my old man" but rarely my mother. She was a pessimist and I wasn't a good son. What did she expect? I didn't visit her as often as I might. Probably thought that father should have left her years before he had. I never felt really close to her. I think I loved her but never told her. Found it very hard to put my arms around her, even when she was crying. I did and she loved me, her only son. Called me "Charlie boy". She was probably very proud of me behind my back. Packed my tuck box and my trunk, sent me off to boarding school. She didn't smother me with affection but wrote me letters. Enclosed ten-shilling notes. Taught other children all her life but never taught me.

Mother was a past master at making a crisis out of a drama. She would always start her sentences with an exclamation mark and finish them with one as well. It was my eldest sister Jane's wedding day at our riverside home in Tansor and the British Summer was doing its best. Gale-force winds and driving rain. Despite father's reassurances, mother thought that the marquee was in danger of jumping the swollen river Nene and ending up on Simpson's farm. So mother rang the George at Stamford.

"Good morning madam," said the manager.

"I'd like you to put on a wedding reception for two hundred and fifty people, " said mother.

"Certainly madam. It would be a pleasure. What date?"

"This afternoon," said mother. I bet she wished she could return to that time, wind the clock back and stop worrying.

The mobile rang. It was the red head. I told her that she had it wrong. There was some dreadful mistake.

"You mean father," I said.

Mother had been found in her cottage. Lying on the floor upstairs in her bedroom. She'd been dead for a day or two. The neighbours were concerned because the curtains hadn't been opened. They thought that she might have been watching Wimbledon on the Tele. She would have been. It was probably one of the last things she had seen. Her heart gave out. She never told us she had a weak heart. Didn't tell us that she was on pills for it.

I kissed her good-bye, kissed her on each cheek in my sister's garden the Sunday before.

"Keep in touch Charlie Boy."

It rained all the way to Troul and Peter's wiper couldn't cope. It didn't really matter because the tears in my eyes and thoughts in my head made the journey a blur anyway. Schedules, such as they were, had gone out of the window. I was Strasbourg airport bound and a plane back to Gatwick at 17.45 the next day. Back to England again, back to see my mother delivered with dignity back to her maker. It was unreal. A nightmare twist to the surreal journey.

In Troul the rain stopped and so did I at one of those typical bar, salle des jeux, cafe type places where people could play the Rapido lottery every few minutes or take it out on the lino-lined football table, spinning skewered men wildly. One moved, they all moved. Not a smart looking person to be seen in the joint unless Claudia Schiffer counted, nearly naked on the wall. The steak was not as tough as the days that lay ahead. The waitress smiled and freckle faced looked happy even though her clothes looked sad. What else could she have expected in a town where vegetables and sledgehammers were sold in the same supermarket aisle and where most of the other shoppers were sun-dried and weatherworn, boiler suited from brawn county? I wanted her to take me upstairs, to lie on a bed with her. I needed to cry on her shoulder, make her sad clothes damp with my tears.

The Sapier Pompiers of Toul were a classy act and they had been out after the previous night's storm cleaning up the damage. Twenty-two of them manned the station in the town and for most it was a full time job. Cars caused more work than fires, but last night's blow had brought them out in strength. They asked me in for a cup of coffee, strong, sweet and black. Perhaps I looked a little storm damaged. Even the tourist office had been effected by the storm. A hasty hand written note stuck to the door said, "Cause orage fermeture exceptionelle". Maybe the wind had broken in and played havoc with their brochures. The blue plastic protective covering around a large window of the Cathedrale Saint-Etienne de Toul was still in somewhat of a flap, the scaffolding shaken not stirred and the streets around littered with the debris plucked from roofs and trees.

My natural urgency to get to as near as Strasbourg airport as possible meant that Nancy didn't get a look in. Heavy skies seemed to match my heavy heart and sight seeing didn't feel right. There would be a lot of mourning in the days to come.

"Keep in touch Charlie boy," she says as I disappear back to France.

Oundle, Northamptonshire ⇥

It is difficult to believe that mother is in there.

Crowson's, the undertakers from Barnwell, gave me the container with mother's ashes in it. The three of us met up, my two sisters and I, and we obeyed her last wishes. Mother wanted her ashes to be spread in the grounds of the Oundle School Chapel.

I took the top off and mother looked grey. Her ash spread like fine powder and blew with the breeze. She stuck to our fingers like a thin silk glove. We spread her through the lush plants and shrubs, around the base of the trees where she had done the same for her mother. Her father too I believed. He'd been the school chaplain, which gave him every right to be there. My mother had loved that place so it gave her every right too.

Besides, it is her last wish. Goodbye Mother, goodbye.

Strasbourg ⇌

I feel disconnected.

My mother's untimely death meant that I got to see my daughter again. We hadn't seen each other for over five years and she travelled over from Hawaii where she lived and worked as a night club singer. She was twenty-nine and had a wit as sharp as a new razor. Once she had been blunt. Once she had been an awkward teenager who didn't understand her parents and whose parents didn't understand her. Meeting again, she was someone to be proud of, someone who cared and someone I loved even more than I used to. Lose a mother and gain a daughter. It was sour and sweet, sad and happy, the right words but in their order wrong.

Mother's passing bought out the hot sun. There were Sun like headlines for the sun. It was hot and as the Telegraph pointed out, temperatures in Britain were higher than those in Hawaii. The front must have followed my daughter. Apart from the heat there were two other things that caught my eye in the Sunday papers as the red head delivered me back to Gatwick. The picture of the crowds on Brighton beach, as disturbing as a picture of those starving masses in Ethiopia. Both crowds seemed to be standing, waiting for something. Obscenely those on the beach were fat through too much, whilst those in the bush bloated by too little. On the right of those crowded on the shore, water, lavish salt water to play in. For the throng in Africa not a drop to play in and precious few to drink. Our lot pink and laughing, their lot dark and crying.

The second thing I took some notice of was a report about France's roadside trees being taken out because Frances' drivers kept killing themselves

314

on them. I was no tree hugger but for the good they did to the air, for the guidance they gave to the routes they lined and because they looked good and were there first, please couldn't France keep its Plane trees? The minister responsible was apparently advocating chain sawing them down and planting replacements elsewhere. I thought a better ploy would be to fine those that hit road side trees and impose a speed limit on all such roads. Maybe then those on the wonderful tree lined routes would appreciate their guardians and maybe drive accordingly. It was the speed that killed and funnily enough trees tended to stand fairly still.

The trees in Strasbourg waved their leaves a little as we came in from the airport. The night plane was late and so rather than trying to extract Peter from the long stay in the dark, I took a taxi to Lingolsheim and the Ibis hotel there. The driver was on a mission and covered the few k's in a few seconds on the wrong side of the road and with lots of muttering. Fine for me having just arrived from Blair's left hand Britain but perhaps not so hot for the taxi man's fellow road users more used to the right. He did charge me one hundred francs which had I thought about it would have been one of the most expensive journeys in the world, but I was tired and sunburnt like a lobster from the English sunshine. I felt disconnected but carried on like an automaton.

In the morning the centre of Strasbourg was not difficult to find with the beacon of the Cathedrale de Notre Dame pointing itself out head and shoulders higher than the rest. Its spire was caged in by a mass of metal tubing. It looked ready for take off. The statue of Gutenberg looked smudged which would not have amused the father of print. His neighbour in the square was a children's merry-go-round which might not have amused him either. The centre of Strasbourg was an island ringed by water, the river Ill (spelt on maps like the English word for not well or in Roman numerals three), and at the west end, Petite France was as much water as it was land. Pretty water side restaurants and houses were bedecked with hanging flowers and snapping tourists in a sort of Hansel and Gretelville.

The glass parliament was shut for the summer holidays but I took the picture of Peter with my suitcase on his back just so I could caption the result, "Peter takes my case to the European Court of Human Rights." There were no storks. I didn't see a stork on a chimney pot. I did see some soft cuddly ones hanging around in a leggy group in a gift shop between the cathedral and the old printer.

As with many of the towns and villages in Alsace, houses looked like mock Tudor cuckoo clocks with flower boxes in every orifice. I knew that I was in "cold winter" country because of the log piles and the steep roofs. Germany was never far away and in fact that part of France had been German as much as it has been French in recent history; for 52 years from 1870 to1918 and from1940 to 1944. The place names were certainly not French with "bach" playing a lot on the road signs. Oberlauterbach, Seebach, Sarlbach, and a broad list of other bachs.

I had tea in Wissembourg and knew that I was in a foreign land in a foreign land. It arrived as a cup of hot water with a tea bag on a string in the saucer just like in France.

"Bitte" said the waitress when I was paying her.

"Yes it was rather" said I which confused her.

The overnight campsite looked like an early Butlin's resort. Camping Fleckenstein was a sea of tents, caravans and huts around a lake in the Parc Regional des Vosges du Nord. It was pine forest to pine forest thick with scantily clad Prussian types. I pitched my tent and went back into Lembach and found the auberge de cheval blanc for an evening meal. The prawn salad, which was actually a prawn kebab, cheese and half a bottle of milky coloured Alsace for the whoopee-it's-summer-and-let's-get-the-tourist-where-it-hurts price of 230 francs. I shared an outside table with a middle aged German couple who whispered a lot. When they left he said his name was Alf.

Alf Veedasane I think, but I didn't catch hers.

Metz ⇥

The Alsatian wakes me at first light. It isn't the dog barking. I think the talking is German but actually it isn't. It's Elsassisch.

When a campsite of those proportions stirred, I stirred with it. According to the Alsace camping guide it was number two in the region with slots for 750 visitors. I didn't wait for the alarm call. It was provided at five forty six by some unhappy camper. He had gone to get something from his car and forgotten to deactivate the alarm system. I could feel his blushes from a hundred yards away. The site was so packed that I heard my next door neighbour turning over. Before lights out the previous evening, I heard him reading a bed time story to his three year old Natalie and then, a bit later, I heard the one he read to his thirty year old wife, Ingrid. Thank goodness he didn't get his wires crossed. In Elsassisch it wasn't easy to tell although intonation had a language all of its own.

The morning was pine forests; a wooded roller coaster but not high, nothing over five hundred metres and not too low either. At Bitche I'd expected to find a lot of hard women, instead it was hard men. Bitche was a town and an army camp with a stark grey citadel overlooking it. There were a lot of stark grey police about and the equally black and white press. A girl's burnt body had been found, apparently the result of a road accident, where the guilty driver may have tried to get rid of the evidence. She was only sixteen.

The forest ended and the farmland took over again and big round bales littered the fields like giant droppings. The occasional road sign warned of the leaping deer. Picasso-like designs showed the antlered beasts stretching

317

themselves to cross the road in their triangles. There should be others to warn of the big green John Deeres. They were a more common sighting.

Sarreguemines sounded dangerous in an unexploded way, so we didn't dwell and pressed on westward. The sandwich lunch at Saint-Avold was chicken and mayo. I'd spotted a sporting goods Hypermarket on the way in and was determined to call and purchase some new tent pegs. The previous night's efforts had been abysmal. The current pegs had about as much strength as paper clips. They bent when I selected them for tent holding up duty and when I dared to show them the wooden mallet, they became like Gwyneth Paltrow on Oscar night, incapable of standing up straight and doing the job properly. They bent double and looked like musical notes, crotchets or quavers, great for Covent Garden but certainly not the sort of anchor on which to base any camping venue. The new pegs were like R.S.J's (rolled steel joists) and when I uncovered my hammer to help them do their job, I was sure I'd hear them say "Come on. Hit me. I'm hard."

Metz had a big cathedral I wanted to see. Its campsite by the river Moselle was one of the best. I was welcomed and then a girl on a bicycle led me to my slot (No 47) right on the riverbank. I made friends with the five white geese who appeared and helped me to enjoy my light supper at the waterside table. John Poulsen from Arizona joined me. He was a wiry fifty-eight year old who was cycling from Hungary to Belgium. He had retired as the lineman from the county. He'd got a shack in Mexico and had a hankering for one in Brittany. He chewed on a thin cigar and called me sir. I did neither. We drank a bottle of red wine and some more and told each other our traveller's tales and got on just fine. Like two pilgrims who'd never ever meet again sharing a life in an hour or so.

It's not until I hear myself talking, telling my story, that I realise I have a story to tell.

Verdun ⚔

The stained glass windows in the cathedral St. Etienne in Metz are vibrant with the bright morning sun punching out the Chagall designs of the sixties and those of four hundred years earlier with equal impact. The nave roof seems to reach up to heaven and there is the scent of fresh flowers rather than burnt candle wax which makes the huge place more alive than dead. Stained glass needs light, like film needs a projector and that day's matinee is a powerful and colourful thriller. I pray for mother.

The hot sun shone on Verdun. That such horror, man made, not enforced by nature, should have existed in Europe almost in living memory was mind blowing. There were memorials everywhere lest we forget. The screaming head of Rodin's statue outside the station was most evocative of what bad we did to each other. The restored cannon, polished shells and marble carved lists of fights from 450 to 1916 served to remind how many times we'd got it so wrong.

There was a phone box, a red English telephone box, not far from the tower that had tried to protect the town on the river Meuse. If I started dialling and tried to dial one million numbers, I still wouldn't have dialled up the number of dead that piled up defending or attacking that place for just two years of the First World War.

It was not in Verdun itself that I sensed the magnitude of that grave chapter in history. North I ran into other monuments, a suitably solid one for Andre Maginot, the man behind the line and a stone carved dead lion that marked the spot beyond which the enemy could not advance any further in 1916.

The Ossuaire de Douaumont was an enormous grey stone structure with its centre pointing skywards, a giant finger pointing to God, a temple for the dead and containing the dead with row upon row of crosses in its front well kept lawns. The fort de Douaumont was set up on the highest ground to defend Verdun. Its gruesome history with both French and German occupants, was still told with tours of the underground fortress for sixteen francs a look. I didn't want to.

To my mind the most vivid testament to the unbelievable carnage was that which was created at the time. It was still there all around nearly one hundred years later. It was what was done to the landscape. Hills and hollows, dips and bumps, craters and mounds, the result of fierce bombardment beyond belief, a macabre unplayable golf course, where all the fairways were bunkers. Hilltops had been blown away, villages taken off the map forever and the stone mason's chisel made blunt by the letters of a million deaths. My Rough Guide to France summed it up well.

"The battle of Verdun opened on the morning of February 21st 1916 with a German artillery barrage that lasted ten hours and expended two million shells. It concentrated on the forts of Vaux and Douaumont, which the French had built after the 1870 Franco-Prussian War. By the time the main battle ended ten months later, nine villages had been pounded to nothing. Not even their sites are detectable in aerial photos of the time. The heavy artillery shells ploughed the ground to a depth of eight metres and, although much of it is now reforested, there are parts even today that steadfastly refuse anchorage to any but the coarsest vegetation."

But why Verdun? The Rough Guide again gave a good account.

"Long a frontier town, in the aftermath of German victory in the 1870-71 war Verdun and its environs became the most heavily fortified military region in France, the linchpin of its northeastern defences. For this reason, and in order to break the stalemate of trench warfare, the German General Erich von Falkenhayn chose it as the target for an offensive that, in 1916, was the most devastating ever launched in the annals of war. His intention was "to bleed the French army to death and strike a devastating blow at the morale of the French people". He advanced to within 5km of the town, but never succeeded in taking it. Gradually the French clawed back the lost ground, but final victory came only in the last months of the war in 1918 and then only with the aid of US troops. The best part of a million men died in the battle, both French and German, to say nothing of the numbers scarred for life by their experiences. But it was particularly devastating for the French: the battle was fought on their native soil against the enemy who had humiliated them so badly in 1870, and it decimated the country's young male population. Most of the names inscribed on the thousands of sad memorials that stand in every village, hamlet and town of France belong to men who died at Verdun."

It didn't seem right somehow that the sun shone. It should have been gloomy or overcast, raining at least but not sunny and bright. Not Hawaiian shirts at a state funeral, shorts and sandals where black ties, black suits and black leather shoes should have been worn. If those battlefields did nothing else other than remind us of the utter stupidity of war and the stubbornness of war makers, then the million or so who died there will still have died in vain.

At least the tarmac roads in that part of Alsace-Lorraine seemed to be weeping their black tar tears in sympathy at the slaughter all around them. Like black treacle the surface oozed under the heat and weight of the many giant tractors on corn cart. Tipper trailers of golden grain and flat four wheelers stacked with straw bales, all hurried for the safety of the store.

It is ironic that there is such a golden harvest from earth so tainted, so scarred for life.

Charleville - Mezieres

Life's a beach in Saint Quentin

The day's journey in Peter was another roller coaster, past dozens of toiling tractors and trailers with the only stop worth a mention being at Charleville-Mezieres. A grand cafe au lait in the Place Ducale next to the hustle and bustle of the Thursday morning market was just the place to take in the rather grand architecture. Charles of Gonzaga, aged twenty-six, commissioned the brother of the architect of the Place des Vosges in Paris and basically told him to copy it. Started in 1610, it took twenty years to finish and its format used all the fours. Four exits or entrances to the square, four windows on each floor, four floors in each building and four buildings in each "block". It was a handsome square and I could be forgiven for thinking that I was in the capital.

Arthur Rimbaud (1854-91) was Charleville's most famous citizen even though he hated the place. He lived and travelled until he was thirty-seven and died in Marseille. He wrote poetry such as "Le Bateau Ivre" and "Une Saison en Enfer" (a season in hell) penned in his Mother's farmhouse. "Le Bateau Ivre" ran as follows.

> Comme je descendais les fleuves impassibles,
> Je ne me sentis plus guide par les haleurs:
> Des Peaux-Rouges criards les avaient pris pour cible
> Les ayant cloues nus aux poteaux de couleurs.
> J'etais insoucieux de tous les equipages,
> Porteur de bles flamands ou de cotons anglais.
> Quand avec mes haleurs ont fini ces tapages
> Les fleuves m'ont laisse descendre ou je voulais.

Born the same year as Oscar Wilde, Arthur Rimbaud died nine years before Wilde. They were writers from the same age but not necessarily the same planet. Four extracts taken from the writings of both men revealed their differences.

A.R. "I went out under the sky, Muse! And I was your vassal."

O.W. "We are all in the gutter, but some of us are looking at the stars."

A.R. "Black A, white E, red I, green U, blue O: vowels. Someday I shall recount your latent births."

O.W. "I can resist everything except temptation."

A.R. "O seasons, O chateaux. What soul is without flaws?"

O.W. "A poet can survive everything but a misprint."

A.R. "I found I could extinguish all human hope from my soul."

O.W. "Experience is the name everyone gives to their mistakes."

Puppets, those were the other things Charleville was famous for according to the bumph from the tourist office. I didn't see any. I wasn't looking hard enough. Maybe everyone in town had strings attached. I knew I did.

Right up from the underground car park bang in the middle of St Quentin, I emerged with my bags on to a beach. Even allowing for some pretty duff geography, I knew that the town was at least a hundred miles and probably more from the sea. So why all the sand? I think it must have been the new mayor Monsieur Pierre Andre who perhaps hadn't been able to shake off the communist tendencies of his predecessor and his belief that everyone should be able to go to the beach. "Beaches for all" he must have cried and the trucks of sand rolled in to his city's centre. It was a jolly good idea and if it hadn't been for the light rain storm, I too would have slipped on to la plage at Place de Hotel de Ville and joined in the game of volley ball or whatever.

Having made St Quentin from the previous night's campsite, I was taking a train to Paris and the overnight sleeper to Tarbes. So by 8.10 the next morning I'd be back in the High Pyrenees for a week or so.

I'm going back for Michel's walk.

Payolle ⇌

Walk. What walk?

Quite a lot went on in the Pyrenees at that time of year. It was fete season and the notices advertising the various attractions appeared as thick as badger's bristles at all the key locations. The village bar was awash with them.

The day's walk at Payolle was not one of those marked down as a key event in the calendar. Not many had branded the date in the diary with a triple underlining and a "not to be missed" scrawled across the page. Those that did turn up must have seen the advertising poster as it flashed past on the side of Michel's battered Espace or at the event itself as it appeared in dayglow through the swirling August mists.

Admittedly it wasn't all the fault of the promotional campaign. The weather played a pivotal role and the misty drizzle and near freezing temperatures weren't really fair for something that wasn't being held in the salle de fete. The actual participants were very plucky. They were, all eight adults and twelve children, literally plucked from the passing day trippers and "invited" to stroll for the heart around the lake following the red and white marker tape that we had put out at various strategic points the evening before. The event tent had more holes in its covering than there were holes in Blackburn Lancashire. Thank God it wasn't very windy and that the precipitation's and sheltering occupants were both only light.

I had travelled back for the do from Northern France and I was sort of expecting what was unfolding. The responsibility had fallen on the shoulders of one man who I respected enormously. But ask him to organise anything and the words brewery and piss-up would have to feature in the same sentence.

The mayor had been asked but didn't show. True it wasn't the same one that sent me off. He'd lost his seat of office in the last elections because he too had been shy with his re-election campaign. Various medical types were supposed to be there, it being for the heart, but they hadn't got the heart to turn up or maybe they'd only got the message off the pigeon's leg the night before.

The "event" had all the agonising elements of a damp English church garden party but without the people. The PA system worked part time. Why a PA system was needed in the first place was baffling. When and if any one talked in anything above a whisper, the man on the mike thought a question was being asked. The choir was great because they gave a spirited performance of mountain choral pieces and actually doubled the numbers of those attending the after walk festivities. The local newspaper did arrive but went off to the local bar presumably to find some local news.

I supposed different people did different things differently. Before a sizeable journey, most would check to see that the fuel and oil in the car were OK, the water fine and the tyre pressures correct. The organisers of that do obviously woke up on the morning of the trip and thought, "Now where's the car?"

I couldn't have blamed anybody for the flop and the less than two hundred Francs raised (one hundred from me as guilt money). I couldn't because what was done, arranged, organised, call it whatever, was done in the very best of faith. It was done by good, honest locals, people who were supporting me, a stranger in their midst, in my egoistic voyage around France. Those guys, and more particularly that one guy, was the very best that God put on the Pyrenees and even though he couldn't organise his way out of a paper bag, his heart was as big as a red double-decker London bus and I loved him.

The local pressman took a photo of the three of us in the bar at Payolle. We had been explaining that the day's event was all about helping to promote a healthy heart. It was a good shot of Momo, Butler and me.

It's a good shot of Momo's cigarette as well.

French Bread ⇌

I have my Laguiole in its leather pouch on my belt as always. It's travelling with me.

The weather was still as thick as a widow's shawl. That morning while trying to retrain my wayward climbing rose, I moved one of the ugly carved masks from somewhere in the Pacific and upset a bird's nest from inside. Three tiny feathery bundles were tossed out on to the ground with their beautifully built nursery smashed to pieces around their little yellow-edged beaks. I felt like an utter bastard and tried to rebuild their lives in an earthenware pot on the wooden balcony not many inches from their previous home. I could hear their mother in some distress near by and I hoped that the new arrangement would work out for them. I felt really bad about it and fixed those masks to the balcony so they wouldn't fall down for future generations.

When I was invited down to the locals for a drink or a pair of teeth (apéritif) and some grub, I knew that the rest of the day would be written off. Midday was normally the starting gun and there wasn't a hint of any real food until about two or three. Those that were not invited to eat realised it and drank up and went. I'd been to some dos where the drinkers obviously expected to become the eaters but it was often a sort of game. Drinkers could only become drinkers and eaters if they'd had you as drinkers and eaters at theirs. If you were only a drinker then so were they. I never saw eaters only, unless they were at the wrong do. In that social scene you were either a drinker or a drinker and an eater. According to your category you eventually got the nod from your host and mine confirmed that I was a drinker and an eater.

The rest of us in the same boat could all relax knowing we were there for the kill.

The fire was lit, even though it was August, because the mountains were still playing funny games. Our host used the sort of wood that would best be described as summer logs. It was like asking a girl to dance because you had to. She was the last one there and all your mates were on the floor with all her friends and you were left with, well, the runt of the litter. Our host's fire was the same. The flames didn't really want to dance with the log and there was a lot of hissing as opposed to kissing.

The 'a pair of teeths' were never that sophisticated. No "Sex on the beach" or "Tequila Fresa" but rather Richard (pronounced aptly as Rick Hard) or Pastis, both alcoholic aniseed, with water. The alternative was neat whiskey of dubious branding, all supposed to be from Scotland but by way of Andorra or Spain or the back of the lorry on the way to Andorra or Spain. I stuck to the red wine because whiskey didn't agree with my heart and because after five or six glasses of Pastis, the meal tasted like everything had been marinated in extra strong Listerine mouthwash.

The meal eventually got underway with the ritual getting out of the knives. It was a game of "My Laguiole is bigger than yours" or "Mine's sharper" or "Mine's got a cork screw on it" or "Mine was given to me by Brigitte Bardot in recognition of services rendered." If you had forgotten your own knife to go with the provided fork, then everyone looked at you as though you'd just done an enormous fart in a crowded lift.

Unless soup's on, one plate normally did for everything and therefore the cleaning of the plate between courses was left up to the appropriate morsel of baguette provided. French bread wasn't intended just for eating. It had many domestic uses, some of which included pointing the way or emphasising a point during a discussion on the way back from the baker. It was a formidable dishcloth, knife cleaner, spilled wine sponge, stain remover, sink de-scaler and draft excluder. The knob end or quignon could be forced over the nose with the fore finger stuck into it where the nostril might be, in an attempt to make those around laugh as I went "Haa, hee, haw" and did my General De Gaulle impression. Old bread was quite good for lighting a fire but obviously our host didn't have any old bread that day.

Inter course often lasted longer than the course itself. Smoking during inter course sessions was always permitted.

Wine came from the same bottle. When the bottle was emptied, it was whisked away and refilled from a plastic vat hidden out of sight. In that sensible way, no one ever knew how much they'd actually consumed and instead of that great clinking glass mountain waiting to be recycled the next morning, the host could say "Well we only had one bottle" without really lying.

Good, bad or indifferent, the substance of the meal, the food, would always be commented on. Eating was a serious business and not just a means of refuelling the body. The "Ouse" and "Ares" from those seated around a table when the particular dish arrived were as an important part to a meal as a kiss or handshake on meeting. Say nothing and people would think I was unwell or foreign or both. Conventional table manners, the sort of table behaviour that was expected when I'd gone to my grandparents for Sunday lunch, went out of la fenetre. If I didn't start as soon as my food hit my plate or I decided against having an elbow or two on the table, then once again, I could have been in danger of drawing attention to myself.

Another strange habit was that of not eating the vegetables with the meat. I'd thought that a nice horse steak would have gone down a treat with some sautéed potatoes and maybe a haricots verts or two. At the sort of local meals I'd witnessed, I'd be very lucky to see two vegetables on the table. It might be rice and salad (lettuce) or potatoes and salad (lettuce) but never meat and two veg. The locals would always wolf down their horse and then help themselves to the spuds afterwards. Salad (lettuce) was a course on its own and cheese, always a great talking point, came before anything sweet.

The Pyrenees must have invented cheese making with the fuss made over the stuff. They did respect it and most would eat it on its own with a knife and fork, slicing it like a piece of meat rather than coagulated milk from vache, chevre or brebis.

Puddings could be anything from the wobbly school, through tarts to a simple piece of fruit all on its own. Coffee was invariably small, strong and black and the eau de vie, something that every host had lurking at the back of his booze cupboard, was invariably small, strong and clear. Eau de vie couldn't be purchased; it arrived in an unlabelled bottle with the donor tapping the side of his nose with his forefinger and an expression like a smug smuggler. It was rocket fuel and actually numbed the gums on its way down to rasping the oesophagus and eventually setting fire to the stomach. It was tossed down like medicine, never sipped. A visiting English friend of mine once sipped his and he couldn't talk for an hour or so afterwards. Don't ever sip it I was told. Take it down in one, just like jumping out of an aeroplane.

The level at which the conversation was pitched would be in direct proportion to the consumption of wine. It started out fairly sensibly with topics as varied and safe as the weather, the holidays and the Tour de France and would tread, after several litres of rouge, on more unsteady ground like which butcher produced the best cuts of meat and why can't the British stay in Britain. Then after everyone had developed a red wine Salvador Dali moustache with attractive matching dark stained teeth, the slurred talk might move into the rather unnerving, indeed unsettling sphere of "If I catch you snogging my wife again, you're dead meat."

I should hasten to add that this last outburst isn't aimed at me, nevertheless it is a good time to wend my way back up the mountain to see if the home I wrecked that morning had somehow pulled itself together.

French Songs ⇒⊦

My wind up radio takes exactly fifty-six winds for thirty-four minutes of music. Sometimes it's thirty-four too many.

In my electricity free mountain retreat I did have a wind-up radio that also worked by solar power when the sun shone on it. Right then a rain driven version would have been more useful.

I'd always been a fan of serious pop music. Stones, Beatles, Pink Floyd, Led Zeppelin but not the Osmonds. I'd seen Cream in concert, The Who and Bob Dylan. Paid to sing along with E.L.O., Ian Dury, the Spencer Davies Group, Van the Man, Jools Holland and even Duke Ellington.

I'd met Jimmy Hendrix at the Norman Cross Motel on the A1 when he was on his way to play the bulb sheds in Spalding one August Bank holiday. We bought each other drinks. He chatted up my girl friend. She was gorgeous and had a mini skirt the width of a fan belt. I put him right about the bulb sheds.

"Flowers Jimmy" I said. "Not light."

"Are you experienced?" he said to me presumably in some reference to his new LP (Long players then, not albums).

"I'm a young farmer." I heard myself say. But I was the coolest young farmer on the planet.

I reckoned that I should have been Mick Jagger or Eric Clapton. There was a time when I could have made a career out of being a John Lennon look-a-like. I spent the best part of eighteen months carrying a guitar around Australia in 1968/9. I couldn't play it but it looked good. Music had always been important to me. But when I tried to tune in to something suitable on the French airwaves, I remembered why I didn't take a radio with me on tour.

French music was deguelasse. The words "Popular French Music" in a record store somewhere were a lie. It was no wonder that when I trawled the radio stations, I'd hear a lot of English language stuff filling the void. I wondered why, because their composers had access to exactly the same musical notes. There wasn't a copyright on them. They had presumably got the same white ones and the same black ones on their pianos as their British or American counter parts. So why did they find it so difficult to put them in the right order?

Perhaps I was being a little unfair and it was not their tunes at fault but rather the language they had to compose for. The French language had been used to good romantic effect by the likes of Maurice Chevalier, Charles Aznavour and Sasha Distel. In their own Franglais way each "liddle sung" made a girl or two (and maybe boy), go weak at the knees. Francoise Hardy sounded vulnerable and some stuff by Serge Gainsbourg, especially "Je t'aime" which he wrote for Jane Birkin, was just sex being performed on a forty-five. But those performers were only the froth on the top.

It seemed to me that the great French songwriter (because it couldn't always be the fault of the performers although they took the rotten eggs) wrote songs in the knowledge that there was always an "er" up the sleeve. If things weren't going to plan in the rhyming steaks, an "er" or two were added. Lyrics with made up French words such as bicycletter, cigaretter, and poubeller stated to appear. Some performers carried it off very weller and made it sound as though it was just the way they would speak to their partners over breakfast. Apart from the "er" there was the rolling of the r's. The most famous exponent of the technique was Edith Piaf. Where as she did it well, there were lots who copied her ability but they didn't have her vocal agility.

Sadly some French singers just couldn't sing and they relied on over production to hide the fact that they couldn't hold even a middle C for longer than it took to strangle a cat. I heard some backing vocals that I simply could not believe and there was one played with regular monotony in the local bar by Nostalgie. It sounded like a group of quacking ducks. It was the truth. In another rib tickling French "classic" the drummer seemed to go completely berserk and I swear you could hear him being forcibly taken out so that the dreadful singer could regain centre stage for the agonising conclusion.

Even Sir Cliff Richard made Johnny Hallyday look like an inebriated karaoke crooner. Some of the songs of France's number one rocker needed serious lifting in line with his enhanced cosmetic appearance. If he were British, Hallyday would have been on holiday for the last thirty years.

There was a place for it in the sound proofed booth called Euro Pop and once in a blue moon when someone had forgotten to shut the padded door behind him or her, something burst out and tried to win us over. Plastic Bertrand cracked it once, but he may have been from Belgium, and Jean Michel Jarre might still be in there somewhere.

The jolly, beret-wearing rascal with his red neck scarf and accordion was fine in small doses. But steady. It was only ever as background noise to the cafe chat or Maigret film and never to be taken seriously. Likewise potential French rappers should take note and leave the English expletives to those that had mastered the language. There was nothing so funny as a foreigner trying to swear in the Mother tongue and it wouldn't matter how many "ers" were put after that unspeakable word because Eminmem would always do it so much better.

If music be the food of love then France should just stick with the cooking.

Back To Saint Quentin Via Paris

I am going to ogle France's top super model.

She had been up there for years and that day was no different. She greeted me with her little, ever so slight smile with her hands resting just beneath her chest. She looked Italian, which was probably because she was and, like so many stars I'd only seen on film, she was much smaller than I thought she was going to be. I was disappointed. I supposed she had to be kept somewhat in the dark, which made the flash of cameras from the throng around her like a fireworks display.

Her name was Mona Lisa and her home was at the end of a long corridor of Italian oils, mostly depicting not very nice things that happened to our Lord and his followers. She was in the Denon wing of the immense Louvre museum in Paris and I paid 45 francs (before 3pm) for the visit. What the Louvre had that the rest of Paris didn't was masses of people. I guessed most must be away on their holidays because the streets seemed to be relatively calm and quite a few shops had signs in their windows saying things like "Out to lunch until September".

My lunch was at the Michelin two star Laurent in Avenue Gabriel not a spit from the Elycee Palace. It was there I met Jean-Paul Courant from Ogilvy One, his business card said he was President of Oglivy One Brand Practice.

Jean-Paul was a professional in "relations marketing" which despite the term didn't mean he was an expert at putting cousins in touch with their lost aunts. He was an expert in putting brands in touch with their customers. He looked after the interests of people like Nestles, Unilever and Kleenex and made sure that their worldwide branding message got through to their

336

customers. He travelled widely (it was Mexico last week) and his experience at Ogilvy had come from his work at the sharp end with Unilever and the Channel Tunnel.

He used the Tunnel project as one way to emphasise the differences between British and French attitudes. In France over 700,000 punters took up shares in the venture. The French saw it as exciting technology, a chance to invest in innovation, another Concorde or TGV. The British on the other hand stepped forward with just 150,000 takers. The British reserve and keeping British reserves seem to have sprung from the attitude that "We don't need a tunnel." As it happened, in investment terms all punters lost out but that was not the point. The French looked upon the Chunnel as an engineering challenge, never mind the politics, let's get digging. The Brits saw it as a giant enema, another back passage to "over there" they didn't really want. Although they didn't put their money where their mouths were, the politicians on both sides of La Manche wanted a tunnel so it would have happened no matter. Left to the people to decide I expect the thing would be only three-quarters finished with a hole at the Calais end but no sign of any earth moving in Kent.

Not surprisingly the talk got on to advertising and I wanted to try and identify the two nations different consumers with a "it-worked-for-them-but-not-for-us" example. In the days of International and pan European brands was there perhaps an example I asked?

"Persil," said Jean-Paul with a flashy white smile and his own pan European accent. Apparently the soap powder that washed whiter, ran a TV ad that featured a teenage lad going on his holidays to Spain. Along with his favourite T-shirts, his Mum had packed some of her favourite washing powder in a plastic bag, so the favourite T-shirts could stay looking good. Obviously the Spanish customs official stopped the lad and found the plastic bag containing the white powder and after the innuendo there were, eventually, jolly smiles all round.

In France, according to J-P, that campaign just wouldn't work. The advertisers were concerned that the 'drugs' label, albeit not a real one, could some how taint the brand in French consumer's eyes. There were big differences over what we smiled and laughed at.

"But what about sex?" said I to Monsieur Courant. "No thank you," said he. "I'm a happily married man with two sons." (He didn't actually say that although he was married and had two sons). The French still believed that it was OK for sex to sell and they didn't attach quite the same 'tacky' label to sex as a sales tool. A pretty girl licking an iced lolly with the look on her face as though she had just won the lottery and been propositioned by Brad Pitt, was fine for Cannes but perhaps not so hot for Canvey Island. Nudity in France was as common as corruption in politics but where the one called for a cover up, the other didn't. How many holidaying British parents have had to explain to their questioning young in the back what those posters meant? The ones seen pasted to the back of nearly every sign post from Calais to Corsica offering the chance of a chat with the young lady concerned.

"But why would she want to talk to you Daddy?" asked Samantha innocently as another pair of female French buttocks disappeared in the rear view mirror.

It was dangerous to pigeonhole but having got the ear of the man whose business was world-wide consulting, communication and connections (it said so on his card) it would be a pity not to try and discover more about the us and them.

"Coronation Street," he said. "It would never work in France". It was apparently not aspirational enough for the French. Unlike the British, the French didn't want it told like it was. They wanted it told like they wanted to imagine it could be. They wanted to improve themselves, not look at themselves at their everyday worst. Maybe that was the reason for the legions of French hairdressing establishments and all those underwear shops.

As a marketing man who had worked on both sides (England and France as client and agent) J-P understood the language and its use. The British would never say, "Well thanks for the presentation and what a load of rubbish it was. Goodbye." After a duff presentation, the conversation in the British boardroom would be more along the lines "Well thanks for the presentation. We'd like to consider your proposals and we'll certainly get back to you at the earliest opportunity."

Jean-Paul said that the French tended to speak their minds which for me was great because he paid the luncheon bill from the wonderful Menu du Pavillion of Joel Robuchon and said he'd like to see me again. He was either genuine or very good at his relations marketing job. I suspected it was both.

338

I then took the train to Saint-Quentin, back to Peter in his underground car park and a short journey to the town's municipal campsite. The evening's snack was a dull salad at the restaurant-brasserie La Bresilien in the town.

Life's full of contrasts.

Arras ⇥

Every November at the service of Remembrance, when we start to sing 'O Valiant Hearts', I find it difficult not to cry.

The fields of Picardy looked pretty much like the fields of the Eastern Counties, big, well farmed and cared for. That was where the similarity ended. It was not only the farmers that cared for their land; it was their government as well. The British government didn't seem to care about British farming anymore. I supposed it was because it was no longer a major industry with masses of employees. It didn't carry the vote power it once enjoyed. Farming issues wouldn't make or break British governments anymore.

Napoleonic laws of France had kept land ownership in the hands of many. I'm not sure if it was the rule every time, but certainly where I lived in the Pyrenees, when I died my property would be divided equally between my wife, if I had one, and my children. It couldn't go just to the eldest son or just to the wife and exclude the other members of the family. The cake had to be cut and shared out equally. It could create a confusing situation as I found with a field opposite to me. It was difficult to negotiate with thirteen different sellers for one scrap of mountain pasture. However the old rule had meant that farmers in France still carried a lot of political clout. There were a lot of them and everyone knew or had a relative who was involved with the land. The President of France and its Prime Minister wouldn't dare to upset such a powerful force. In France farming issues could well change the government.

Our Prime Minister's only apparent contact with farming was the egg on his face and the inconvenience to his budget of the compensation he had to pay out to an industry he didn't really want; a blot on the landscape of a politically spun country. It was a real pity but that was what it looked like from over there.

The combine harvesters were out in force (not protesting) and I could see their dusty trails, like field dragons as they reaped what was sown. It was not all air-conditioned cabs and press button computer control from the driver's dashboard. I saw one sun-dried, dust-coated driver with a rather pretty cafe umbrella over his platform, keeping the sun but not the chaff off his head.

On the road out from Peronne and towards Albert, I stopped and dwelt a while at the tiny Gordon Cemetery which epitomised that line by Rupert Brooke. "If I should die, think only this of me, that there is some corner of a foreign field that is for ever England." Scotland would have been more apt in that particular case with the names on the stones reading like the roll call of a highland gathering. Solid Scots names, Muir, Irvine, McDonald, McCulloch, McGregor, McLeod, Robertson, Millar, Duncan and the rest. There were one hundred and two British soldiers buried in the well kept corner of a foreign field, most of them from the Gordon Highlanders, all of them slain on the opening day of the battle of the Somme on the 1st July 1916. There was not one that I could see who had celebrated his thirtieth birthday.

In Peronne, where I had taken a late breakfast or early lunch (salad de gesiers but with an added egg), I went to see the museum they had put together showing the history of the First World War. It was the sort of place to take your children so they could see the newspapers and newsreels of the day. They could see the uniforms and medals, look at the maps and drawings, the sculptures and the photographs, the cigarette packets and the post cards home. What they might fail to see was the stark list, like a gruesome balance sheet, that showed each country's contribution in manpower to the war effort. Next to the column giving the numbers sent to fight, was a column with the numbers of those killed and next to that, the percentage mortality rate. It made horrendous nonsense. I didn't jot them down exactly and they will be a matter of public record but I came away with the three bottom line figures which read seventy point something million, nine point something million and over thirteen percent.

As good as it was, the museum visit felt too cosy, too much like turning the pages of a history book, too clinical. The only horror of war was depicted by the dark drawings of trench life. The old film footage didn't look real. Children came out and asked for a Magnum ice cream when perhaps they shouldn't.

They understood horror. Spielberg horror and Disney thrills got to them, but the Great War was too much to bring to life those that went to their death.

Le Tommy Brasserie in Pozieres had tried. In production terms it was a low budget affair. Two tailor's dummies decked out in Aussie battle dress greeted me at the door. There were more in various stiff posses in "the trench" in the back garden where I sipped my tea from a Tetley's tea mug to the sounds of wartime songs and the recorded memories of old soldiers. The owners of Le Tommy had turned the Great War to their advantage, so too had the proprietors of the Poppy a few villages away. I couldn't really blame them. If it was tasteful then it was tasteful in a very nearly tasteless way. Some of the memorabilia was for sale and two hundred francs would secure a fair sized shell case. Just how many lives or limbs it had accounted for didn't seem important any more. It would look great on someone's mantelpiece. French, German and British tin helmets lay rusty and full of holes in the garden not far from the hand chalked black board menu offering "Fish et frites" for 35 francs.

Arras town centre was very gentrified with cobbled streets and squares and elegant dwellings above arched topped alcoves fronting shops and cafes. The town hall looked like it should be the cathedral and the sad grey lump of a cathedral looked as though it had seen better times. It was in its way a testament to tenacity and had been up and down as many times as a whore's drawers. Started and stopped in the 18th century, it became a nearly finished cathedral in the reign of Napoleon 1st. The First War saw three quarters of it destroyed and restoration started in 1920 and was finished by 1934 just in time for it to be destroyed again ten years later by a bomb in the Second World War. Whilst the outside was grey and sombre, the inside was lighter and had the feel almost of a vast railway station.

That night's campsite was in the Southern suburbs of the town off a very drab street like so many that were on the outskirts of rebuilt towns. I walked into the centre because Peter's clutch was losing it again and I wanted the exercise. It was only a mile or so but then for some reason, when I walked back again, I went off in completely the wrong direction. I think I skirted most of Arras by the time I eventually found my little tent. I was hot, hungry and getting footsore. But good gracious, I was the lucky one.

No one is trying to shoot me.

Lille ⟐

It is really a very strange feeling. My grandfather had fought for the ground I am standing on.

The Canadians, who fought at Vimy ridge in early April 1917 and dislodged the Germans from the strategically important vantage point, have been rightly hailed as heroes. For three years others had tried and failed but four divisions of the Canadian Corps did it but not without sustaining 10,602 casualties and 3,598 dead.

What was so spooky about visiting that part of northern France, was that my grandfather had been there before me. It was him that had been making the history that I was witnessing. While I was peering through a camera to capture that moment, he would have been looking down the barrel of his service revolver hoping to capture the enemy. While I was walking upright over the neatly cut grass, he would have been crawling on his stomach through the ripped open earth. While I was breathing the clear French air, he would have had the stench of death in his nostrils and the fear of the phosgene gas at any moment.

My grandfather had always been one of my heroes. He was the stuff of Boy's Own made flesh. Even the history books gave him a mention and his colleges in the Northamptonshire Regiment had christened him "the intrepid hero". Chapter ten of a little book called 7th (S.) Battalion Northamptonshire Regiment 1914-1919 gave the following account of Vimy in 1917.

"The trenches in this area were in a poor condition and the battalion was kept busy draining the line and improving the dug-out accommodation, which was far from adequate. Situated in front of the British lines was a shell-beaten tree known as "The Lone Tree", and on the top of this tree Lieutenant Berridge hoisted a red ensign during one night. This action caused considerable annoyance to the enemy, who endeavoured without success to shoot it down; and as the days went on it seemed particularly suitable that the flag of the merchant service should float over the shell-pitted No Man's Land, which was rapidly coming to resemble an ocean of water and mud."

For his part in the Great War, my grandfather was awarded six decorations for gallantry including the DSO and three MC's. Even more important than that, he survived and knew old age and his great-grandchildren. So many with him there at Vimy eighty-four years previously never had the joy of watching their own children grow up, so many took their last footsteps there.

The area around the ridge was now the Canadian National Vimy Memorial and it was where the memory of 66,655 Canadians who died in the First World War was kept alive. The vast monument itself was the most moving piece of sculpture that the living could carve for the dead. Over 11,000 names of Canadians killed in France, but whose final resting-place was not known, were etched into the walls. Steps led up from all sides to the centrepiece, two giant monoliths towering skywards. There was much symbolism to the sacrifices made with vast carved figures representing Peace, Justice, Truth, Knowledge, Gallantry and Sympathy. Perhaps the most heart-felt of all was the lone cloaked figure standing at the front of the monument, a young woman in mourning, like the then young nation of Canada, as she looked down on to the tomb of a dead soldier. If cold, hard, carved stone could make a man cry then that surely was where he would weep.

I could see for miles. Looking west and south towards Arras, I could see the grassy shell holes as hollows beneath the re-grown trees. I could see too some of the trenches preserved to help us understand. Looking east and north I saw, miles away on the horizon, the man made scars of other mines, the coal mines of northern France.

Lens was north and I mused that I would need a pretty strong lens to find anything of interest in it. It reminded me of the sort of dreary working town where some of the shops had names like Etam or What She Wants. Sadly it probably was not what she wanted at all but rather what she could afford. The town had been worth fighting over. My grandfather had passed that way also and the account of his foray to Lens was in the regimental history book.

"The same evening "C" Company reoccupied the houses they had been ordered to abandon; and 2nd Lieutenant Morris and 2nd Lieutenant Berridge occupied a further eight rows of houses on the outskirts of Lens before the battalion was relieved by two battalions of the 46th Division, the 6th and 8th Sherwood Foresters."

Peter and I passed through with every gear change sounding like we'd just dropped a galvanised bucket full of knives and forks out onto the road beneath us. I could see Lille before we actually got to it. It took time to penetrate the outskirts because I was determined not to get sucked onto the frightening major road that would lead to the centre in moments, or if we missed the turn, off towards Paris. We did it by compass and back streets, which rebuilt my directional confidence, my in-built GPS, after the previous evening's mystery tour of Arras. It seemed a more appropriate way of doing things, treading as I was in my grandfather's footsteps.

The Tourist Office pointed me in the direction of the Hotel Brueghel, right in the shadow of St Maurice and as near to the heart of Lille as it was possible to get. The landlady was blonde and charming and for 375 francs I got room 302 with a small bed, loo and shower. For that price I could also use the old metal lift. I expected to go down, right down to the coal face as it did look like the sort of thing miners went off to work in.

King and Large arrived at eight on their holiday way from Amsterdam to Grasse down near Cannes. King (him) and Large (her, although she wasn't) had been friends of mine for some years. I first met Large in her capacity as the greetings card buyer for Woolworth's. In her Marylebone office at Woollies H.Q. she was the hardest nut in the pick 'n mix bowl. She never smiled. If she liked something that was shown to her, she would rarely let it be known in front of the sales man. I don't think I ever heard her say those two words that were presumably banned in the Woollies Buyers Guide, namely "That's nice". To admit to liking something was to send out the wrong signal. If she did hint at the possibility of trying something, her terms were so tight that it would have been more profitable just to pay Woolworth's the money and not bother with supplying them the product. Anyway like all good salesmen, I kept trying, kept that foot in the door, kept being a persistent pain in her in-tray until eventually I got her out of the H.Q. and into something more comfortable, namely Royal Ascot.

Ladies Day it was and what a different person she turned out to be. She was human, female, laughed and had fun and instead of saying no, didn't say the word once when asked if she'd like another glass of Champagne. However she still wouldn't buy anything from us so we offered her a job, putting into play that adage if you can't beat them, get them to join you.

Large was really a King because that was the name of the man she married, but she kept her maiden name and therefore its tough Woolworth associations. She did well for our business after the culture shock of moving from poacher to gamekeeper and from something as big and formal as a government to something like the village hall committee.

King was a lawyer and rugger bugger, a man of few words, which could be mistaken for shyness. What he did say was always good to hear and he obviously had a great deal more charm and power of persuasion than I did when it came to selling. She had said yes to his proposal. Then again he was offering far more than a selection box of Christmas cards.

In the Place du General De Gaulle, we eat seafood sitting outside in one of the square's busy restaurants and enjoy the first supper of their holiday, another plat du jour for me.

Bath Via The Tunnel Sous La Manche ⚊⊹

Like running a marathon, Lille is the pain barrier bit after thirteen miles. If I can get past Lille then maybe I'll complete the course.

The dropping galvanised bucket noise under Peter at every attempted gear change was concerning. So concerning that I sought out Lille's Piaggio dealer away from the centre and on the road named Dunkerque. Capitulation was not on my agenda but when I reached the dealership, a little hand written sign told me that every one was on holiday. The dealer's name "Desir" was fairly descriptive of what I felt. I "desired" to throw something heavy through their showroom window. It wasn't their fault. I wanted to drive Peter through their plate glass. Abandon him. Abandon the tour.

Like those before me on the road to Dunkerque, I felt a sense of being cut off, but unlike them I could hop on the TGV at Lille Europe and evacuate to Waterloo without getting my feet wet. Leaving Lille at 11.41 and arriving in London at 12.43 and despite what time the clock showed, the trip took two hours. The French were always an hour ahead although some would say light years. All the space age trappings of Lille Europe under the big boot shaped building and the smooth, fast TGV journey through to Calais were in contrast to the difficult, bumpy and slow re-entry into the atmosphere that our sleek craft seemed to encounter on emerging into Kent.

Graffiti was an international language. It was sprayed for those that flashed past it and had to work either from right to left or left to right. Most that saw it wouldn't understand it. It was communicated in a language like Esperanto, broad with it's meaning but narrow with its usage. So even though the letters were familiar, it was difficult to make them sound right. Some of the messages were works of art, fat over blown-up tyre like letters that had taken their composer time and skill. Others were just quick scrawls, no more than a dirty mark on a wall. No one ever witnessed the performance. Graffiti arrived like art in a gallery behind closed doors. It was often dangerous art and the doer risked being done or, worse still, electrocuted, run over or broken to pieces after the big drop. Roof top designs needed a vertigo free hand. It was like asking Hockney to paint and bungy jump at the same time, a big splash against a wall.

Graffiti at its best needed to be studied from a train or motorway. On runways the odd number and letter appeared, but self indulgent script writing on those strips of concrete was discouraged for obvious reasons. A jumbo turning left rather than right because of graffiti might result in some more serious and widely read headlines. Signal boxes, defunct carriages and some still on the move, factory sides, bridges and lock-ups, anywhere that showed its canvas to its passing public, could carry the message what ever it was. Chinz, Wotiz, Bong, and Flickhead sat in amongst obscure messages and the downright rude. I wrote my own message in the condensation on the window. 'Failure' it said.

Train journeys made me think. Running through to my final destination it was dusk. Uncertain light faded fast on the outside of the moving train. I could see my blurred face in the double glazed window, as it became less of a look out and more of a mirror with lines running through it. Lines and sleepers. Tiddle-de-dee, tiddle-de-dum, tiddle-de-dee, tiddle-de-dum. Trees skipped along my eyebrows and platforms skimmed my chin. The background was full of people reading or eating or listening to music on little black earphones or snoozing, some with noisy plastic bags from supermarkets filled with fizzy drink and sandwiches. I thought they were out there but they were in the carriage. I was there too. It was only my impression that was outside and like a dream it flirted with me every time I winked at it.

Soon it was dark outside. The council lights flew by like shards of bright sparks wind blown off the bonfire right through my nostrils or in one ear and out of the other. Pitch darkness outside sealed the window and what I saw there was what I got, only perversely in reverse. Could that have been mother and decorated grandfather? Were those my children with my grandchildren? They and strangers were all travelling with us on the same train, their tickets paid for by us but when we pulled into a station, not necessarily our stop, they disappeared, while those outside on the platform climbed aboard and took their seats. We pulled out back into the dark and those that had joined us had bought their spitting images for the ride. When we did get into the station of our choice, our destination, I thought they got off with us. But I couldn't be sure. I just didn't know. Who was to say my shadow wasn't peering in on the empty seat still warm with my impression? It was there from Paddington to Bath when I looked left and before I left. Why not from Bath to Weston-Super-Mare and on to the seaside?

Not sunbathing but basking in the shadows somewhere. There is something about this journey to see the red head that makes me feel incredibly nervous, incredibly sad. Will it be my last?

Back To Lille ⇥

I ring Sylvie and she tells me that World War Three has started.

Sylvie sounded almost hysterical on the phone. I had called her on my return to Lille to see if there was any body I should be arranging to visit for another PR opportunity.

"No one will want to meet you today," she said urgently. "America is being attacked."

I took the stairs down to the hotel lobby, not wanting to be caught out in the tiny cage lift during a nuclear war, and joined a small group of other residents and staff who were glued to the TV. I thought that we were watching a Bruce Willis disaster movie. What was happening couldn't be real could it?

Vieux Lille is still standing; its cobbled streets have seen destructive armies come and go. It knew its spoilers and its saviours, their causes right or wrong. But not Manhattan, its Twin Towers put to rubble by fanatics most likely on the whim of some obscure quasi-religious bearded weirdo in his desert home.

Today I got my first parking ticket, stuck on Peter's windscreen, it looked ridiculous. It won't ever get paid.

Dunkerque ⚓

"You should have stopped in Armentieres," says the mechanic in Armbouts-Cappel just outside Dunkerque.

He reminded me of the Irish man who when asked the way said "Well I wouldn't have started from here." Despite his advice to see me turn tail and retrace my steps virtually back to Lille, he agreed to look into the noisy gear change problem. Seven minutes later he had it sorted with a self satisfied smug grin.

"Nowsharge" he said unlike the infamous Mademoiselle from Armentieres.

It was pretty much the same thing that the three 'Speedy' men said an hour later when the clutch cable came off altogether. I lurched into a 'Speedy' roadside workshop.

"Nowsharge" said the 'Speedy' lads and the cable was reconnected.

There was a charge at the restaurant Au Bon Coin in Malo-les-Bains where I had a wonderful fishy supper, hot fish starter, fillet of Turbot with a choron sauce, a bottle of Brouilly and goat's cheese and coffee for one franc less than four hundred. I had the place to myself between 7 and 8 and I hadn't had anything since the French breakfast in Lillie that morning. I was staying on a windy seaside campsite for less than four pounds.

Dunkerque's beach or more accurately the sands at Malo-les-Bains tapered off into the Channel very gradually and walking on them in the mini gale, I could just about picture the surreal scenes in 1940 described by my travelling companion, The Rough Guide.

"The evacuation of 350,000 Allied troops from the beaches of Dunkerque from May 27 to June 4, 1940, has become one of those heroic wartime legends which conveniently conceals the fact that the Allies, through their own incompetence, almost lost their entire armed forces in the first few weeks of the war. The German army had taken just ten days to reach the English Channel and could very easily have finished off the job. Unable to believe the ease with which he had overcome a numerically superior enemy, Hitler ordered his generals to halt their lightning advance, giving Allied forces trapped in the Pas-de-Calais enough time to organise Operation Dynamo, the largest wartime evacuation ever undertaken. Initially it was hoped that around 10,000 men would be saved, though thanks to the low-lying cloud and the assistance of over 1750 vessels - among them pleasure cruisers, fishing boats and river ferries - 140,000 French and over 200,000 British soldiers were successfully shipped back to England.

In France, the ratio of Brits to French evacuees caused bitter resentment since Churchill had promised that the two sides would go bras dessus, bras dessous ("arm in arm"). Meanwhile the British media played up the "remarkable discipline" of the troops as they waited to embark, the "victory" of the RAF over the Luftwaffe, and the "disintegration" of the French army all around. In fact, there was widespread indiscipline in the early stages as men fought for places on board; the battle for the skies was evenly matched; and the French fought long and hard to cover the whole operation, some 150,000 of them remaining behind to become prisoners of war. In addition, the Allies lost 7 destroyers and 177 fighter planes and were forced to abandon over 60,000 vehicles."

The rows of bright beach huts were the only sign of current regimentation and the only other occupant, a man flying one of those two handed giant kites that lifted him off the ground then dumped him back again. He looked like he was trying to evacuate but couldn't make up his mind.

Funny how things happened, because just as I'd paid the bill for my extravagant evening meal, my mobile rang and a female French voice asked if I'd like some supper. I said no thank you but nevertheless she on the phone and he in the background would be coming to meet me, there in the restaurant, immediately. She was Jocelyne Cazeel, he was Dr Henry Delbecque and I was whisked away to his house and given melon-flavoured ice cream and more red wine.

He had retired, was 'en retraite', which sounded not too inappropriate for someone living in Dunkerque. He'd been a heart doctor and he now spent his time helping people to give up smoking and lead more healthy lives. He started the fun runs for the heart, Parcours du Coeur, which were held in over sixty-five locations in France every year. He was the president of an organisation whose notepaper was only just wide enough, Association de Flandre Maritine Pour L'Accompagnement et les Soins Palliatifs. Jocelyne Cazeel was the secretary. Quite what they actually did, I couldn't immediately ascertain, but I believed that the good doctor was like a councillor for those suffering. His association was there for care but not medical treatment. His care for me was very welcoming and the half bottle of red and melon ice cream, an unusual nightcap.

Back on the beaches it was blowing a hooley with rain to match but with a bottle and a half of wine inside me, my little tent looked as welcoming as Father Christmas's knee to a precocious four year old with a long Christmas shopping list. Only the ghosts over the sand dunes would have joined in with my rather bad singing " Inky-pinky-parlez-vous."

I am pleased that red wine is good for the heart.

Calais ⇌

Flemish style architecture makes the town halls of northern France look like red brick buildings with knobs on.

The coast between Dunkerque and Calais looked industrious with large confusions of concrete and steel, intermittent cranes and piers sticking out into the water, chimneys and the rusty piles that corroded on sea shores when their use was spent. At Gravelines, nuclear power was being generated. I couldn't tell. None of the animals grazing near seemed to have two heads.

As children our seaside holidays were, I supposed, quite genteel, middle class summer breaks. It was Mrs Whatmore's three quarters the way up Charmouth hill, just where the climbing lorries used to have to change down to their lowest gear which tested Mrs Whatmore's window panes and her best china in the sideboard. We had one side of the house and my auntie Mouse and uncle John and their girls had the other. The fortnight was too short a sentence filled with punctuation marks such as mackerel fishing, fossil hunting, the whist drive, crabbing, trips to Lyme Regis (when wet), walks up Golden Cap, playing in the park, my sister breaking her arm and Dorset knobs.

We were a family that pretty much made its own entertainment, we thumped Mrs Whatmore's old piano and her Bagatelle. We used to tease her terrier and her window dressing son Ted. It was mostly sunshine and it must have been hot on some days because my grandmother, my mother's mother, had to take shelter in the wooden beach hut we hired on Charmouth beach for the two whole weeks.

If Charmouth in my ten-year-old mind was as I described, then Calais was everything we would not have been allowed. The brightest light in Charmouth in the summer of '59 would have been the one that couldn't decide if it was red, amber and red and then green. Its nearest competition was that orange flashing sphere, the Belisha beacon, which at least had only two choices on and off, on and off, on and off.

In Calais every working bulb served to highlight the opportunity for spending money. "Bureau de Change" - "English money taken" - "We'll melt down your jewellery" - "Gold fillings extracted" – It was that sort of place and only thirty miles from England, it was abroad for those that wanted the tax free benefits of Europe without all that funny foreign language stuff. Calais was Heathrow-on-sea and its shops and cafes catered for the catering classes. Moules and frites or Welsh rarebits (not croque-monsieur although they were on the menu) if you preferred for less than a fiver.

"Our waiter inside speaked English" which wouldn't have mattered one bit to Ken and Liza just over for the day.

"We've done real good on the savin's what it would've cost us" they said in a language that even a trained UN interpreter would have had some difficulty with. Market forces had made Calais what it was, the most "British" town in France, union jacks at every turn, bitter beer in pint glasses and the pound much more welcome than the imminent Euro.

Kiss-me-quick Calais had one of those over the top Flemish style wedding cake towers over the top of its town hall and the gardens around were pure French municipal chocolate box. The gardener had a three-wheeled Piaggio to help him, a younger version of Peter, so we stopped to say hello. Rodin's burghers looked on.

Although Mary Tudor got very passionate about the place, I am not sure she'd be so impressed with it today.

Boulogne-Sur-Mer ⇌

We all stood in silence by the war memorial remembering last Tuesday's outrage.

From Calais via the D940, the coast rose from the sea to become quite spectacular. I drove through Sangatte expecting to see hordes of would-be illegal immigrants queuing to take their turn to enter the Channel Tunnel. I didn't see any although there was a load of empty police busses and I didn't suppose their former occupants were playing volleyball on the beach.

We stopped at Cap Blanc-Nez to see the sea whipped by the wind and but for the white flecks riding each wave, it would have been difficult to tell where the sea ended and the sky began. The Cote d'Opale was aptly named although Cote d'Concrete Bunker would have done just as well. Hitler's Atlantic Wall, the bunkers that were supposed to keep us out, looked like overgrown football boot studs.

In Wimereux the whole town stopped at midday when the church bells rang and the siren sounded, its mournful wail for people in distress. A small group of about forty people had gathered around the war memorial, some clutching bunches of flowers, some more elaborate bouquets and some just their shopping bags. The fat policeman stopped the traffic and we were all silent for a few minutes in respect for those who had died in America on the previous Tuesday. It was a moving and genuine gesture and I guessed that the same thing was happening all over France and the rest of the civilised world.

At Boulogne-sur-Mer Julius Caesar assembled his fleet in 55BC and set off to conquer Britain. The busy fishing port wasn't called that then

358

but Gesoriac and the place became a significant hub in the cog that was the Roman Empire. Caligula had a B&B there and Emperor Claudius was an in-transit passenger on his way to Britain. The port became the most important on the Atlantic side of Europe and therefore an obvious target for the barbarian hordes snapping around the crumbling empire and indeed a stepping stone to fight over ever since.

Henry VIII took time off from wife worrying and besieged the town. Later and back under French management, Napoleon used it as his base for invading England so Nelson gave it a bombarding. In 1914 it was a front line base and so the Germans threw a lot of flak at it and in 1940 when the Germans used the port as a submarine base, the Allies raided the place 487 times. It was remarkable that with all that action, Boulogne stood, old with new and looked quite good despite the knocks.

History recounted that its inhabitants must have been a pretty tenacious breed. In 1544 three thousand Boulonnais resisted thirty thousand English troops until they were betrayed. Napoleon awarded the first Legion d'Honneur near there in 1804. In 1827 the local vicar, one Monsignor Benoit-Agathon Haffringue, should have been given a medal for without any architectural skills, he decided to build a cathedral. In it I went to see the white Madonna and child who were sitting in a rowing boat. Mother and child both wore red crowns. In her hand was a red heart while the child carried an orb of the same colour. From 1943 to 1948 the float was carried through France from Lourdes back to the Cathedrale Notre Dame de Boulogne and became the focus for a religious revival that travelled with it. The boat sat on an old four-wheeled trailer whose rubber tyres would still pass an MOT.

Peter's much smaller tyres have got me to a camp site just out side Etaples and I hope they'll get me safely all the way back to Lourdes, not far from where I live.

Le Touquet-Paris-Plage And Azincourt

I think I remember that father used to come here on golfing and business trips years ago.

Le Touquet was a French seaside resort conjured up in the sand dunes and pines in the 1920's so that blokes from Britain could gather in twos or fours to play golf "sur le continent". It was a theme park for adults with grand hotels with names like Le Manoir and Le Westminster, a casino, an airport for the Cessnas and lots of shops and places to eat. It might like to think it was the Cote d'Azur but it was as much like Cannes as a tin with beer in it.

The car numberplates told a tale with PRAT 1 and TO55ER on a Jag or two. If not being descriptive of what he was, the numbers might tell us who he was. We could all see that M1 JON or HENI 5 were both in town. The English conversation was always loud, never quiet or spoken like the Queen. If labels had to be applied, and they were certainly worn, then Nouveau-Riche-on-sea would be as good as Flash-your-Cashville. It was empty bottles of white wine turned upside down in their ice buckets. Bad form. It was asking for a cafe blanc in a way they knew was absolutely right.

"Cafe noir is black in it, so cafe blanc is white right." Wrong mate. But in Le Touquet it was right to be wrong and as long as they kept paying, it would stay that way. Le Touquet-Paris-Plage was how my map denoted the place, but then that was far too many French words to remember when the golfers got back home.

"My Edward had a lovely trip this weekend and he had a hole in one in the Torquay" I bet he did and he wasn't anywhere near the golf course at the time.

Not far away the French were given a really good seeing to in Azincourt. I didn't know why Henry V called it Agincourt unless it was to add insult to considerable injury. October 25th 1415 didn't start particularly well for the English army and by all accounts they expected to be beaten easily by the French who outnumbered them by four to one. The three or four things in favour of the English however were to turn events to their advantage. The weather was wet (no change there then) and the French knights were heavily armoured on their horses which would have been OK had not the horses got stuck in the mud. Knights dismounted and they too got stuck in the mud. The English bowmen, with their long bows, were a formidable force and they were able to rain arrows down on the French stick-in-the-muds. The French king, Charles VI, was barking mad so the French leadership at Agincourt was given to the Connetable d'Albret while the English had the fearless Henry V leading them. It was no wonder we won. The French lost ten thousand men, which must have been horrendous. Eight thousand were deemed as gentleman and the cream of French nobility.

Azincourt wasn't exactly highlighted on the map. "Come and see where we got really well and truly beaten up by the English." The village was full of cardboard cut-out medieval soldiers and the Centre Historique Medieval explained what happened in an audio-visual way with added props. The white-haired lady who ran the front of house was very friendly considering and no doubt had to be reasonable at English to get the job. The battlefield itself was like any other farm in those parts, but then it was six hundred years after the event.

The Hotel Flandres in Hespin looked like the town's best and was pretty well populated with other British visitors and five very noisy bikers from Holland. They had an early start on the Sunday morning and obviously wanted everyone else staying in the hotel to get up and wave them off. It was tempting and I thought about giving them the two-fingered salute from out of my window. I remembered from one of my history lessons that the form of abuse was originated by the English long bowmen who held two fingers up at the French, the two fingers that pulled back the string on the bow to such lethal effect at Agincourt.

Flicking V-signs at the Dutch bikers is probably not the best thing to do from out of the bed room window at six in the morning. I'm not sure if the five leather-clad heavies will understand the historical significance of my gesture.

Le Treport

There is nothing so confusing as a seaside town in the pouring rain. It goes against the grain, baffles the childhood memories, makes a lie of the past.

It was south to Crecy-en-Ponthieu from Hesdin often toiling through winding lanes, France's damp, still-leafy innards, and then out into the open fields of potatoes, beet and maize. The cloudy sky was as moody as a teenager and the big black and white cows were lying down which must have meant rain. And when it came, the showery bovine prediction, Peter's windscreen wiper did two inches of glass and, very helpfully, eight of bodywork just below the screen. The wiper blade would not stay on the windscreen where it was needed but seemed to have taken on the duty of car washer, limp and useless and so annoying.

Sixty-nine years before Agincourt, Edward III had a result at Crecy. With the Earl of Northampton and the Black Prince, the English invasion and Hundred Years War had an early victory with England's new secret weapon, the long bow. Apparently gunpowder was used for the first time in Europe at the battle but perhaps no one thought it would catch on.

"Steady lads. Stick with your bows and never mind the fireworks."

Philippe IV of France went forth but came second. From the watchtower on the edge of the battlefield I got the King's eye view of the lay of the land and a partially graffitied plan gave me some idea of how things were. Obviously the farmhouse on the right wasn't there, nor the grain drier or those trees or that road. The village on the left wouldn't have had the meubles warehouse where it was and the electricity lines in the distance wouldn't have been invented yet. Apart from that the landscape hadn't changed at all.

From Crecy and past some quite grand looking mini chateaux it was but a few beats of a big bird's wing to the Parc ornithologique du Marquenterre. There on marshy land next to the sea and the Somme, a reserve for birds had been created. I paid 60 francs plus 25 for the guidebook and armed with my mother's mini binoculars, I went to see what I could see. There were more ducks than England had ever had at cricket. Scaup, Gadwall, Pochard, Teal, Mallard and Water Rail were all autumn visitors. Geese and swans galore were out in the wild but safe from the chasseurs' guns. The Spoonbills and Egrets had their own enclosure, netted over, which made me think zoo like thoughts for a moment. Maybe like little children in the playpen, it was for their own protection for without doubt there were some loose cannons in those parts. The road signs to the reserve were riddled with bullet holes, a French joke no doubt.

Just as September was blowing in the autumn, so Peter and I slipped across the Somme and into Normandy. Le Treport was a smart seaside town like the Ford Zodiac was a smart car. Both had had their day. Rain didn't make seaside towns look any prettier but even when it stopped for a while there was no real change. The cliffs looked grey not chalky white and even the colourful front was muted. The hotel Riche-Lieu was fine, the best I'd expect in a fading resort that used to boast the best and probably the nearest beaches to Paris. I couldn't say if they were still the best but they were certainly getting nearer. La Manche's munching would mean that in a millennia or so, Paris would be twinned with Le Treport whether it liked it or not. The Eiffel Tower would become a lighthouse; Le Riche-Lieu no longer worried about the fruits de mer on its menus.

I had skate and a bottle of St Emilion and watched the world blow by outside. Mrs Darth Vada walked her Scottie dog along the front. The wind kept her hood up and Scottie, what ever his name was, tight on his lead. Not because of his keen pace but rather the wind off the sea causing near strangulation. Did I see Mrs Vada talking to her dog?

"Keep me down Scottie."

The trucks in the car park opposite were enjoying doing wheelies around the few parked cars. I was trying to work out why and how many there were. Like Zebra, seen one and you'd seen them all. But look more closely and one was smaller, shorter than the others were, and another had got dents, different battle scars from the rest. They seemed to be moving the beach from A to

B and must have been working to fight the town's erosion and a drop in the ocean.

There was a biscuit with my coffee, a free gift, wrapped to go in the saucer. After I'd bitten into it I read the wrapper. Its main message said "Speculoos" which was mildly worrying there only being a shower in my room. Better that than the shower I had become used to in my tent.

I gaze across the wild sea and think about the red head over there on the other side. God how I must love my own company!

Dieppe

Oscar Wilde ran away to Dieppe. Maybe he too watched the bird lady.

The French seemed to like their nuclear plants but the one between Le Treport and Dieppe generating electricity for the EDF could have been powered by legions of hamsters on their treadmills. The high fence and rolls of barbed wire keeping out the animal rights lot rather than those who were just looking for a plutonium relationship. The place wasn't glowing incandescently or humming unduly and apart from the security ring fence there were no "Keep out. Danger radio active waste produced here" signs. There was a single railway line in and out, so everyone hoped the guy who worked the signals had always had a good night's uninterrupted sleep before he clocked on.

If the previous night's biscuit had a silly name, my cafe at the Cafe des Tribunaux in Dieppe was just as daft. It had "Kimbo" printed on the cup. If it had not been for the last night's film on the French Arte channel about Oscar Wilde and the extraordinary coincidence of taking a plat du jour at the place he escaped to in Dieppe, the "Kimbo" thing would have gone unmentioned. How appropriate I thought, like a mean, smutty schoolboy, that Oscar presumably went there because it wasn't only Bosie's legs, he liked akimbo.

The newspaper office was only a spit from the Alpine-looking cafe but because the clock had just struck twelve, no journalist would be available until three. I sat in the unusual and welcome sunshine and took a hot-melted goat's cheese on toast with salad and three small glasses of rouge. I watched the bird lady feeding them, an excited gaggle of pigeons and seagulls with fearless sparrows bobbing about around the edges waiting for their crumbs.

The bird lady was quite mad. She didn't want the sea birds to have her food but didn't know how to organise it. Waved her paper bag at those she didn't invite. She wore a battered hat. They always did. She would need to move in land quite a long way to solve her conundrum.

The interview with the journalist, called Johnny, was short and sweet but I hoped some use for the heart cause. Sylvie rang and wanted me in Paris on the twentieth for an interview with someone from a national TV channel. What did they want to talk about? Not my adventures around France but my heart attack.

"Ow was et for you Mester Perridge?"

"Loads less fun than sticking sharp needles in my eyes thanks."

Sylvie was worried that my French might not be good enough. Quite right too, so she was going to give me a morning's coaching which I hoped would take me just beyond the kindergarten stage.

Fecamp was about half way between Dieppe and Le Harve. One side of the town, the west side, looked just like Coronation Street-on-sea. Rows of red brick semis. The east end had a working class marina and the whole seaside town was fronted by a beach with stones on it the size of Granny Smiths. There was a promenade that kept the salt water from the town and on it was a statue of a woman looking out to sea. She was wearing clogs and a gown with a hood but the poor girl's face had gone, blown away by the wind no doubt. It wouldn't have been local vandals. The most exciting graffiti read "Psyco Katz" and it was painstakingly executed in biro on an Artex wall. The statue reminded those that knew that years before fishermen had gone off to Newfoundland, leaving their loved ones behind, waiting and watching, staring out to sea, praying for a safe return or the chance of joining them.

There was a casino below the cliff top campsite where I was staying and I dropped in, moth like, attracted by the bright lights and the promise of untold riches. Not for that casino the dinner jacketed or plunging neck line glamour that gavotted among the gaming tables of Monte-Carlo. In Fecamp it was slot machines. How on earth I thought I could beat them was beyond me. The things were built for the express purpose of extracting money from those dull enough to feed them. OK a percentage had to be paid out occasionally and some dumb Herbert thought he'd won. I tried. One hundred and fifty francs in less than fifteen minutes. I lost a quid a minute and at that rate there had to be better ways to spend my money. But not in Fecamp.

The campsite would probably have been great on the few days of the year when the sun did shine. Its layering gave each camper the terrace of their choice between cliff top and seaside, but that evening it looked like so many paddy fields.

I zip myself in and the wet wind gets up.

Le Harve

It is one of the worst showers I have ever had.

I went to bed damp and got up wet. All the uncomplimentary things I thought about Fecamp had come true. It was pay back time. It was the worst night in a tent that I had ever had. The storm got up at about the same time I went to bed and it blew all night. At 10.15 that morning it was still blowing and the rain was so hard that I swore Peter had developed hundreds of new dents on his blue bodywork.

All night the little tent shook like a spaniel trying to get dry and when it wasn't shaking, it was quivering like a jelly on a vibrating plate. With several force nine blasts, the two poles that made up the frame changed their shape. My flimsy home for the night changed from igloo to windsock, from windsock to pancake, back to windsock and then to igloo once again. My sleeping bag was a big green sponge and my pillow that was wrapped with my towel to try and absorb some of the water, could only become fish food. The wind blew up under the waterproof outside cover, which was cheating, and in through the see-through net lining that wallpapered the living quarters. The sea, not very far from my feet, had turned from something I could understand Moses parting, into a boiling soup pot that spat a lot. Try as I might to keep out the elements, I hadn't a bailing vessel big enough.

My condition made me feel vindictive towards Fecamp. The place stank and I never wanted to see it again as long as I lived, even if it became a sub tropical zone with free plat du jours every day and wine thrown in for nothing. The guide for the place made me smile cynically. "Discovering Fecamp (to be seen again and again). The museum of New Foundland fishermen and fishing." The fact that the local fishermen left the place and risked drowning, said much about the town. "The fine art museum". Some not very fine art and some carved fish bones. "Benedictine Palace." True Hammer Horror surroundings with a brew made from boiled down oilskins, the fish bones not fit to turn into fine art and other dubious local ingredients. "The Abbey, the Church and the Chapel of the Haly Trinity " (that was how they spelt it)," Sainte-Etienne and Notre-Dame-de-Salut", in that order, were all grey, dark and dank. "The ducal Palace" (the small d for ducal was theirs) I could not find. "The Town Hall" I didn't want to. "The fountain of the Precious Blood" sounded just desperate. Whose I wondered? No mention was made of the faceless and forlorn would be escapee standing on the shore looking for her knight in shining armour or sailor in what ever colour oil skins, to come and rescue her from a Fecamp worse than death.

The only way I could exit the camp site was to collapse the tent, something the wind had being trying to do all night, leaving everything in it and bundle the whole lot, like some enormous bag of dirty washing, into the back of Peter. The rain was the wettest I'd been lashed by since records began and had there been anybody else on the camp site to watch my Napoleon-withdrawal-from-Moscow-look-a-like-competition, they would have given me first prize after having wet themselves had they not already been in that state by just being there. I did fall over several times and honestly, for all the good they were doing me, may as well have removed all my clothes and completed the decamp at Fecamp altogether in the all together.

As if things couldn't get any worse, Peter's gears had come out in sympathy again which that morning made both driver and the driven very noisy travelling companions. Elderly pedestrians, those that had obviously been blown off course, looked really scared when we approached. A lot of little French dogs did things on pavements out of sheer terror rather than the normal well thought out now-I'll-do-it-right-here pile usually found fouling the walk ways. With an engine that sounded several decibels louder than a taking off Concorde, prompted by awesome gear changes, no effective windscreen wiper and the inside of the cab misting up because of the sponge like driver, our progress from Fecamp to Goderville was a hazardous affair. It was difficult to tell just what colour the lights were until it was too late. Spray on the windscreen made everything look like a bad oil painting. I had therefore an impression of red on occasions and the resultant impression of angry French drivers sounding their klaxons. No one actually hit me or collided with Peter, although I expected plenty wanted to.

At Goderville I stopped for two grand cafes au lait in a PMU bar and tabac and left a trail between door and bar, bar and table like that of a melting iceberg. I was sure some of the locals thought that I'd just swum ashore, the result of some tragedy at sea and when I asked how much further it was to Le Harve (the harbour) I could see the lady behind the bar actually dialling for the coast guard.

Le Harve arrived still in the pouring rain and because of the noise coming from Peter's gearbox, other road users got out of the way. Even a bendy bus thought twice before bending in front of us. A gear change too far happened on the Cours de la Republique at Le Rond Point. We stopped. No shouting, hitting, pushing, pleading or even trying to surprise the gear lever would prompt a response. We came to a halt and so did all the traffic behind us. I didn't know if bus drivers were supposed to leave their vehicles unmanned but thank goodness that one did and the two of us pushed Peter out of the main traffic lane and into a relative backwater. It was the sort of backwater people could live in. Shops, cafes, bars, and the hairdresser of course, a couple of underwear shops, an insurance office and a Singer sewing machine centre. I thought about sewing machines and whether they had gearboxes and if so, perhaps one could be used to good effect on Peter. Such was my challenged mechanical ability.

Once a Piaggio always a Piaggio and no one wanted to know. I pretended once that Piaggio was Peugeot, but was soon rumbled. They hadn't made a three-wheeled Peugeot that they'd admit to. Even if I had got a valise full of money and waved it in front of them, unless I found the right man, it was " I'm sorry it's not one of ours Sir " ("Je suis desolee. C'est ne pas une Renault.")

The one thing that did work however was the Mondial Assistance provided as part of the insurance cover through AGF. I'd had more than my money's worth and dear old Mondial Ass could have put me on the moon for the amount it must have cost them to low load Peter to his various saviours. Roadside assistance had been one of my better investments. Mine cost £170 for a year and I reckoned that I got that back every time Peter broke down and had to be winched off to the repairer's yard.

Once on the back of the rescue truck we trawled around Le Harve and its neighbours trying to find someone who would be prepared to have a look at Peter. You'd think we were trying to pass on a notifiable disease the way most receptionists greeted us. After some time a "back-street" garage in Harfleur, where the receptionist was also the mechanic, tea boy, accountant and managing director, agreed to take Peter in for a "look". I could tell that the recovery truck driver was a happy man by the way he punched the air, goal scoring footballer style, and kissed the consenting mechanic firmly on both cheeks.

I got a Mondial Assistance paid for taxi to an hotel, Hotel Grand Parisien, right opposite the station in Le Harve and peeled off my still soggy clothes for a hot shower. I'm not sure but I think that even the people in the busy railway station across the main road could hear me singing from the hot steamy recess in room twenty-five.

It is one of the best showers I have ever had.

On TV In Paree

I haven't been on the telly before and somehow I don't think I'll appear after today's encounter.

The train journey from Le Harve to Paris took about two hours so I was in Sylvie's office by ten and being coached in French before you could say "Jaques Ribensin." The sort of sentence supposed to roll fluently in French off my English tongue for the TV interview, went along the following lines.

"After my cardiac infarction and the cardiologists confirmation that the blood test had shown as much, I was kept in intensive care until angioplastie could reopen the shut down artery and a stent could be placed in the offending area."

It wasn't exactly " Bon jour. Qu'est-ce que c'est le plat de jour?"

I had, with Sylvie's help, prepared a script and written down most of the words as they sounded. Funnily enough quite a lot of jargon was the same in both languages, "indigestion", "angioplastie", "attack cardiac" which sounded worse than a heart attack and much worse than "infactus", so I used it. It was the genders that got me as per French usual. Un infactus. A masculine heart attack. What happened if you were not a bloke? Tough. In France you could only have a masculine heart attack. Un infactus. "J'ai un infactus". Not the easiest sentence to roll naturally off the tongue and it didn't much to Sylvie's disappointment. She was standing in the corner out of camera shot miming her socks off and, on several dreadful pauses, when interviewer Jacques Ribensin may as well have been posing a question to the Wailing Wall, Sylvie's mimes became audible.

"J'ai un infactus" she mimed and whispered and shook and looked as though she had indeed had what she was trying to get me to say.

Jacques, the interviewer, wasn't having any coaching from the wings or scob sheets and so the interview may well have gone down in France Deux TV history as one of the great "non" interviews. Maybe they had the equivalent of " It'll be all right on the night" or " Auntie's Bloomers", those cheap television shows that rely on showing the cock ups that occurred while making the expensive television shows. May be I'd get on the French variation for while Jacques clearly knew the questions he was asking and I fairly clearly knew the answers I was giving, the two had absolutely nothing to do with each other at all. It must have been worse than interviewing a politician or a child, who at least tried to play around on the same pitch. If Jacques was doing football then I was probably preparing an egg salad. That was how far apart we were. The only two things we agreed on were the start and the finish. I looked forward with interest to the result and thanked God with my heart, stent and all, that the broadcast wasn't going out live.

Before the TV fiasco, Sylvie had arranged a plat du jour at a Swedish style restaurant by the name of Comptoir de Saumon & Cie. There was pretty much anything available as long as it came with "saumon" and some of that Swedish crisp bread on the side. Jean-Marc Monternot was the other person chosen to talk about his "attack cardiac" although clearly he would be able to answer the questions as they were put to him in a language that he and the viewers would understand. He and Sophie Lamijeon, a PR. person from the Association Cardiologie (Ille de France branch) joined Sylvie and I at the French-come-Swedish joint. It was one of those lunches where I left feeling not totally satisfied. It was like riding a horse, not an old nag, but something with a bit of spirit that was just bursting for permission from its rider to open up and go. Lunch was like that. We would have liked another bottle of wine, cheese perhaps, but we were all holding back because it was business, heart business, and we were, all four of us being extra good for our hearts.

The train back to Le Harve was late leaving St-Lazare for some reason the station public address system tried to explain. Not for the first time that day did I find myself not understanding what was being said. At the station it wasn't the language but rather the means by which it was being relayed and the resultant echo. The girl whose job it was to make the announcements could have been speaking to us in Swahili, or her own made up tongue. I bet if I ran into her at a drinks party, I would have been able to understand every word she said. Or would I?

"Hello. My name's Charlie."

"Bertran stibing ut plit firm force is ve tooths hirty sex fur lee harve et je lappels Francoise."

Le Harve is in darkness when I get there and my mood isn't much better. Peter's boite de vitesse (gearbox) is apparently terminal. The train from Paris might stop at Le Harve, the end of the line, but I cannot let the Plat du Jour Tour do the same.

GARAGE DES VALLÉES

Ventes Réparations Toutes Marques

5, Chemin des Vallées   76700 HARFLEUR
Tél. 02 35 45 45 65   Fax 02 35 47 40 56

GARAGE DES VALLÉES TERRIBLES

Ventes Réparations Toutes Marques
Dans La Mesure De Nos Abilités Trés Limitées

5, Chemin des Vallées   76700 HARFLEUR
Tél. 02 35 45 45 65   Fax 02 35 47 40 56

Le Peyras ⚊⚊

I don't know if my number is up this time.

There I was in the bar next door to my hotel in Le Harve, the one right across the road from the station, and this man came in and sat down opposite me. It wasn't as if there weren't any other tables in the place, there were, but he came and sat down right in front of me, in my booth. What made it stranger was that I was half way through my meal. There were still a couple of mouthfuls of entrecote on the plate and the salad (lettuce) remained pretty much undisturbed on the side.

The guy wasn't a beggar. He didn't behave like one. No lighter on the table with a note that said please pay ten francs or whatever for the lighter because the guy who had just put it there was deaf and dumb. I saw quite a lot of deaf and dumb people working the cafes like that and I could sometimes catch them out by asking for a gold coloured lighter rather than the silver coloured one they left as the sample. Nine times out of ten they'd give me a gold coloured one, their hearing miraculously restored by the prospect of the ten franc coin.

The bloke opposite me looked rather smart. A suit, which was worrying, like he'd come to collect money rather than beg for it. The bloke, "the suit", wanted to give me money or rather he wanted me to "make" money by following his advice. In the bar there was a TV screen but rather than news of the Americans trying to find Bin Liner, the screen was full of squares and numbers. "Rapido" was a lottery game that could be played every five minutes. "The suit" passed me three Rapido slips for games 193, 194 and 195 that were due to be played within the next half an hour. Each slip had two boxes, grille

A with numbers one to twenty and grille B with one to four. The idea was to pick eight numbers from grille A and one from grille B. Simple as that. So "the suit" had done it for me. For game 193 he had marked 7,8,9,10,12,17,19,20 and 4. All that had to be done was to give the ticket to the barman with the stake money and if all the numbers came up, I'd win ten thousand times my money back. Ten thousand to one but in real terms it was more like a several millions to one shot. There was a sliding scale downwards so that if five numbers came up in grille A and one in grille B, I could still win six times my stake.

"The suit" said to me to put 50 francs on game 193. So I did. All the numbers came up. I won five hundred thousand francs. I'm not sure how I felt other than I finished my meal.

It was game 194 and "the suit" passed me another slip with 1,7,8,12,14,15,16,17 and 3. He said go for another 50 francs, which I did and within the five or six minutes I'd won another 500,000 francs. I ordered another pichet of rouge. Rapido game no 195 was due and on the slip "the suit" had selected 5,7,9,10,15,16,18,19 and number 2 and he was right again. I'd just added another half million French francs to my winnings.

So I was about £150,000 the richer than I was twenty minutes before (I'd obviously got to go and get the dosh from Rapido H.Q. because the bar understandably didn't carry that sort of cash) and I offered "the suit" a drink. Well it was the least I could have done.

"No thank you," said he. "I don't drink and I don't gamble."

"But the numbers," said I. "You had all of them spot on."

"No," said he. "The numbers are always spot on. It's you that's not."

And with that he got up, slid out of the booth and away into the night. I thought that was justice for my lost fifteen pounds at the casino in Fecamp and then, just as I was ordering the small black espresso, just as I was thinking wasn't life funny and a new gear box for Peter would be no problem, I woke up.

On my way over to the station I paused for a second or two outside the bar, the one running the Rapido games, but I couldn't see the man of my dreams, "the suit", which was probably just as well.

The day's reality was eight hours on two trains. Two hours to Paris from Le Harve and six on the Nivea TGV from Montparnasse to Tarbes. After Bordeaux the TGV label became a misnomer and the initials TAP (train s'arreter partout) would have been more fitting. We pulled into places that I swore Monsieur Michelin hadn't mapped. It gave the locals (population in most cases no more than 12 and a dog) something to stare at as well as exposing them to the Nivea range of skin care products. No one got on or off the Nivea express at the back of beyond halts, so we could only assume that the driver had relations he wanted to wave at. He obviously came from a big family whose procreation, unlike the train, didn't stop.

Nivea, the skin cream people, sponsored the TGV or TAP because the outside of every carriage was covered in their graffiti. Nivea needed the lines. We slid our way southwestward on what had become a sort of "Avon calling" journey, knocking at the door of any station that would have us. The "Ding dong" that we heard from the platforms outside, the one that precedes the announcement, was totally appropriate. "Ding dong". "Not today thank you." I'd travelled in the 101 Dalmatians train, a sort of high tec spotted dick, but it was the first time I'd taken the tube as it were. Once inside the cream express, it was only those outside that could get the message as we squirted past, wrinkle free and as smooth as a baby's bottom.

At Tarbes it was nearer to 10 pm than 9.30 and Butler was kindly there to greet me. He whisked me back to Sainte Marie de Campan where friends and supper were both waiting to be served.

I have failed. Peter, abandoned in Le Harve, I return to the mountains to lick my wounds and feel sorry for myself again.

Here And There But Going Nowhere ⇥

It is six months to the day that I slipped off the Nivea express.

When the little wren tapped at my window and then hopped from log
to log in nervous search, I knew that it was my mother. When I heard the
woodpecker's laugh like some naughty child at the back of the classroom,
heard but not seen up in the woods, I knew it was my mother. The evening
owl hoot, that was her too and the cawry crow lolloping up the valley. I knew
she was there. Don't ask me how but I knew. I fed the birds; of course I did,
with crumbs and sometimes whole baguettes gone too hard and leftover
stews and the cut-off fat from the leg of Spanish ham. My mother liked her
yoghurt but dairy products without the power to keep them would soon lose
their appeal.

She was there keeping an eye or two on me and I loved her for it. When I
looked up from my rough outside table where I sat and wrote, I could see the
white-capped peaks mottled as the sun got the better of the snow. The sound
of water accompanied the dead but dancing leaves, downed from last autumn
and blown from here to there and there to here in a harum-scarum vortex by
the strong and gusty wind. The March sun was strong (a thermometer on my
wall might show mid twenties) and Spring was given another starter's gun in
what had in the past weeks been false start after false start. To your marks
once more but the date made it somehow more official, the first day of spring
as far as the calendar was concerned.

The shepherds too sensed the seasons change, it was light at six thirty
in the morning and dark by half past seven at night, so the scales tipped in
favour of the lighter hours and darkness lost more than its fair share for a few

months at least. The rams arrived at Sainte Marie-de-Campan to get their bills of health, their medicals for the mountains, so their horns of plenty might make mountain passes at even the scraggiest of ewes. Their owners, the farmers from around, gathered with their beasts on ropes and formed a queue behind metal barriers, the sort used to control the crowds on Tour de France day. There was no hurry; no sense of urgency and everyone would be seen in turn under the old grey slatted market roof. The vet was there and each ram was given the once over, prodded in the right places, marked with an ear tag that made some rear up in complaint. There was a man at an impromptu desk, a table, taking money and making notes and another with a drenching gun to give each animal a dose of something good. The farmers, twenty or thirty of them with their hangers on, were sturdy, outdoor types. Most short and stocky with weathered faces and working hands which guided the rope halters around the bony heads of their particular prize tup. If it were the other way round, and rams led their men for inspection, I wondered how many would get the seal of approval?

The village bar did a roaring trade and Magali was rushed off her feet with orders for gal pan and gal peen, café and pastis. The triumphant rams waited outside for their owners return. Did they count men to get to sleep? Penned up in tin trailers or in pick-up trucks or beaten up old vans, they awaited their masters and dreamt of the day, not too far ahead, when they would be set free up in the hills, the high pastures of the High Pyrenees. For the rams of the valley spring was stirring.

The first weekend of the previous month I thought that spring had sprung already. Back in early February it was Momo's birthday. His fiftieth. Fifty years a Frenchman. The fires, the grass fires set ablaze on purpose by the mountain shepherds flared across impossible slopes all night, a moving firework show to announce Momo's big day. The smell and smog of burnt pasture hung in the valley and grass that was brown through unseasonable lack of water had paid the price and was turned to soot. The rock escarpment en-face became smutty, black and grey, cooked to a turn by ancient fire with the certainty that phoenix like green shoots for spring would push their verdant way through their family ashes. But then came more snow.

Even in the last week of February when the Christmas lights were coming down in Bagneres-de-Bigorre, the weak sunshine was hinting at spring and the circus had come to town. Zavatta posters appeared like a colourful case of chicken pox and trees, once plane, became a bright hoarding. Lampposts where dogs would dain to dally were dressed as roaring paper tigers. Little French pooches wouldn't dare to cock a leg under the fierce stares. The red Zavatta van ran around the town brashly broadcasting the bill through loudspeakers on its roof. It was the van that somehow spoke, the van and not the man inside. The spectacle, the thrill, drew the breath in and prepared it to be amazed. Monsieur Zavatta, like the travelling medicine man of old, would hold the crowd spellbound under his tent for an hour or so and all for a few Euros, not ring side Francs anymore. The travelling circus was as natural in those parts as goat's cheese, stooped French widows, fat four wheel drive cars and snow. Long live Zavatta! Long live his tigers! And long live the snow so it seemed.

Sadly I missed his show. There were two performances in Bagneres, one in the evening and the other a matinee. I got my timing all wrong unlike Monsieur Zavatta's trapeze artists. It also snowed some more so spring was once again put on hold. Maybe I'd get to see inside the big top one day. Maybe one day I'd be thrilled.

Like Zavatta, his tigers and the rams, I must soon be on the move, and the tour, like the spring, was under starter's orders and ready for the off once more and when the time was right.

Winters get harder the older we get.

Back To Le Havre And Onto The Normandy Beaches

It's a nervy moment but on the second or third turn of the ignition key, Peter purrs into new life outside Le Monaco Hotel right next to the port in Le Havre. I'm bloody well going to do it. I'm not going to give in.

Trying to find a replacement gearbox for Peter proved as difficult as finding someone to replace it. No one seemed to want to know. Garage after garage shook their heads in the wrong directions. Mechanics sucked air in through their teeth until their gums hurt with the cold draft. Even Monsieur Piaggio in Paris couldn't see an obvious solution other than to buy a brand new machine. We seemed to live in an age where anything outside the ordinary was frowned on by the ordinary. If it was broken, throw it away and get " a sensible" one, one that won't "bother" us, one that required "minimum effort". Anything for an easy life. Peter had been taken to a garage in Harfleur and what they had hoped would be a "minimum effort", "easy life" job, turned into one of new gearbox proportions. The Garage des Vallees didn't want to know. They didn't want broken Peter on their premises. So much for their "Ventes Reparations Toutes Marques" claim. I felt like quoting the Trades Description Act to them, but I knew that wouldn't do any good.

Thierry the car breaker actually came up with a solution. He told me that the scruffy man I'd purchased Peter from had another three-wheeler of similar vintage. Butler and I hastened off to find the fellow. Sure enough in one of his out buildings there was a rusty red three-wheeled Piaggio covered in layers of dirt. It hadn't been used for years but the scruffy man said it would go, given some work. We explained that it was probably just the gearbox we needed and the scruffy man looked as though he already knew what we were after. We adjourned to the scruffy man's scruffy farmhouse kitchen and accepted a ludicrously strong glass of something alcoholic. One glass led to another. And another. And another. We talked about who we knew and what a pity it was that the Franc had been replaced by the Euro. The scruffy fellow was still getting used to Francs. He said he still talked in old Francs. Eventually we meandered our way back to the business in hand. Yes, he said, he thought that he could help us. We should however come back and see his son. His son was a mechanic.

" Quelle surprise," I think I slurred to Butler as we pulled away from the place several hours later.

Peter was blue. The forlorn machine in the scruffy outbuilding was red and a few years older. The scruffy man's son agreed to go to Le Havre and scoop up broken blue Peter bringing him back to Bagneres. He would then take the working bits from the red wreck and transplant them into the blue one. Like all transplants, it wasn't cheap, it wasn't quick and it wasn't easy. It wasn't just the gearbox either. The whole engine had to be transferred because the gearbox was not compatible. There were anxious moments during the operation. Bits didn't fit and blue Peter with the red machine's guts had an engine that didn't take petrol in one aperture and oil in another, but rather one tank for a mixture of the two. The new engine didn't seem to have quite the same pulling power as the old, but the scruffy man's son got the job done although the scruffy man himself negotiated the price in old Francs which made the number of noughts look obscene.

The new blue Peter, complete with a new sign on the back that explained to the frustrated following driver that "It's incredible! I am doing a tour of France", was loaded onto a trailer and taken back up to Le Havre. The journey with the scruffy man's son and a friend of his, took the three of us twelve hours. They simply unloaded the little three-wheeler outside Le Monaco Hotel, had a quick fish supper with me, said "Bon courage", shook me firmly by the hand and then set off back home, another drive through the night of at least ten hours.

Understandably rebuilt, most of Le Havre was sadly a monument to the cement mixer. What war destroyed, peace time had ruined. On the bright spring Sunday morning the beachfront area was bristling with walkers, joggers, cyclists and scooters, those micro silver machines punted along with one foot on and one foot off. Old and young, human and canine, the sea front was being used as only sea fronts could be in celebration of a fine day, less of the concrete and more of the ozone.

Peter putted on, as excited as any beach side jogger, his replacement engine and gearbox seeming to do the job. At Harfleur, as if in homage to the home of the garage that had claimed to be able to fix anything, we came to a stuttering halt. Was Peter going to give them another chance to rebuild their tarnished reputation? Had they seen the little Piaggio parked up over night and spiked his guns somehow? Fuel I thought, but it was the spark plug lead that had jumped off. Hurled itself out of action. Recklessly jump stopped. I felt like a serious mechanic as I pushed it back onto the one and only plug. With a turn of the key, we were back on the road again. Simple, the practical engineering bit.

The Pont de Normandie was a pretty impressive bridge that cost five Euros to get over for a normal vehicle. Peter was allowed over for nothing.

"C'est gratuit." said the toll taker from his booth window looking down on us as though Peter was a snail. Which, as it turned out, he was.

The big humpback-bridge across the Seine between Le Havre and Honfleur would take a Porsche or Ferrari microseconds to cross. A Renault what-you-may-call-it would do it in minutes. A blue Piaggio called Peter took nearly half an hour. We were actually moving for twenty minutes. Moving with the engine in the traditional way for fifteen and for five, with me out and pushing. We didn't go anywhere for ten. We were stationary, quite still apart from the sideways buffeting given to us by the extraordinarily quick traffic that skimmed past us inches away. Getting out to move the vehicle was fractionally more frightening than being stuck sitting in Peter's little cab. The thin tin panelling gave a false sense of security. Outside, high up on the bridge I felt exposed. I was exposed. Exposed to the elements, the swollen mud coloured Seine and the constant threat of a French maniac driver either in his Porsche or Ferrari or even the Renault what-you-may-call-it, ramming into us, catapulting us down into the mouth of the Seine miles below.

If they had charged us the five Euros toll, I would have wanted my money back. The ride was not supposed to be a scary one but it was. The mechanical problem that time was not as simple as a disconnected spark plug lead. It sounded stupid but the prolonged climb up the Pont de Normandie in second gear probably made the hard working engine too hot, so it stopped for a breather. It started again after a rest but while it recovered, the driver didn't. It was not as though I could have pulled off onto the side. The hard shoulder to cry on was very soft indeed. Air thin really with a watery base to it way below. Pull over and I'd end up in Seine. We made it, but it was, in Normandy speak, nearly a bridge too far.

On the north side of the Seine estuary everything was waiting to be refined. The skirts of Le Havre bristled with things of a petro-chemical nature. On the south side everything was much more refined. Honfleur, Trouville and Deauville with not a hair out of place and all very neat with Sunday afternoon French café society at its spring sunshine best. A dozen oysters or maybe just the six sitting at the water's edge wondering, but not worrying too much, whether it will be Chirac or Jospin in June.

On the relatively flat Peter didn't falter although his progress was slow even with less weight to carry. I'd only one tin trunk with my camping kit and a small case for my clothes rather than the two tin trunks stuffed full I had hauled pre the Le Havre breakdown.

At Benouville we crossed the new Pegasus Bridge and stopped for half an hour at the memorial. The battle around there was the stuff that schoolboys of my age used to dream about. Behind enemy lines, parachuted in to take Gerry by surprise, 10,000 troops became the first to liberate Normandy. Heroic stuff with Major Howard at the fore and fierce fighting to make sure that the D Day landings could be successful. One thousand of those that dropped in by parachute or glider died in the fighting and they were remembered at the Pegasus Memorial.

I didn't get the same sense of dreadful conflict that was in my face at Vimy Ridge or Verdun but none-the-less I was told that it happened. The First World War fields were like arriving at the scene of a road accident that had just been cleared up. I could still see the tyre marks, the rubber on the road. The scars were there for all to see what warlike men could do. At Pegasus there were no signs, no marks of war, just a place name on a map and things to jog the memory in a museum.

At Arromanches, on the beach like stranded whales, their physical presence made history unavoidable. Giant concrete blocks lay half submerged in sand and sea as their own memorial to a remarkable structure, a floating port created to support the D Day effort. From there fighting men and machines came and went in their hundreds of thousands from sea to land and land to sea.

Almost as though it had been planned, when I returned to my hotel room and flicked on the television, the opening sequences of "Saving Private Ryan" were being broadcast on TF1. I'd been to the Normandy beaches, now I was seeing the movie; it was really very strange.

It is very strange being back on the road again.

Granville ⇌

Over Granville the seagulls fire, one or two long opening bursts and then their machine gun cries. Bird echoes bounce off the buildings in Hitchcock like horror. Theirs is not a pretty song.

The spring tide was riding high but the waves slapped half-heartedly at the port's seaside defences. The casino, a dull yellow Lego built building that had to look successful, housed the "machines a sous", the unpredictable fed by the predictable, fruit machines played by fruit cakes. It was right opposite where I was staying.

The day started appropriately enough, all misty and damp at the well kept Ryes War Cemetery near Bazenville, inland from the Normandy beaches and on the way to Bayeux. Surrounded by French fields, some just ploughed, others grass or growing food, the neat rows of white gravestones stood like a permanent crop for those young men harvested before they had ripened nearly sixty years before. The military ranks were drawn, regimented, straight lines. But every stone was an individual. A name, an age, most twenty something, and an inscription. I wandered the rows and read.

"Say not good night but in some brighter clime bid me good morning"

"To live in the hearts of those you love is not to die, Eric"

"Doomed to know not winter only spring"

"We will meet again some sunny day"

"He scarce had need to doff his pride or slough the dross of earth"

"My dear Bob. May some kind hand in that distant land lay down a flower for me? His wife Susan"

I found a daffodil growing on the fringes in the long grass under the trees and I picked it for Bob from Susan, feeling as though I was being watched. But I wasn't. I was all on my own apart from six hundred and thirty British, twenty-one Canadians, one Australian, one Pole, and three hundred and twenty six Germans. They were all there around me in that peaceful resting-place. On my way out, I caught the words on a Scottish sergeant's headstone.

"Not goodbye dear, just goodnight. Wife Lily and baby Janet"

They made the tears break the thin cover they had been keeping. I had to wipe my glasses dry to see where I was going.

At Bayeux, for 6.40€ in the centre Guillaume le Conquerant, I strolled the length of the famous tapestry, lit up in its own glass case; I peered at it from within a darkened room. It was an extraordinary band of linen, over two hundred feet long, apparently embroidered by the nuns of Kent in a naïve but detailed style. If you had asked a class of five and six-year-olds to draw the story, the images would have looked similar. Norman knights like stick men in chain mail, some with the heads lying next to their bodies. Weird beasts, like griffins and dragons, adorned the tapestry's borders. Had I been more attentive during my Latin lessons at school, I might have been able to translate the old words that tell the story of Edward the Confessor, William of Normandy and Harold; 1066 and all that. But I couldn't and just looked at the pictures instead. They painted a vivid account. Bloodshed was a common feature of daily life, then as now. Today "News at Ten" Gaza Strip; one thousand years ago the Bayeux Tapestry, Kent coast.

Leaving the linen, Peter and I headed southwest and stopped briefly at Balleroy. The Chateau there was very grand. It looked just like a giant hot air balloon in the shape of a very grand seventeenth-century French chateau. I parked in the drive and waited for lift off, but nothing happened. The balloons had gone up from here in times gone by. The French home of Malcolm Forbes, wealthy American news magnate and therefore like a magnet, attractive to the rich and famous keen to show their mettle, Chateau Balleroy would have been a great place to party with or without balloons.

If after partying all night in St Lo, I had climbed the stairs in the main square, I would have found myself going nowhere. The stairway to heaven looked as though it should have had a concrete multi-storey car park attached, but it didn't. The ruin of the gate to the town's old prison stood adjacent to the newer stairs to nowhere and it was a memorial to the dead of the last war. An urn contained the ashes of some of those sent off from there to concentration camps. French Resistance fighters shot and soldiers who died were named, and General de Gaulle was pictured. Steps to nowhere and a shut gate didn't say much for St Lo. But I could imagine Samuel Beckett there, tending to the wounded and thinking lots.

At Coutances, I took a cup of hot water with a tea bag in it. The Catherdrale de Notre-Dame could be seen from miles away and acted like a beacon to that part of rural Normandy. Its stone was as light in colour as my tea, which I drank never the less before the last leg to Granville and the sea once more.

The seagulls are not my mother although their cries could be her in anguish.

Le Mont-St-Michel And St-Malo ⇒

People are outside on the cobbles snapping at the moon. I can see them from my window table. They are trying to get the walls; some stonework or the white blue crossed flowing flag into the picture so that back in Osaka, Harrogate or Jacksonville they can say, "That was the moon over St-Malo."

The Route de la Baie was our route for the day. Like millions before I was making a pilgrimage to the Mont-St-Michel. From afar the Mont looked like a mysterious, mist-shrouded pile. It was the sort of place that filmmakers, space and time travellers, hobbits and yellow brick road walkers might look to as their final destination, their goal. The Mont was made even more pert by the flatness that surrounded it and its nipple, the spire of the abbey, pointed proudly to heaven. I thought I was there but from when I first saw it to when I arrived at its base and walked through its big front door, seemed to take forever. It grew bigger like a pimple that on Monday was just a minor bump, an irritation that by Friday had turned into Everest sitting on your face.

Like it's twin Carcassonne, Mont St-Michel felt as though Walt Disney might have built there. I'm afraid I got nothing of the magic of old religion. The so-called sacred place was sacred to the tourist. I went away carrying the vision of the young Japanese man, the subject of a photograph by his girl friend. He stood on the ancient steps into the abbey in a John Travolta "Saturday Night Fever" pose, arm extended upwards, finger pointing to God. But unlike the spire above him, his stance seemed almost blasphemous. He was pointing at God without even knowing it. Being rude, like staring. Then, as I looked out over the thick stone wall, I saw a crocodile, a long chain of people walking out across the wet sands from the island towards the firmer, greener land. I thought that that was how it must have been. They died getting there in days of old, swallowed by the tide, and now they came by coach.

I too got the corny picture, the Mont on Peter's back, riding him like a steamed pudding on a plate. We then took the fifty Ks to St-Malo via the coast, flat as a nervous karaoke singer's opening note. Where the windmills should have been, their four sails had become for sales.

The Americans rebuilt St-Malo, the walled citadel, after they had helped to destroy it in the Second World War. It was old worldly and charming but with every mod con. Fast food and old wine, cobbled streets and beaches, battlements and boutiques, a cathedral and a sex shop, St-Marlo within the walls had lots for the masses and as a result, masses for its lot.

The Hotel de France et de Chateaubriand, whose ashtrays I'd nicked in the past, was a wonderful old place. I stayed there every time I passed through St-Malo and every time the girl behind the reception desk gave me a room bigger than my house. It was 454 that time with two beds and three windows all looking out over the sea. There was a table and chairs that the Royal Family would be happy sitting on and pictures on the wall, old prints, that any gallery would be glad to have in their old prints section. It was not fashionable or chic and its floorboards creaked under thin carpets. The bathrooms were from the 1950's, but they worked well enough with water from the present day. There was a marble-topped tallboy in one corner of my room and a tiny wrapped boiled fruit sweet, a welcome from the management, the family that still owned their great anachronism.

My dash to St-Malo, cutting off most of the Cotentin peninsula bit of Normandy, missing out Cherbourg, was so that I could catch the ferry back to England. I was going back as a foot passenger for Easter, just for four days, there and back again.

Missing my mother, I want to see my father. I want to see the red head again. Give her some eggs for Easter.
"Fertilised or unfertilised," she'd say with that bold bright smile of hers.

Le Val Andre ⇥

My broken toe doesn't make me limp anymore.

I sat on the front, up on the long promenade and looked out to sea across the wide beach. I remembered breaking my toe on that sand. I ran into the back of a French girl. Bent my second toe all the way across my big one. Bent it at a right angle. Stubbed it on the back of her leg during a game of beach volleyball. Dr Carpier shrugged when I showed it to him.

"Oui. It's broken," he told me. There was nothing he could do about it. It had been like it ever since, straighter but still an ugly reminder of happy days.

Le Val Andre was pretty much the same as when I had last seen it back in the sixties. The island of rabbits was still there out to sea, the beach, the prom, the casino and the Rotonde cinema. The crepes were now being served in cafes rather than through the open windows of beach side houses but they still smelt and tasted just as good. There was no Bertrand though and sadly no Odiele to play havoc with my hormones. The Beatles were still on the radio and the French were still musing at the lyrics of Yellow Submarine. It didn't look as sophisticated as I remembered. But that was all to do with me rather than Le Val Andre.

The road from Le Val Andre was simple but got itself complicated around St Brieuc. Peter's new even slower status really got to the other road users on the motorway type routes. I did try to keep him off them and while we got into the centre of the city without too much trouble, leaving it and heading for Paimpol involved several kilometres of very frustrated other drivers. Hooting was how they'd take it out on us mostly. The really frustrated would resort to hooting and sign language. On the normal thoroughfares the new sign on the back ("It's incredible! I am doing a tour of France") prompted quiet a few friendly hoots. Short beep-beeps and waving and smiles rather than long aggressive blasts that I could tell were meant to blast us off the road.

At Crukin, just before Paimpol and just after the ruined Abbaye de Beauport, the manager of the municipal campsite was certainly one from the friendly hooting camp. I felt like a wise man, who had found his star hovering over head. I pitched my tent and headed off for fish.

We were smarter than fish. That was why we ate them. That and they tasted good as well. Of course some of them did eat us occasionally, but I bet we didn't taste as good as they did. We were probably a bit like very salty sushi, with bones and swimwear of course. The fish I had for the plat du jour at La Cotriade (meaning the fish stew in English) was wonderful. Pretty as a picture, it arrived on a square frosted glass plate, a whole chunk of Turbot on five green fingers of asparagus. The bases of the spears were tightly wrapped in bacon. Had chef been corny he might have made Turbot and asparagus look like a whole hand. He wasn't and he didn't but I had to hand it to him, his plat du jour was one of the best I'd had in a long time. At nearly 30€ for the plate, so it should have been and for that I expected Britney Spears to be the waitress.

I was under canvas once again, well nylon really, for the first time since wet Fecamp, so a Turbot and five fingers of asparagus were perfectly in order. I looked up over the harbour and the gently nodding boats. A vapour trail had spread wide in the sky, like a girl's belt. There was no buckle, just a cloudbank to hide what might have been and when I looked up again after four or five minutes, the slate had been wiped completely clean. No birds, no bird's belt, just clouds.

I know that it makes my pee smell funny, but that's Brittany spears for you.

Treguier And Morlaix

The viaduct sweeps over Morlaix so rail passengers can easily get vertigo by just looking down on the town centre.

I camped. It rained. You could imagine the composer of those old Janet and John books. "See Charlie camp." "Charlie has a tent." "See it rain." "The rain is wet." What the author wouldn't have written was "See Charlie's fist." "He shakes it at the clouds."

It was raining when I woke up at six and it rained all day. Now it might have stopped but it didn't, as punishment for me using the disabled person's shower and loo at the municipal campsite. How the disabled used the disabled person's shower at the municipal campsite was beyond me. The manager tapped on the side window of Peter's cab as I was pulling away from my pitch with a soggy load. I must have looked guilty because of the disabled shower perhaps, but all he wanted to do was shake me by the hand and wish me well for the trip.

Damp rather than Fecamp wet, we went slowly to Treguier. Breton fields in those parts looked like what my father would have called market gardens. The sea was never far away and glasshouses and polythene encouraged growth where they could.

It was market day in Treguier. There were two, separated like a split-level grill, one on ground level by the little harbour and the other up the hill under the shadow of the cathedral with a holy spire, a spire with lots of holes in it.

The old town was as soggy as a windscreen washer's shammy. Trade wasn't brisk as open-air markets tended to respond better to just that. Open air, not air partially clogged with big wet drops of water. The cathedral of St Tugdual was dry inside but oh so gloomy. Christ hung on his cross in big, impressive style over the entrance to the cloisters. The sign told me "In flamboyant Gothic style, built in 1461, completed in 1468, the cloister is in a quadrilateral shape. The fine lace-like work was fortunately restored in 1910." Monks would have got wet had they been tempted to loiter in the cloister that day.

The candles on fire at the feet of St Yves created the bright spot in the cathedral. The venerable old saint (died 1303) was the patron saint of lawyers. I probably didn't realise that lawyers had a patron saint. Heaven knew they needed one and there he was. He charged of course. Like those he represented. It was 1,2 or 3€ for a candle to place at his feet and that was without the light or a prayer. Somehow appropriate. St Yves was supposed to be incorruptible (weren't all saints?) and presumably that was why the cathedral had honesty boxes rather than live staff taking the money from its visitors for post cards, visits to the cloisters and indeed candles to place at the feet of St Yves. Imagine not paying at the shrine of the patron saint of lawyers?

The rose coloured granite coast wasn't seen in its best light given the dull wet weather. Although some of the rocks had been eroded into Moore like shapes, the ones I saw wouldn't have been given space in the gallery along side those from Corsica. We took our steady route to Morlaix through the Celtic like landscape made even more so by the road signs in French and Breton. The BZH graffiti was spread about as a reminder that even in that untroubled land, some of its people still wanted to be set free.

Morlaix was a pleasant town with a traffic problem. The boats were fine in its port and the trains were able to glide by on a viaduct high above the rooftops. It was just the cars that clogged its streets. The Hotel D'Europe I found after several slow circuits and at 35€ for a decent room, I looked forward to a dry night. The sign in the en suite bathroom made me smile. "This is a very old house so be gentle when flushing the toilets."

Peter's windscreen wiper packed up mid afternoon, which once again made every thing I looked out at rather pixelated. I knew why it was though. I hadn't paid to see the cloisters in the cathedral at Treguier and the patron saint of lawyers had gone to work.

I cannot escape the long arm of the lawyers

Loudeac ⇥

I don't know what it is, but there is something undeniably attractive about real working class people.

I really wanted to get further west to Brest but only for the schoolboy jokes. The Plat du Jour Tour had to turn towards Rennes where an invitation to join a French family weekend celebration condemned all the jocular stuff about bosoms back into the recycled bin.

The route south from Morlaix to Loudeac took a gentle road through woods to Carhaix-Plouguer. The place names sign posted to off the beaten track often looked as though we weren't in France. Coat-Guern, Goureac and lots of places began with Ker, which was understandable, as ker was Breton for house or town. Pleyber-Christ might have been attractive but it sounded like a bad oath.

A long slow road (N164) took me into Loudeac and right bang into the middle of Brittany country. Shania Twain played in the bar beneath my room and the unattractive locals took their bevies with the smoke as thick as their accents. At five in the afternoon the bar had twenty or so mixed souls grazing at its face. Chain-smoking schoolgirls in black jeans with multi-pierced ears and mini rucksacks full of homework, gnarled old men with poor teeth and cheap shoes and younger stock in leather and denim. Nearly all shook hands or kissed or did some of each when they arrived and no one left without a word. In that unglamorous gold fish bowl all the occupants seemed to know each other, all swam in the same water and made the same small bubbles. It was only me that felt like the fish out of water in that place. Hotel Sympatic was its name and if I'd been able to stay there for the rest of my life, I'd have been just fine.

The church, the eglise Saint-Nicholas, was 18th century pure Italian, a prophet for the pizza parlour. On the top of its tower sat a dome, half an apple, and down in the town square by its side a mosaic salmon leapt from a fountain, another fish out of water. Le Cheval Blanc was a good place to eat in town although once inside it turned Irish from the look of the posters on its walls.

That is Brittany. A little bit Irish.

Rennes

I have to buy a jacket and a tie. I can't go to the celebration looking road worn.

Through the woods, more like a forest, the trees were on parade. Past myths of Merlin, eau de vie, the very source of eternal youth, past saw mills and to lunch on beef and beef, by mistake, at a full restaurant in the square at Plelan-le-Grand.

The Carre's house in suburban south Rennes, Chartre de Bretagne , was in the Alle des Tennis so I didn't look for a skating rink or piscine to find it. I listened for the particular plonk, plonk of balls; tennis balls struck by catgut or man-made fibre to make a racket.

I cut the grass using the doctor's tractor, his mini ride on mower. Like Peter with a soft-top. He was at work at his practice but I didn't have a chance to rehearse, in at the deep end right or wrong. The English could cut grass. The French were sloppy. Madame Carre, that was Anne, arrived from her work at the town hall. She did the P.R, the internal communication stuff, for the four thousand three hundred that kept Rennes on its municipal feet. She was bubbly like champagne and petite and Puck like too. In panto she'd play Peter Pan and do it well without the strings. I kept the ride on mower going to beat the evening dew and avoided the trees, wooden traffic cones on the green highway, and the blow up plastic pool. Their house was fine, middle class comfort, much better than the average and bigger too.

Antoine (17) and Sophie (11) were at home but the doctor, Pierre-Jean (not Jean-Pierre) arrived back at nine thirty. Friday was a heavy day like most. Forty consultations before the weekend off. Pierre-Jean had the bedside manner, even in the sitting room. Quiet, confident and the smile. Those practised hands, clean, nimble long fingers with just one band of gold but hands that knew how to save a life and shake a hand. Pierre-Jean worked for seventy hours a week. He did the Paris march, joined the doctors in revolt. He worked, he said, from January 1st to mid October for the government. Two and a half months toil was his. His to dispose of his disposable, as he would. Twenty Euros a head was what he got. A plumber or a sparky got more and of course there was nothing on the black. No false patients to claim for. No way to fiddle a thing. He and his wife worked hard for their holidays, two months a year, spent in Meribel (skiing), Corfu (skin diving) or somewhere else. Their photo albums and their memories were never far away.

Their children were central to their lives. Their success was paramount and Antoine, their son would an engineer. Not just a grease monkey but at the top of the tree. He was clever and so was Sophie, but she was too young to know what to do other than to race downhill on her skis to win the fastest time for her age. A gold medal for the region. Medal or not, Sophie got stroppy, was at a 'difficult' age apparently.

The weekend was special in the Carre's diary. Pierre-Jean's father, called Jean himself, was celebrating his golden wedding anniversary and the clan Carre was gathering. In Gilbert and Sullivan style sisters, cousins and aunts assembled at the Cocq-Gadby, one of Rennes oldest restaurants, and ate and drank and danced.

Foie Gras grille en Terrine Chutney de Fruits

Blanc de Turbot braise au Champagne Puree de Fenouil aux Poires Pigeon farci en brick de petits Legumes

Tulipe Glacee au Miel de Chataigner Ronde de Fruits Rouges

Coteaux du Layon

Quincy Haut Corbin St Emilion 95

Eau et Café

We met at eight and left at two and the evening was exactly the same as hundreds of the same throughout Europe. A family gathering at a posh restaurant. Nephews with their hair too long, suits and trainers. Uncle so-and-so, without his wife that time. She had been playing up apparently and so stayed at home with the children. Cousin such-an-such had just come back from Guadeloupe but her sister hadn't. Great Uncle what's his name had had another hip and Jacques, the one from Paris, was still hitting the bottle too hard, although he'd given up the fags.

Out came the digital cameras so they could see what was happening just seconds after it had. It was a dangerous device because it meant they could change what they didn't like. The music played, arranged by Anne who loved her notes, and the tables were moved so that the happy couple, fifty years together, could dance and show the family that it was possible.

Jean Carre was an architect. He had created thirty thousand apartments in Rennes and all had their history, but that night he was celebrating a one off fifty-year achievement, something that had lasted longer than his concrete constructions, something better than his rabbit cages.

I was honoured to be there, at the party. A guest unknown until the previous night and there I was in the bosom of the family. Suitably dressed by a Rennes men's wear boutique with striped tie and linen jacket. Welcomed, nodded to, danced with, kissed even on the cheek, made to feel like one of them, related in some way even though I wasn't.

The restaurant had seen better days. The Presidents of France had been there in their time; their photos were on a wall. Its image had slightly tarnished; weddings, birthdays and first communions were fine but President Jospin, I wasn't sure he'd ever be feasting there.

On Sunday, wet and windswept, the hardcore of the family was invited to Pierre-Jean father's house for lunch. It was exactly the type of house I expected a seventy-six year old architect to live in, designed back in the sixties and almost past its sell by date. The '89 La Tour du Pin Figeac wasn't. The pictures on the walls told a story. One painted in a concentration camp with paint made by the artist, Jean's father. There were some scenes of spectacular Brittany. Jean was an artist. He sketched and drew the view from his hospital bed the Tuesday before.

He was a great man, a great French man, prominent nose, glasses and moustache; short in stature but big with authority. He didn't speak English he told me and had only been to Torquay with the Rotary Club but then he recited "Run rabbit, run rabbit, Rennes, Rennes, Rennes. "

The Carres made Rennes a special place but even without them, it was a capital city. I learnt the following about it: -

1.   Edmond Herve, long standing left wing mayor of Rennes, was Minister of Health during the 1985 scare over infected blood supplies. Just how many people had died of A.I.D.S. as a result of the scandal was not certain. Monsieur Herve was sorry but some say he was not sorry enough.

2.   PSA Peugeot Citroen was the city's biggest employer with 12,000 workers and many more in support around. The trees opposite the main factory found it difficult to grow when the wind blew in their direction. Apparently it was something to do with the paint for the Citroen cars they were producing there.

3.   The miracle of Our Lady in the Basilique St Saveur happened back in the hundred year's war. When the English were trying to dig their way into Rennes, the statue of the Virgin with her arm raised to heaven suddenly changed. Her arm pointed earthwards to where the English were tunnelling. As they emerged the French were waiting to bop them on the head.

4.   The Rennes Museum of Fine Arts had one of the most striking paintings I'd seen. "The newborn" by Georges de la Tour was painted in 1645 and was a masterpiece. Mother glowed at her new baby, wrapped up like a present for her, whilst the midwife or whoever looked on with intimate respect. Disturbing was Paul Seruisier's "Solitude", but not as disturbing as the March of Death by someone who had taken his place in the queue he depicted. Picasso's "Bather at Dinard" couldn't have taken him long to do but was fun, whereas Eugene Amaury-Duval's portrait of Isaure Chasseriau made me turn around once I'd left her because I knew she'd still be there, looking right at me, staring me out even though my back was turned.

5.   The Saturday market in Les Lices was just heaving. Flowers and fruit and veg of all sorts. That was where the knights of old used to joust (Les Lices aka the lists) but they couldn't swing a cat there now with all the crowds, let alone a big spiked metal ball on the end of a chain.

6.   Le Notre, the gardener who created Versailles, designed the gardens of Thabor. He wouldn't have included the concrete table tennis or the out door football table, the one with the players stuck firmly on to spinning metal rods.

7.   The Dreyfus affair was sorted out in Rennes, away from Paris and other more dynamic cities where the political hot pomme de terre might have caused trouble on the streets

8. In 1994 the revolting fishermen burnt down the Palais de Justice. It had been rebuilt but the fishermen were still revolting.

The Carre family doesn't eat beef anymore. Mad cows roam Breton fields too.

Angers And Chateau Bauge ⇒

Mel shows me the photograph of her and Francois standing at the foot of her impressive staircase. Francois is dressed in full hunting regalia, the whip limp in his hand. Mel's looking adoringly into his eyes. She is wearing black lace La Perla underwear and high heels. Nothing else. I can instantly tell who is wearing the trousers.

From Rennes to Angers was about two pages of my Michelin atlas routier et touristique. That was 150 kilometres as Peter went. Angers showed me more tapestries hanging in its old castle, one that still looked like a proper fort with big thick walls and a moat. I could imagine the cauldrons of boiling oil. The tapestry, which was what most trekked there to see, was based on the last book of the Bible, the Revelation of St John the Divine. The spectacular hanging clothes depicted the Apocalypse. Finished in 1382, the work was thought to be the largest tapestry in the world. It was certainly the most thought provoking. I walked past and was dwarfed by seventy different scenes. There were seats, tiers of them on the back wall, so that visitors could, if they wanted to, sit and ponder like students what it was they were looking at. A guided tour was probably the best way to do it but the next English speaking version wasn't due until half past four when I had to be somewhere else. The Apocalypse Tapestry hung in the aptly named Gallery of the Apocalypse and the lighting suited the occasion. It was heavy going. Bart Simpson wouldn't rate it and the cluster of French school children being told all about it, looked as though they would rather have been with Master Simpson. It was heavy going but it was bound to be. I didn't know an Apocalypse that wasn't.

I stayed in Angers at the cheap and cheerful Hotel des Lices and ate at La Ferme just next to the cathedral St Maurice. The builders seemed to be following me around France, as once again a religious building was partially shrouded in metal tubing, wooden planks and masses of netting and polythene. The aptly named Maison d'Adam was also next to the cathedral and not covered up, in fact bits of it were giving away too much information. It was an old half-timbered building with wooden carvings, various figures in various poses. A medieval flasher gave some of the tourists something to titter at, if they knew where to look.

We left Angers without looking back and followed the Loire towards Saumur. It was a wide span of water in places and looked like a river in flood. There were lots of islands and mud banks all the way along its course. The road by the side of it was a levee, a bank to prevent flooding, and we putted past houses at bedroom height. At Les Rosiers-sur-Loire Peter and I crossed the river and headed south to Doue-la-Fountaine.

It was only a few miles from there that Melinda Lowis and her two children Casper (11) and Elektra (9) had their light coloured stone chateau. Mel and my sister Kate were among the first girls to integrate with an English Public school and they served their time at Uppingham together. I knew that my sister didn't really enjoy her time there. Mel, on the other hand, made good use of the favourable odds and the ratio of at least twenty-five boys to every girl. If Mrs Marcos collected shoes then Melinda collected boys and then moved on to men. She exuded confidence. There was more than a hint of Thatcher about her and when the local bakery stopped producing bread to Mel's own English recipe, the sinking of the Belgrano was re-enacted in the little village shop. Mel wasn't perhaps the flavour of the month for a lot of women who saw her as an unnecessary attraction for their men. But Mel couldn't help being attractive in the same way that Madonna couldn't help performing. My Mother would have called her, probably did call her, "A naughty girl." Mel was pure theatre though and it was a performance I enjoyed. I didn't join in; I didn't participate, run up on stage with her. I stayed firmly in my seat. I was too wacky for Mel to even consider as a bedroom conquest, which was actually fine by me. I would never be one of Mel's poodles.

She'd been in her chateau for eleven years and seemed very contented with her Frenchman, Francois, who came into her life a few years ago. He was a local farmer, landowner more like, but actually made money from money because his family invested their Francs wisely several centuries before in what had become blue chip stocks and shares. Apart from Mel, his passion was hunting. Mel didn't hunt, well not on horseback, and was cast in the role of the wicked English woman, the Extra Terrestrial. She'd had visits from local wives and had fingers wagged in her face by them. Mel quite enjoyed that type of field sport.

Her French accent was the envy of Francois' Parisian friends. They seemed to think that saying the words without any attempt at a French accent was frightfully chic. To me she sounded just like an English woman struggling with the pronunciation. The other extraordinary thing was that whilst Francois talked to Mel in French, she replied in English. They seemed to understand each other perfectly.

When she first came to the area, she started to make wine. In Mel style she made something different, something with bubbles and she hired a van, put on a short skirt and flogged her bottles in England. It was hard work and her children missed her so her vines were let out to a French wine professional. Her main income was from the gites that she had made by converting her unused out buildings. Brits would pay £1500 a week to stay in a gite there in August, which was good money even in Euros. There was always Francois too. He presumably could be counted on occasionally for help with the folding stuff.

On Thursday Elektra and I went to the Zoo. The Troglodyte caves that littered that part of the Loire and were once home to cave dwellers, Trogs presumably, were the home to wild animals of a different type in Doue-la-Fountaine. Most memorable was the hungry tiger who watched me feeding popcorn to the throng of greedy goats. The big striped cat would much rather I was feeding the throng of greedy goats to him. Some would say it was a bit cruel putting animals in cages. Putting animals in cages right next to their lunch was probably torture. Bars between hunter and hunted weren't right although in the vulture's enclosure we could easily have become the snack, because there were no bars. We strolled through the area and the scrawny-feathered raptors looked at us down their awful beaks and weighed us up. The vulture enclosure was not the place to have a turn, come over all faint and pass out. I could just hear them chortling to each other, Johnnie Morris like, "Look boys. It's the treat you can eat between meals without spoiling your appetite." Elektra was quite brave in offering one perched sample about the same size as her, a piece of popcorn. The big bird looked but didn't touch thank goodness. I didn't really relish the idea of imparting the news to Mel that unfortunately the vultures were picking over Elektra's carcass and that Casper therefore was now an only child.

The stay at the Chat Bauge is fun and it was kind of Mel to have me without having me. Her life in La France Profond is doing her good and there's no danger of her becoming a Trog just yet.

La Rochelle And The Ile-De-Re

La Rochelle is like a beacon for the south. Its name means that I'm well on my way home.

After waving goodbye to Mel and her nippers, the lunchtime stop was at Bressuire. I bought one of those things the French call a sandwich but which should more accurately be called half a loaf of French bread with a piece of ham inserted somewhere in its middle. I sat in the light sunshine in a square opposite an ugly great church and munched on my lunch log. The crust played havoc with the roof of my mouth and after eight painful bites, I let the birds have the rest. The monolith that was the ugly great church's tower was like a big bird nesting box with pigeons and jackdaws jostling each other for the prize nooks and crannies that the drab stonework offered. I tried to look inside the place but what was available to pigeons wasn't to people. The door was locked.

There was a roundabout just north of La Tardiere and it was there, after having pulled over to examine the map, that I needed to use my dog-eared Mondial assistance card. Peter would not start. I turned the key and just got a click. Turned it again for another. Battery I thought, and it was. Depannage Automobile Fontenay came out with his big breakdown lorry and got me going with the jumbo jump leads and told me where to find his garage in Fontenay-le-Comte about 20k's away. I got there slowly and once again stopped the engine. It would not restart but just clicked at me, like someone tutting. Monsieur Depannage knew the problem straight away and produced another battery from one of the wrecked cars he had presumably rescued from the side of the road. I turned the key and Peter sprang into life.

Monsieur Depannage gave me the battery for nothing because he said he liked what I was doing and besides his son lived in Notting Hill Gate and worked in the City.

"So why did you come to Fontenay?" asked the journalist from the Ouest France newspaper the following morning.

"Because of a dud battery." I replied which probably wasn't the best response.

The only thing of any real significance in the town was the Chateau de Terre Neuve where Georges Simenon lived for three years, but that too was a bit of a dud not being open until May. The young waitress in the hotel didn't understand why they should consider changing the magret de canard offered on the menu to Maigret de canard. I thought it was a hilarious idea but then after having nothing to eat all day and being stuck into a bottle of wine; I was bound to laugh at my own joke.

South of Fontenay the landscape became like the Somerset levels. The land was criss-crossed with water. The fields sometimes looked like the flowing stuff as the wind swept through the young green crop and forced a land locked ebb and flow. The sunlight caught the dark side of the bending green shoots and then in an instant their lighter side would shimmer in the breeze. The hedgeless fields looked like a big green sea at play. Young corn rippled in the right light and looked even more like the sea than the sea.

Vix had its fix of electioneering. Like thousands of communities throughout the country, the candidates for President were fixed in Vix onto a mobile tin hoarding. Each numbered and in glorious colour, the posters proclaimed who was who and for what each stood. There was the familiar alongside the unknown. Smiling Jacques Chirac and a couple who looked like they should have been offering things for sale on a television-shopping channel. The racist Le Pen was right next door to a smiling coloured lady who presumably he wouldn't ever vote for. Some of the locals had already cast theirs and moustaches grew where whiskers shouldn't. Comments had been scored onto some of the posters but my French wasn't good enough to translate. I got the general gist.

Like a tightly coiled spring in spring, La Rochelle was taut for summer action. Wound up and ready to go. The streets in mid April were already pretty full but the cool breeze kept the lid on things. It was a great resort with something for everyone, kiss-me-quick to bateau chic.

It was a simple rule and nine times out of ten it paid off. When I was faced with a harbour front full of restaurants all offering their plat du jour's on boards outside; all looking pretty much the same, all well used, I'd go into the one where the person at the front of house spoke to me. Where they seemed pleased to see me. "Bon jour Monsieur" or "Bon soir" would do. I was hovering around the menu board outside, looking at the bits of fish inside. It was the tenth board I'd pretended to read from start to finish. I'd looked at so many fish, I was beginning to think I might prefer a piece of lamb and then the friendly voice of welcome made me feel just that and in I went. Of course the food that followed could be a load of old rubbish but at least I was made to feel wanted.

Crossing to the Ile-de-Re via the toll bridge, I thought that I might get away with the two Euro motorbike charge. Peter however, was paid the ultimate compliment and charged nine like any other proper four-wheeler. Unlike the last major bridge venture, he behaved like a proper four-wheeler as well. The residents of the Ile-de-Re, the full timers, called France "The continent" or "The other side". The island, which had only had a bridge to and from it for the past ten years, had undergone a transformation. House prices had soared through their curved orange tiled roofs. One million Francs was the starting point for anything within the walls of the principal town St-Martin-de-Re. Further north to Loix, where Prime Minister Jospin had a pad, or in Les Portes, and estate agents were talking Cote d'Azur dosh. Paris car numberplates spelt Paris money.

I met and stayed with two shoe sellers, Edouard and Keri Carre. They bought their single storey house there last September within the walls of St Martin, the capital. In common with all the properties there, they could not change anything on the outside of the building without an official nod of approval. All brick paintwork had to be white or cream and all window shutters regulation blue or green. The island's planning permission was quite strict which kept the island, or bits of it, the attractive place it was.

Edouard (French) married Keri (South African) at a wedding ceremony in the African bush back in December. Keri's father was big in shoes and his brand Tsonga (The T wasn't pronounced) was named after the tribe who allegedly saw that the leopard had leather pads on its feet and so invented the sandal for their own. Tsonga was a family affair with Keri's sister selling the brand in America and Keri and Eduoard starting out on the Ile-de-Re. They worked at the markets on the island every day during the spring and summer months and that was one of the reasons they chose to live there. There were plenty of tourists and seven months of open air selling if they were lucky. Their idea was to try out the market before branching out as the distributor for the whole of France. I bought a pair of deck shoes from them, blue buckskin for 45€. People did expect to pay less on a market and that was why their prices were pretty low for something that was hand made, albeit in Africa. The bubbly Keri reassured me that the chains that kept the workers shackled to the floor were quite long. She was joking of course.

Eduoard and Keri were prepared to have a go at starting a new business, obviously encouraged by Keri's father, but the average twenty something French university or college graduate often had no higher ambition than to become a "fonctionnaire", someone who worked for the state. It was a thirty-five hour week with twenty-eight days annual holiday or more; probably a subsidised lunch for 4€, little stress, the nearest thing to a job for life, limited prospects and a pension at the end of it. The hassles involved with starting up a business did seem to provide a barrier for entry to some, but then maybe that was a good idea. If they were not prepared to fill in the forms and take the financial risk, they probably were not cut out to be an entrepreneur.

The bustling harbour of St Martin-de-Re was the hub of the little capital. Its cobbled streets were made shiny by the soles of tramping tourists. Intruding cars were frowned at whilst bicycles were more plentiful than boats. A folksy band played to the Sunday crowd and we ate fish and drank the local dry white, chilled from an ice bucket. The queue that kept the richest man in those parts rich, was a fat one for the time of year. He was the ice cream maker and seller and his emporium was legendary. After lunch we wandered the streets and climbed the little square church tower, up the narrow wooden stairs controlled by traffic lights, up through the bells and out into the island's sunshine. From the top the view confirmed the feeling that we were abroad, cut off by the sea. The walls of the old town and its prison were still intact, but the inmates wouldn't get to see Devil's Island like those who passed that way before. We strolled, no one was in a hurry on a fine spring Sunday afternoon, and sauntered into the new gallery of Marc Coroller. His paintings attracted us. Edouard was a trained photographer and piano player and Keri had a degree in fine arts. I was just a sucker for a picture I liked. I liked the canvases. They were actual canvas from ship's sails and the way in which the artist had created his "Architectures d'ocean" was different. I did a deal but had to leave the picture in the safe custody of my hosts.

It looks good hanging on their seaside wall. A distant yacht tilting on the horizon, a lone figure, a man, standing on some wooden decking in front of a piece of architecture that grows from the sea all around it. Half bunker, half toaster, a number 35 is marked on the building's side.

Saintes ⇒

Eighty thousand pounds back in 1717 was like tens of millions now. She was a very wealthy woman but probably not a matrimonial prospect.

Nothing moved or squeaked on the Ile-de-Re without the newshounds from Le Phare de Re reporting it. The newshound I saw was Nicolas Gillette and he'd had a close shave that morning. I hadn't. The newspaper, like the island, was sweet. It looked like a broadsheet version of a parish magazine. Its paper quality was as thick as a carpet. I would just need one page to light a fire rather than the five or six from the Sud Ouest, which caught up with me on my way back through La Rochelle. Their photographer was an old pro, brown leather jacket, cigarettes and a lens the size of the tower he snapped me in front of. The girl who asked the questions looked about fifteen.

Rochefort on the Charente was, as it should have been, all shipshape and Bristol fashion. In the seventeenth century it was the place where the French navy mustered and made its ships, munitions and ropes. The big ship-shaped dents were still visible in the ground where the wooden hulls were put together. The Corderie Royale was the longest building in France and might help to solve that old chestnut of a question, how long was a piece of string. At least 372 metres would be a fair enough answer, because that was the length of the building in which the French navy made their rope.

In Saintes there were more bits of ancient Rome and if I stuck my head out of the window of my room at the Hotel Du Centre and looked left, I'd get a crick in my neck but a great view of the Arc de Germanicus built in 19 AD.

I drove Peter right up to the beautiful doorway of the Abbaye-aux-Dames, which was hidden away in the back streets of the town. We tourists often visited

415

those wonderful buildings and marvelled at them without understanding their history. The Abbey's was rich and précised thus: -

Julius Caesar conquered the Gauls and found a race of Celtic people living near the Atlantic. Mediolanum Santonum (Saintes) was their capital and La Rochelle their port.

At the end of the 4th century, St Martin founded a monastery there.

In the 6th century under the pontificate of St Pallais, the great church-building bishop, the monastery enjoyed a period of great prosperity.

Ravaged by the Normans, it was destroyed in 814 by a violent earthquake that also changed the course of the river Charente.

In 1047 Geoffroy Martel and Agnes de Bourgogne founded an abbey for women. Thirty abbesses taken from France's high aristocracy oversaw the power and influence of the abbey until 1792. The popes, bishops of the region and the kings of France and England gave the abbey money, privileges and rights. It could mint its own money. In 1717 the incumbent abbess received 80,000 pounds in rent. The abbesses became called Madame de Saintes and wielded wide political and religious power.

Apart from the Normans and the earthquake, the bastards, brigands paid by the English, ravaged the place in 1327 and destroyed the abbey but not the church.

In1648 fire did its bit of damage but the mother of Louis 14th told him to cough up for the repairs, which he did.

In 1792 the French revolution dispersed the 85 nuns and melted down the 14 silver bells. The church became stables and military warehousing with a new first floor dormitory.

In 1924 the town bought the church from the Ministry of Defence for 10000 Francs.

In 1942 the restoration work was finished and the church was re-consecrated to the parish of St Pallais.

The history of the abbey reflected the history of the Church itself. A decline in influence and old Christian feudalism binned. In 1950 the bishop of La Rochelle said "…the good times enjoyed by the abbey should not give rise to nostalgia for Christianity as it was. The Church in the 20th century may not have the territorial power that it had formerly but it seeks to serve God and mankind… may the Lord be praised for the splendours of this ancient stone church…" The church I photographed with Peter in its doorway had become a museum to religion, a musty edifice, a thing of beauty but a shadow of its former self. No longer the factory for faith, its production lines had been mothballed.

The TV, religion's replacement, in the bar above my head was filled with the salt and pepper smoothie Patrick Poivre d'Arvor reading the news with his almost lisp.

"Tres bonne soiree a tous," he said with the old pro's smile just after telling us how many were feared dead in a plane crash in Korea. As usual the flames were filmed, the charred on their stretchers. If they could, they'd bring us the smell of burning flesh.

"Excellent soiree a tous."

Jarnac And Backhouse ⇁

I prefer Armagnac.

The plane trees in plain and pretty towns looked like sprouting candelabra, their wooden tops docked and stubby like bitten fingernails or the pom-pom ends of French poodle's tails. Pollarding it was called. The green shoots of recovery, as someone once said, clamoured for the sunshine and bum fluff leaves moved up a gear to push their transpiration.

From Saintes heading east following the Charente to smart Cognac, the river was as unrushed as the famous drink from those parts. It was not as slow as Peter but that was because we were heading back into hilly country once again. Peter and hills were like a camel and the eye of a needle, easy to pass through but only with a lot of faith. In little Jarnac, under the shadow of Napoleon's own brand, I took a plat du jour outside. My mobile rang and I spoke to my friend Barton just off for a week's salmon fishing in Scotland. At the next table Eric Ezendam and his wife from Amsterdam were having a drink.

"Ezs goud ter her dee inglish speeken preplee," said Eric to me, which was friendly of him. There were quite a few Dutch in the area.

Jarnac was the place where Thomas Hine & Co made their brands of Cognac. The original Tom came to France from Dorset in 1791, was interned during the French revolution because he was an alien and shared a prison cell with someone called Hennessy, which presumably gave him the taste. It was also a little twist of irony, as Hennessy owned Hine. After his release he married Mademoiselle Delamain, the daughter of a Cognac maker, and in 1817 the brand Delamain became Hine.

There was much mystique, hype and general marketing bravado surrounding the Cognac makers, not least who actually made the stuff and who owned the brands. Hine was fairly small and produced just less than half a million bottles a year. Hennessy flogged three million. Hine and Hennesssy were no longer a family business although Bernard Hine, presumably a great, great, great, great relative, was given the title of brand ambassador for the label that carried his name. Hine had become part of a luxury goods empire, L.V.M.H, which sold handbags, after-shave and booze. Some of their bottles were shaped like handbags and some of their after-shave smelt like Cognac. A blurring of the brands perhaps but something that the new British president of the company, Mark Cornell, would no doubt be looking into.

Florence was my guide around the chais (cellars) where the smell was as potent as the liquid that produced it. The no smoking sign on the door into the underground store was for real. If she went home, smelling like a brewery, she could actually come up with a very good reason why. I didn't tell Florence that I really preferred the taste of Armagnac. It would have been a pity to extinguish her enthusiasm.

I used to live just down the lane from the Backhouses: Sara, David and their three children. David's studio was practically in my back yard (the back yard I used to rent) and he used to create his sculptures in the lazy Somerset backwater, on the banks of the Frome. Every so often he would disappear to his French house for a while. He'd had his bit of France, a converted barn, for sixteen years. In Somerset I didn't really know David. He didn't think that anybody there really knew him. For sure, the man I found right on the edges of the quiet and wooded Perigord Vert wasn't the same man I used to see in church occasionally or ambling down the lane to and from his work. He had the same gait, the walk of a man who thought his hips were bad and that slightly stiff turn of the neck, so that the shoulders moved in the same direction as the head. He had the same beard and short-cropped hair and the same ET like fingers, digits almost too big, too mechanical to knead the clay or bend the wire. He had the same way of telling me things and the same voice, but what he said was different. David Backhouse had changed. Rural France had rekindled his gypsy spirit. He became less of the parish and more of the world. He was already over sixty and set to make his indelible mark on the London landscape.

Pretty much his whole creative output at that moment was focused on the project "Animals in War". A new monumental sculpture would adorn Park Lane to commemorate the animals that fought with Britain in the twentieth century. An ox, elephants, camels, horses and of course the mule would all feature. Wasn't he worried that he might have missed out some obscure helper, I asked examining his working model? What about the rat or dolphin, possum or bat? David wanted a public debate with letters to the press. I wondered where the line might have to be drawn. I could almost hear it. "Dear Sir. It is a well known fact that when I escaped from Colditz, I evaded capture by riding on the back of an ostrich". David wasn't sure whether his dog would end up a German shepherd or some other breed. Public monuments were partially built on politics and a committee was constructing the one that David had designed. Jilly Cooper wanted her say just as much as the boss of the R.S.P.C.A, Mr Parker-Bowles and chairman McCrum. Everybody had a view and in order to ensure that everybody got a view was proving to be a lengthy process. So when would we see the finished thing? August 2004 said David and he hoped that Royalty would unveil it. In the mean time money with six noughts behind it needed to be raised. It was already coming in (the Duke of Westminster had coughed up £150k) and asking the British for money for their animals was a lot easier than asking them for money for their old people.

David and I went out to the local hotel for our evening meal and put the world to rights. We probably drank too much wine and laughed and cried a little too. His tears for his personal reasons and mine brought to the surface with the news from David that Fred Chant had died. Dear Fred from Frome was the churchwarden at Orchardleigh. He wrote in the Parish magazine under the pen name of 'the sparrow'. Fred always had time, always asked how the children were and my father. He was an old soldier too, used to drive tank transporters. He always said the words on Remembrance Sunday and read the lesson in his distinctive local accent. He was a good man. I helped him occasionally. I was his assistant churchwarden. I didn't know he'd gone.

David had David as a builder. David the builder looked like the sort of chap who back in Britain might well be selling the Big Issue. Thin, long, lank hair, trilby hat and a face like Ronnie Wood of the Rolling Stones. David was also a musician, drummer, in a band that covered Bob Marley. They'd got a gig in Perigeux soon, Lion in Zion in Dordogne. Apart from the building and the drumming, David was the local philosopher. "Freedom in Britain is taken for granted," said David. "In France there is no freedom." "Britain is male, France is female." There was more." France is the most policed country in the world." More. "Money counts in England. Who you know counts in France." David loved France and had lived there for over twenty years, free or not.

David (Backhouse) lets David (builder, drummer, and philosopher) get on with it while David (Backhouse) gets on with his sculpting. The Animals in War Memorial is unveiled at Brook Gate, in Park Lane, London by HRH The Princess Royal on November 24th 2004.

Oradour-Sur-Glane, Brantome And Riberac

It's difficult to believe that a war crime was committed in the small town. It looks more like a natural disaster has overtaken the place.

Oradour-sur-Glane was a real ghost town. On the morning of June 10th 1944 it was probably pretty much like any other small town in France under German occupation. It had several cafes, hairdressers, doctors, a post office and even a tramway going down its main street. By the evening of the same day the whole town lay in smouldering ruins. So fierce was the heat from the fire that the church bell melted. The ghost town wasn't created by some freak event of nature. The six hundred and forty two inhabitants that were killed there on that day were not over taken by some natural disaster. They were burnt and shot by two hundred SS soldiers.

The town, although it felt like a gruesome stage set, was a war memorial. I could see the rusting Singer sewing machines in the derelict remains of most of the houses. Rusty bicycles and old cars rested where they were torched. It was a dreadful reminder of a dreadful moment in history. The notices said "silence" but the birds sang which didn't seem right.

David and I made the grim pilgrimage and then in complete contrast lunched at the Hotel de la Poste in postcard pretty Brantome. The meal was as simple as a pig; most of it was a pig, pigs head pate followed by cote de porc.

On the riverfront just across from the ancient abbey there was a shop that sold even more ancient bits. A little Welsh man ran it and he was big into fossils. I would have liked the sabre toothed tiger's fossilised skull, but settled for a several million year old piece of rock from the Middle East with star fish impressions impregnated into it. My sister Kate might like it as a birthday present and David said he would deliver it to her in Bath on his next return.

The route to Riberac followed the Dronne at its leisurely pace and the countryside whispered Sussex to me. We stopped and found the rather grand Hotel de France and its evening dining room, polished floorboards not good for leather soles. Formal and hushed, the asparagus to start and then fish and fennel with goats cheese to follow and a Jurancon sec, the white wine of kings.

I expect the Nazis drank it too.

Chateau Meaume ⇒

I leave Riberac market in a straw boater, the sort worn by Maurice Chevalier.

The Friday market in Riberac had everything anyone could possibly want and lots they wouldn't. I was rather glad that it finished by lunchtime because the piece of tarmac where Peter had parked safely for the night had turned into a flower stall. I was up and out too late; the market had been trading for an hour at least. It looked rather like the little Piaggio's funeral surrounded as he was by blossoms in tribute to a life of ups and downs. The flower trader was intent on trade and therefore would not move a single stem to let me out until the clock struck one. I wandered through the bazaar, the colourful mix and listened to the banter some unfamiliar and lots from the Home Counties. There were a couple of English people selling their pottery and another doing her home-made honey, extolling its virtues to those that already knew, those that didn't care and those who thought it would be something sweet to take home. How right they were. A Maurice Chevalier straw boater was all I purchased, that and two cups of coffee. Peter was finally released when the flower seller had had enough and we headed off south and west to claret country, Peter smelling like a bunch of flowers and me singing "Sank evan four liddle gulls."

It was a bit like an Agatha Christie novel. The guests arrived at Chateau Meaume (pronounced like Naomi but without the e sound on the end and with an m not an n at the start, so actually not a lot like Naomi at all). It was the sixtieth birthday party luncheon for Alan Johnson-Hill and the thirty or so guests trooped into the immaculate grounds of the house. I was appointed assistant bar man, assistant to the host, but due to an inappropriate power cut to the outside kitchens; the host was busy re-fusing the situation. Thus I got to meet, or at least hand a glass of cool rose to, nearly everybody. The roll call was like an ex-pats who's who. Many from Hong Kong were ex pat experts, so removed from their original roots that they'd forgotten where they were supposed to be. The language was English, even the few French spoke it and it was delivered in an accent that our Queen would have been totally at ease with. The Johnson-Hill's garden became the scene for an English garden party. Blazers and frocks, Britannia didn't waive the rules and one charming gentleman, Peter Edwards a Hong Kong lawyer, arrived as he always did, in his Rolls Royce, the chauffeur a retired Ghurkha, the roller a soft top.

Sue Johnson-Hill, Alan's beanpole wife with gallons of energy, had decked out the worker's dinning room and drawn up a seating plan. On my right was Mrs Lillian Barton of Leoville Barton, producers of a fine St. Julien appellation. In Medoc terms it didn't get much more top drawer than that. Understated and not flashy, Mrs Barton was exactly like her wine, full bodied and like the label on her bottles she exuded an air of confidence that came from generations of doing the best. Her family's 'chateau' was one, a big building with towers, whereas others just described a wine domain with a house. Mrs Leoville Barton didn't live in a misnomer. On my left sat Claire from Condom. She did live in a misnomer.

Hamilton Narby, with a Canadian twang, dressed in black but produced white at Chateau Guiraud. His hectares ran along side those of d'Yquem, the most famous Sauternes producer in the world. He had some tales to tell. The one that made us laugh the most was about his 'best' skiing accident. At the end of a fast downhill run, he had overshot through the safety barriers and landed, like a cartoon, on top of a moving coach. Spread-eagled on its roof, the passengers inside were concerned about the unauthorised hitchhiker. He had dented the roof and done a fair bit of damage to his own insides. He had made a full recovery but didn't like travelling on buses any more.

Bob Watts talked about his Graves and Esme with his gentle stutter, who'd been in the wine business for years, were both a delight. Jill James and her husband, David Thomas; nearly everybody was invited because of wine and most were there to enjoy it and toast Alan Johnson-Hill. "Happy Birthday" we all sang in that rather self-conscious way that grown ups develop even after all those years of practise.

The other houseguest, apart from me, was Peter Beale from St Tropez. He was an international mix and mixer, intelligent, wealthy and slightly mysterious. I didn't understand everything he said even though he said everything in perfect continental English. He was talking investments and pulled up something on the Internet, which he thought might be of interest. I couldn't tell. "The Weil homomorphism is a mapping from the ring of invariant polynomials of the Lie algebra of a Lie group, G, into the real characteristic co homology ring of the base space of a principal G-bundle." Apparently the guy that wrote those words was making some serious bucks but sadly not taking any more money to invest in, what ever it was he invested in, just at the moment. Peter was currently into writing and he had just done a screenplay for Michael Caine but not a lot of people knew that. He had an art gallery in Paris and a great pair of colourful shoes to match. His boyish charm made a fool of his pensioner's pass and he still had an eye for blondes and I could imagine that some of them still kept an eye on him.

The cottage guests, there being cottages in the grounds, were there to photograph their new mail order catalogue. Win Green marketed a range of delightful play tents for children, up market Wendy houses in the shape of forts or circus big tops or commando style bivouacs. Their designs were made for them in India and they were starting out on that road called building a business, exciting, early days for them.

That part of France was two or three weeks ahead of Britain, not in attitude, but in season and spring was well and truly sprung. Good for photographing catalogues and good for the growing vines around.

The light green leaves were already working to produce their tiny bunches, like new born babies, so vulnerable. A frost could be ruinous and precautions were hard to take. If Monsieur Jacques Frost was even hinted at, hot candle tubs were put between the rows and even helicopters were called up to hover above the young crop to stir the freezing air in the hope of diluting its terrible effect. Fingers crossed, not that year. Maybe one in ten.

Alan had 150,000 vines on thirty hectares, which represented one third of his piece of France. A vine should produce a bottle of wine and Chateau Meaume was sold by the case to Majestic Wines back in Britain. It cost £5.99 a bottle but I paid "rien" and, probably due to my host's generosity, had over thirty quid's worth at Majestic prices. I got to taste the 2001, still resting in steel tanks, and they said it was going to be the best year yet for that Bordeaux.

It was not an easy business; the Johnson-Hills were self-taught and employed eight full-timers and lots of others when the work demanded.

Their domain was immaculate. Rose bushes, in tradition, grew at the end of the rows of vines. The question why was as deep routed as the vines themselves. Not for the bees, vines did it to themselves, self-pollinate. Not for the bugs either. If the rose and its bush had got an infestation then the vines next door would, so the idea that the rose provided some sort of early warning system was not a sound one. The rose came from the same family as the vine and I liked the idea of families sharing the same plot. I also liked Alan's other explanation. Like him it made sense. In days past when oxen pulled the plough that kept the weeds down between the rows of vines, at each end the beast would turn and grab a mouthful of precious vine leaves, a bovine snack. Prickly rose bushes discouraged that sort of behaviour.

There is gold in them thar Johnson-Hills. They don't seem to have a prickly side to them at all. Young for their years, their enthusiasm like their wine is superior.

Bordeaux ⇥

I wake with a jerk, a reaction not a person. It's ten minutes past midnight. I know because my wristwatch tells me. I'm in the hotel room over looking the Place Gambetta.

The shock election result must have hit home because the kerfuffle in the street beneath me was already imploring a vote for Chirac rather than Le Pen. Someone had got hold of a loud hailer and someone else was banging a drum and between them, they seemed to have gathered quite a noisy crowd.

Apathy had crept up and kicked La Republique in the goolies. Actually the republic hadn't got any and those she thought she might have had, had been inked out. Le Pen was mightier and the right in France had, it seemed, become righter. At least Britain had an excuse for voting in Tony Blair. There just wasn't any decent alternative. But in France there were several candidates and a Jospin v Chirac final was predicted as a left v right tussle. Jospin was finished. He could retire to the Ile-de-Re and leave "the continent" that left him. It was a pity because left versus right was somehow a fair fight. We all knew where we stood. Now it was going to be right versus far right, although as the wild man of tennis said," You cannot be serious." Come the real thing, Chirac was bound to be mightier than Le Pen, wasn't he?

In common with a lot of French voters, I'd forgotten that the day before had been polling day and didn't see any signs of actual voting anywhere. I left Chateau Meaume and chugged to St Emilion where they were as good at getting money out of visitors as they were at putting red wine into bottles. A salade nicoise and half a bottle of 1998 Chateau Martet number 29233, a merlot from Sainte-Foy harvested by hand on 23rd or 24th of September '98 and bottled on 25th or 26th of May '00, or so the label told me, cost 40€. I supposed that I was paying for the location as much as anything else and right opposite the Eglise Monolithe in the sunshine wasn't bad. The church was carved out of the rock that looked like those big, rough, light brown sugar lumps that the smart French sometimes put in their coffee. The early signs of summer things to come were already apparent with the Americans and Japanese marvelling at every cobblestone and the British and Dutch drooling in the estate agents windows.

Bordeaux itself was in turmoil. Once across the wide Garonne, the work being done to give the city trams was giving it jams. Behind the rising clouds of dust the old buildings of Bordeaux looked very grand and not at all like the hotel I found squeezed between two restaurants, like a limp burger between two plump bapps. It was central however and I was able to park Peter outside in the street and walk in the Sunday afternoon sunshine to the Esplanade des Quinconces where something was going on.

Brocante, bric-a-brac, dusty brocante, was heaped into the square and offered for sale by a battalion of stallholders to a regiment of Bordelais. Visiting Martians would have been puzzled to find such a weird collection of other people's things. An old horsehair chaiselong looked reasonable but an oversized rusty cement mixer was strangely out of place. Name it and it was there in the dusty municipal square. I was just so pleased that my Aunt Rosemary wasn't with me because it would have been car boot sale heaven to her. Some stalls were busier than others and while some looked more like impromptu antique showrooms with Persian rugs on their welcoming duckboard floors, others took the pile it high and let 'em rummage approach to selling. The guy selling 50's retro gear, jukeboxes in the main, had created a 1950's style coffee bar, which was fun. There was one woman trying to sell a new car and even though she had an official slot, I think she'd got her dates wrong.

The best old thing in the square, but it wasn't up for sale, was the Monument aux Girondins. It was an over the top mighty bronze statue come fountain featuring large naked men and women gambolling in the spraying water. Leaping horses with a Boadicea type were driving a chariot towards the queues at the ice cream stall. Apparently the whole thing was dismantled in the war and hidden because of a threat to melt it down. The only thing currently melting was the ice cream that the Boadicea type was trying to get to, but just couldn't.

The Grand Theatre on Place de la Comedie was also nearly surrounded by tram works but still managed to look impressively big, impressively mock Roman. Just the sort of place on whose steps I could imagine a winning President waving to the cheering crowds. That was of course if Chirac did get back for another try. I couldn't believe that France really wanted Le Pen waving in victory to any body.

Not being able to cast a vote anyhow, I roll over and go back to sleep.

Villenave-D'Ornon ⇒

Poor Magali looks so uncomfortable. She's fit to burst.

Trying to find the centre of the place was like trying to find the middle of the galaxy. Unlike Bordeaux itself where I knew I had reached roughly the centre, Villenave-d'Ornon didn't seem to have a heart. It was one of the southern suburbs of Bordeaux and even though it had probably got all the right bits, its architects hadn't really assembled them in the right order.

Dominic Quignon lived in an apartment somewhere in the sprawl and he had to come and find me rather than Peter and I finding where he and his wife Magali lived. We rendezvoused in the giant car park of the Geant Casino, which despite its name was not a large den for gambling but a hypermarket. As it turned out I was but a stones throw from where Dominic and Magali had their home. It was a ten-year old flat in a mini two-story block of four. It was spacious for two, soon to be three, with two bedrooms, bathroom, separate loo, dinning/sitting room, kitchen and a separate utility room. Both bedrooms and the living area had their own balconies that overlooked the communal gardens below, so when it was hot, they could sit and eat outside on their ledge. The place was worth about £60,000 and they rented it from a work colleague. They would really like to buy a house with its own garden, but that close to Bordeaux the starting price for something pretty average would be about £80,000.

Magali was heavily pregnant and her first baby, a girl, was due in about three weeks. The hot weather (25 degrees) was not very comfortable for heavily pregnant women and she wanted to get the process over and done with. Monsieur Quignon met Mademoiselle Kroop while he was doing his

National Service. He thought that he was sent to Toulon by mistake. He should have gone to Toulouse, that was the plan, but by going to Toulon, he met his future wife across the military bedpans there. Magali was a regular military nurse but currently on leave and fighting her own rather special battle of the bulge. Dominic was back in civvies and nursing in Bordeaux where he was currently in urgencies (casualty) for his thirty-five hour week. There wasn't much he hadn't seen coming in off the streets of the city. He enjoyed his work because it wasn't routine.

My left ear wasn't being routine either. It was blocked. Magali rang a local doctor and I got an instant appointment; no inquest from a protective switch board; no will a week on Friday be OK; just come on down. Dr Dantin saw me as Tintin, because I was wearing the T-shirt that said so, and he gave me a prescription for some antibiotics. He didn't agree with my raising funds for the heart foundations because he felt that the money would be used to run the organisation rather than help the heart. I tried to explain that a shovel was needed to get the coal to the furnace but I was not sure my translation was that good. I think I left him with the impression that I was driving an old steam train round France.

I took Dominic and Magali out for supper, somewhere local, which was packed and pretty good and we ate and drank well for twenty-four euros a head. Magali got tired, which was understandable, so we weren't that late.

We went to the seaside the following day, out west to Arcachon, which if said quickly sounded like a sneeze. Not far away the giant sand dune, the Dune de Pyla, was over 100metres high and probably not the sort of neighbour anyone would want to be on the wrong side of when the wind got up. The seaside seemed packed with holidaymakers and Dominic explained the staggered system the government had adopted.

France was divided into three zones, A, B and C. Zone A contained such key places as Lyon, Montpellier, Nantes and Toulouse. Zone B had Marseille, Lille, Tours, Poitiers and Strasbourg and zone C Bordeaux and Paris. What the authorities tried to avoid was everybody going on holiday at the same time. Chaos for the roads and the staggered system helped spread the workload for hotels, shops, restaurants and the like who were catering for the holidaymakers. So from April 6th to 21st zone A had its hols, from April 1st to 14th zone B took its turn, with zone C off between April 13 to 28th. The holidays in February were staggered too and actually the scheme sounded sensible. If of course you happened to be a fonctionnaire living in zone B with a crush on one living in zone C, it would mean you only got one day of the April holiday together, but what a night April 13th would be.

Where the whole idea fell apart was in the summer when from June 30th to September 4th the whole of France went away. I wanted to conduct a promenade poll to make sure that only zone C people were on holiday in Arcachon. Dominic and Magali didn't think it would be a very good idea, so I didn't.

Tom Kennedy wasn't taking his zone C holiday. He was Her Majesty's Consul in Bordeaux and I met him very briefly for a photo call for the Sud Ouest newspaper again. Apparently as soon as the election result was announced, albeit the first round, and Le Pen was in the running for President, British Embassies in France had queues of French nationals asking how they could become British citizens. It was not as though the jackboots were marching up the Champs-Elysees but the shock result had had its waves.

The newspaper didn't print Mr Kennedy's name with the picture, which is a pity. Maybe they thought he didn't look like a Consul, maybe they just forgot.

Sauternes And Castlejaloux ⇒

I look at Chateau d'Yquem rather like a schoolboy with his face pressed up against the window of Hamley's toy store.

In sweet Sauternes, despite my still deaf ear, I heard the high pitched whistle of the swifts and swallows, I never knew which, as they swooped past the old office of degustation. Lunch outside was right opposite in the Auberge des Vignes, where for 18€ I ate three courses; salad, veal and cheese but I didn't drink the local brew. Hamilton Narby's family domain, Chateau Guiraud, gave me half a glass, a small aperitif, during my brief visit. I'd met him at the Johnson-Hills and he'd said to drop in, something he was quite good at doing, particularly on the roof of buses.

His wine had its moments too and in a reasonable year his 85 hectares should yield 120,000 to 130,000 bottles. The year before saw only 40,000. A bottle of Hamilton's nectar would cost about £25 for a 1996,'97 or '98. A 1989 on the other hand would be nearly 61€, about £40, for a bottle. Sauternes was expensive stuff. Hamilton had twenty-nine full time employees at the chateau and a general manager with an appropriate general manager's name, Xavier Planty.

Sauternes most famous occupant was d'Yquem. The chateau was next to Hamilton's, although it was very difficult to find. There were no signposts for d'Yquem. There didn't need to be. It had its own landing strip and serious visitors to d'Yquem arrived from the air. A very discreet name on the front gatepost was the only evidence that I'd arrived on three-wheels at the home of the world's finest sweet wine makers. I was the owner of a very rare and expensive bottle of d'Yquem. I purchased a 1949 at auction because not only

435

was it a good year for me, the year I was born, but it was also one of the finest years for Sauternes. So having shelled out several hundred pounds on my bottle, I sort of felt that when I passed the doors of the place it came from, if I popped in, I'd be made welcome. I supposed it was a bit like buying a packet of Duchy biscuits in Waitrose and dropping into Highgrove to let the Prince of Wales know. It might have helped if Peter had wings. He didn't so we scuttled off.

It was amazing given Peter's snail speed just how quickly the French landscape changed. One minute we were surrounded by soil mixed with gravel and grapevines, months away from their noble rot. It was land probably worth anything up to a million pounds a hectare. The next we were amongst tall, straight pine trees in sandy soil that couldn't be given away.

Castlejaloux had some old half-timbered houses and apart from farming, tapping pine trees in the Gascon forest for resin, plugging D'Artagnan and Armagnac to the tourists, not a lot else happened in the town. Something must have been happening the evening I pulled in and asked for a room at the hotel I chose. They only had one left and if they had called it 'The All For One And One For All Suite' they would not have been exaggerating. It was big. I took it at 55€ for the night, so didn't eat out. I had had lunch and a sip of Hamilton's brew that left the sweet taste of success in my mouth.

I'll open and drink my fine bottle of d'Yquem on my sixtieth birthday. I wonder where that'll be? I wonder who will share it with me?

Condom =+

Finally just finished reading the Peter Carey book an account of the Kellys in Van Dieman's land think it would be a good thing to recount my visit with the Wadsworths thus with no offence to the Booker winner.

Castlejaloux to Nerac all morning through the woods and out into the big open fields where farmers toiled on adjectival tractors as I toiled in Peter. Bail up! said she in Nerac pulling alongside waving her paper in my face she wanted me to pull up and talk about the adventure the adjectival tour which I did. Isabelle Guin was her name she would I thought if she could get more than a story out of me but she did not.

We slipped into Condom and fell out the other side to find Lafitte just as described so well by Freddie on the adjectival phone after the municipal pool and tractor show room hang a right prepare your bottom for the adjectival bumps. The dogs barked all seven of them and Freddie and Claire came out to say hello the place felt like a home even though I had never seen it in my life before.

Mohamed was there the good retainer and I was put in the pigeon house which was done for guests comfortable roomy interesting with books and oil painting monolith on the wall the lavatory the most comfortable I will ever sit on being high so my legs being long almost cannot touch the floor and my knees not around my adjectival ears.

Freddie made the first drink of the day which took the dust from the travellers throat and I got to know the big man who was over three score years and ten he had had the dodgy heart like me but was living proof that it will not cut you down need not take you in your prime. Claire was Freddie's second and twenty years his junior but Claire was really Freddie's first he thought the world of her.

Who they did not know was not worth knowing and the Far Eastern Economic Review and Hong Kong's finest jewellery emporium had given them a foot hold on the adjectival ladder of power the rich and famous the down right influential. Said someone fit in Nigel Lawson if you can but some one must drop off the perch before even he an ex exchequer could be squeezed under the adjectival wire.

Peter and I took a run to Monluc for Armagnac a switch back route to St Puy and back then Freddie rode me out to Montreal home of fierce rugger men and on to Labarrere where Protestants walled themselves in behind fortifications and the seven o'clock bell was rung by the verger or whoever as we entered and then his own adjectival phone rang for him.

Claire had prepared a feast she was a foodie and knew her chefs and cooks abroad while Freddie did his duck breast on the open kitchen fire we three ate like adjectival royalty and the dogs didn't do too bad at all.

We mount a sortie to Fources on Saturday and found a rose bush and two vines for Claire to plan into her gardens and Mohamed to care for water and weed. Then Freddie in the soft top showed me Flaran and the Cistercian Order the place he said where God had gone from but where with a little imagination I could hear the monks still eating and pacing in the glorious cloister praying. Back to Lafitte for outside luncheon ham roasting on a turning spit piano playing and distant cuckoo some where in the woods beyond. Lafitte and Freddie and Claire as comfortable as a pair of slippers out side of Condom with its light cathedral stone screen not made of wood and funny post cards for the tourists innuendo for all the Johnnies and the Johannes and the Joans.

Them Wadsworths was noble of true colonial coin.

You come again says Freddie who sits up late to put me right. Reckon I will says I right back.

Mont-De-Marsan ⇥

A Sunday night in Mont-de-Marsan at the end of April is a must for anybody who doesn't want to miss anything. I can confirm that they won't miss anything at all.

On Sunday the only place to eat was a Moroccan kebab eat in or preferably take away. I'd never had a doner kebab before. Cooked things on a stick yes, but not the rather fatty meat that looked like a giant sizzling reconstituted lollypop turning round slowly on a skewer. Hacked off with a giant scimitar, I always remember the warning I was given in Glasgow years before, "Donner eat that son." If I was going to become a veggie, then the time was right to sign up and take the pledge. The place looked clean but that was the sort of thing I'd expect my mother to have said. The man was smiling and his fat and happy wife was out the back. She emerged from time to time through the beaded curtain to check out the front of house activity. She was the boss. The bespectacled daughter was there at the sharp end along with her Father. I pointed to the top shelf behind the glass counter.

"C'est gateau," the bespectacled girl said shyly. It had looked like Tapas to me.

"Puis-je voir la carte, s'il vous plait?" I asked in my best take away French.

"Non," said the bespectacled one. Monsieur came to the rescue seeing that the chance to turn a Sunday evening shilling, a euro even, might well be just about to walk out of his door.

"Brochette" said he in with a broad Moroccan grin.

"Vin," said I smiling back.

"Bien sur," said he.

Brochette sounded a lot more digestible than kebab but that was what it was, kebab, and beggars on a Sunday night in Mont-de-Marsan could not afford to be choosers.

The corridors of the Hotel Richelieu smelt of pee as though some of the guests hadn't made their rooms in time. The lift was dreadfully slow, Schindler's lift according to the manufacture's nameplate. The corridors were long and dark but I'm pleased to say I did make mine in plenty of time.

The Sud Ouest offices in M-de-M were right next door to the hotel and on a wet Monday morning they were as about as keen on my story as George W was on Bin Liner. I think that I won them over even though the tired Monday morning journo did at one stage suggest that it might be better for the heart to walk around France rather than use Peter. It probably would have been a lot quicker, I said. The Piaggio was as uncertain as Shindler's lift I heard myself saying and regretted it almost immediately.

My sense of humour isn't theirs. Just one of the many differences between us.

Aire-Sur-L'Adour ⇒┼

I am going to a bullfight.

The little town of Aire-sur-L'Adour was en fete. I missed the Sunday night fun which, judging by Monday's total lack of life on the streets, must have been quite a good shindig. The tumbleweed was out in force when Peter and I rode into town. I knew that things must have been or were going to get exciting because the inside walls of the Hotel de la Paix were covered in clear polythene. Other catering establishments in the town had similar precautions and the PMU watering hole had encased its bar in wooden planks, the sort used for making coffins, which was perhaps a bit of a warning. I found lodgings at Chez L'Ahumat and booked in for three nights. May 1st was bullfight day and I was in Hemmingway mood.

Tuesday was hot and sunny; an encouraging symptom of the encroaching south, and the evening arrived where most would gather in the big marquee specially put up for the occasion not far from the town hall. A band was tuning up or maybe even playing. The thing about fete bands in those more southern climes was that they all sounded the same, brassy but not all at the same time. Their members tended to stand in a circle and the next tune they played was decided at random by the cornet or trumpet that hadn't run out of puff. He started and the rest caught up. What they played was exactly like bull fighting music. The musicians looked exactly like bull fighting types, Basque berets, white trousers and shirts, red neck scarves and red faces and horns for those that knew how to blow them.

There was a man with a big drum who might well end up someday with something called repetitive beat syndrome. There was also one unfortunate who had had his instrument surgically grafted to his body. It was a tuba but bigger and had a resonance that sounded like a giant didgeridoo. It looked like a cross between a vast old-fashioned listening horn for the very deaf and a satellite dish. It was white and sponsored by Ricard, according to the stickers on it; the people that made that drink that brought on madness. The guy seemed quite attached to it, which was just as well. Whether he took his food and drink through the thing I could not ascertain.

The evening in the fete marquee went well enough. The local Corrida band gave way to the star attraction, something of a five-piece combo that seemed to think it came from Mexico. All the hombres dressed just like the Cisco Kid and the lead singer was a cross between Flamenco furls and flounce and the girl behind the Tapas bar. That band too contained a lot of trumpet and even the curvaceous lead singer got hold of one at one stage. The crumpet with the trumpet.

I thought it must have been the drink but it couldn't have been because I really hadn't had that much. One minute the band was definitely hailing from somewhere like El Paso and the next they had metamorphosed into the Spanish Blues Brothers. The lead singer was in a natty double-breasted number with a dark pork pie hat and shades. I was confused but not as confused as the band.

The Tuesday night, actually Wednesday morning, streets of Aire-sur-L'Adour were in complete contrast to the Monday afternoon ones. Music played, people drank, people danced, people tried to talk, people drank, people danced, people kissed, people were sick. Such was the fete. At about three in the morning, I'd had enough. I left the Hotel de la Paix, certainly a misnomer at that moment, and headed back to my room at Chez L'Ahumat where pretty soon the only sound from room 11 would have been snoring with maybe just the odd sleep grunted "Ole!" dreaming of the next day's bulls.

May the first had arrived and it was a holiday in France. By the look of the media and the general hysteria surrounding the fact that the nation had let Le Pen enter the two-horse race for President, May Day had been renamed anti Le Pen day. A red dread of Le black Pen day. He and Madame Le P were busy laying flowers at the feet of Joan of Arc, which I thought symbolic for other reasons. Didn't she get her fingers burnt in the end?

Like a teenager I didn't get up till nearly midday, which was disgraceful, and I walked back to the fete marquee and into the sounds of the local fete band once more. Whether they had been to bed or not remained an unanswered mystery but they were there, in their circle, playing bull like tunes. I noticed that occasionally some of them just wandered off to chat to loved ones or acquaintances gathering in the big tent but that their absence didn't seem to affect the overall quality or quantity of the sound. What the tunes they had played did hide, was the sound of rain falling on the marquee.

For 19€ a head a fete lunch was served and I joined a couple from Dax on a round table set for ten. They looked very Spanish and she was wearing several items of what could only be described as bullfight jewellery. She didn't have a ring in her nose but her bracelet and cufflinks were bull themed. I tried to see if she was sporting a Buliva watch but I think it was something far more expensive. Even though places weren't reserved and people in their parties sat down to eat and drink at tables of their choice, no one sat at the long table in front of the stage, the scene of the previous night's concert. That had obviously been "kept" for the towns' elders; the mayor, the fete president and their ladies and other visiting dignitaries. Our table, the two from Dax and I, became the overflow for the officials, the benefit being free wine, excellent service and, if it could be deemed a benefit, a seat next to a picador. Now I think that's what he was. I didn't have any Spanish other than si and ole and Rioja. It was the way he ate his veal that gave him away. Details need not be gone into but I detected that he was getting in a bit of pre-fight practice with the piece of meat on his plate.

The fight itself was due to bully off at 16.30 and so the crowd meandered down to the towns bull-fighting arena on the wet banks of the Adour. The rain wasn't hard, it was drizzling and damp and during lunch official eyes were being raised and official shrugs being given, which indicated that the fight could be called off. It was. The three matadors and six bulls would all live to fight another day and my 75€ place, the top price for a ticket, would, so I was told be refunded to me in the post.

I wandered back to the Hotel de la Paix where the fete band was playing in the bar. No one seemed too bothered that the fight had been called off, besides it would happen all over again in June.

I'm not going to a bullfight.

Biarritz ⇌

Peter is limping. It seems that he has sensed that the end really isn't that far away.

Maybe it was tempting fate, but the drive south and west rather than just due south meant that the finishing posts would be delayed for another few days. The Tour should include the Atlantic coast in the southwest corner of France. The temptation to cut the corner and head for home was considerable. What swung the decision and the compass needle in that direction, was the imminent arrival of the red head at Biarritz. It was therefore Biarritz airport or bust or, more lustfully, Biarritz airport for bust.

Crossing the Adour bought a tear to my eye. My stream, the source that gushed out of the ground just a few feet away from where I lived and cascaded down the mountain passed my home, flowed into the Adour. I was crossing my water, however many millions of parts to one it had been diluted didn't matter, it was mine and as I looked down I could see the very wet stuff that only days before had been pushing off down passed my shuttered windows at the unoccupied Grange.

I knew I was getting south because place names started to look Spanish. Orthez, Escos and Oraas. There were a lot of names ending in os or even osos and pelota, paella and piperade started to get more than their fair share of mentions. The rain, however, sadly didn't stay mainly on the plain. It was one of those days where one minute I was hot, the next cold. I was dry and then I was wet. The sunglasses came out of their case and went back in again more times than I changed gear. Actually I was nearly prevented from doing that ever again when having climbed up the hill leaving Aire-sur-L'Adour, the clutch cable snapped. It went twang right outside a garage and a chap in overalls and a baseball cap helped me. He looked just like Radar out of the TV version of M.A.S.H. and he found another bit of wire and after several attempts of fiddling with the clutch pedal and its cable, engineered the desired effect. I gave Radar 5€ for a drink and he smiled for the first time that day, which was nice.

The roads became more serious in an up and down sort of way and the Pyrenean foothills started to make Peter cough. I didn't know how he was going to cope with the real thing when I pointed him up it. We chugged along under heavy skies and crossed the old bridge that gave Orthez its mention in history and its place on the map.

I'd always had a soft spot for Biarritz and an even softer one for its neighbour, St Jean de Luz. Like the favourite restaurant, it was not just about the food. My associations with Biarritz were essentially of coming and going "home", either back to England or back to the Pyrenees, travelling cheapskate and leprechaun like. Biarritz was an Atlantic seaside town, which was once rather more posh than perhaps it was currently. European royalty no longer lounged in its bars or if they did, they were not wearing their crowns. Ryan air had made it a breakaway weekend resort. It was grand though with smart shops, great surf and beaches, a casino, some good seafood, a very grand hotel or two and some reasonable smaller ones. Soft-top jeeps were at home there together with the Ferrari and lots of motor scooters. It had rugby and pelote and bull fights not far away. The early May population was young and old in equal mix with the scales tipping ever so slightly in the favour of widows. The locals looked healthy even in the wind swept and damp streets and most had a tan. Biarritz was slightly exotic. If it were a cocktail it would be a gin and French, if Champagne a Moet not a Crystal.

Normally at airports it was limos or taxis or at least some conventional four-wheeled form of transport that scooped people up. Peter and I met the red head and we stashed her bag in the back along with the tin trunk and tent and headed off into town. I supposed that I had become used to travelling slowly, used to hoots of encouragement or derision, the pointing fingers, the gestures of support or disbelief. The red head wasn't. She simply couldn't believe just how slow Peter was. The redness of her face soon matched the redness of her hair but we made the Hotel Maitagaria and parked Peter facing down the sloping road outside. Once again the battery seemed unwilling to provide enough juice to start the little motor. I didn't care. I had a new best friend. Two was company and three-wheeler was a crowd. I could leave slow flat Peter on the kerbside and concentrate on my much racier girl friend. At least her battery wasn't flat. We were both very pleased to see each other again.

The Hotel du Palais on the front at Biarritz called itself one of the leading hotels of the world. Its setting was pretty impressive and the building itself was an over-the-top pile created from the ashes of the Villa Eugena built for his Empress by Emperor Napoleon the third. The hotel's brochure was as lavish with its language as the interior was extravagant with its fittings.

"Cradled for over a century by ocean waves paying court to its golden beauty, Le Palais is the embodiment and fulfilment of a long ago promise, an invitation to taste the sweetness and harmony of the land, where the gentle caress of Time gives way to a full appreciation of the magic of the moment... multilingual ballets of images and ideas move around intertwine, enlightened and enlivened by everything from gourmet refreshments to the preprandial tournaments in the Rotonde, the heart of the hotel."

Not worried about the preprandial tournaments in the Rotonde, the red head and I went there for lunch.

Jean Marie Gautier was the chef and he came out of his kitchen to meet us and posed with Peter for a photo outside, much to the bemusement of the bellboys and other regiments of reception staff. Monsieur le chef didn't speak any English and when I asked him what he had just had for his own lunch, I was sure he replied, "Bake head beans", but I might have misheard. He was very dapper and his food was wonderful even though for the price of it, two people could have flown backwards and forwards from France to England at least twice. It was the red head's birthday treat and, because we both sensed that the Plat du Jour Tour was nearing its end, a double cause for celebration. We hardly dared think about it. Was it really nearly the end of the Tour? What was going to happen next? We both got drunk just thinking about it.

After the lunch Peter refused to start which was no surprise really. He probably quite liked showing off, sweeping up the hotel's drive, past the security guard and up to the entrance to be greeted by the doorman more used to Range Rovers and Mercedes than three-wheeled mechanically challenged wheelbarrows. So the red head and I left him in the smart car park where the hotel flunky had parked him and we walked back to our more humble lodgings.

Fate rolls the dice for us. We aren't very good at doing it for ourselves.

King's Cross To King's Lynn

My sister rings to say that father has been admitted to the mental hospital in King's Lynn.

Timing was everything. I took the last available seat on the plane out of Biarritz on the Wednesday. Had it been full I would have travelled back on the Thursday to catch the doomed 12.45 train from King's Cross to King's Lynn on Friday. It was easy to say after the event, but I genuinely did think about the horror of a train crash as we pulled out of King's Cross, left platform 9a with a pretty full load. Sister Kate and I grabbed the rear two seats (2nd class) of the rear carriage. We rumbled north. Minutes later we rushed through Potter's Bar over the points which in exactly twenty four hours would be the cause of mayhem, as the rear carriage, our carriage, flipped off the rails and scythed sideways through the station.

I looked at the animated Asian traveller and his friends sitting at the table opposite, gabbling excitedly. I thought how vulnerable we all were on this parallel Harry Potter's Bar line, unrestrained people in a metal tube, less secure than eggs in an egg box, laughing, talking, reading or just sitting quietly. I heard the chatting and remembered it well. I saw the bodies, mine included, swaying and our heads moving not of their own volition but because the train called the shots, the train played "Simon says". All of us East Anglia bound for a good look at King's College Chapel, the Fens, England's finest cathedral or a sick father. Just two revolutions on the clock face by the little hand and seven would die where we now lived and browsed the Times. In only twenty-four hours the Thunderer would be using the lines that we were on. Their luggage tossed across the derailed wagon like confetti at a wedding.

Their bodies beyond their own control, rag dolls not even crash test dummies, without restraint, so vulnerable. On the rails and tickety-boo, every thing going forward as it should but off the rails and wrong momentum, no longer in the chosen seat, back to the engine. Their back was broken, something had pulled the stop cord, the spinal cord, and their carriage slid into the station at a grotesque angle as they slid from this world to the next. If they had bought a return ticket, they had been doubly cheated.

Shirley met us off the train and took us to Charterton House, King's Lynn's nut bin. Thank God that father was not there. He'd flown over that cuckoo's nest and been sent to the Queen Elizabeth Hospital in another corner of the Wash. Father was unwell. He wasn't robust but a long way from bedlam. Those that did not know him might have thought he was barking.

"Give him some tickets for rugby" croaked my father to me after the doctor in A and E had extracted yet more blood from my old man's old man's arm. I knew what he meant. He knew just what he meant. But the doctor with his blood must have thought that he was confused. He wasn't. My father wanted the good, over worked doc to accept tickets to watch a game of rugby football at Twickenham. That was all. Not mad, just generous. The occupational therapist was confused as well.

"What do you do when you are at home Mr Berridge?" she asked quite innocently and just for the record.

"Shoot," growled my father, which presumably sent that expert back to her textbooks even though we knew exactly what he meant.

Seeing one's noble father reduced to a hospital wreck was so upsetting. Dignity went down the tube with the catheter. Father, dear father, who had always had control, didn't any more. He sat, propped, waiting in his own wet pyjamas. He smelt ill, smelt of heart drugs and hospitals. Even though the kind nurses did their busy best, it really wasn't good enough for my father. I hated it. He hated it. We all hated it but none of us knew just what to do to make it better. If he had been an old gun dog, the vets would have kindly put him down. He might be going to bounce back. He had before. The MC he won in the field was typical of his tenacity.

When I left him after my all too brief visit, he shook me by the thumb; I found it hard not to cry. I wanted to see him again well and upright in his home in charge, in control, my father, not Frederick Berridge, the misnomer in felt tip pen, a feeble patient or NHS trust client. No one had called my father Frederick even though it was his first given name. He had always been called David (his middle name). But the sick old man the nurses tended was just another Fred.

The pause button of circumstance once more suspended the Tour. Peter was poised on hold at Biarritz airport, parked absurdly, like the thin blue filling to some chunky metal sandwich, between two sleek machines each with an extra wheel. Three or four, it made no difference there, parked.

He needs help, will need help when and if he comes out of hospital.

Pays Basque ⇒

I leave father with a promise that I'll be back as soon as possible. Back to look after him. The red head understands. I think.

Pathetic Peter in Bayonne, old Bayonne, with its half-timbered houses, narrow streets and chocolate river. The Hotel des Basses Pyrenees clinging to the city wall with its simple Pays Basque feel and a bedroom from before the war, which war would be anybody's guess.

The Pays Basque was basking in May sunshine. Everything was growing. The beasts stood up to their hocks in lush green fodder and they feasted on the rich new food and the air, the scent, was full of the result. Eau du flatulent vache. The route from Bayonne, south and east, climbed up and down but mostly up and Peter had to get down to first for several hill climbs. The tarmac road twinkled at me like it was made with a mixture of asphalt and diamonds, guiding me like the masses before, pilgrims on their way to northern Spain following St Jacques de Compostelle.

St Jean Pied de Port clung to the Spanish border and I could sense the throngs whose feet had brushed the cobbled stones and crossed the narrow bridge on their pious way. I picked up a post card and read the words.

"Will anyone ever be able to number all those men and women who trudged through that gigantic itinerary of converging roads leading the pilgrims to the remote province of Galicia? Despite the dust or mud that covered those rocky paths, they braved the jeopardy represented by brigands, wolves or rivers in spate, their eyes riveted on the Milky Way, which mysteriously appeared in the sky every night reminding them of the way to follow. Be they rich or poor, their bourdon, their dark woollen mantel and a writing from their parish priest were the only things they carried on the way they trod. Hoping to save the miserable footwear they possessed, they often crossed barefoot through the worst passages because it is well known that the pilgrim's first prayer comes from his feet. But what were those brothers of eternity seeking? Was it Santiago the Apostle they were looking for? Was it the remission of a terrible sin or was it simply their place in Heaven? By submitting spontaneously to such a Calvary, some of them were giving thanks for some child saved from disease or for one of those vows pronounced on a battlefield. For some, the pilgrimage meant a penal sentence. For others, that was only the response to their desire to discover the world. One thousand different pilgrims mean one thousand different reasons to get there. What did they find once they had reached Galicia? Themselves, undoubtedly. The rest only regard their conscience. Have a safe journey, all you who are in quest of the ultimate."

Not the ultimate for me that day but rather a Galette with Bayonne ham and a Kronenbourg and a walk around the old place, stretching the legs before stretching Peter some more.

The signs said that we were taking the Routes du Fromages, the curds and whey on the curves and way. The Basque lettering in those parts looked Russian and the A's all had apt hats on them that looked rather like Basque berets. At Oloron-Sainte-Marie I found the municipal campsite and pitched the tent for what I hoped was to be the last time.

Monday evening in Oloron was like Monday evening in a lot of backwater France. Everything was shut and I was glad of the Galette at lunchtime because I turned in without another bite to eat. I remembered my first night on tour had been a foodless affair. So it was with my last. It wasn't always thus in Oloron and over the Romanesque door to the town's cathedral, the medieval carvers had depicted some of the culinary activities in Bearn. Pig hunting and killing featured prominently together with grape picking, salmon fishing, cheese making, duck bleeding, omelette whisking, leg of lamb carving and home made bread cutting. The historical tympanum made my mouth water but I couldn't find a single stuck pig or bleeding duck to get my teeth into that evening. I wouldn't starve.

I thank God for the plats du jour I have had. One a day at least. God how spoilt I am.

Lourdes And Home ⇒

Nuns wear Nikes.

Through the woodland by winding road we climbed and fell on our lonely way. Four cyclists, a parked Mercedes, an enormous tanker and a K reg British Volvo estate were all the traffic we encountered for several hours. All of them looked at Peter and me as though we were from another planet.

Arundy was brisk with a morning market and over the Grand Crème taken in the bustling square, I realised that today the Tour would reach its end. The thought like the coffee tasted good and so without much delay, we pressed on for Lourdes.

I first visited Lourdes not long after buying the Grange and was moved and appalled all in the same sentence. The friends that had been staying with me suggested irreverently that a visit to Lourdes might cure me of persistent smoky fire syndrome. As master of the house, I was also naturally captain of the fireplace but try as I might in those early days of holiday mountain life; I could not achieve anything other than a room full of wood smoke. Great for curing the ham but not so good for the other house guests. Those that stayed with me could smell the smoke on their clothes for weeks after they had returned to their less polluted drawing rooms. One sniff and a knowing nod between those that had been smoked out, "You've been to the Grange haven't you?" After that first Lourdes visit there did seem to be more flame to the fire and less smoke in the room, then again it probably coincided with much drier raw material and logs cut to the right size. Burning small green trees on an open fire with their roots and branches hanging out into the room was perhaps a trifle ambitious. Lourdes focused me on fire.

For many believers Lourdes was the last chance. The doctors had drawn a line under their notes and had had a quiet word with the next of kin. There was often nothing further that medicine could do and so faced, in Sinatra speak, with the final curtain, the sufferer made the trip to Lourdes. I could see them bed ridden with all the medical paraphernalia, the tubes and drips still attached, being wheeled to the place where St Bernadette talked to the Virgin Mary. They were there to take the water or be bathed in it and they were hoping, presumably praying and believing that by some miracle they would avoid what the doctor had said was inevitable.

The Roman Catholic Church wasn't one for hiding its light behind a bushel and if any evidence were needed concerning the exploitation of the believing masses, then call Lourdes to the witness box. Exhibit one. Crutches hanging from the roof of the Grotte, the cave, altar, where Bernadette heard her voices. Exhibit two. The hundreds of personalised "thank you" marble plaques inside the church built over the Grotte, paid for by the grateful. Exhibit three. The wax mountain of candles burning and burnt in offering and exhibit four, the street vendors and shopkeepers selling every possible souvenir imaginable and some you'd rather not. A bleeding Jesus winking from his cross, a St Bernadette loo seat cover. Grotte rock and plastic jerry cans for taking some holy water home for the journey or back to the neighbours who couldn't make it or the wilting houseplants. It wouldn't surprise me if McDonald's in Lourdes didn't do a pilgrim's lunch, St Bernadetta burger and chips. It would have to be lamb of course. The saint was a shepherdess.

There were supposedly more hotel bedrooms in Lourdes than in any other town in France. I wasn't sure if that included Paris. There was little question of no room at the inn for the modern day pilgrim and there were certainly more nurses and nuns in Nikes per square foot than there were penguins in the Antarctic.

The RC Church must have made a fortune out of Lourdes and the millions of visitors must have helped the local economy. The place had little dignity and even at the holy of holies, the Grotte, the crowds were reminded to keep quiet by a loudspeaker system going "Schhh" every few minutes. There was little to do with the sort of religion that I could understand, but if one terminally sick person had visited the place and as a result of their belief had been cured, then I applauded Lourdes.

In a normal car or other sensible form of road transport, I wouldn't sense the uphill struggles. The route from Lourdes to Bagneres-de-Bigorre seemed tough in second and third for most of the way with me praying hard that our brief visit to Lourdes would somehow get us miraculously back home.

I couldn't really burst into tears when I arrived at the Café Londres in B de B at just after two p.m. and asked for a table in the tree lined square opposite. My emotions, like Peter's little two stroke, were on overdrive. I rang the red head. I rang Barton and Leech but they were all out to lunch. I rang anyone to try and share the moment with them. It was however just a Tuesday lunchtime and I couldn't expect whoops of delight, brass bands, flags, garlands of flowers and champagne. I just had a simple plat du jour rounded off with goat's cheese in oil and then I got on up the valley.

At the village bar in Sainte Marie-de-Campan, Magali was talking to a travelling sales man, ordering up more coffee or fizzy drink. My entrance didn't surprise her. She didn't rush out into the street shouting and waving her arms "He's back! He's back! He's made it!" It was "Oh 'ello Charl. Wet do yew went?" I wanted a cider. Actually I wanted some counselling. I was beginning to think that I hadn't been anywhere. But I drank the cider and reminded myself that that was why I loved that part of rural France. Nothing changed. I could have walked into the bar with a bunch of Martians just having pulled up outside in our flying saucer and Magali would have said, "Oh 'ello Charl. Wet do yew went?"

From the bar I started Peter's little motor for the last time and we crawled a bit further up the valley to the Butler's house, a bed for the night for me and a garage for Peter. His mileometer read 66,345. On July 15th two years earlier it read 54,810. We had travelled 11,535 kilometres or 7,170 miles together.

It seems like we have been to the moon and back rather than for a slow drive around France.

Brancaster

Up And Running

"Let's go visiting." Father wants to visit the well, return the favour.

They let father out to my care on July 15th, two years to the day from when I'd set off on the Plat du Jour Tour. He shuffled somewhat uncertainly out of the aptly named cottage hospital at Wells-next-the-sea and eased himself stiffly into his old Volvo estate car, the one with nearly two hundred thousand miles on the clock and a horse on the bonnet. I'd never really understood why father had a silver coloured racehorse attached to the front of his car. He wasn't a breeder, trainer or owner. I guessed it was a left over trophy from the "his 'n hers" days with his "unsuitable" second wife. She had a silver dog on the bonnet of her BMW which some might say was wholly appropriate.

One of the many stories that my father created concerned the silver coloured mascot. He came out of a pub on the edge of the Fens, one he used for one of his "pit stops", and found that a vandal had removed the mascot and left a hole in the bonnet. He rang the police from his mobile in the pub car park.

"My horse has just been stolen." Father added to Cambridgeshire's crime statistics.

"Right sir. How many hands?" replied the officer down the telephone.

"What ?" said father.

"How big is the horse sir?"

"What?"

"The horse you are reporting stolen sir. How tall is it?"

"About four inches," said father.

From the cottage hospital, the replacement nag led us home to the unsuitable flint cottage in Brancaster. Father seemed pleased to have been let out. Right away he threw himself back into normal life and once again he tried to assume control. What we took for granted, the simple action of opening an envelope or packet of biscuits or even the slightly more challenging box of "Eat Me" dates, father found a real Beachers Brook. Every little task, no matter how menial to the able, took time. Anything that required dexterity, like dialling a number on the push button phone or writing an address with a pen, was given the sort of concentration that brought on a headache. Actually two, one for the onlooker as well.

They said it would and they were right. Looking after an ancient father whose weak heart didn't get enough blood to his old brain was just like running a toddler. A bit more difficult, because the toddler was eighty and had been there before. He had already learnt to walk, understood complicated words like "bus conductor" and "corrugated iron". I couldn't put this one back in his play pen or baby bouncer, to give myself a little time to call someone on the phone for a top up on normal conversation. Normal conversation was difficult. Father's speech was not clear and he was deaf. Nearly every sentence therefore that each of us uttered had to be repeated.

Two days after his release father set his sights on travel, something he had always been good at. In sickness and health he had clocked up a fair mileage. We took the Volvo down to Auntie Rosemary in her Kent pile. She was deaf too and rather eccentric. She had just made out her Will and left the lot to her part time gardener, Shane a failed green grocer, with G-O-D-I-S-L-U-V tattooed onto his knuckles. God was a three-letter word and so was love according to the legend carved on Shane's fist. The lot in auntie Rosemary's case was a lot, between five and ten million, which should make Shanes' knuckles dance for joy.

Anyhow, Auntie Rosemary in the back and father in the front, off to Rye to buy some fish for supper. Father had got his plastic bottle to pee into, his bag of sweets and a bottle of Orangina. Confusion set in sometimes, but so far I had managed to keep the two bottles in their respective roles. It was only the bag of sweets that was meant for sharing and Auntie Rosemary tucked in with delight whenever father waved the bag over his shoulder and under her nose.

The drive from Maidstone to Rye was hilarious. Not the drive but the conversation from the one hundred and fifty-five years of human experience sharing the inner Volvo space with me.

"Hector farmed there you know."

"What?"

"Hector. He farmed there and died on his horse."

"Hunt?"

"What?"

"Hunting?"

"East Kents."

"What?"

"East Kents."

"Where?"

"What?"

"Where?"

"What?" And so it went on until I said, as loud as I could,

"Rye."

"What?" came the double-barrelled reply as a salvo from father and Auntie Rosemary.

"It's Rye!" said I at so many decibels it nearly blew the sunroof off altogether.

We stopped and bought three sea bass and Auntie Rosemary asked the nice fisherman whether he had got crabs.

"Not last time I looked Luv" said he.

"What?" says Auntie Rosemary as I hustle her out of the little quayside stall and back to the car where father is standing, his trousers round his knees, holding the Orangina bottle.

Rows ⇥

"Stop being so kind to me." I think father means what he's saying.

One night we had a pretty major row. It started lukewarmly enough with an almost throwaway line about how the pasta was prepared. It bubbled and simmered along not too seriously, involving some cutting remarks about the sauce that went with the pasta and then started to boil quite vigorously when the flavour of the ice-cream was brought into question. By the time the coffee of dubious origin was served, steam was coming out of ears and safety valves were in danger of blowing.

Father you see was going through his second divorce, trying to make legal his break with the "unsuitable" wife, the one with the silver dog on her bonnet. They hadn't spoken a kind word to each other for several years and they'd lived apart for over two. Father married her some fifteen years previously when infatuation crept up and offered him a big bite from its apple. When he was in hospital the divorce proceedings were put on hold but now that he was out and within shouting distance of a telephone, his lawyer had been told in no uncertain terms that he was "Bloody useless" and that he should "Get on with it." I could feel the noughts multiplying on the inevitable legal bill and wondered what it was all about. His money, such as it was, was all wrapped up. He and his "ex" had split the financial proceeds from their house sale, and every month Father's bank account paid her handsomely. I guessed he wanted an actual set of divorce papers to frame or file, and in a perverse way he felt he owed his first wife, my mother, the satisfaction of a divorce from his second. Even though she wasn't there to see it. It wasn't as though he wanted to get married again. Well, not for the time being.

His blue touch paper started to fizz because he was frustrated by his frail physical condition, his less than razor sharp mental agility and the rather reduced home comforts now around him. On the one hand he ripped into his rather slow country solicitor for not getting on with it and on the other hand he treated his "ex" (sometimes referred to as "Mother") as a long lost bosom friend.

"Of course she can use the beach hut," he mumbled through a mouth full of muesli without any thought for the implications. Father was nothing if not generous, but his generosity hadn't always served him well. In his current state he was batter and bowler at the same time and that was one of the reasons we argued.

I could, should probably, just have let him do exactly what he wanted. It would be a bit like giving a four-year-old a box of Swan Vestas and a can of unleaded. I didn't want to see him hurt himself but the damage limitation process caused hurt of a different kind. Take his car insurance for example. He "thought" that his old Volvo was insured for any driver but it wasn't. Fortunate therefore that none of the various "any" drivers he let use the thing hadn't had an accident. The fact that father was not allowed to drive, no longer had a license and couldn't physically do the job, seemed irrelevant to him.

"I'm insured" he insisted adding as an afterthought, a sort of knock out blow "Comprehensively."

One of the reasons he would find it difficult to negotiate the Norfolk highways was that he could not see. We went for an eye test in Hunstanton a few days after he came out of hospital and the gentle Srilankan optician said,

"Please read the lettuce."

"What?" said father.

"The letters," said I interrupting so as not to cause unnecessary misunderstanding.

"What letters?" said father. He was as blind as a blindfolded bat and both eyes were heavy with cataracts. Another poke in the eye.

Our rows were like those of a husband and wife, those futile debates where both were right and which slipped quite quickly from the point of disagreement into the realms of "You shouldn't have bothered to come back from France." (Father to me) or "Perhaps you'd like me to take you back to the hospital then." (Me to father). When his short fuse burnt out and he couldn't find the loud words to crank up the drama any further, he'd start to cry, just tears without sobs. Or he'd teeter from the room into the tiny hall to grab for his plastic bottle propped up by the blue front door and he peed on to the stone floor, once again missing the point.

But the bad words were soon forgotten and we slipped into the routine of carer and cared for. We'd give each other little presents that said we were both sorry. A bunch of fresh flowers, a ginger cake from me to him and he would delve into his tattered wallet and hand me a tenner or even fifty pound note and we would wish that that was the end of it. Until the next verbal skirmish.

"It's not how I'd do things," he said to me as I tried to retrieve the position with the man from Sky who hadn't been paid for some months. Dear Father was right. It wasn't how he'd have done things because sadly he couldn't do very much at all.

"You don't understand." Father bellows angrily and he's right. I don't. But nor does he. He's never really understood.

Beside Myself, Beside The Sea ⇒

The electric fire that hangs on the bathroom wall spits at me when I turn it on.

I put one of Mr. Tesco's finest meals (duck a la orange) into the oven and all the lights went out. Father noticed because the Newsnight he had been watching went blank.

"There's no news," he said to me once I had tried to reset the trip switch to give the system another chance with the juice. After a second and a third failed attempt at getting the oven to work, the duck was put into the freezer and I made quite a good cheese, potato salad and coleslaw sandwich for us both, which we consumed in front of Paxman.

"There's no news," said father again but with a different meaning than before.

The unsuitable cottage needed a makeover. The electrical wiring was unsafe and the whole place was damp. For over thirty-five years father had rented the cottage as a holiday home. Woodworm and worse had taken the place apart. At a recent barbecue we held in the little untidy garden one guest did a rock too far on the wooden kitchen chair that looked like a piece of Emmental cheese. He landed in the flowerbed with a cloud of sawdust and much tittering. The second or third bottle of red helped to break his fall and covered his embarrassment and our own. Even father under his battered Panama hat had to smile. Pure slapstick at its best. It was surprising just how the woodworm had survived the damp.

The Parish Magazine, the font of all local knowledge, carried some small advertisements and because they were being featured in a semi-Holy publication, they were somehow themselves not far from Godliness. So father instructed me to get a couple of builders round. Far from having Our Lord's warrant on their vans, the two chosen ones arrived and were just like any other normal jobbing builders. Basically it wasn't anything that time, money and skilful effort couldn't sort out. We weren't looking for miracles, just someone who could make the place more habitable. Terry's quote turned out the best and the fact that one of the nurses in the Wells cottage hospital was his girlfriend counted even more in father's eyes.

"She's the one that cut my toenails. Pretty little thing," Father said when interviewing Terry for the job. Father loved the opposite sex and would always ask waitresses, check out girls and nurses their names and where they had come from and how long they had worked in that particular job. It was his chat up technique and nine times out of ten it worked. He charmed them and they would end up giving him extra portions or packing his bags for him or, in nurse Ruth's case, cutting his toenails.

Trying to get the landlord to agree to improvements to the little cottage was like trying to get blood out of a stone. He owned a lot of property in the village and most of it was in need of attention. The landlord himself looked as though he could have done with a serious makeover. He was a scruffy looking fellow always in a flat cap and Harris Tweed jacket, cavalry twill trousers and brogues, all new in 1960 something. He was nearer eighty than seventy and he didn't look anyone in the eye when he mumbled in their direction. Every Tuesday he arrived in the village in his rusty Vauxhall and spent an hour or so in his vegetable patch, a piece of unwanted garden adjoining another of his unloved cottages next door to ours.

"Good morning Mr Turnip," I said in a loud voice.

"Arr. Yes." He replied uncertainly, looking up from his weeds.

"Father would like a word with you so when you've finished your watering perhaps you'd like to call round."

"Arr. Yes."

He didn't of course. Hadn't been inside the place for over thirty-five years.

We wrote to him. Listed the things that Terry said needed doing. Enclosed a copy of Terry's quote. We didn't ask the landlord to pay, although it would be nice if he contributed. We were just asking permission to make improvements to the cottage. Put in a downstairs bathroom, cure the damp and make safe the wiring. The landlord sent our letter back with his scrawling in Biro written on it. He didn't want the cottage "turned into a palace". Went on to suggest that if father didn't like living there, he could always move on. Father was undeterred.

"We'll buy the place. Buy them all." Father had tried this ploy before but Mr Turnip and his "Trust" were not in the market to sell.

Kim lived at number one. It was the little cottage on the end of the row. She had long blonde hair; a rat like yappy dog called Boo and spent most of her life as high as a kite on the wacky backy. She was part hippie and part gardener and she had a stall (table actually) outside in the street with a few potted plants and organic vegetables for sale. There was an honesty tin where people could put their 50p's. Kim didn't say much other than "Hi," a well-meant greeting and a state of mind. Father made her cry with one of his bursts of indiscreet energy.

"How would you like a new landlord?" he said to her in passing. We had to pass her front door to get to ours.

"What?" said Kim.

"I'm going to buy the lot and knock down your end bit so we can get the cars in." Father, who couldn't stand him, was being more like George W. Bush than the President himself. Kim ran off down her garden crying. Later I pushed a note through her letterbox explaining that father wasn't going to be her new landlord and that he was not about to buy her cottage. Sorry the note said; it was probably the drugs that made him go off on one. Kim of all people should have known that.

He took a mug of tea. I made it for him in one of those frilly bone china mugs with flowers painted on its side. He held the mug in both hands after it had cooled. Ignored the prissy handle. He wrapped his fingers around the china and raised it to his lips. Long before the mug reached them they pouted. He sucked at the tepid tea, made a sharp little intake of breath. Took in a mouthful through his thin lips, barely moved the mug away and then swallowed. It was as though the effort of swallowing the liquid was immense. Eyes shut, concentration furrowed in the brow, the sip of tea went down. The noise of relief followed with an exhalation of air from the lungs, a contented sigh, triumphant breath. He looked at me over the top of the china mug, hands clasped around it, ready for the next intake. I was annoyed. Irritated by the way he did things. The way he drank his tea made me cross. It was silly. How could tea drinking be so infuriating? It was. Because I loved him.

"That's good." He said it as though it was simply the best meal he had ever had in his entire life.

"Bloody man." He said thinking about something other than the tea.

"Who is?" I was expecting the landlord's name.

"Blair," said father darkly.

"What?"

"I want you to send him five pounds."

"Who?"

"Duncan-Smith." Father was nothing if not surprising. After his "never underestimate a quiet man" speech at the party conference, father wanted to send I.D.S. some money to let him know he had his backing. He liked him, but then like all those desperate for some sort of opposition to the Blair thing, even a quiet man would do.

Driving to Burnham Market along the narrow top road through Thompson's ground father said something to me about how I didn't really look after him very well. Maybe the frustration of the non-compliant landlord was getting to him. Maybe it was Blair.

"Well you're doing a bloody awful job," were his exact words. Something inside me snapped and I jammed my foot on the brake pedal of the car so furiously that the old Volvo slewed to a surprised halt. Father's frail frame lurched forward violently. His head so nearly bashed into the windscreen that for one of those dreadful time breaks I could see his skull impacting with the glass, imagined it bouncing off like a grey football, leaving its impression like a frosted spider's web. I had punished him with my bad temper for something that he hadn't meant to say. Or even if he had meant it, I wasn't big enough to take it. I felt terrible. I had wanted to hurt him, to chastise him for being incapable. Hurting the ones I loved. I was becoming quite good at that. His seat belt had prevented any physical damage and my action was like shouting at a child. Frightening for both of us.

We're both becoming grumpy old men.

Daily Help

"I'm so much better dear." Father tells Teresa the good news most mornings.

Teresa arrived every morning at nine. She'd done her stint of cleaning and, in the winter, lighting the fires at the golf clubhouse. She came to the cottage on her bicycle to get father his breakfast of muesli, orange juice and tea. She gave him the pills to keep him going. Some days, and if he was feeling well enough, he would get up and take his breakfast downstairs in front of the coal fire. Increasingly he would have it in bed. Teresa would chat with him.

"Mornin'," she'd sing happily. "How are you today?"

"I'm so much better dear." It was father's daily response to the daily question.

"Think I'll stop taking those pills."

"You can't do that! The doctor won't like it." She sounded like a girl from Norfolk although she had grown up in Kent.

"Better have them then dear. Doctor's orders. You're the boss. " It was pretty much the same conversation most mornings.

Teresa was the boss. In father's mind she called the shots, ran the house and made sure that he stayed alive with her twice-daily visits. She had acquired the job almost by accident. She had looked after the cottage when it was just a holiday home and had been there for father when he first arrived to claim the place as his principal residence. When he had left his second wife. Teresa had been propelled in rank from part time caretaker of the property to daily help for its occupant, from a private to a general in father's muddled view. Teresa had coped well for a few months until father's condition meant that he'd stay in bed for most of the day. It was then that I got the phone call, the one that told me that father had been taken into hospital. He had pneumonia.

When I arrived from France to be with father all the time, he didn't see the need.

"Teresa is the boss," he said to me.

"She is," I agreed, "But you can't live here on your own any longer."

"Of course I can." Father was adamant. He really did believe that he could survive on his own, didn't need constant care. I found it unbelievable that he thought that way. I didn't know if he was just being stubborn or naughty or genuinely thought that he could continue to live on his own in such unsuitable surroundings. I knew that he was a fighter and that his pride wouldn't let him admit defeat. I didn't understand the elderly, hadn't had to cope with their special needs. I was on another learning curve. So was father.

If Teresa was the boss, then I became a sort of non-executive chairman. Father would issue his orders to her in the morning and then she would come and talk to me about them.

"He wants that downstairs extension built today." Teresa relayed the day's task. We'd look at each other and smile. Teresa knew that he wasn't well, understood that his mind was all over the place. So the two of us played the game, watched over his restless soul and gave him his daily care. Protected him from himself.

The firemen were on strike for more pay. Father was dead against their claims.

"Blair mustn't give in," he growled. Teresa arrived for her evening visit, "Just to see if I'm alive," said father. The TV was showing the fire fighters standing next to their stations with banners and blazing braziers. Father said "Good evening dear," and then gave her a ten-percent pay rise. Just like that. Teresa didn't have to ask. Hadn't mentioned money at all. Her seventy pounds a week wage (now seventy-seven) equated to fifteen pounds an hour. He chatted to her about her day's shopping in Lynn, the impending war and her donkey. She took her anorak off and had two glasses of the red wine. Father liked that. Eventually Teresa wobbled off home because after two glasses she got like that. Before she went, she did his eye drops. Dripped the liquid onto his cheeks like tears. He liked that too.

Father had Sky. Every channel that was gong, although he only really wanted the sport. After I had gone to bed and if he had been enjoying a whiskey, father would wander the airways with the remote control. He was searching for something. I could hear the channels output, catch the canned applause, the music, the fabulous offers, the long putt, the L.B.W. appeals and the news. My father had an obsession with the news; needed it like his pills. Often I'd drift off to sleep with the television down the short, steep stairs giving father what he thought he wanted. He watched then went to bed. Crawled up the Eiger steps, clinging to the vital handrails. I'd wake up and lie there, listening to every painful step, ready to jump out of bed and help. He'd make the top and shuffle to his room.

"Bugger Blair", he'd say or "Good night darling", and I'd know that he was safe for another few hours.

In one of David Attenborough's 'Life of Mammals' programmes, at night lions roared their claims to territory. Father's nocturnal noise was similar and he too roared when he was awake and lying in his bed. He roared as he breathed and the roars sometimes became "Bloody hells" or other longer phrases that I couldn't quite get. When he slept, he was quiet but sadly most nights he roared a lot. Like the bush lions to let me know he was there. Let me know he was alive and that that was his territory. I didn't really want to be there, knew that he didn't want me there either. I had to be though. Had to for him. Had to for me.

In the morning I heard him talking to Teresa.

"I watched a lot of German women doing their housework with no clothes on." Father had channel hopped and leapfrogged into something continental and pornographic.

"There's not a lot good on the telly these days," says Teresa, having to repeat the statement.

Lunch Breaks ⇌

"Cheers darling." Father toasts me loudly and I'm getting used to be called darling by him in public.

Pub lunches were pretty much a vital part of the daily routine. It got us out and as often as not we'd walk to the Ship in Brancaster, which was just around the corner. In normal stroll terms, two minutes maximum. Father took somewhat longer but the exercise was good for him. It was his ambition to walk down to the clubhouse (the Royal West Norfolk Golf Club house) for lunch but he would need to have set off just after breakfast in order to arrive in time for lunch.

Some days at the ancient club house we sat at a giant round table sipping our red wine over looked by the roll of honour, gold letters on polished wood, royal names, peers of the realm, double-barrel captains and the like. Father always told me two stories once the steward had bought us a roll each and the soup of the day. The first was how he became a member. He applied in the normal way and for his profession put down "Potato Merchant" on the application form. He was turned down. The R.W.N.G.C. was not ready to open its stiff portals to a mere purveyor of spuds. Rank uncertain, potato merchant didn't come between Air Vice-Marshall and Rear Admiral. Unabashed or unmashed, father went to see his father, my Grandfather, who was the farming neighbour of the old Duke of Gloucester, Prince Henry, the old King's brother. Various communications ensued with the result that my father was accepted as a member at a pace never before seen in the corridors of the famous links clubhouse. The Duke proposed my father as a member and in those days the committee wouldn't have dared to ignore a royal command.

The second story concerned the banning of dogs from inside the clubhouse. They used to run free, roam at their leisure, packs of Jack Russells and Labradors, cocking their legs on the old chairs and generally behaving like their owners. The then steward (passed on to eternal service in that even greater club house in the sky) kept cats and it was the pack of Whippets belonging to somebody double-barrelled that ate the cats that caused the secretary to issue a ban.

As we ate our lunch and father recounted his two stories, other members wandered over to the table and shook him by the hand.

"Good to see you David. Thought we'd lost you," said one stalwart referring to father as though he was a wayward golf ball. Father had a great conversation with the fellow in the plus fours and the two parted with a promise of a further reunion to drink some whiskey in the cottage.

"Who was that?" I said to father not having been introduced.

"I haven't a clue," said father, adding as an afterthought, "We have got some whiskey haven't we?"

"Another drink darling?" The steward is smiling at me.

Very Social But No Service ⇒

*"Are you allergic to anything Mr Berridge?" says Sara to father. "Red tape."
He replies instantly.*

We were out and about one day, 'The Brancaster Dodgy Heart Brigade', and father announced that he needed to go "Biggies". "Biggies" was a term that I grew up with. It was the opposite of "Littlies" and came from that unwritten dictionary of parent speak for children that included such words as "tassel" and "noddy" (men's and/or boys bits), "tibbit" (telephone and/or post boxes) and "belchiemakey" (fizzy drink). It meant that we would need to find a public lavatory with some paper and fairly soon.

Like the red blotches on the landscape they often were, a Little Chef soon came into sight and I eased the old Volvo into the disabled slot right near the entrance. Father disembarked to go and do his "Biggies" and I followed at a suitable distance as the minder and chauffeur. When after some time father reappeared from the Little Chef's smallest room, he had the sort of smile on his face that said the "Biggies" exploit had been a triumph and some. The "and some" was apparently a result of his encounter with the obligatory spotty youth employee. As father had stumbled his way into the red eatery, he had asked the helpful baseball hatted lad where the lavatories were. Now father's speech was sometimes very strange. He had a hiatus hernia that made him sound like he was trying to talk through a bucket full of soapy water. Anyhow despite his simple enquiry, the spotty youth with impeccable company training said "Smoking or non-smoking?" As I think I pointed out as we pulled away from the disabled parking slot, "If it wasn't before, it certainly would be afterwards." That was "Biggies" for you.

Sara, the head honcho of the local social services, paid us a visit one-day to see how we were doing. Sara's manner and her presence had made Father think of her as the chief executive of his life. He treated an audience with her as a way of putting right the NHS system, easing his doctors work load, finding the silk dressing gown he had lost in one of the hospitals, sorting out Tony Blair's ineffective government and lifting the threat of war with Iraq. Sara carried a lot of responsibility on her broad shoulders. She did have a very good bedside manner and you could tell that she'd been used to getting her way with those that she thought needed her social service. Her voice was rehearsed and reassuring with just a hint of an Anne Robinson. She negotiated in an if-I-do-this-for-you-will-you-do-that-for-me sort of style. Win win I think it was called. She had father eating out of her hand after the meeting and he promised Sara that he would be bathed twice a week by her cohorts. She promised too to send details of an organisation that provided temporary care when the current carer needed to go away for a few days. Sara left the cottage and father felt as though he'd had another very successful board meeting.

They do say that actions speak louder than words but Sara's visit didn't result in any action at all. The "bather" never appeared. There was no letter from her either, no minutes of the meeting that father could read as confirmation that it had taken place. The social services were pretty stretched anyway and when and if the "bather" did turn up at ten to two on a Tuesday afternoon while father was watching the last day of the second Test, my old man would probably tell the "bather" just where to stick the bath plug. Father took his baths at 6 am, twice, sometimes three times a week. He managed most of the job on his own and because of one of those mechanical hoists, an electric chair he called it (although for obvious reasons it wasn't). He ran the white hot water from the Sadia, a giant boiling tank suspended from the bathroom wall midway between bath and washbasin, which had a swivelling pipe at its base allowing flow either to the bath or to the basin or on to the bathroom floor between them. The steam that it emitted was more abundant than the water and the Sadia's suspect and diminishing efficiency offered about a bucket full of molten fluid per session. It was so hot that it would boil an egg. I lay in my bed next to the bathroom, a thin and dripping wall away, listening to my father's washing efforts and prayed that he wasn't about to do a Princess Margaret by simmering his feet. The bath itself was old and its bottom had a rough scouring pad on it where smooth enamel used to be. Cold water came from a single tap over the bath once you could turn it on. Once on it then became unwilling again to turn off.

But the point was, it was father's bathroom, it was available when he wanted it and he could use it with or without social service sanction. Actually he used it when I was in there quite often which I didn't mind one bit. I was just rinsing the shampoo from my hair, lying prone in the bath, enjoying the invigorating back scratching exercise, my legs up over the end lurking dangerously near the Sadia's white hot outlet pipe when up went the door latch and in came father. It was OK. He wanted a pee or a shave or "biggies" or all three. Fine with me in there but probably a little bit less comfortable for the red head on a weekend visit trying to wash her red hair.

"Oh!" she said, the hue of her bare skin instantly matching the colour of her hair "I won't be long."

"Nor will I dear," said father carrying on with his bathroom business. I explained to her that he was not very good with the eyesight but apparently that was not the point.

Quite how the social services "bather" would cope when he or she got round to it, I really couldn't imagine but I didn't worry because there was no sign of them getting round to anything that was talked about.

Life in the unsuitable cottage is suitable enough and better than death anywhere.

Prostrate ⚒

Father is pinning so much hope on the operation.

An early September sun slid down under the salt marshes at 7.40pm and the chill in the evening air said that summer on that North Norfolk coast had had its day. The sky streaked into an impossible watercolour wash and the few feathery clouds turned to gold leaf. The V formations of talking geese flew past on their missions. The children on the slatted wooden balcony at the White Horse in the Staithe belched and squealed with giggly delight at their naughtiness. Too much cola and not enough restraint. The waning sun was playing on one of the most romantic canvases in the world, the Norfolk sea and sky.

That morning I had taken father to the Sandringham Hospital so that his prostate could be sorted out. Mr Eaton was officiating and he seemed quite confident that father would benefit from the surgery. I was present at the first interview, the one in Mr and Mrs Eaton's house. Because father had wanted me at the consultation, I heard the firm slap of rubber as the surgeon snapped on his man made gloves. I pretended to study the pictures above Mr Eaton's mantle piece, the family photos and old oils, my back turned on the groping surgeon and my father prone and talkative as ever.

"I've had this done to me before." He growled at the urologist who wasn't quite sure what father meant but whose bedside manner was as smooth as his KY jelly.

The explanations and write-ups were never like the real thing. Even though father shuffled into the private hospital with all the confidence he could muster, when I saw him again an hour after surgery, he looked very uncomfortable. It seemed to me he had been set back in that dreadful game of health snakes and ladders. He'd climbed out of last Spring's pneumonia and had been making real progress only to slither down the prostrate snake. He shook in his bed, shook as though he was cold and I had to get the nurse and a doctor to come and administer to him.

"Bloody hell," he moaned several times and it probably was. He had a drip and a catheter replumbed into him and although Mr Eaton deemed his work a success, it was the sort of triumph that came with a price. Father had paid three thousand pounds for the use of the room and operating theatre. Mr Eaton's fee would arrive in due course. If the surgeon's skill would mean that father could take back control of his bladder then the misery and money would both be worth it. They wrapped him up in blankets and he looked like that shot from ET in Spielberg's film, the one where big, sad, confused, lost eyes looked up, pleaded for home. Father's too were imploring me for help, wanted to go home, to be scooped up and smothered with tender compassion.

I don't know if it will help him or not.

Faith ⚊⚊

He confesses to me. Tells me about the affair he had. I don't really want to know. I am not worthy to hear his confession.

Beside his bed, father had a pile of books. The latest, Harry Potter and the Sorcerer's Stone, the Koran and the Rough Guide to the Internet. He had stopped reading the paper, although the Parish Magazine was still given a good going over. Father had lost his faith. Or so he said.

When Shirley came to see him, which she did every so often, the two of them would talk about old times. Shirley had found God. She was what would be labelled as a born again Christian. I'd be in the kitchen making the tea for them and then I'd leave them to their talk and go for my walk off down to the beach. Shirley was trying to get father back from the abyss. I'd hear snippets of their conversation as I waited for the kettle to boil.

"I've lost my faith. I don't believe in God anymore."

"That can't be true David." Shirley had the sort of voice that was so soft, so quiet. She knew she had found God and didn't need to shout about it. She had a saintly smile as well.

"Pardon dear?" said father.

"That can't be true David. God is keeping you here for a reason." Shirley spoke up a bit.

"Well I'm damned if I know why."

"Read your Bible David."

"Pardon dear?"

"Read your Bible."

"I'm afraid I don't believe in the Bible anymore. I'm looking at the Koran dear. That and Harry Potter." Shirley was temporarily silenced. The kettle boiled and I made them tea.

The beach was my new escape. I could walk there most days. I'd leave the cottage when father was in bed or occupied with a visitor. Across the road in the village shop I'd buy some sweets for the journey and chat to the smiling girl behind the counter.

"Hello Charlie," she'd say. "How is he today?" I'd always say that he was making progress, pay for the sweets and then head off along the beach road, past the parish church.

The bank that cut through the salt marshes ran along side the narrow road. When the high spring tides came in, the road would be covered, cut off by the sea, but the bank and its footpath acted like a bridge. From up there the Staithe could be seen away to the east, marked out on the flat landscape by the pin-prick masts and white sails of the boats as they bobbed about on the high water. To the west salt marshes ran away to Thornham. Waterfowl and sea birds played in the pools; fat geese grazed the tough grass. The sky was always big. No mountains to look up to. Cloud maybe, or just the blue North Norfolk sky with the unseen skylark whistling while I walked. When the wind blew, the beach was often marked with kites. Brightly coloured sails, like giant commas, floating in the air above the sand dunes. I couldn't see their controllers but knew beneath the noisy sails hung a person trying to ride the waves or steer his wind cart across the sands. In summer kids' kites trailed their tails as excited mums and dads watched their little treasures take their dreams to the air. The Royal West Norfolk golf clubhouse silhouetted against the sky was the only substantial building on the beach. There were the public lavatories and the wooden shack selling ice-creams, teas and coffees, kites and buckets and spades. The beach shop only opened from Easter (if the weather was OK) until September but the clubhouse was open all year. Open to members only.

If the tide was in, the waves wouldn't be apparent until I arrived on the beach, walked past the car park and clubhouse and got on to the soft sand. If the tide was out I couldn't see the sea. The wet sand would stretch away to the flat horizon and from the distance I'd hear that low roar, the power of the North Sea out there somewhere. I'd nearly always turn right, head east along the beach and walk to Norton's Pool. It was at the entrance to the Staithe and a bowl in the tidal mud where the retreating seawater became trapped. Deep enough at low tide for yachts to moor in and for Labradors to swim after sticks. The walk along the beach was never the same. Like the shifting sands joining Scolt Head, my mood would vary, swing from this to that. Some days I would wonder what I was doing with my life. Not sure what was going to happen to me next. I would think about the red head and wonder if my future should be tied up with hers. Some days I would just marvel at my surroundings; get drunk on the sea air and the beauty of that coast.

I would nearly always call at the beach hut hidden up in the moving sand dunes. Slip back to my child hood, as I stood high on the dunes surveying all the magnificence around me. The sea (I could see it from up there), the black stubborn wreck of the SS Vina, the marshes and the land beyond, the gentle rolling Norfolk country side with its hedged fields and woodland copses. The beach hut, a wooden garden shed really, lay half buried in the sand. It was the private place where we would change into our swimwear.

"Mummy, Mummy. Can I go for a swim now."

"Wait until your lunch has gone down and be careful not to go out of your depth." Mother was always careful. We'd keep the windbreaks, deck chairs and Calor gas cooker to boil water for tea. Sun cream in sandy topped, plastic bottles, a bucket, shrimping net, towels and a football. Cricket stumps and tin mugs, a punctured rubber ring and some clothes pegs. They'd all be in the beach hut even after all those years. It was a place where I could taste the memories like a picnic. It was a place where the moving sand would soon obliterate everything.

My walk took two hours. Shirley had gone and father had put himself to bed or got Shirley to help. I looked in on him.

"Good walk?" He asked.

"Wonderful." I replied. "Didn't see a soul. How was Shirley?"

"Couldn't save this soul." Father still had a sharp wit. "Need to finalise my Will."

"What's she been saying to you?"

"Shouldn't have left your mother. Made a mistake."

"What's done is done Pa." I said not really wanting to comment.

"Decided not to leave any money to Sue."

"Who's Sue?"

"Girl I had a fling with back in Peterborough." Too much information I thought.

"You don't need to leave her anything." I said reassuringly.

"Told her I would."

My faith in my father didn't slip a cog. I never thought of him as a philanderer. He'd look but surely never touch. If he had I didn't really want to know about it. Besides, he didn't like a man who couldn't control himself.

I remember his advice, my sex education, delivered to me when I was thinking about moving up into long trousers. "I don't like a man who can't keep his cock in his pocket."

Death 2003

I know that you knew your onions. There is a photograph of you with the Queen Mother when you were showing her around a trade show. On the back of the picture you've written "Immediately after this photo, the machine which was over wrapping tomatoes, malfunctioned and the Queen Mother was splattered all over with tomato to which she replied "I also see you make ketchup".

I arrived at the seaside cottage hospital and, as usual, walked into his room unannounced. It was easy to come and go without seeing any staff, as father had been put into a room on his own, right at the front of the building. Through the front doors, past the empty office and his was the first door on the right. The next door lead to the staff rest room where the nurses drank their hot drinks or cuppa soups and read Hello and Norfolk Life. A hushed dignity had crept into the little room where father lay on his own. There was no disturbed newspaper or heap of crumpled tissues. No breakfast tray or half-drunk cup of tea. His dressing gown hung on a peg and he was neatly tucked into his bed, hospital cornered, with the metal bars on the sides of the bed raised up. The morning cleaner had 'done' and the starkly functional room had a time warped feeling. I could have been stepping into the fifties or sixties, slipping back to when I was a teenager or younger. His wash bag lay undisturbed by the wash basin. He hadn't been out of bed. He hadn't ruffled the order of things around him. His 'bible', the pocket diary and address book, welded together by necessity and sellotape, sat on top of his bedside locker next to the plastic jug of water and its matching beaker.

His grey head lay propped up slightly on the white pillow. He looked different without his glasses on. The marks that their years had left were indented on to the sides of his nose. Without glasses, he was as blind as a bat. Night blind too. In the war he led one platoon, or most of it, off the end of a jetty and into the sea. "This way chaps," I could hear him saying with all the confidence in the world. Contact lenses were a new invention and he had one of the first pairs ever made. He was one of several guinea pigs from the forces to try out the new idea. The lenses covered the entire eye and had to be tucked right under the upper and lower lids. They were the thickness of an eggshell and the actual lens in the middle protruded out like an air bubble from the rest of the eyepiece. Putting them in must have been a very uncomfortable business but he used to wear them for sport and to cause a stir. At one particular Army cricket match he had been batting rather well and at tea one of the other players came up to pat him on the back.

"Well played David!" he said. Removing the pipe from his mouth father tapped his left lens with the pipe's mouthpiece.

"Gosh David" said the other player. "I didn't realise you had a glass eye." With a mischievous look he then tapped the other eye with his pipe.

I walked round to the window side of the bed and sat on the NHS chair. The net curtains veiled us from the car park and the road and the green fields beyond and the salt marshes beyond that and then the sea itself. He knew I was there and said something I couldn't understand. It sounded like "Bloody pylons" but it couldn't have been. I knew he was in pain. His face would contort into a grimace when the hurt came and all I could do was watch. Hold his beautiful hand and watch as he winced with pain then lay still again. When he lay still, breathing gently, he looked quite well. At peace, sleeping or dozing. His skin looked baby soft, even had a healthy glow. Then quite suddenly the pain took hold again and distorted everything. The familiar face no longer familiar, no longer at its ease, but transformed into something grotesque, a reflection of what was going on inside. Why couldn't they help him? Please God somebody help him. Somebody relieve his suffering. The nurses could do no more or so they said. A doctor was the only one who could help and the doctor was on her way, would be there within the hour. I fed him little sips of water from a plastic beaker with a straw. Maybe that helped. He was brave. We knew that.

"On the afternoon of 1st March 45, this officer's platoon was attacking enemy positions south of UDEM (MR 9840 – sheet 21). The forward section became pinned down in open ground by heavy and accurate Spandau fire from their front and right flank, and were suffering heavily, all except one man became casualties.

Lieut Berridge went forward to see the position for himself, and tried without success to signal to his supporting tanks. He then crawled 100 yards under intense fire to the nearest tank, and successfully directed its fire on to the enemy position that was holding up the advance of his platoon.

In the meantime enemy shelling had commenced in the immediate neighbourhood of this platoon. Nothing daunted Lt. Berridge collected the remainder of his platoon and cleared the area of enemy capturing 20 prisoners and the MGs which held him up.

Lt Berridge's prompt action and complete disregard for his own safety undoubtedly ensured the complete success of the attack. Throughout the operations on this day this officer's gallantry and leadership were an inspiration to his platoon."

Then my sister arrived with her new man. They had driven from Gloucestershire after last night's phone calls, the ones I thought I should make having spoken to the doctor. I had telephoned both sisters. The eldest arrived, swept into the room, and had every right to be there except that I didn't want her to be, felt somehow that I had sole rights to his ending. It was stupid, selfish of me. She sat the other side of the bed. Her new man found a seat and perched at the foot. I really didn't want him there at all, which was perhaps more understandable. He referred to my father as "Grandpa".

"Hello Grandpa," he said when he first came into the room. He was being friendly. He was supporting my sister, being there for her when I didn't want him to be there with me. But he stayed and the three of us watched as father slowly died.

When nurse Ruth, short though she was, looked me in the eyes and told me straight that father might "pass away", as she put it, "in a few moments", I didn't believe her. I didn't believe her even though her tone was different, her sing song jolliness missing. He'd had a bad night. He'd had bad nights before. Father had been defying the grim reaper since long before I was born. Not near death at birth, nor peritonitis nor a German's bullet (or American's in the back for that matter). Not the North Sea, nor car crashes nor heart attacks nor the triple by-pass op. I had seen him in hospitals before. As big hearted as he was, it was sadly his heart that started to let him down but his sheer determination not to give in confounded the medics. I remembered visiting him in the Royal United Hospital in Bath and seeing the words "Berridge Reckless" written in bold felt tip pen on the name board above his bed. We laughed at the apt description and laughed even more when we discovered Mr Reckless was the consultant looking after him.

In the end, however, the eighty-year-old heart had just had enough. It could not sustain its frame, which actually wouldn't have minded a few more years. There was still so much to do, to get things sorted, get things done. Good for boy scouts but being prepared was not for father. Not now and he'd be furious that his time had come, if it had. Even though the undone chores were myths, not important. The landlord, the building project, seeing Paul the financial adviser, the divorce, the RFU debentures; in father's oxygen starved brain each took on the gravity the size of a decision to invade Iraq which too had given father sleepless nights.

I had never seen a dead body. Didn't really want to either. His portrait in oils had looked down at me from the cottage wall, a confident thirty-six year old, proud with regimental tie, pipe in hand and a long way from the frail old man gently propped up in bed at Wells-next-the-sea, sides up to stop him from slipping out but not from slipping away.

"What will he die of nurse?"

"He'll die of death," she might have said with handbook precision.

"Why will he die?"

"It will be death." It will be his last decision.

"He'd have liked a bit longer."

"We all of us want more."

"I'm dying," he said to us quietly, suddenly. What could we reply? Lost for words. We couldn't say something trite like "Well we all are I guess," or we couldn't sound over jolly. "Oh get on with you. You'll be up and about this evening." We certainly couldn't agree. "We know." We knew that he was because he had said so and therefore it was real to him. We said nothing of any importance, just lip service. Awkward bedside manners.

"You can call for the hearse." Father's last words. Why I should remember his first I didn't know but I did. I must have been told them when I was a child.

"What were your first words daddy?"

"Get your feet off the table Mike." Mike was his twin brother already in heaven.

Three o'clock, afternoon teatime, or a minute or so before on the Saturday May 17th father died. My other sister missed him by half an hour or so. A wrong turn from London, her driver feeling pretty bad about it, she was too late and devastated. I greeted her at the hospital entrance, threw my arms around her and before I could tell her that she had missed him, she knew, read the tell tale signs scrawled like wet graffiti on my face, saw my distress. She ran past me and into his room hoping that I was lying. I wasn't. Father always thought her time keeping was erratic.

Doctor Gorrod said he might go once the injection of the awfully named Diamorphine took away his pain. Took away his life. One minute alive and sipping through the straw, little sips of comforting water to quench the thirst. A thirst for life. Another few ticks and tocks, the jerk of the second hand as it loitered just for a second at each stop. Any second could be the last. It was less than a stop between living and dying. One moment I was holding a hand that had warmth, stroking skin that was glowing baby soft and alive, the next, when the little vein in the neck stopped dancing, the skin turned quickly cold and hard, tinged with grey and blue. The worst thing of all, the mouth gaped like a black hole and no longer sucked on the straw. I cried, my sisters too, because what else could we do. I cried because that was my noble father who I would never speak to again. Never shake by the hand, never drink with, and argue with, laugh with or cry with ever again. Cry for him but never with him ever again.

Ever.

Funeral

Here goes.

I stepped out from next to the red head and up to the lectern. I pulled the sheets of A4 paper from out of my inside pocket and unfolded and flattened them on top of the tilting wooden surface. I would have killed for a glass of water. The rows of serious faces stared up at me and I began as I had practised.

I said the words from my heart. By the lectern not far from the font, in front of a full house of God I did the theatre and when I'd finished with an emotional splutter and scurried back to the front pew, I heard in the distance the noise. Like waves on pebbles or traffic's rush from a balloon way above it. It was clapping. Concert hall clapping in that quiet place of worship. The congregation applauded in celebration of my father's life recounted to them by his only son in seventeen brief minutes. Perhaps they were applauding my new status. They say you don't grow up until your parents die. The ovation was his and then they carried him out of the church.

The burial was next to his mother and father in the churchyard at Barnwell. The same church where I had been baptised by my proud grandfather, my proud father suited and owlish with over fifty more years before he was to be the centre of attention in that place. He would have held me by the old font. Cradled me in his arms. Might have passed me carefully to his father-in-law for the reverend gentleman to put water on my forehead. Fifty or so years later and the handshakes and kind words from those I knew and those I didn't came at me because of him. He knew them all and crossed their lives palms with his silver in one way or another.

I cast a whiskey bottle, only half, wrapped in the regimental tie, into his grave, and a single rose I'd taken that morning from next to the blue cottage door in Brancaster. The bugler, note perfect, finished his reveille and we walked away and down to the farm, Castle farm, in the afternoon sun where he grew up to be a man, where I stayed as a boy.

———

Three months passed and the nitty-gritty of what happened next kicked in. Probate and the Will and who got what with questions asked. "Why the barometer for Freddie?" It didn't matter a damn and his Will was done even though his Will would offend. The sorting of the clothes, each picked over in gruesome jumble sale style. "Doesn't that fit you?" and try as I might I knew it wouldn't nor ever would. Dead men's shoes size ten would not squeeze over an alive eleven, shoe horned or not. Extra thick bin bags were filled with suits from the Newmarket tailor, Liberty ties, country cords, unsuitable D.J's and flashy jackets from the flashy days with his flashy wife. She'd sat very quietly at the back of the church. Didn't feel she ought to be conspicuous. I had father's signet ring for her in my pocket, her initials engraved with his, just in case she came up to say hello. Sadly she didn't. I didn't know she had been there until afterwards when somebody said they had seen her mourning at the back. So I posted it to her.

Socks and braces, grey morning gloves and jumpers, most familiar and shaped like the frame they once covered, were bundled into the black plastic and taken to the green Planet bin down the road. Father's clobber, the clothes he stood up and lay down in were posted in a green bin. Posting the bin bags in through the Planet bin's metal flap was somehow more real than the lowering of the coffin. Less showy. More private.

Just me and him or his body-shaped clothes, quietly slotting them away into the Third World via a green skip collection bin stuck in the far corner of the car park at the Ship Inn, Brancaster.

Birth 2004 ⇥

"I need not add that a man who indulges in parenthood at the age of fifty-four deserves all he gets." So says General Stornwood in Raymond Chandler's Big Sleep. So writes my scriptwriting friend James in the little book left for such things by the downstairs loo.

It was after a good curry that the red head felt things stir three weeks before they were meant to. As it turned out her waters had broken before dawn had and so quiet calmly, we made our way to the R.U.H. once again. If death had been a peaceful business then birth was altogether a far noisier affair. She crouched on the delivery bed on all fours and screamed her head off. The experienced midwife brought out of retirement had seen it all before.

"Yes dear I know it hurts," she said as if to confirm the red head's fuss.

"Please tell me what to do." The red head snarled then pleaded through gritted teeth. Squeezed my hand so hard it hurt too. Turned it white.

"So whereabouts in France is your house?" said the midwife to me. We talked like a couple of people sharing their holiday experiences over a cup of tea rather than across a hospital bed with a distressed writhing mother-to-be between us. I told her the high Pyrenees. She wanted more precision.

"Near a spa town called Bagneres-de-Bigorre," I zoomed in for her.

"Been there. Done that," she said.

"Up the mountain a bit. Campan. Sainte Marie-de-Campan," I said it not expecting her to know the name. The red head screamed expecting some attention.

"Gosh I know where that is," said the midwife. "My hubby and I went touring in those parts last summer. Watched the Tour de France as it came through. Very exciting. Very colourful. All those fit cyclists. Not an once of fat on any of them. And they race along, pedal up and down those mountains as though they weren't there."

"Yes. It's quite a spectacle," I said. The red head arched her back with the next contraction. She was sweating like a cyclist in the mountains.

"They do say that more people watch the race than any other sporting event. World wide that is." The midwife was talking about one, looking at another.

"Please tell me what to do," screamed the red head.

"Don't worry dear. Every thing's going just fine."

What a coincidence that all of us in that delivery room had experienced something of those mountains. All three of us had been there and were now together. Witnessing new heights. And pretty soon after that the baby arrived. A new son with a middle name the same as his father's and grandfather's. Even though he would never know his grandfather, maybe not his father that well, he would always carry their names with him. I held him first, before his mother and looked at him. Once again I was lost for words. Couldn't then say what I really wanted to. Couldn't again. Wasn't prepared for death and wasn't prepared for life either.

Now as then just tears.

Now And Then ⇒

The flames in every fireplace were the same.

There is that wonderful stretch of coastline; the beach where, when the tide is out, the sea disappears. Goes off to Norway for the day. The exposed sands, different each time, become the place to be. I walked them nearly every day when I was with my father. Walked them for both of us. And when he went I walked them for myself and my new son, the blue eyed baby that the red head had grown. Maybe I walk on a beach looking for King John's treasure, the crown jewels washed up by the high tide, and I am not seeing the real bounty all around. Too much focus on trying to find something that isn't there, not enough on seeing what is right in front of me. The beauty at the end of my nose of much more value than any imaginary trinket.

It was the same with the journey to and around France. Chasing an imaginary Holy Grail, believing that what lay in the next valley would turn out to be of more worth than what was spread out in front of me. I had to make the journey though, we all of us have to make those trips, because without them how do we really find true contentment? How else do we come to understand our potential? Some will spend their whole lives looking, the outsider looking in, and some, the fortunate ones, will know right from the start that the here and now is far better than the there and then.

Of all the things I thought I might have been - loving son, loyal husband, attentive parent and grandparent, successful businessman, French mountain man, traveller and dreamer - I ended up being a father again. But, as long

494

as my heart lets me, I suppose I should grasp the opportunity the second time around. A fourth chance to get it right maybe. I've become something that I never imagined. I mention my new job title uneasily when other men ask.

With the bright autumn sunlight I see her shadow on the wall talking. I cannot hear what she is saying but I know it's gentle words because her lips are moving slowly, full arms too, gently jogging up and down that tell me she is in conversation. Or her shadow is at least. In deep and happy conversation with you or singing you a song. When you sit on my own knee, nuzzle up to my shirt like a dormouse, sometimes you look directly at me in exactly the same way that my old man had. Delivered one year to the day from when we put father in the ground. My new son Caspar David, your whole life before you and me inside at the end of the slab of English oak writing all this down, my funny life well on its way.

There was still so much to do, to get things sorted, get things done.

Printed in the United Kingdom
by Lightning Source UK Ltd.
121300UK00001B/178-204/A